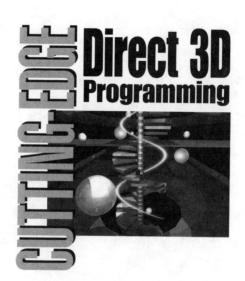

CUTTING-EDGE
Direct 3D
Programming

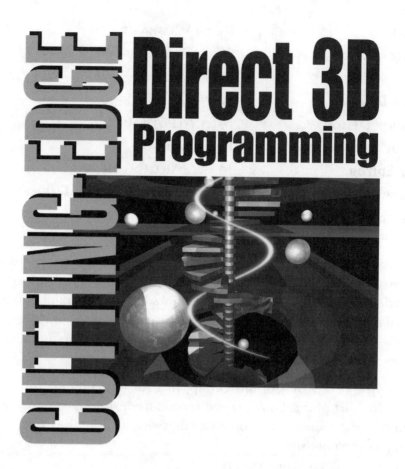

Direct 3D
Programming

CUTTING-EDGE

STAN TRUJILLO

 CORIOLIS GROUP BOOKS

PUBLISHER	KEITH WEISKAMP
PROJECT EDITOR	SCOTT PALMER
COVER ARTIST	GARY SMITH
COVER DESIGN	ANTHONY STOCK
INTERIOR DESIGN	MICHELLE STROUP
LAYOUT PRODUCTION	ROB MAUHAR
COPY EDITOR	MARY MILLHOLLON
PROOFREADERS	SHELLY CROSSEN, KATHY DERMER
INDEXER	JENNI ALOI

The Coriolis Group, Inc.
7339 E. Acoma Drive, Suite 7
Scottsdale, AZ 85260

Phone: (602) 483-0192
Fax: (602) 483-0193
Web address: http://www.coriolis.com

ISBN 1-57610-050-2: $39.99
Printed in the United States of America
10 9 8 7 6 5 4 3 2 1

To the wise and venerable Al Stevens, to whom I am grateful
on a personal and professional level

ACKNOWLEDGMENTS

Thanks to Keith Weiskamp and Jeff Duntemann. Keith and Jeff are unique in that they are publishers that are also programmers and authors. Their insight into this business does not go unnoticed.

Special thanks goes to Scott Palmer, my editor. Like Keith and Jeff, Scott is an accomplished author and understands the toils and stresses of writing books.

Thanks also goes to my long-time friend and colleague Patrick Lujan. Patrick helped me with this project by writing the installation program for the CD-ROM, but that is nothing compared to the help he has been over the years.

CONTENTS

CONCLUSION   395

CHAPTER 10   FULL-SCREEN APPLICATIONS   397

DIRECTDRAW   400

MODIFYING THE RMWIN CLASS   403

INTRODUCTION

The origin of the human race and the details of our early history are the subject of much debate. Early human history is only loosely recorded, but we can make some educated guesses about how we spent our time. For example, it is safe to say that we spent a good deal of time designing and using tools.

When we think of tools today, we think of wrenches and hammers, or, for us programmers, software tools. But the first tool was probably a sharpened rock or bone that served as a knife. From this humble beginning, we eventually designed spears, skewers, shields, and sheaths. We designed vessels for the transport and storage of food and water and slings to carry infants. We invented sewing to hold skins together. Later we invented the wheel. The bronze age saw the introduction of metal pans, swords and shields. The industrial revolution changed the worlds of finance, labor and consumerism forever with the introduction of complex machines that could perform routine tasks consistently and reliably. The last one hundred years has brought cars, washing machines and can openers to millions of homes around the world.

The point is that we have inherited a rich and powerful legacy: a legacy of shapes, levers, pulleys, cams, and gears, and this technical portion of our heritage is fundamentally three-dimensional.

THE IMPENDING 3D REVOLUTION

The two-dimensional desktop metaphor employed by Windows[1] has been successful for word processing and spreadsheet applications because documents and spreadsheets are two-dimensional. For other applications, however, a 2D interface is stifling. Applications such as training simulators, educational software, medical imaging applications, architectural design software, games, and anything resembling virtual reality will all benefit from real-time 3D graphics technology. The desktop metaphor itself might someday be replaced with a 3D metaphor.

3D is not new. Real-time 3D graphics for PCs is new, but it is being adopted quickly because 3D graphics mean that we can stop thinking in 2D, and resume thinking in 3D.

Millions of years ago, a group of our ancestors celebrated the invention of the wheel. The new invention was no doubt put into use right away. Today, low cost real-time hardware accelerated 3D graphics is available for the average PC, and it's time to put it to use.

WHAT IS DIRECT3D?

Direct3D is a DirectX component that supports high performance 3D rendering and animation for Windows 95. Direct3D itself has two interfaces: Retained Mode and Immediate Mode. The Retained Mode interface provides a high level, powerful interface that allows complex 3D scenes to be maintained and rendered. The Immediate Mode interface is a low-level triangle processing layer. Internally, Retained Mode uses Immediate Mode. This book covers the Retained Mode interface.

Direct3D wasn't actually written by Microsoft. It was written by a London based company called *Rendermorphics* and it was called *Reality Lab*. In February 1995, Microsoft acquired Rendermorphics, and began porting Reality Lab to Windows 95. In its current form, Direct3D is fundamentally dependent upon DirectDraw, the 2D graphics portion of DirectX. Direct3D uses DirectDraw for its underlying video buffers and page-flipping mechanisms. Like DirectDraw, Direct3D is written in such a way that it automatically takes advantage of any specialized hardware present on the video card (assuming that you are provided with the correct video driver). When a DirectDraw application runs on a video card that has a rectangle blitter, performance is enhanced dramatically. When a Direct3D application runs on a video card that has 3D hardware, performance is enhanced further. Optimum performance therefore requires a video card with 2D and 3D acceleration. Performance aside, it is not necessary to use an accelerated video card to develop applications for Direct3D[2].

READER REQUIREMENTS

In order to use this book effectively, you must be a programmer, and you must know C++. You don't have to be a C++ expert, but you should have an understanding of features such as classes and virtual functions. Some of these ideas can be picked up by observing the context in which they are used, but it never hurts to refer back to classic C++ books such as Stroustrup's *The C++ Programming Language* (2nd edition) or *Al Stevens Teaches C++*.

You need to be familiar with Visual C++ and MFC (Microsoft Foundation Classes). We will be using only a portion of MFC, so MFC mastery is not necessary.

You will need to know some basic 3D concepts, but you are not required to know a lot of math. You do not need to understand rasterization algorithms, perspective transformations or phong shading to use this book.

SOFTWARE REQUIREMENTS

In order to use Direct3D, you will need Visual C++ 4.0 or greater and Windows 95. You'll also need DirectX. DirectX comes in two parts: the runtime portion, and the SDK. The DirectX 3 runtime protion is included on the CD-ROM that comes with this book. You can get the DirectX SDK from MSDN or the Microsoft Web site (www.microsoft.com/msdownload/directx3.htm)

HARDWARE REQUIREMENTS

For the most part, any machine capable of running Windows 95 will do the job. Practically speaking, however, you should have a fast 486 or a Pentium. Sixteen megabytes of RAM is desirable. Visual C++, DirectX, and the code in this book comes on CD-ROM, so a CD-ROM drive is required. Finally, you'll need a video card that is supported by DirectX.

ORGANIZATION OF THE BOOK

This book has 10 chapters. Chapter 1 is a quick review of Visual C++ and an introduction to the Direct3D AppWizard. Chapter 2 covers key 3D graphics concepts and terminology. Chapter 3 is an introduction to the Direct3D

API. Chapter 4 documents Direct3D application structure. Chapters 4 through 10 cover Direct3D Retained Mode, and present 23 demos. For the most part, each topic is covered by a separate demo. Appendix A discusses the demo programs that are included with the book's CD-ROM.

GETTING HELP

If you have questions, comments, or compliants, you can reach me at stan@rezio.com.

[1] Credit for the desktop metaphor goes to Xerox. Apple gets credited with the metaphor frequently because the Apple Macintosh was the first widely available computer that made use of the metaphor.

[2] I wrote the majority of the code for this book using a non-3D accelerated video card.

Chapter

1

A QUICK
INTRODUCTION TO
VISUAL C++

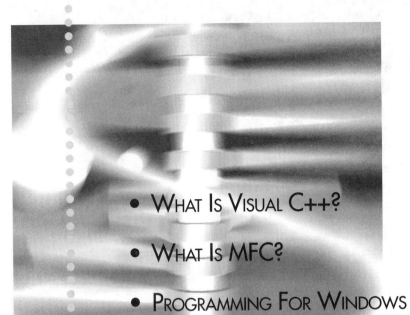

- What Is Visual C++?

- What Is MFC?

- Programming For Windows

- Using The ClassWizard

- Using The AppWizards

- Using The Direct3D AppWizard

CHAPTER

1

A QUICK INTRODUCTION TO VISUAL C++

Since the release of Windows 3.0, hordes of programmers have migrated to Windows from other platforms. Many Windows programmers started with DOS and discovered that programming for Windows is very different. To make matters worse, there were no function libraries, class frameworks, or visual tools to ease the pain of transition.

Things have changed a lot. Visual C++ is an amazing tool that combines a powerful class framework with visual tools that take the drudgery out of designing resources such as dialogs and menus. Visual C++'s ClassWizard allows you to add functions to your project with the press of a button. Visual C++'s AppWizard constructs ready-to-compile projects, giving you a solid starting place whenever you start a new application.

As great as Visual C++ is, however, you still have to be a programmer to use it, and you have to understand some basics about Windows programming. In this chapter, you will learn how to use Visual C++ to create complete applications and easily modify them. You will also learn how to create complete Direct3D applications in this chapter.

It's not a complete Visual C++ tutorial, but it should be enough to get you started if you have some programming background.

DEVELOPER STUDIO

Visual C++ is a set of tools for Windows application development. The flagship Visual C++ tool is Developer Studio. You can use Developer Studio to create minimal applications, add functionality to existing programs, and create or edit resources such as menus, dialogs, and icons. Developer Studio is also a complete compiler, debugger, and editor. Figure 1.1 shows the Visual C++ Developer Studio.

THE WINDOWS SDK VS. MFC

The Windows SDK (Software Development Kit) is a set of functions, structures, and macros that allow programmers to write applications for Windows. The SDK, in some form or another, has been with Windows since Windows 1.0 (yes, there was a Windows 1.0). Written in C, the SDK is known for being hard to work with. Because the SDK isn't object-oriented, it is difficult to extend and forces the programmer to deal with every possible detail of Windows programming. The Windows SDK is included with Visual

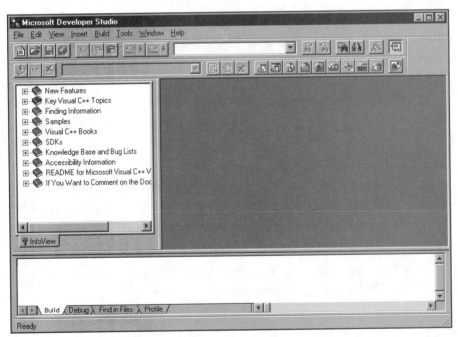

Figure 1.1

The Visual C++ Developer Studio.

C++, but in a way, you're missing the point if you restrict yourself to SDK programming. The real heart of Visual C++ is MFC.

MFC (Microsoft Foundation Classes) is a C++ class library that insulates programmers from the details of the Windows SDK. Microsoft named MFC appropriately. MFC is indeed a foundation, a set of low-level, flexible objects that can be extended to serve just about any purpose. Many of the MFC classes are merely thin wrappers around Windows SDK constructs. By themselves, the MFC classes are not particularly impressive or useful, but their extensibility is remarkable. MFC is also included with Visual C++.

EVENT-DRIVEN PROGRAMMING

The most fundamental difference between Windows and DOS programming is that Windows is event-driven. This means that virtually everything that happens in Windows happens in response to a message or event (in this discussion, we use the terms *message* and *event* interchangeably).

In DOS, you are given an entry point, a place in your program that DOS will execute when your program is started. The DOS entry point is the **main()** function. DOS calls your **main()** function and your program does whatever it needs to do. You don't return out of **main()** until your program is finished. Once **main()** returns, DOS shuts down your program.

THE WINMAIN FUNCTION

A Windows program also has an entry point: the **WinMain()** function. **WinMain()** is a function that you write and that Windows calls when your application starts. Unlike the DOS **main()** function, however, **WinMain()** must perform certain tasks. A typical WinMain function initializes data structures, creates a window, and then runs a *message pump*, which is a loop that continually checks to see if new messages are available. If so, the pump retrieves each message and dispatches it. A typical message pump looks like this:

```
while ( GetMessage( &msg, NULL, 0, 0 ) )
{
    TranslateMessage( &msg );
    DispatchMessage( &msg );
}
```

GetMessage, **TranslateMessage**, and **DispatchMessage** are all functions supplied by the Windows SDK. Messages can be posted by applications or by Windows itself. These messages can be notifications that the system palette has changed, that a key has been pressed, the mouse has moved, and so on. Eventually, the pump translates and dispatches a WM_QUIT message, which signals the program to terminate.

EVENT HANDLERS

An event handler is a function that you write and then register with Windows. After your event handler is registered, each message that has been dispatched via **DispatchMessage** is sent to your event handler. A typical event handler contains a **switch** statement with a **case** for each message that is to be handled. Messages that are not handled are usually passed on to the default Windows event handler. A simple event handler looks like this:

```
long WINAPI WndProc( HWND hWnd, UINT msg, UINT wParam, LONG lParam )
{
    switch( msg )
    {
        case WM_KEYDOWN:
            // code to handle key presses goes here
            break;
        case WM_MOUSEMOVE:
            // code to handle mouse movements goes here
            break;
        default:
            // if we don't handle the message let Windows handle it
            return DefWindowProc( hWnd, msg, wParam, lParam );
    }
    return 0;
}
```

The event handler construct is powerful because it allows you to intercept messages before Windows gets them. You can react to any event that goes through your event handler by adding a **case** statement to your event handler.

On the other hand, the fact that every possible message is handled by one function makes for ugly code. Traditional Windows programs (including the sample programs that come with DirectX) often have massive event handlers that go on for hundreds of lines. An alternative is to write a separate event handler function for each event and then call the function from your event handler. This is often preferable because it allows you to write a set of small, reasonably sized event handlers instead of one huge, complicated event handler. MFC uses this later technique, but with one significant improvement: message maps.

MESSAGE MAPS

Remember that MFC is designed to insulate the programmer from some of the messy details of Windows programming. MFC insulates you from the event handler by supplying its own, and then calling individual handlers that you supply. This is accomplished with *message maps*. A message map is a macro that tells MFC you are interested in handling a specific message. All you have to do is include a message map and an event handler in your code, and MFC takes care of the rest. A message map looks like this:

```
BEGIN_MESSAGE_MAP(OurClass, BaseClass)
    ON_WM_PAINT()
    ON_WM_SIZE()
    ON_WM_LBUTTONDOWN()
END_MESSAGE_MAP()
```

This message map tells MFC that you have a class called **OurClass** that is derived from **BaseClass**. **OurClass** will be handling three messages: **WM_PAINT**, **WM_SIZE**, and **WM_LBUTTONDOWN** (these message are standard Windows messages).

Now you need to supply an event handler function for each message. The **WM_PAINT** message handler, for example, would look this way:

```
void OurClass::OnPaint()
{
    // respond to the WM_PAINT message here
}
```

Finally, the event handlers must be declared within the class. The three event handlers that we are using as examples might look like this:

```
class OurClass : public BaseClass
{
protected:
    afx_msg void OnPaint();
```

```
    afx_msg void OnSize(UINT type, int cx, int cy);
    afx_msg void OnLButtonDown( UINT state, CPoint point );
    DECLARE_MESSAGE_MAP()
};
```

The **afx_msg** macro identifies the functions as event handlers, and the DECLARE_MESSAGE_MAP macro notifies MFC that this class uses message maps.

CLASSWIZARD

Message maps are great because they simplify event handling, but Visual C++ makes them even easier to use with ClassWizard. ClassWizard is a tool within the Visual C++ Developer Studio that allows you to add, remove, and edit event handlers. Figure 1.2 shows the ClassWizard dialog.

From ClassWizard, you select the message that you are interested in handling and then click the Add Function button. ClassWizard installs a do-nothing event handler that you can then modify to your own specifications. ClassWizard makes the addition of event handlers as easy as it possibly can be because the handlers that it installs are ready to compile. The only missing ingredient is your code.

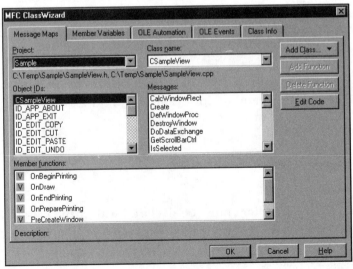

Figure 1.2
The ClassWizard dialog.

The code that ClassWizard adds to your project is a little different than the message map code that we discussed earlier. For example, if you installed the previous message handlers with ClassWizard, the message map would look like this:

```
BEGIN_MESSAGE_MAP(OurClass, BaseClass)
    //{{AFX_MSG_MAP(OurClass)
    ON_WM_PAINT()
    ON_WM_SIZE()
    ON_WM_LBUTTONDOWN()
    //}}AFX_MSG_MAP
END_MESSAGE_MAP()
```

The difference is that ClassWizard inserts text elements that act as book-marks. To the compiler, these bookmarks appear as comments, but to ClassWizard they indicate the location of the message maps within your source code. You can delete the marks and the code will still compile, but you will no longer be able to edit your message maps with ClassWizard.

ClassWizard can also be used to remove event handlers. When you remove a handler with ClassWizard, the message map and the function declaration are removed. It is up to you to remove the actual function body.

We'll use ClassWizard later in this chapter.

APPWIZARDS

While ClassWizard makes it easy to modify projects, AppWizards make it easy to create projects in the first place. Visual C++ includes an AppWizard, for example, that allows you to create new MFC projects. If you activate this Wizard, you are presented with a series of dialogs that ask what kind of MFC application you would like. Visual C++ includes several different AppWizards: one for creating MFC applications, another for console applications, another for creating DLLs, and so on.

The best thing about starting a project with an AppWizard is that the new projects are usually ready to compile. You don't have to add anything in order to compile and test it. By producing a ready-to-compile project, AppWizard saves you the frustration of finding yourself with a large body of unfamiliar code that doesn't compile.

CREATING AN MFC APPLICATION

Creating applications with AppWizard is so easy that we should create one right now just for practice. From Developer Studio, pull down the File menu and select New. The New window, shown in Figure 1.3, will appear. Choose Project Workspace and click on the Create button.

Next, the New Project Workspace window appears (Figure 1.4). This window allows you to use any of the AppWizards that are installed on your computer. We'll use the MFC AppWizard to create an MFC-based Multi-Document application. Select MFC AppWizard(exe). Then enter the name of the project. As Figure 1.4 shows, we will use "Sample" as the name in this example.

Notice that the project name is also used as the directory where the new project will be created. You can modify the path in the Location box to specify another location.

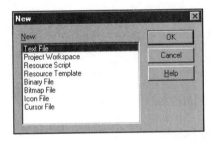

Figure 1.3
The New window.

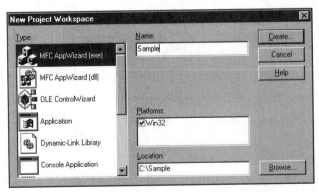

Figure 1.4
The New Project Workspace window.

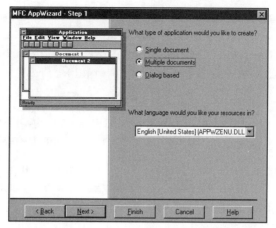

Figure 1.5
The first MFC AppWizard dialog.

After you click on the Create button, the first dialog in the MFC AppWizard will appear. This dialog is shown in Figure 1.5. Here, you can specify if you want to create a Single Document Interface (SDI) application, a Multiple Document Interface (MDI) application, or a dialog-based application. In this example, we'll use the default selection (MDI).

Pressing Next takes you to the next dialog. Dialogs 2 through 5 let you specify more options for your new application, and we will use the default settings. Figure 1.6 shows the sixth and final MFC AppWizard dialog.

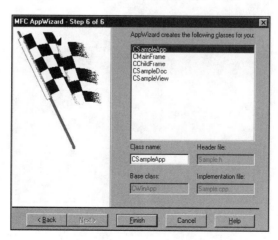

Figure 1.6
The final MFC AppWizard dialog.

The final dialog allows you to override the names of the classes that will be used in the new project. AppWizard creates suggested class names by appending identifiers such as App, View, and Doc to the project name. For our purposes, the proposed names are acceptable. Press the Finish button to proceed.

Before actually creating the application, AppWizard displays a New Project Information window (Figure 1.7) that outlines the settings to be used.

This is your last chance to review your choices. Pressing the OK button creates the application. You can compile the new project by pressing F7, and run the application by pressing F5.

ADDING AN EVENT HANDLER

Now that we have a working application, we can modify it with ClassWizard. Using the MFC application that we just created, select ClassWizard from the View menu. Figure 1.8 shows the ClassWizard dialog.

The ClassWizard dialog has five tabs. The Message Maps tab should be selected, as shown in the figure. The dialog shows any installed event handlers

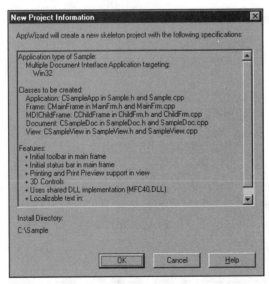

Figure 1.7
New Project Information window.

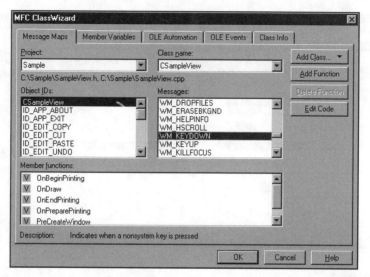

Figure 1.8

The ClassWizard dialog.

for the class shown in the Class name pull-down control. The list box labeled Object IDs contains the class name and a list of menu IDs. You add event handlers by selecting one of the menu IDs or the class name and selecting a message from the list box labeled Messages. Pressing the Add Function button creates the new event handler.

Let's create an event handler that will report keystrokes. This can be done by installing an event handler for the **WM_KEYDOWN** message. Windows posts a **WM_KEYDOWN** message when any key is pressed.

Make sure that the **CSampleView** class is selected in the Class name box and in the Object IDs list box. Select the **WM_KEYDOWN** entry in the Messages list box (you'll probably have to scroll through the messages to find **WM_KEYDOWN**). Once you have it selected, press the Add Function button. AppWizard adds **WM_KEYDOWN** to the Member functions list box and adds the new event handler to your code. Now press the Edit Code button. ClassWizard will display a window with the new code. Figure 1.9 shows the new event handler.

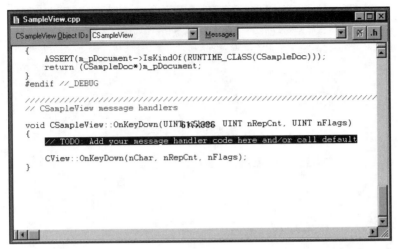

Figure 1.9

Our new **WM_KEYDOWN** event handler.

Pay attention to event handler code

Pay close attention to the code that ClassWizard places in new event handlers. ClassWizard will indicate the best place to put your code by inserting a comment at the location. Sometimes, this code goes before the call to the base class member function, and sometimes it should go afterward. In some cases, ClassWizard will instruct you not to call the base class function at all.

The only thing that the event handler that ClassWizard creates for you does is call the base class version of the same member function. We can add our code where ClassWizard has left a comment to indicate the best place for our code. For this example, we'll use a TRACE debug macro to display information about the messages that are received. Modify the event handler to look like this:

```
void CSampleView::OnKeyDown(UINT nChar, UINT nRepCnt, UINT nFlags)
{
    TRACE("WM_KEYDOWN message received  ");
    TRACE("keycode=%d  repeat=%d  flags=%d\n", nChar, nRepCnt, nFlags);

    CView::OnKeyDown(nChar, nRepCnt, nFlags);
}
```

Now, compile and run the application. Once the application window appears, press some keys. The **Debug** window in Developer Studio will display the TRACE messages.

Note: This example only works when the project is compiled in Debug mode and executed from Developer Studio because TRACE macros have no effect in Release mode.

A CUSTOM DIRECT3D APPWIZARD

Visual C++ allows you to write custom AppWizards. Custom AppWizards can be written to generate just about any application imaginable. The CD-ROM that comes with this book includes a custom Direct3D AppWizard that you can use to create fully functional Direct3D applications.

Custom AppWizards are special DLLs (Dynamic Link Libraries) that have an AWX extension. AppWizards can be installed by copying the AWX file into the Visual C++ template directory (usually c:\msdev\template). The Direct3D custom AppWizard can be installed either by copying the Direct3DAppWiz.AWX file from the CD-ROM's Direct3DAppWiz\Release directory into the \msdev\template directory or by using the CD-ROM's installation program.

After installing the custom AppWizard, get into the Developer Studio and choose New from the File menu; then select Project Workspace, and press the OK button. The New Project Workspace window will appear. Scroll down to the bottom of the Type list-box and select Direct3D AppWizard as shown in Figure 1.10. You'll also need to enter the project name. For this example, we'll use "Sample3D." After you enter the project name, press the Create button. Now, the first Direct3D AppWizard dialog shown in Figure 1.11 will appear.

The first dialog is an introduction to the AppWizard. Press the Next button to proceed to the second dialog shown in Figure 1.12.

The second AppWizard dialog allows you to specify the 3D object that will be displayed by the Direct3D application that you are creating. By default, the Swirl object shown on the dialog will be used, but you can select another object by selecting Let me choose an object and entering the object

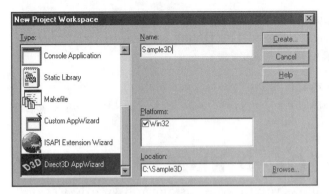

Figure 1.10
Selecting the Direct3D AppWizard.

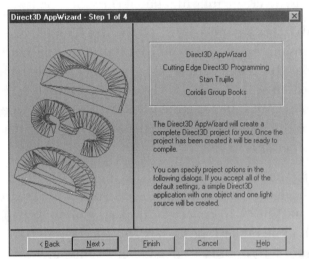

Figure 1.11
The first of four Direct3D AppWizard dialogs.

name in the Object edit control. You can also use the Browse button to locate an object (Direct3D object files have an X file extension). For this example, we will use the default object. Pressing the Next button will take you to the dialog shown in Figure 1.13.

The third AppWizard dialog lets you choose what (if any) types of light sources you want in the application. We'll talk more about light sources later. For now, we'll just use the default directional light source.

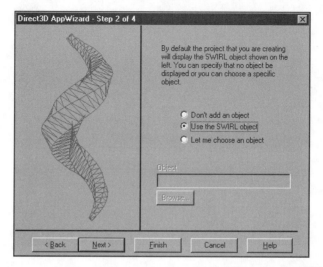

Figure 1.12
The Object selection dialog.

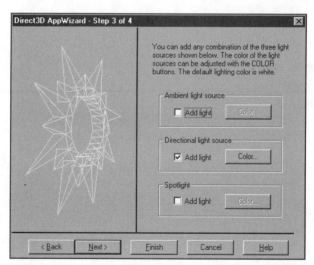

Figure 1.13
The Lighting selection dialog.

The color of the light sources can also be adjusted from this dialog. By default, each light source uses white as its color. Press the Next button to go to the fourth AppWizard dialog, shown in Figure 1.14.

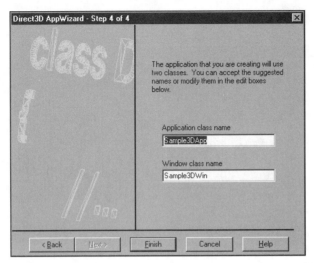

Figure 1.14
The class names dialog.

The fourth dialog lets you override the class names that the AppWizard suggests. Accept the defaults and press the Next button.

Now the AppWizard displays a confirmation dialog (Figure 1.15) so that you can review your choices.

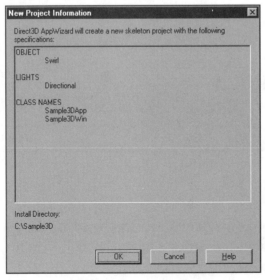

Figure 1.15
The Direct3D AppWizard confirmation dialog.

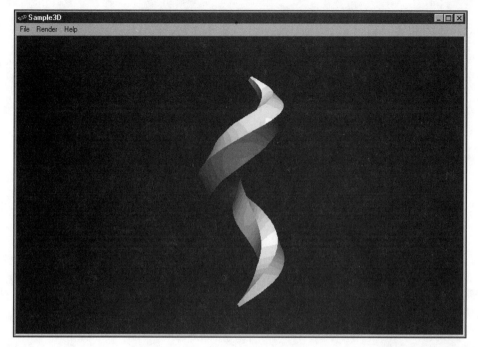

Figure 1.16
The new Direct3D application.

Visual C++ creates the new project when you click on the confirmation dialog OK button. Compile the project by pressing F7, and execute the new application by pressing F5. Figure 1.16 shows the new application.

WINDOWS CODE, AND WRAPPING UP

Windows code has a distinct look. Event-driven programming isn't the only thing that Windows newbies have to adjust to. One of the reasons Windows code looks different is because Windows programmers often use *Hungarian notation*. Hungarian notation uses variable prefixes to identify the type of each variable, and is useful in languages that have little or no variable type checking.

One key features of C++ is strong type checking. This means that C++ solves the problem that Hungarian notation was intended to solve—with one improvement. With C++, the compiler does the type checking, not the programmer. The leaves you free to concentrate on more important things (like 3D graphics). The code in this book doesn't use Hungarian notation.

Another departure from tradition is that the classes in this book are arranged so that the public member functions appear at the top of the class. This is because the public interface is usually the topic of interest for users of the class. Private data members and functions are included near the bottom of each class because they can't be used by derived or external classes anyway.

You'll have ample opportunities to apply this chapter's concepts as you create Direct3D applications throughout the rest of the book.

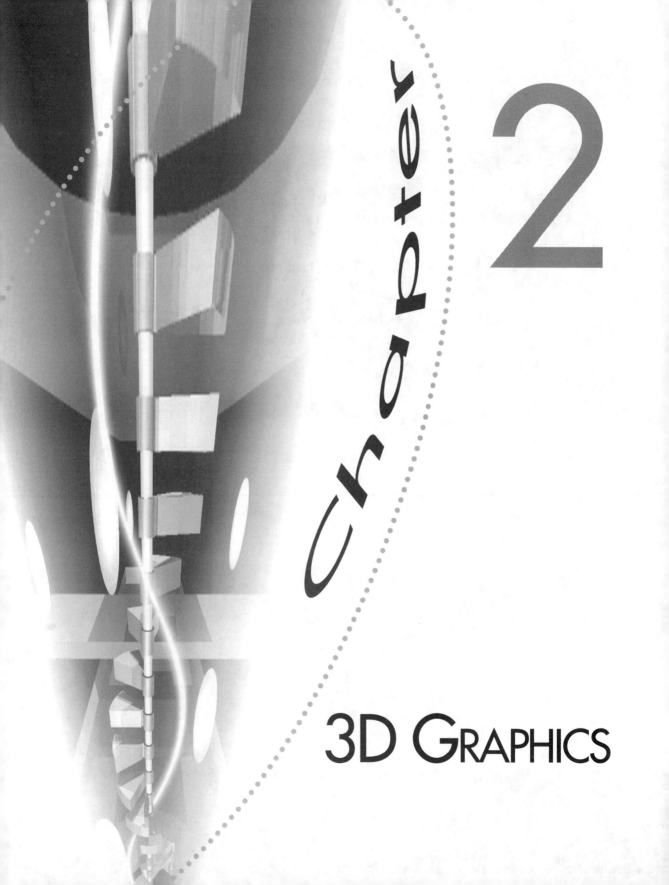

Chapter

2

3D Graphics

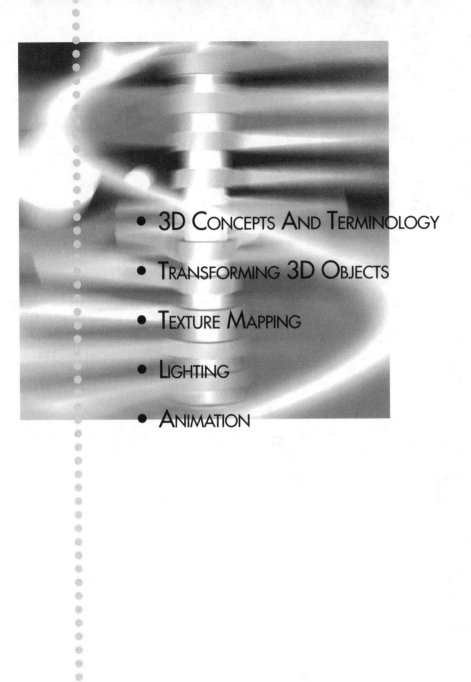

- 3D Concepts And Terminology

- Transforming 3D Objects

- Texture Mapping

- Lighting

- Animation

2

3D GRAPHICS

Volumes have been written about 3D graphics and, in a way, this chapter is another installment. However, most of the literature on 3D graphics shows how to implement particular algorithms. A smaller portion of the work addresses how to best represent and manipulate graphical constructs. Because we are using Direct3D, many 3D conceptual issues have already been addressed. Still, you need an understanding of key 3D concepts in order to use Direct3D. We'll talk about those concepts in this chapter.

3D COORDINATE SYSTEMS

The goal of 3D graphics is to present a two-dimensional representation of a three-dimensional scene. The presentation is in two dimensions because the medium on which the scene is viewed, a flat computer screen, is two-dimensional. So, 3D graphics means preparing two representations of the same scene: a three-dimensional representation that remains unseen and a two-dimensional representation that displays on the screen. We will talk about the unseen, three-dimensional representation first.

Representing objects in three dimensions can be accomplished by using a coordinate system that provides three separate axes. These axes are usually named X, Y, and Z.

There are two common variations on the 3D coordinate system: left-handed and right-handed. The difference between the two is the behavior of the Z axis. In the left-handed system, distant coordinates (appearing far away from the viewer) have larger Z values, while closer coordinates have smaller Z values. In the right-handed system, the Z axis is reversed: Distant coordinates have smaller Z values and closer coordinates have larger Z values. Direct3D uses the left-handed system, so we'll use it in this discussion. Figure 2.1 shows the left-handed coordinate system. The arrows represent the direction in which values increase along each axis.

Any point in 3D space can be described with a set of three values. These values indicate the point's location along each axis and are shown in this book using angle brackets like this: <1,2,3>. The values indicate the point's location along the X, Y, and Z axes respectively.

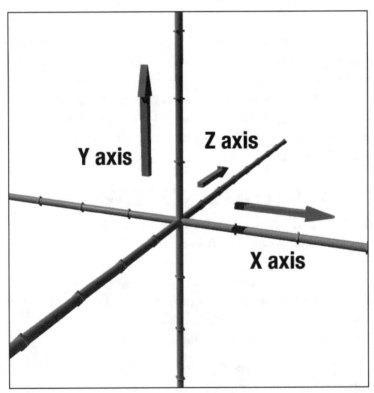

Figure 2.1
The 3D coordinate system.

THE ORIGIN

The point at which all three axes meet is called the origin. A point located at the origin has X, Y, and Z values of zero <0,0,0>. The farther a value is from zero, the farther the point is from the origin. Points located to the right of the origin have positive X values, and points located to the left have negative X values. Likewise, points located above the origin have positive Y values, and points located below have negative Y values. Figure 2.2 shows some labeled points

In the figure, the points are represented with spheres. This is just for visual effect, since a point is a location and not an object. Figure 2.3 shows a set of labeled points that appear at various locations along the Z axis.

VECTORS

A vector, like a point, is represented by three values, but a vector describes a direction and a velocity and not a location.

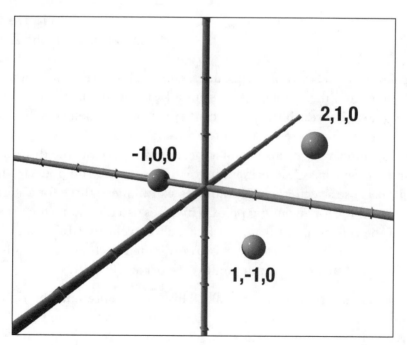

Figure 2.2
Some labeled points.

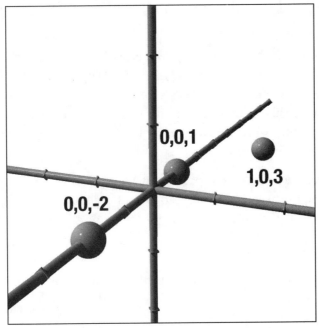

Figure 2.3
Some points along the Z axis.

Take, for example, the following values: <0,1,0>. If we treat these numbers as a point, then the numbers represent a location that is one unit above the origin (units are arbitrary: they can represent centimeters, miles, etc.). If, however, we treat these same three numbers as a vector, we are given a direction and a velocity instead of a location. In this case, the direction is up and the velocity is 1. Representing vectors with three numbers is a little sneaky because a vector actually requires six numbers: three for a starting point and three for an ending point. This gives us a direction (the orientation of the second point from the first), and a velocity (the distance between the two points). Vectors can be represented by three values only if it is understood that the starting point is the origin (0, 0, 0).

Let's look at another vector: <2,0,0>. This vector represents the right direction because the vector starts at <0,0,0> and travels to the right along the X axis for two units. Because the <2,0,0> vector represents a line twice the length of the <0,1,0> vector, the <2, 0, 0> vector's velocity is twice that of the <0, 1, 0> vector's velocity. Figure 2.4 shows the two vectors we have discussed so far.

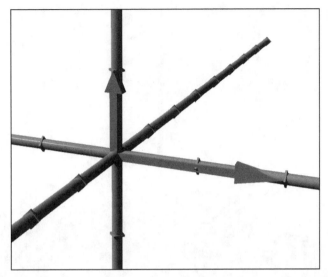

Figure 2.4
Vectors <0,1,0> and <2,0,0>.

It is important to remember that vectors and points are different. A point specifies a location; a vector does not. Locations are used to define a vector, but a vector does not define a location. The vectors in Figure 2.4 are placed at the origin because that is how they are represented numerically, but the arrows in the figure could appear anywhere in the coordinate system.

PLANES

A plane is a flat surface that extends to infinity. A plane is not a square or a rectangle, because squares and rectangles have edges and corners. A plane's size is undefined. The simplest way to represent a plane is with an axis and an intersection value. For example, a plane represented by a Y value of –3 is located 3 units below the origin, and extends out indefinitely along the X and Z axes. That is, the plane intersects the Y axis perpendicularly at –3. A portion of such a plane is shown in Figure 2.5.

Notice that by representing a plane with an axis and a value, we are unable to describe a plane that is not aligned with an axis. If we want to describe a plane that cuts across the Y axis at a 45 degree angle, for example, we need a more sophisticated representation.

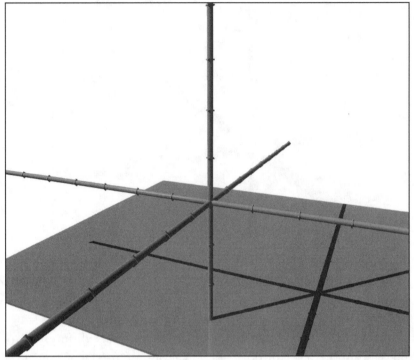

Figure 2.5
A portion of a plane intersecting the Y axis at –3.

We can use a vector to describe the orientation of the plane. If we want a plane that intersects with the Y axis at a 45 degree angle, we could use the vector <0,1,–1> to define a plane that is tilted toward the viewer (the plane is perpendicular to the vector). This vector alone doesn't define a plane, only the orientation of the plane. We still need to indicate where the plane is located. Again, we could use a Y value of –3 to indicate that the plane crosses the Y axis three units below the origin. Figure 2.6 shows a portion of this plane.

VERTICES

Vertices are points that are used to place objects such as faces and meshes in 3D space (we'll talk about faces and meshes soon). Vertices, like points, are locations, so they are not visible. Still, Direct3D supports a mode in

Figure 2.6
The plane placed at Y= –3 and oriented with the vector <0, 1, –1>.

which vertices are drawn as dots. This mode is of little practical value because it's hard to determine what's being drawn based on vertices alone. In fact, scenes rendered in this mode look like 3D "connect the dots" puzzles. (Great—hand me a pencil!)

FACES

In Direct3D, a face is a flat graphical element that is defined in terms of vertices. Each vertex defines a corner of the face. All of the vertices in a face must exist in the same plane; they must define a face that is flat. Faces with vertices that do not exist in the same plane are invalid and cannot be drawn.

The simplest form of a face is defined with three vertices. The resulting triangular face is easy to work with for several reasons. First, it is impossible to define a set of three vertices that do not exist in the same plane, so the

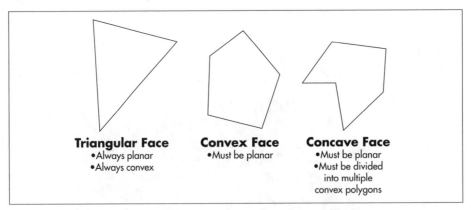

Triangular Face
•Always planar
•Always convex

Convex Face
•Must be planar

Concave Face
•Must be planar
•Must be divided
into multiple
convex polygons

Figure 2.7
Some sample faces.

face cannot be invalid. Second, triangular faces are always convex, and convex faces can be rendered more efficiently than concave faces. Figure 2.7 shows some examples of faces.

 Direct3D uses triangles
Internally Direct3D Retained Mode divides non-triangular faces into triangles because the Immediate Mode interface (that does the actual rendering) accepts only triangles.

Faces are usually the only visible objects in a graphics system. Some graphics systems are capable of drawing curved surfaces but most, including Direct3D, use collections of small, flat faces to represent curved surfaces.

MESHES

A mesh is a collection of connected faces. Typically a mesh represents one object in a scene. A mesh can have one or more faces and can be very complicated. Figure 2.8 shows an example of a mesh. If you look closely at the figure, you can make out the individual faces.

NORMALS

Normals are vectors used to calculate colors for faces and meshes. There are two types of normals: face normals and vertex normals.

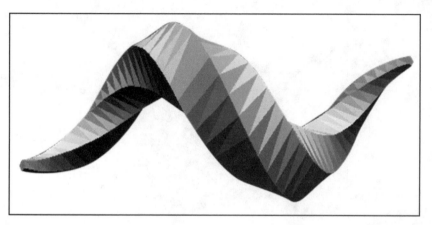

Figure 2.8
A rendered mesh.

A face normal is a vector that is perpendicular to the face. The normal determines the color of a face and which side of the face is visible. Figure 2.9 shows a cube with arrows representing the face normals.

Vertex normals are vectors that are assigned to each vertex in a mesh. The orientation of each vector depends on the orientation and size of the adjoining faces. Figure 2.10 shows the vertex normals for a cube.

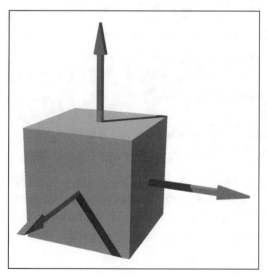

Figure 2.9
Face normals for a cube.

Figure 2.10
Vertex normals for a cube.

The use of face normals versus vertex normals depends on the rendering method. Some rendering methods use face normals, others use vertex normals, and some rendering methods don't use normals at all. We'll talk about rendering methods later in this chapter.

In most cases, Direct3D calculates and uses normals automatically, so it's not necessary that you know they exist. There are situations, however, when normals can be over-ridden to achieve specific rendering effects. We'll talk about normals again in Chapter 8.

TRANSLATIONS

Now, we know how to place objects in three-dimensional space. We can specify vertices, define faces using vertices, and define meshes using faces. Now what we need is a way to move the objects around. There are three common operations (or translations) that can be used to move objects: *translate*, *scale*, and *rotate*. Using these three operations, it is possible to place an object in any location and give it any orientation.

Before we proceed, let's construct a simple scenario that we can use as we discuss the translate, scale, and rotate operations. We'll use a simple mesh: a cube. Our cube is centered on the origin and has dimensions of 1 by 1 by 1. Figure 2.11 shows this cube.

Notice that because the cube is centered on the origin, each side of the cube extends ½ unit away from the origin. Notice also that each face (each side of the cube) is aligned perpendicularly with an axis.

TRANSLATE

The dictionary defines *translate* as: *to express in another language*. This definition has nothing to do with 3D graphics (that will teach you to look things up!). For our purposes here, translate means *move*.

Let's say that we want to move (or translate) our sample cube up from the origin by two units. We can accomplish this by using a translation of <0, 2, 0>. Figure 2.12 shows the result.

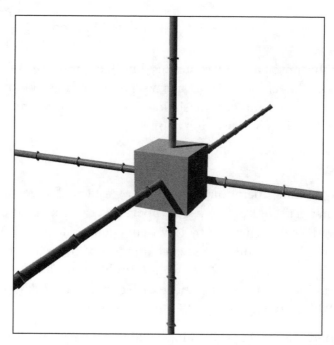

Figure 2.11
Our example cube.

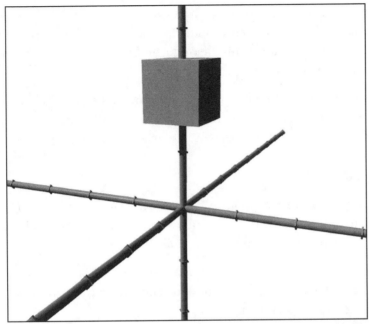

Figure 2.12
A translated (moved) cube <0, 2, 0>.

Objects can be moved along several axes simultaneously with a single translation, so it isn't necessary to perform a separate translation for each axis of movement. For example, a translation of <2, 2, 0> would move the cube two units to the right and two units up.

SCALE

Performing a scale operation on a mesh or a face changes its size and location. First, let's look at how a scale operation can change the size of an object. If we take our sample 1 by 1 by 1 cube and scale it by a factor of ½, our cube would be ½ units long in each dimension (or ½ by ½ by ½ units). If we used a scale factor of 2, we would double our cube's dimensions, producing a cube that is two units long in each dimension (making our sample cube 2 by 2 by 2 units). Figure 2.13 illustrates these scale operations.

As mentioned previously, performing a scale operation can also change an object's location. In Figure 2.13, the cube is centered on the origin. Had it

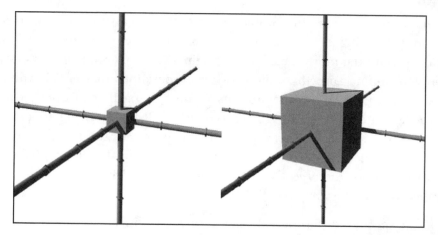

Figure 2.13
The result of scaling a 1x1x1 cube with scale factors ½ and 2.

not been, the cube's location would have been affected as well as its size. A scale operation doesn't scale the object directly: it scales the object's vertices. With a scale factor greater than 1, vertices move away from the origin. With a scale factor less than 1, vertices move toward the origin. Figure 2.14 uses the same scaling factors as Figure 2.13, but this time the cube is located to the right of the Y axis and the resulting cube is moved away from the origin.

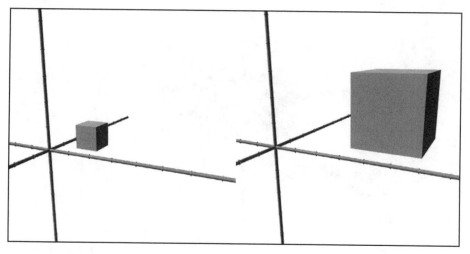

Figure 2.14
A cube that has been sized and moved by a scale operation.

Often, this effect is not desirable because if you want to scale an object without changing its location, you have to move the object to the origin, scale it, and then move it back to its original location. Some graphics systems (including Direct3D) allow for scale operations that enable you to resize an object without changing its location, regardless of whether the object is centered on the origin. This is accomplished by using a local, or object, axis. Scaling objects on a local axis produces the same effect as scaling an object centered on the origin: the size of the object changes, but its location (the object's center) stays the same. By default, Direct3D scales objects using the object's local axis.

You can specify a different scale factor for each axis. This allows objects to be stretched and shortened. Scale factors of 1 have no effect on an object's vertices, so 1 can be used for any axis that should not be modified. If we take our original cube and perform a scale operation using <2, 1, 1>, we will increase the cube's width without affecting the other dimensions. Figure 2.15 shows the result.

ROTATE

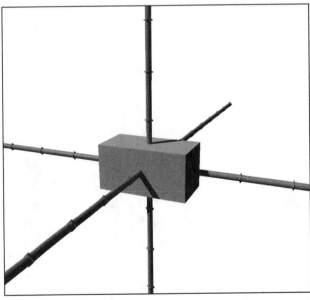

Figure 2.15
Using multiple scale factors <2, 1, 1>.

ROTATE

The Rotate operation allows us to assign orientations to objects. Rotating an object requires that we determine the axis of the rotation and how far the object should rotate.

We can use a vector to describe to the axis of the rotation and a value to describe how far the object should rotate.

Let's go back to our sample cube and rotate it on the Z axis by 45 degrees. Rotating on the Z axis means that the cube will turn as if it had been speared by the Z axis and is now free to turn in only one direction. We can express this with the vector <0, 0, 1> and the number 45. Figure 2.16 shows the result.

TEXTURE MAPPING

Texture mapping gained a lot of attention with the advent of ID software's smash hit, DOOM. DOOM wasn't the first implementation of texture mapping, but it was certainly one of the most popular.

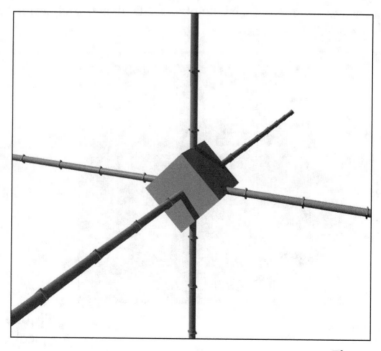

Figure 2.16
A cube rotated 45 degrees around the axis <0, 0, 1>.

Texture mapping is the application (or mapping) of a texture onto a face or set of faces. This mapping takes place with regard to the object's location in 3D space. We can't just slap a texture on a face without regard for the object's distance and orientation from the viewer. Such a scene would hardly be convincing. We will talk more about texture and perspective later in this chapter. For now, bear in mind that correct texture mapping requires textures on distant objects to be applied differently than textures on nearby objects.

THE NATURE OF TEXTURES

A texture is a two-dimensional grid of color values. Textures are often stored in familiar file formats such as BMP, PCX, or GIF. Just about any 2D image can be used as a texture. Figure 2.17 shows a typical texture.

Keep in mind, while you can use any image as a texture—not all images make a *good* texture. Good textures usually aren't much to look at by themselves, but they can bring realism to the objects. Images that are complete scenes usually make poor textures because you don't expect to see an entire scene when you look at a single object. 3D objects such as mirrors or pictures are exceptions to this rule.

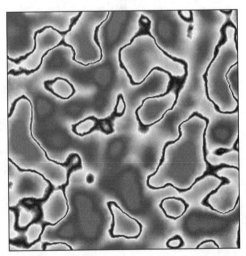

Figure 2.17
A typical texture.

TEXTURE SCALING

Textures can be applied to objects in a number of different ways. One way to vary a texture is to alter a texture's scale. If a texture is applied with a large scale factor, only a portion of the texture will fit on a given object. If the scale factor is small, the complete texture will appear on the object as a set of repeating tiles. This second effect can be quite useful for situations where you are representing large objects that have a similar overall appearance. Figure 2.18 is an example of the same texture applied using different scale factors.

TEXTURE WRAPPING

Texture wrapping determines the manner in which the texture is applied to objects. The simplest wrapping method is one in which a texture is applied as if fired from a gun. The individual colors in the texture shoot straight through the object and come out the other side. This method is usually called a flat wrap (a bit of a paradox, since you can't wrap an object with something that is flat). Figure 2.19 applies the texture shown in Figure 2.18 to a cube using a flat texture wrap.

This method is frequently used on large objects, especially when the viewer will only see one side of the object. Flat wraps are easy to use because they require only that the direction of the texture application be specified. Because flat texture wraps apply textures to objects in only one direction, the sides of the object usually appear striped.

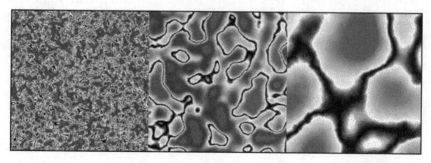

Figure 2.18
Texture scaling.

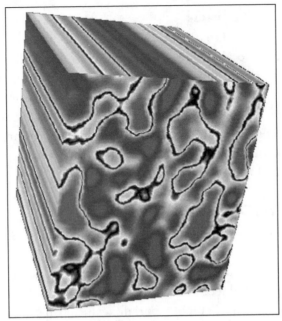

Figure 2.19
A texture applied with a flat wrapping method.

Another common method is cylindrical. Cylindrical wrapping methods apply a texture to objects by bending or warping the texture into a cylinder. Figure 2.20 is a cylindrical wrap. Notice the "seam" where the texture edges meet.

It's important to remember that the texture wrapping method and the shape of the object being textured are completely independent. You can just as easily apply a flat wrap to a sphere as a spherical wrap to a cube. Direct3D supports flat, spherical, and cylindrical texture wrapping.

We'll study texture wrapping methods in more detail in Chapter 5.

TEXTURE ANIMATION

Rendering the same object with different textures or different texture wrap settings is called texture animation. A simple example is to apply the same texture to an object, but change the texture location with each animation frame. This causes the texture to move across the object. This technique is useful for representing a moving object such as a conveyor belt. Another

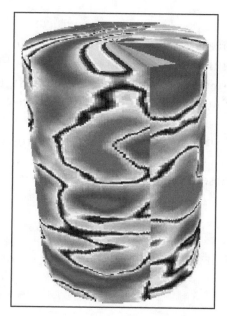

Figure 2.20
A cylindrical texture wrap.

example is to change the scale of the texture. These two methods are easy to implement (because they require only one texture), but are limited in usefulness.

A more powerful texture animation technique is to use a different texture on an object for each animation frame. If, for instance, you wanted a scene with a television (and the television needed to be on), you could apply a different texture to the television screen for each screen update. This technique is very effective, but requires a lot of memory if the sequence of textures is long or if the texture is large.

LIGHTING

Our translated, scaled, rotated, and textured objects can exist in a 3D world and never be seen if they remain in the dark. Before we can expect to see anything, we need to provide a light sources. When we view a final output, the objects in the scene will be rendered according to the qualities of the light sources contained in the scene.

COLOR

All light sources have a common attribute: color. Normally light sources are white, meaning that all color values are on at full intensity. Lighting systems vary from one graphics package to the next, but most use RGB (Red, Green, and Blue) values to define light source colors. In Direct3D, each RGB value can vary from zero (off) to one (on), so a white light has an RGB setting of 1, 1, 1. A red light has a 1, 0, 0 setting. A blue light has a 0, 1, 0 setting. Colors besides red, green, and blue can be represented by using mixture of these three colors. For example, yellow has an RGB setting of 1, 1, 0.

LIGHT TYPES

Light sources come in several forms. Typical light sources include ambient lights, point lights, and spotlights.

AMBIENT LIGHT

The simplest light source is an ambient light. Ambient lights have no location and illuminate all of the objects in a scene with the same intensity. These lights are handy because they are easy to use. Ambient lights are often used in combination with more sophisticated light sources.

POINT LIGHT

A point light emanates light in all directions. Point lights have a specific location but no orientation. Point lights are fairly demanding in terms of processing time due to the requirement that light emanates in every direction. The cost in processing time is often worth the price, however, because of the realistic effects that point lights create. Point lights are sometimes called "omni" or "omni-directional" lights.

DIRECTIONAL LIGHT

A more computationally efficient alternative to the point light is the directional light. Directional lights have orientation, but no location. The rays of light that a directional light produces are parallel to each other. Directional lights tend to make scenes look as if the light source is very far from the objects in the scene.

SPOT LIGHT

Spot lights have orientation and location, and produce light in the shape of a cone. The cone characteristics are determined by *umbra* and *penumbra* angles. The umbra angle defines the cone of light where the spotlight fully illuminates. The penumbra angle defines a cone of diminished light around the umbra cone. A spotlight's penumbra angle is always greater that the umbra angle.

Direct3D supports ambient light, point light, directional light, and spotlights. Direct3D also offers a variant on directional lights, called *parallel light.*

PERSPECTIVE TRANSFORMATION

At the beginning of this chapter, I mentioned that the goal of 3D graphics is to present a two-dimensional representation of a three-dimensional scene. We've covered manipulating the unseen, 3D universe; now we'll discuss producing a 2D version of the 3D world.

The conversion from 3D to 2D requires a perspective transformation. A perspective transformation ensures that the final output looks and behaves correctly. Correct behavior means that objects closer to the viewer appear larger than distant objects. It means that objects or portions of objects located outside the scope of the scene are not drawn. It requires that we decide when an object is too far away or too close to be drawn at all.

3D TO 2D

Going from 3D to 2D requires that we partition 3D space in a way that a 2D version can be easily produced. This means that we need to decide where the viewer, or camera, is situated, and how much of the scene the viewer should see. These settings are represented by a *viewing frustum*. We can think of the viewing frustum as the base of a pyramid. The viewer is located as the very top of the pyramid and looks toward the center of the pyramid's base. As the size of the pyramid base increases, more of the scene is visible, but the objects appear smaller. As the size of the pyramid base decreases, the objects in the scene appear larger, but fewer objects fit into the scene. The size of the pyramid base is determined by the viewer's angle, or field-of-view (FOV) setting.

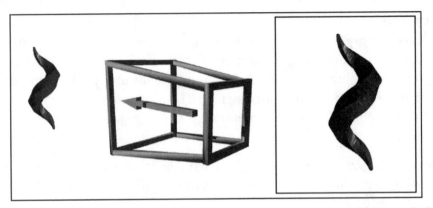

Figure 2.21
The viewing frustum and the resulting image.

Figure 2.21 shows a scene from two different angles. The image on the left shows a representation of the viewing frustum. The arrow indicates the direction from which the scene is viewed. The right side of the figure shows the image that results from the frustum configuration.

Using different viewing frustum settings is similar to changing the lens on your camera. Using a telephoto lens lets you see objects in the distance, but you can't take a picture of your family without standing 400 feet away. On the other hand, you can use a wide-angle lens for close-up shots, but it isn't very useful for bird-watching (unless the bird you are watching is in a cage).

HIDDEN SURFACE REMOVAL TECHNIQUES

An important issue in 3D graphics is determining which objects are visible and which are hidden by other objects. Rendering a scene without concern for which surfaces are closer to the viewer than others results in confused final images. Algorithms that solve this problem are called hidden surface removal techniques. There are many hidden surface removal techniques, each with it's own merits. The technique employed by Direct3D is called Z-buffering.

Z-BUFFERING

Z-buffering uses a memory buffer to keep track of which surfaces are closest to the viewer. The Z values stored in the buffer do not necessarily correspond to the Z axis; instead they represent how far surfaces are from the viewer. As the image is drawn, Z values are compared with Z values in the Z-buffer. If the value in the buffer indicates that the surface being drawn is closer to the viewer than any existing surfaces, then the new surface is drawn over the old surface. If the new surface is farther away than an existing surface, then the surface is not drawn.

Rendering performance can be optimized by sorting the surface in front-to-back order. This improves performance because objects in the front of the scene are drawn first and hidden surfaces don't have to be drawn at all. Luckily for us, Direct3D Retained Mode performs Z-buffering (including the sorting optimization) without any intervention from the programmer.

Z-BUFFERING: PROS AND CONS

Z-buffering is regarded as one of the simplest and fastest hidden surface removal techniques. It is also accurate to the pixel (yes, some algorithms are not) and handles complex scenes efficiently. The major drawback of Z-buffering is the amount of memory a Z-buffer requires. Z-buffers must be at least as large as the output image and can have bit depths of 32 bits. As an example, a program running in a 800 × 600 mode with a 16-bit Z-buffer requires almost a megabyte of memory for the Z-buffer alone.

RENDERING METHODS

Once a scene has been modeled in three dimensions and converted to two dimensions it is ready for rendering. This final step produces the image that will be visible on your screen and is called *rendering* or *shading*. A number of different rendering techniques exist; let's go over some of the more common techniques.

WIREFRAME

A wireframe rendering doesn't look realistic at all and doesn't require all the steps we've discussed. Wireframe modes draw only the edges of the faces in the scene, representing them with straight lines. Figure 2.22 is a mesh rendered in wireframe mode.

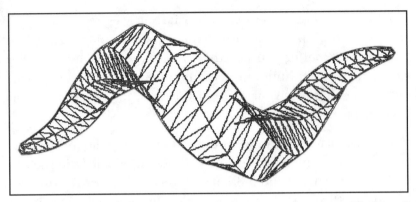

Figure 2.22
A wireframe rendering.

UNLIT

Unlit rendering gets its name from the fact that it doesn't take light sources into consideration. Faces are drawn using the assigned face colors and textures without consideration of light values or face orientation. Unlit scenes can be rendered quickly but objects tend to appear as silhouettes. Figure 2.23 show an unlit object.

FLAT

Flat shading provides output more realistic than wireframe or unlit output. Flat shading takes light sources into consideration at the face level. A

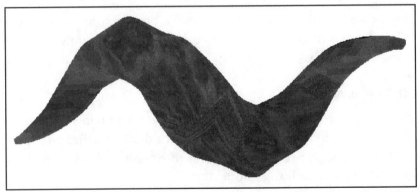

Figure 2.23
Unlit shading output.

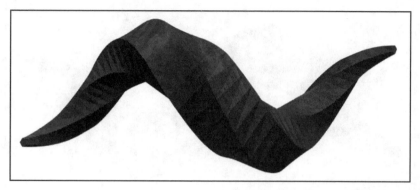

Figure 2.24
Flat shading output.

normal is calculated for each face and used to calculate lighting attributes for the entire face. Flat shading requires more computational power than wireframe or unlit modes. Figure 2.24 shows a scene rendered with a flat shading mode. Notice how each face is easily discernible.

GOURAUD

Gouraud shading is similar to flat shading except normals are calculated for each vertex instead of each face. The faces are then shaded by averaging light intensities over the face. This tends to round the appearance of meshes, and individual faces become indistinct. Gouraud shading provides realistic output, but can make objects look vague and loosely defined. Because vertex normals are used and face intensities are averaged, Gouraud shading is more computationally demanding than flat shading. Gouraud shading was used to produce Figure 2.25.

PHONG

Phong shading is an improvement over Gouraud shading. Like Gouraud, Phong shading uses vertex normals, but instead of averaging to calculate facial values, normals are calculated across the entire face. This extra work provides a precise, predictable appearance. As you might imagine, Phong shading is slower than Gouraud shading. No figure is supplied because, at the time of this writing, Direct3D doesn't support Phong shading.

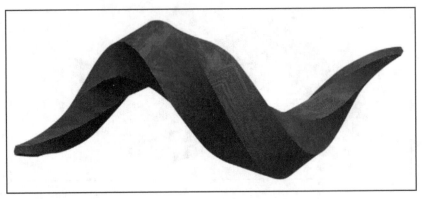

Figure 2.25
Gouraud shading output.

RAY-TRACING

Ray-tracing produces the most realistic output of any rendering method. In fact, ray-tracing is known for its photo-realistic and even hyper-realistic output. Ray-tracing uses an entirely different approach than the methods we have discussed. The ray-tracing algorithm automatically calculates shadows, reflection, and refraction (other rendering methods do not automatically perform the calculations). Unfortunately, ray-tracing is notoriously slow. Single images can take hours or even days to calculate. Needless to say, ray-tracing isn't well suited for realtime graphics and is not supported by Direct3D. Figure 2.26 is a ray-traced image (produced with POV-Ray).

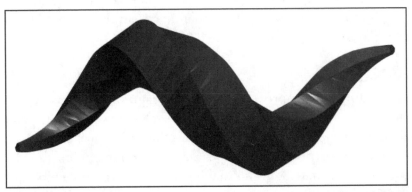

Figure 2.26
A ray-traced scene.

ANIMATION

Realtime 3D graphics are no fun without animation. 3D animation can be accomplished in two ways: motion attributes and key-framing.

MOTION ATTRIBUTES

One of the simplest ways to achieve animation is with motion attributes. A motion attribute is a translation, rotation, or scale factor that is applied to an object or set of objects for each screen update. Motion attributes are useful for simple repeating motions. Once a motion attribute is assigned to an object, the object will move according to the attributes, without any further intervention.

KEY-FRAMING

The term *key-framing* comes from a traditional animation technique where only certain "key" frames in an animation are drawn. The remaining frames are produced by creating intermediate poses between the key frames.

Key-framing in 3D graphics means that you define the positions of objects in a scene at key times in an animation. The computer holds the responsibility of placing the objects in the remaining frames.

Key-framing requires you to determine the number of frames in an animation and to define keys at specific frames. For example, if you wanted to create an animation where an object travels from the top-left corner of the screen to the top-right corner and then to the bottom-right corner of the screen, you would perform the following steps:

1. Define the number of frames in the animation (we'll use 30 for this example).

2. Specify that in frame 1 the object should appear at the top-left corner of the screen.

3. Specify that in frame 15 the object should appear at the top-right corner of the screen.

4. Specify that in frame 30 the object should appear at the bottom-right corner of the screen.

In Direct3D there are two modes for key-framing: linear and spline-based. Linear key-framing means the animation motion between key frames is linear; the objects travel the shortest path between key frames. Spline-based animation uses curved paths to travel between key frames.

Using our example, linear animation would cause the object to travel directly from the top-left corner of the screen to the top-right. At frame 15 (when the object reaches the top-right corner) the object will turn abruptly and travel to the bottom-right corner. A spline-base animation would cause the object to round-out the corner at frame 15. The object would act as if it was anticipating the fact that it was going to have to make the corner.

In both linear and spline-based animation, the objects in the scene are exactly where you specify at the key frames.

CONCLUSION

Although graphics packages vary from one to another, there is usually a body of concepts and terms that they have in common. The concepts and terms in this chapter are fairly universal and apply to most graphics systems. In the next chapter, we'll introduce Direct3D. We'll look at how Direct3D implements the common techniques, and how it differs from other graphics packages.

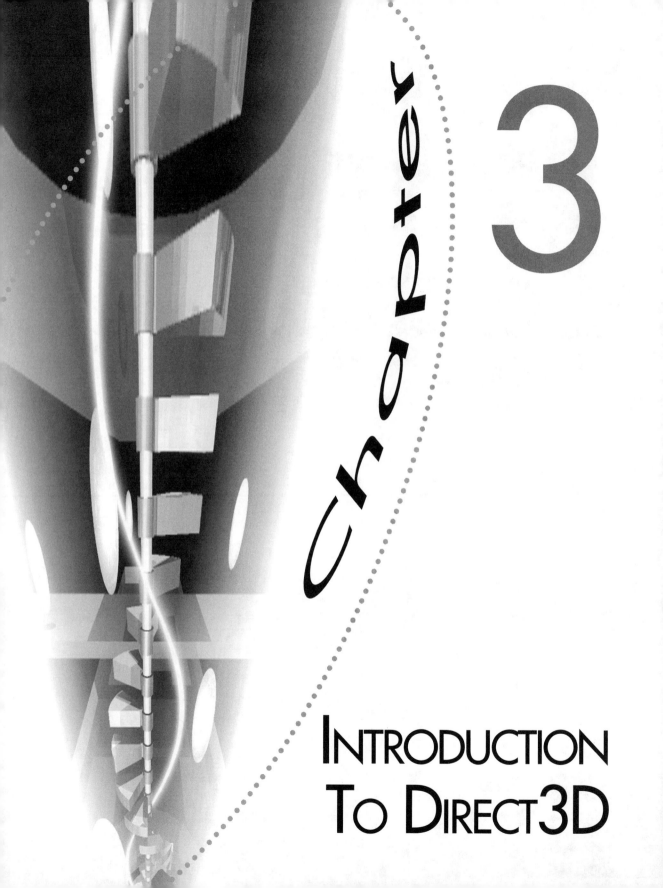

Chapter 3

INTRODUCTION TO DIRECT3D

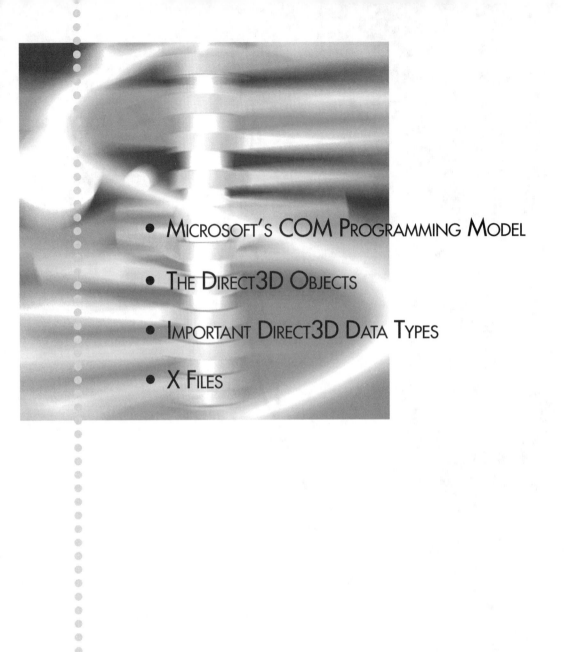

- MICROSOFT'S COM PROGRAMMING MODEL

- THE DIRECT3D OBJECTS

- IMPORTANT DIRECT3D DATA TYPES

- X FILES

3

INTRODUCTION TO DIRECT3D

In this chapter, we'll take a look at Direct3D. We'll talk about the concepts and terminology that Direct3D employs, and we'll look at the Direct3D API itself.

DIRECT3D

Direct3D is a collection of Microsoft's Component Object Model (COM) interfaces that represent graphical constructs such as meshes and faces and application constructs such as viewports and devices. We'll talk about each interface in this chapter.

Although we will be discussing interfaces and member functions, the purpose of this chapter is not to provide a reference manual. We aren't concerned with parameter lists or return values, just the functionality that an interface provides through its member functions.

Before we jump into our discussion of the Direct3D interfaces, you need to be familiar with Microsoft's COM. The following is a short discussion of COM. By convention, COM interfaces are named with an "I" prefix ("I" for "Interface"). In our discussion, we'll omit this prefix.

COM

Microsoft's COM (Component Object Model) is a programming model designed to allow the development of completely portable, safely upgradable software components. COM's vision is that software components should be as easy to install as hardware components. Snickers aside (that sure doesn't sound like the hardware components I've installed), COM is the foundation of APIs such as OLE and DirectX.

COM uses an object-oriented model that is different from the model used by languages such as C++. The COM model is more strict. The COM version of inheritance, for example, is limited compared to the C++ version. Also, COM objects do not allow public data members. All interaction with the object must be done through member functions.

A COM component is made up of an object and one or more interfaces that access the object. The object provides the actual functionality that the COM component supports but cannot be accessed directly. COM objects are always accessed through interfaces. A single object can support multiple interfaces. Figure 3.1 illustrates the object/interface relationship.

The figure illustrates the application's relationship with the COM object. The application uses the COM object only through the interfaces that the object supports.

COM objects support multiple interfaces in order to allow the object's functionality to be upgraded or extended without risk of "breaking" existing programs.

COM also supports a feature called lifetime encapsulation. Lifetime encapsulation means that COM objects control their own destruction. When

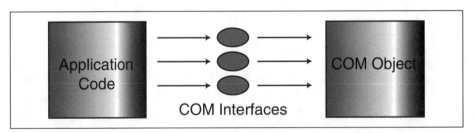

Figure 3.1
COM objects and interfaces.

an object detects that it is no longer needed, it destroys itself. In order for this feature to work properly, programs are charged with the responsibility of notifying objects when a new pointer to the object is created and when one is destroyed.

All COM objects are derived from the **Iunknown** COM object. **Iunknown** supplies three member functions: **AddRef()**, **Release()**, and **QueryInterface()**. **AddRef()** and **Release()** are the member functions that increase and decrease an object's reference count. The **QueryInterface()** function is used to retrieve auxiliary interfaces for an object (or to determine that the interface is not supported). One of the **QueryInterface()** function arguments is a Globally Unique Identifier (GUID) that identifies the interface that is being sought.

All of the DirectX API's are built with COM. This does not, however, mean that you must be an expert on COM to use DirectX. In fact, using COM objects is similar to using C++ objects. The following guidelines point out some of the rules that should be observed when using COM.

- COM objects and C++ objects cannot be derived from one another. The closest you can get to deriving a C++ class from a COM object is to "embed" the COM object into the C++ classes and write "wrapper" functions for each COM member function.

- Anytime a copy of a COM object pointer is made, the object's **AddRef()** member function should be called to notify the object of the additional reference. This doesn't apply to object creation. Usually the DirectX API supplies a function that creates the COM object and calls **AddRef()** for you.

- Anytime a COM object pointer is no longer needed, the object's **Release()** member function should be called.

- The **QueryInterface()** member function isn't magic. **QueryInterface()** will return interfaces to an object only if the object supports the interface. Attempts to obtain arbitrary interfaces from an object will fail.

If you want to know more about COM, you can download the specifications from the Microsoft Web site (www.microsoft.com).

DIRECT3DRM: THE MASTER INTERFACE

As I mentioned earlier, Direct3D is a collection of COM interfaces. All the various interfaces that make up Direct3D depend on a single master object: **Direct3DRM** (RM stands for Retained-Mode). The **Direct3DRM** object represents Direct3D itself. The interface is created with the **Direct3DRMCreate()** function. For example:

```
LPDIRECT3DRM d3drm;
Direct3DRMCreate( &d3drm );
```

The **LPDIRECT3DRM** type is a pointer to a **Direct3DRM** interface. The **Direct3DRMCreate()** function creates the object and initializes the interface pointer. Once the **Direct3DRMCreate()** function returns successfully (we'll talk about return codes later in this chapter), the **Direct3DRM** interface is ready to use.

CREATING DIRECT3D OBJECTS

The primary purpose of the **Direct3DRM** interface is the creation of other Direct3D objects. Most of the **Direct3DRM** member functions have "Create" prefixes. The object creation member functions are:

- CreateAnimation()
- CreateAnimationSet()
- CreateDeviceFromClipper()
- CreateDeviceFromD3D()
- CreateDeviceFromSurface()
- CreateFace()
- CreateFrame()
- CreateLight()
- CreateLightRGB()
- CreateMaterial()
- CreateMesh()

- CreateMeshBuilder()

- CreateObject()

- CreateUserVisual()

- CreateShadow()

- CreateTexture()

- CreateTextureFromSurface()

- LoadTexture()

- CreateViewport()

- CreateWrap()

It is certainly not necessary to use all of these functions. Some are virtually identical to each other. For example, the only difference between the **CreateLight()** and **CreateLightRGB()** member functions is how the color of the light source is specified.

Because the **Direct3DRM** interface is needed in order to create other Direct3D objects, **Direct3DRM** is usually the first object that a program creates.

MODIFYING THE SEARCH PATH

Another role of the **Direct3DRM** interface is to allow you to modify the search path that Direct3D uses to look for files. The path can be examined and modified with these member functions:

- AddSearchPath()

- GetSearchPath()

- SetSearchPath()

By default, Direct3D installs c:\dxsdk\sdk\media as the search path. You can override or append this path using the search path member functions, but the changes that your program makes will take effect only during the course of your program's execution. This path will not be installed on an end user's machine, so your programs should not rely on its existence.

Changing the default search path

The default search path is stored in the Windows registry and can be changed using REGEDIT, the Windows 95 registry editor. You can find the search path entry by searching for the "D3D Path" entry.

CONTROLLING THE UPDATE PACE

Finally, the **Direct3DRM** object defines a **Tick()** member function. **Tick()** controls the rate at which a program runs. Each time the **Tick()** function is called, Direct3D updates animated elements in a scene and renders the results. Calling **Tick()** often updates the scene often; calling **Tick()** infrequently slows the program. In addition, the **Tick()** member function takes a single parameter that controls the animation rate within a scene. For most situations, using a value of 1.0 is desirable, but a program's pace can be fine-tuned at runtime by using different values.

DIRECT3DRMDEVICE: THE DEVICE INTERFACE

Direct3D devices are objects that create rendered output. Direct3D supports a number of device types. Programs can either choose a device from a list of available devices, or instruct Direct3D to select a device automatically. The two main types of devices are software devices and hardware devices. Software devices allow programs to run on computers that are not equipped with 3D accelerated video hardware. Hardware devices are available only on computers with 3D hardware and allow Direct3D to make full use of the features that are present on the hardware.

A device is represented with the **Direct3DRMDevice** interface and can be created using the **Direct3DRM** member functions. There are three ways to create a device:

1. Create a DirectDraw "clipper" object, and then create the device with the **CreateDeviceFromClipper()** member function. This is the simplest and most reliable method to create a device.

2. Create a DirectDraw primary surface with a back-buffer (to allow page-flipping), and create the device with the **CreateDeviceFromSurface()** member function. This method is used to initialize Direct3D applications that will be running in full-screen mode.

3. Initialize Direct3D Immediate Mode, and create a device with the **CreateDeviceFromD3D()** member function.

Once a device has been created it is used to specify rendering settings and perform the rendering of scenes.

COLOR MODELS

Both software and hardware devices come in two varieties: RGB and Ramp. The RGB color model supports colored lighting, while the Ramp color model does not. Reduced overhead allows Ramp devices to out-perform RGB devices. Ramp devices are also called "mono" devices because of their monochromatic treatment of light sources. This can be misleading, however, since only the light sources are monochromatic in Ramp mode. Meshes and faces enjoy full color capability in Ramp mode.

RENDERING OPTIONS

Devices can be used to modify rendering options. The **GetQuality()** and **SetQuality()** member functions, for example, allow you to specify the rendering mode (Gouraud, flat, etc.) that the device will use to render scenes. Individual objects can override the device settings only if the rendering scheme they specify is more primitive than the device scheme. The default rendering setting is flat.

The **GetShades()** and **SetShades()** member functions let you control how many different shades of a given color a device uses to render scenes. This setting often varies depending on the bit depth of the current video mode. The default number of shades is 32, but this is low for 24- and 32-bit modes. It pays to experiment with different shade values (values must be a power of 2) when determining the best setting for your application.

The **GetDither()** and **SetDither()** member functions let you turn dithering on and off. Dithering is a technique that simulates a greater number of colors than are actually available and is useful for video modes that support few colors (usually 256 or fewer, but even video modes that support sixty-four thousand colors can benefit from this technique). Dithering is enabled by default.

DIRECT3DWINDEVICE: THE WINDEVICE INTERFACE

The object that provides Direct3D's device support is an example of a COM object that supports multiple interfaces. The **Direct3DRMDevice** interface that we discussed is one interface through which a device can be used. The **Direct3DWinDevice** is another. The **Direct3DWinDevice** interface represents devices that are supported by Windows. Figure 3.2 illustrates the Direct3D device object and its interfaces.

Because the **Direct3DWinDevice** interface is merely an alternative interface to a Direct3D device, applications use the existing device to retrieve the **WinDevice** interface. This is done with the **QueryInterface()** member function. The code looks like this:

```
LPDIRECT3DRMWINDEVICE windev;
device->QueryInterface( IID_IDirect3DRMWinDevice, (void**)&windev );
```

The **device** variable is a pre-initialized pointer to a **Direct3DRMDevice** interface. The device's **QueryInterface()** member function is used to retrieve

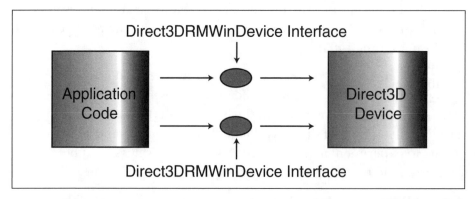

Figure 3.2
The device object and its interfaces.

a pointer to a **Direct3DRMWinDevice** interface. The **IID_IDirect3D-RMWinDevice** is the GUID (Globally Unique Identifier) for the interface that is being requested.

The **WinDevice** interface supports two member functions: **HandleActivate()** and **HandlePaint()**. Both of these functions notify Direct3D that certain Windows messages have been received. A Direct3D program should call the **HandleActivate()** function whenever a **WM_ACTIVATE** message is processed. Whenever a WM_PAINT message is processed, a Direct3D program should call the **HandlePaint()** function.

DIRECT3DRMVIEWPORT: THE VIEWPORT INTERFACE

Viewport is the Direct3D term for a camera. A viewport determines the location and orientation from which a scene is viewed. Viewports can be used to adjust field-of-view settings, front and back clipping, and perspective transformations. Viewports can also be animated to simulate situations where the user is traveling through a virtual environment.

A viewport is represented by the **Direct3DRMViewport** interface and can be created using the **Direct3DRM CreateViewport()** member function as follows:

```
d3drm->CreateViewport( device, camera,
            0, 0, device->GetWidth(), device->GetHeight(),
            &viewport );
```

The **d3drm** variable is a pointer to a **Direct3DRM** interface. The **device** variable points to a **Direct3DRMDevice** interface. The **camera** variable is the frame that will determine the viewport's location and orientation. We'll talk about frames later in this chapter.

FIELD OF VIEW

The field-of-view (FOV) setting can be adjusted with the **SetField()** member function. The default FOV is 0.5. Smaller values reduce the angle of the viewing frustum, causing a telephoto effect. Larger values increase the frustum angle and provide wide-angle effects. Negative values are not permitted.

CLIPPING

Viewports control front and back 3D clipping. The **SetFront()** and **SetBack()** member functions can be used to define an area in front of the camera where objects will be visible. Objects located outside this area will not be rendered. The default front and back clipping settings are 1 and 100 respectively.

DIRECT3DRMFRAME: THE FRAME INTERFACE

Direct3D Retained-Mode relies heavily on frames. The use of this term tends to cause confusion because of the existing use of the word to describe a single image within an animation. The Direct3D meaning of frame comes from "frame of reference." Frames are used to place objects in 3D space. Objects such as meshes, faces, cameras, and light sources by themselves have no means of locating or orienting themselves. Instead, these objects are added or attached to frames, and they receive their location and orientation from the attached frame—when the frame moves, the objects move.

FRAME HIERARCHIES

A Direct3D scene is defined as a hierarchy of frames. Each scene contains a root frame and any number of child frames attached to the root frame. Each child frame can have children of its own. Frames are represented by the **Direct3DRMFrame** interface and are created with the **Direct3DRM CreateFrame()** member function. For example:

```
LPDIRECT3DRMFRAME newframe;
d3drm->CreateFrame( parentframe, &newframe );
```

This code declares a pointer to a frame, and then initializes the pointer with the **CreateFrame()** member function. The **parentframe** variable is a pointer to the frame that is the parent to the new frame. Specifying NULL for the parent frame creates the root frame for a new scene.

Child frames inherit characteristics from parent frames. One inherited characteristic is the "frame of reference." Child frames are attached to parent frames, so they follow the parent frame—when a parent frame moves, the child frame moves. This allows for powerful "sub-object" animation. For example, if you want to create and animate a helicopter (complete with spinning blades, naturally), you would create a frame for the helicopter body, and then create child frames for the helicopter blades. The blades can be animated by applying a rotation to the frames to which the blades are attached. The helicopter body can be animated by translating and orienting the frame to which the helicopter body is attached. Because the blades are children of the helicopter body, they imitate the body's movements.

Frames aren't limited to using their parents as their "frame" of reference. Many frame member functions allow you to indicate which frame should be used as a reference frame (regardless of child-parent relationships). The flexible nature of frame hierarchies is one of the reasons whyDirect3D Retained-Mode is so powerful.

FRAME POSITIONING

The **Direct3DRMFrame** interface offers member functions dedicated to positioning frames. **Direct3DRMFrame** provides the following member functions:

- AddRotation()

- AddScale()

- AddTranslation()

- GetOrientation()

- GetPosition()

- LookAt()

- SetOrientation()

- SetPosition()

The **GetPosition()** and **SetPosition()** member functions allow the frame's location to be inspected and assigned. The **GetOrientation()** and **SetOrientation()** member functions allow the frame's orientation to be specified. The frame interface also provides a **LookAt()** member function that orients a frame to face, or point at, another frame. **LookAt()** is convenient for situations where a camera or light source follows another object.

The **SetPosition()**, **SetOrientation()**, and **LookAt()** member functions assign attributes to the frame object without regard for the frame's previous settings. The Frame interface supplies **AddTranslation()**, **AddRotation()**, and **AddScale()** member functions to adjust a frame's setting instead of replacing them. **AddTranslation()** adjusts a frame's location according to the translation provided. **AddRotation()** adjusts the frame's orientation by adding the supplied rotation to the existing rotation. **AddScale()** resizes a frame relative to its current size.

FRAME MOVEMENT

The frame interface provides member functions that adjust a frame's position on an on-going basis. These functions specify motion attributes that will be applied to the frame with each update of a scene.

The **GetRotation()** and **SetRotation()** member functions are used to manipulate a frames rotation attribute. Rotations applied with **SetRotation()** take effect on every scene update.

MOVE CALLBACKS

Having the ability to place a frame, or assign motion attributes is great, but it can accomplish only so much. Interactive graphics require that the objects in your scene respond to each other, as well as respond to input from the user. The frame interface allows for this runtime adjustment by using callbacks. Callbacks are functions that you write and install, or register, with Direct3D. After you register your callbacks, Direct3D will execute the callbacks whenever a new scene is about to be drawn and allow you to make last-minute changes to the objects in the scene.

Callbacks are installed with the **AddMoveCallback()** member function. Each frame object can install multiple callbacks. Callbacks are called in the order they are installed. To remove callbacks, use the **DeleteMoveCallback()** member function.

DIRECT3DRMMESHBUILDER: THE MESHBUILDER INTERFACE

The **Direct3DRMMeshBuilder** interface is a high-level, convenient mesh manipulation tool that offers 38 member functions for creating and modifying meshes. Meshbuilders, as their name implies, build meshes and are not meshes themselves. They can, however, be used as convenient substitutes for meshes. Meshbuilders can be added to scenes as visual elements. When meshbuilders are added to a scene, they create and use an internal mesh. Meshbuilders are created using the **Direct3DRM CreateMeshBuilder()** function as shown below:

```
LPDIRECT3DRMMESHBUILDER meshbuilder;
d3drm->CreateMeshBuilder( &meshbuilder );
```

LOADING AND SAVING

The **Load()** member function lets meshbuilder objects load meshes from disk, program resources, or memory. The **Load()** function will also load any textures applied to a mesh as long as the texture's location is supplied in Direct3D's search path.

Load() allows for the use of a callback function whenever an attempt is made to load a texture. This allows programs to override the default attempt to load a texture, making it possible to load textures from specific directories or from a program's resources.

The meshbuilder **Save()** member function allows you to save meshes as text, binary, or compressed files.

RENDERING OPTIONS

Meshbuilders allow for the manipulation of mesh qualities such as color, texture, and rendering options. Some meshbuilder member functions used for rendering mesh options include:

- GetPerspective()

- GetQuality()

- GetTextureCoordinates()

- SetColor()

- SetColorRGB()

- SetPerspective()

- SetQuality()

- SetTexture()

- SetTextureCoordinates()

- SetTextureTopology()

The **SetColor()** and **SetColorRGB()** functions can be used to assign colors to the faces in a mesh. No **GetColor()** function is supplied because there is no guarantee that all of the faces in the mesh will be the same color.

The **GetQuality()** and **SetQuality()** member functions can be used to set the rendering mode of the mesh (wireframe, flat, Gouraud, etc.). There is a limitation, however. Direct3D will "demote" the render quality of a meshbuilder if the device on which it is to be rendered is configured to use a more primitive rendering mode. For example, if a device is configured to use the wireframe mode, then any meshbuilders that use flat or Gouraud mode will appear in wireframe.

The meshbuilder **SetTexture()** member function assigns specific textures to the meshbuilder. The **GetTextureCoordinates()**, **SetTextureCoordinates()**, and **SetTextureTopology()** member functions allow texture attributes to be assigned. It is usually preferable to use a texture wrap instead of these functions. We'll talk about texture wraps later in this chapter.

The **GetPerspective()** and **SetPerspective()** member functions can be used to turn texture perspective correction on or off. Texture perspective correction insures that textures appear correctly given their location and orientation from the viewer, but it brings extra computational overhead as well. In general, perspective correction is desirable when a texture appears on large faces, close to the viewer. Correction can be safely turned off if a mesh doesn't get close to the viewer. You'll know it's time to turn on perspective correction if it appears that textures are drifting and sliding across mesh faces during animation.

FACE ACCESS

The **Meshbuilder** interface also allows face modifications and additions. For example, a list of the faces that make up a meshbuilder can be retrieved with the **GetFaces()** member function. The number of faces in a mesh can be retrieved with the **GetFaceCount()** member function. Faces can be created and added to a meshbuilder with the **CreateFace()**, **AddFace()** and **AddFaces()** member functions.

VERTEX ACCESS

Meshbuilders allow the vertices used by the mesh to be accessed. The number of vertices in a mesh can be retrieved with the **GetVertexCount()** member function. All of the vertices in a mesh can be retrieved, modified, and assigned using the **GetVertices()** and **SetVertices()** member functions. The vertex access functionality is powerful since the shape of the mesh can be modified using the vertex functions.

TRANSLATING AND SCALING

Objects rely on frames for their locations, but meshes can specify how they are situated in relation to attached frames. The meshbuilder **Translate()** member function allows you to specify offsets for a mesh's location. This allows you to attach multiple meshes to a single frame without having the meshes occupy the exact same space.

The **Scale()** member function applies a set of scale factors to a mesh. The scaling takes place on the mesh's local axis, so the mesh is scaled as if it were centered on the origin. Different scale factors can be used for each axis, so meshes can be stretched and reduced.

PERFORMANCE

Because of the power and ease of use that the **Direct3DRMMeshBuilder** interface provides, meshbuilders are the obvious choice for many tasks. In terms of performance, however, the **Meshbuilder** interface is lacking in some situations. If you use a meshbuilder to load and configure a mesh, and then use the resulting mesh in a scene without frequently modifying its qualities, then using the **Meshbuilder** interface is fine. However, if the qualities of a mesh (color, texture, vertex positions, etc.) change often during the course of execution, meshbuilders perform poorly. We'll talk about the alternative to meshbuilders next.

DIRECT3DRMMESH: THE MESH INTERFACE

The **Direct3DRMMesh** interface is designed for speed. Unfortunately, the mesh interface is not nearly as easy to use as the meshbuilder interface. Meshes can be created with the **Direct3DRM CreateMesh()** and **Direct3DRMMeshBuilder CreateMesh()** functions.

MESH GROUPS

The **Mesh** interface is dedicated almost exclusively to the manipulation of groups. A group is a collection of faces within a mesh that can be treated as a single entity. The group creation and modification member functions are:

- AddGroup()

- GetGroup()

- GetGroupColor()

- GetGroupCount()

- GetGroupMapping()

- GetGroupMaterial()

- GetGroupQuality()

- GetGroupTexture()

- SetGroupColor()

- SetGroupColorRGB()

- SetGroupMapping()

- SetGroupMaterial()

- SetGroupQuality()

- SetGroupTexture()

These functions are all pretty straightforward to use—once you've created one or more groups. Groups are created with the **AddGroup()** member function. **AddGroup**() requires that you supply mesh attributes at the vertex level. This means that you must supply vertex locations, normals, and texture coordinates in order to create mesh groups. Once one or more groups have been created in a mesh, each group's settings can be changed quickly and easily.

VERTEX ACCESS

The **Direct3DRMMesh** interface provides **GetVertices**() and **SetVertices**() member functions for the manipulation of vertex positions. **GetVertices**() is used to retrieve the current vertex settings. Once vertex settings are retrieved, the settings can be modified and re-installed using **SetVertices**(). This is the recommended technique to modify the shape of a mesh in time-critical situations, such as vertex animation and morphing.

Like **Direct3DRMMeshBuilder**, the **Direct3DRMMesh** interface provides **Scale**() and **Translate**() member functions.

CREATING MESHES WITH MESHBUILDERS

Meshbuilders can be used to create instances of the **Direct3DRMMesh** interface. Typically a meshbuilder is used to load a mesh from disk, to assign colors, textures, adjust faces, vertices, and normals. Then the **Direct3DRMMeshBuilder CreateMesh**() member function is used to create a **Direct3DRMMesh** object. This technique is convenient, but it means that all of the faces in a mesh belong to one group. Defining a mesh with multiple groups requires that the **AddGroup**() function be used.

DIRECT3DRMFACE: THE FACE INTERFACE

Meshes are sets of faces, so creating a mesh means creating faces. Most of the time you will modify existing faces rather than create new faces directly. The **MeshBuilder** interface, for example, allows access to existing faces with the **GetFaces**() member function. It is, however, possible to create faces from scratch and add them to a Meshbuilder. In either case, face attributes such as color, texture, and vertices can be adjusted. Faces are represented by the **Direct3DRMFace** interface.

The **Direct3DRMFace** interface provides **GetColor()** and **SetColor()** member functions for inspecting and changing the color of the face.

FACE TEXTURES

Textures can be applied to faces using these **Direct3DRMFace** member functions. Those functions are as follows:

- GetTexture()
- GetTextureCoordinateIndex()
- GetTextureCoordinates()
- GetTextureTopology()
- SetTexture()
- SetTextureCoordinates()
- SetTextureTopology()

We'll talk about textures in more detail when we talk about the **Direct3DRMTexture** interface.

FACE MATERIALS

The appearance of a face (shiny, dull, etc.) can be adjusted using the **GetMaterial()** and **SetMaterial()** member functions. We'll talk about materials later in this chapter when we talk about the **Direct3DRMMaterial** interface.

FACE VERTICES

The vertex settings can be manipulated with these **Direct3DRMFace** member functions:

- AddVertex()
- GetVertex()
- GetVertexCount()
- GetVertexIndex()
- GetVertices()

The ability to add vertices to a face makes is possible to create concave faces. This could cause trouble since the underlying Direct3D rendering levels cannot draw concave faces (or even faces that have more than three vertices). Fortunately, Direct3D Retained-Mode automatically divides faces into triangles.

DIRECT3DRMTEXTURE: THE TEXTURE INTERFACE

In Direct3D, textures can be applied to faces and meshes or added directly to a scene as a background image or decal. Textures can be loaded from BMP files, PPM files, from a program's resources, or from memory. Textures are represented with the **Direct3DRMTexture** interface.

CREATING TEXTURES

The easiest way to create a texture is to use the **Direct3DRM LoadTexture()** function:

```
LPDIRECT3DRM texture;
d3drm->LoadTexture("texture.bmp", &texture );
```

LoadTexture() takes the name of a BMP or PPM file as an argument and uses the bitmap file to create a texture.

Textures can also be created and loaded from a program's resources by using the **LoadTextureFromResource()** member function as shown below:

```
LPDIRECT3DRMTEXTURE texture;
HRSRC id = FindResource( NULL, MAKEINTRESOURCE(IDR_SAMPLETEXTURE),
    "TEXTURE" );
d3drm->LoadTextureFromResource( id, texture );
```

The **Direct3DRM LoadTextureFromResource()** function takes a resource ID as a parameter and creates a texture from the resource indicated by the **id** variable.

Internally, Direct3D uses DirectDraw surfaces to represent textures. The **LoadTextureFromSurface()** member function allows existing DirectDraw surfaces to be used as textures.

TEXTURE COLORS

Once an instance of the **Direct3DRMTexture** interface has been created, the **GetColors()** and **SetColors()** member functions can be used to control how many colors Direct3D uses to represent the texture. Together with the **GetShades()** and **SetShades()** member functions, you have precise control over how a texture is rendered.

The number of colors in a texture (the setting controlled by **GetColors()** and **SetColors()** functions) determines the number of distinct colors present in the texture itself. The **GetShades()** and **SetShades()** member functions control how many shades are used to represent each color in the texture. For example, if a texture has only two colors, the **GetColors()** member function will return the value 2, and the **GetShades()** member function will return the value 16 (because 16 is the default number of shades). In this example, each of the two colors in the texture will be represented by 16 variations of the color.

Reducing either the number of colors or shades that a texture uses will reduce the clarity of the final output but allow specific textures to be favored over others. For example, if a texture uses many colors but is used in such a way that its clarity isn't important, its colors and shades can be reduced, reserving more colors and shades for a texture whose appearance is of more importance.

DECALS

A decal is a texture that is added to a scene without being applied to a face or a mesh. Decals are rendered into a scene with respect to their location, so they grow and shrink depending on their distance from the viewer. Decals also obey hidden surface rules. If a decal appears behind an object, it will be occluded by the object.

Decals have one major drawback: they always appear facing the viewer, so they cannot be viewed from different angles. This limits their usefulness considerably. If they could be oriented away from the camera, they could be used, for example, to represent paintings in a museum scene or monitors on the deck of a spaceship.

Nevertheless, decals are great for rendering two-dimensional images into scenes. Effects that are computationally expensive to implement with meshes and faces can often be simulated efficiently with decals (explosions, for example).

The **Direct3DRMTexture** interface offers a number of decal manipulation member functions.

- GetDecalOrigin()
- GetDecalScale()
- GetDecalSize()
- GetDecalTransparency()
- GetDecalTransparentColor()
- SetDecalOrigin()
- SetDecalScale()
- SetDecalSize()
- SetDecalTransparency()
- SetDecalTransparentColor()

Most of the decal member functions are used only with decals. The transparency member functions, however, are used to control transparency for decals as well as textures that are applied to meshes and faces.

DIRECT3DRMTEXTUREWRAP: THE TEXTURE WRAP INTERFACE

A texture wrap is an object that describes a manner in which a texture can be applied to a mesh. Texture wraps control the wrap style (flat, cylindrical, spherical), the wrap orientation, and texture settings such as scale and origin.

A texture wrap is created using the settings mentioned and applied to a meshbuilder or mesh object. Texture wraps determine how the texture is to be applied to each face. This saves a significant amount of work because a mesh might have thousands of faces.

Texture wraps are represented by the **Direct3DRMTextureWrap** interface and are created with the **Direct3DRM CreateWrap()** member function.

DIRECT3DRMMATERIAL: THE MATERIAL INTERFACE

Materials determine the behavior of light on faces and meshes. An object can be made to appear shiny, dull, or even appear as if it were emitting light by applying different materials.

Instances of the **Direct3DRMMaterial** interface can be created with the **Direct3DRM CreateMaterial**() member function. The **Material** interface allows the adjustment of three settings, specular light power, specular light color, and emissive light color. The resulting material can then be assigned to faces, meshbuilders, and meshes.

SPECULAR LIGHT POWER

Specular light is the light that reflects off an object and produces specular highlights. The behavior of specular highlights influences the appearance of an object. Small, bright highlights make an object appear shiny. Larger highlights give objects a plastic appearance. Little or no highlights make objects appear dull.

The behavior of specular highlights can be controlled with the specular power setting. Small values produce large specular highlights, and large values produce small highlights. The **Material** interface provides **GetPower**() and **SetPower**() member functions to control this setting.

SPECULAR LIGHT COLOR

The color of the specular highlights can also be adjusted. By default, specular highlights are white. The highlight color can be adjusted with the **GetSpecular**() and **SetSpecular**() member functions.

EMISSIVE LIGHT COLOR

Emissive light is light that emanates from the object itself. Emissive light is useful for representing light sources such as lamps or neon lights. By default, objects have no emissive light (an emissive light color of black). The emissive light color is controlled with the **GetEmissive**() and **SetEmissive**() member functions.

Emitting light in Ramp and RGB color models
The Ramp color model does not support colored light, but emissive light is not dependent on light sources, so objects can emit colored light in both Ramp and RGB color models.

DIRECT3DRMLIGHT: THE LIGHT INTERFACE

Direct3D supports five different types of lights: ambient, point, directional, parallel, and spotlight. The only setting shared by all of the light types is color. Every light type supported by Direct3D can be assigned locations and orientations, but some light types ignore the settings.

Lights are represented by the **Direct3DRMLight** interface and are created with the **Direct3DRM CreateLight()** and **CreateLightRGB()** member functions. Both functions require that you specify the color and the type of light, although these settings can be changed at any time.

Light sources get their location and orientation from frames, so they must be attached to a frame before they can be used in a scene. The **Direct3DRMFrame** interface provides an **AddLight()** member function for attaching lights to frames.

AMBIENT LIGHTS

Ambient lights are the easiest lights to use because they have only one setting: color. While ambient lights must be attached to a frame before they can become part of a scene, they ignore the frame's location and orientation. For this reason, ambient lights can be attached to any frame in a scene.

A scene can have any number of ambient lights. The resulting ambient light level is the sum of the ambient light settings. For example, adding three ambient lights to a scene where the lights are colored red, green, and blue respectively is the same as adding a single white ambient light.

POINT LIGHTS

Point lights emit light in all directions, so their orientation is meaningless. Their location, on the other hand, determines where the light emanates from.

DIRECTIONAL LIGHTS

A directional light is the opposite of a point light. Directional lights have orientation but no location. Directional lights produce parallel light rays, so they have no location from where the light originates. The parallel rays of a directional light point in the direction indicated by the frame to which the light is attached.

Directional lights offer better performance than point lights and are useful for simulating distant light sources.

PARALLEL LIGHTS

The parallel light type is a variation on directional lights. Parallel lights also produce parallel light rays, but instead of casting light in only one direction, parallel light case light in two opposite directions.

Both orientation and location affect parallel lights. The orientation determines the two directions in which light is cast, and the light's location determines the plane from which the light is generated.

SPOTLIGHTS

Spotlights produce light in the shape of a cone. Spotlights use a frame's location to determine the origin of the light (the tip of the cone) and a frame's orientation to determine the direction of the light.

The light that a spotlight produces is described with two angles: the umbra and penumbra angles. The umbra angle defines a cone in which the light is at full intensity. The penumbra angle defines a larger cone that determines where the light ends. The light level in the area between the two cones varies depending on its proximity, gradually changing from the spotlight's color to black (no light).

The umbra and penumbra angles can be adjusted with the **SetUmbra()** and **SetPenumbra() Direct3DRMLight** member functions.

DIRECT3DRMSHADOW: THE SHADOW INTERFACE

Direct3D is designed for performance. This means that other design goals, such as precision and realism, are sometimes sacrificed. Direct3D's shadow support is a good example of a design sacrifice because the rendering techniques used in Direct3D do not account for shadows. Shadow support comes in the form of an object that is added to a scene that emulates a shadow's effect. This emulation is only a rough approximation and has several limitations.

A shadow is created by specifying the following items:

- The object casting the shadow.

- The light source used to calculate the shadow's characteristics.

- A plane on which the shadow will appear.

The fact that a light source must be supplied points to the first limitation: each light source that is to cast a shadow must have its own shadow object. Shadow support is not a feature that can simply be enabled.

Another limitation is that the location of the shadow is defined by a plane. This means that you can't cast a shadow over a complex object. Convincing shadows in Direct3D require flat surfaces.

Shadow objects are instances of the **Direct3DRMShadow** interface, and are created with the **Direct3DRM CreateShadow()** member function. The Shadow interface offers one member function: **Init()**. The **Init()** function is rarely necessary because the **CreateShadow()** function performs the same purpose and is easier to use.

DIRECT3DRMANIMATION: THE ANIMATION INTERFACE

In Direct3D, the term *animation* has two meanings. Animation is the movement of objects in a scene, but animation is also the name of an interface that supports the creation and playback of key-framed animations.

CREATING KEYS

The **Direct3DRMAnimation** interface allows the construction of an animation sequence based on *keys*. Each key is a translation, rotation, or scale factor that is to be applied to an object at a specific point in an animation. The Animation interface can then produce an entire animation based on a few keys by calculating an object's settings between the key frames.

The Animation interface supports the construction of key frames with these functions:

- AddPositionKey()

- AddRotateKey()

- AddScaleKey()

Each of the addkey functions requires a time and a translation. The time indicates the point in the animation when the key is to take effect. The translation is the position, rotation, or scale that is to be used at the key frame. The total length of the animation is determined by the key with the largest time value. Keys can be removed from an animation with the **DeleteKey()** member function.

SETTING TIME IN ANIMATIONS

Once an animation has been constructed, the **SetTime()** member function can be used to determine the current location within the animation. The values sent to **SetTime()** depend on the values used to install the key frames.

The time values are floating point numbers, so keys can be installed anywhere in an animation—even if the total length of the animation is 1. This also allows an animation to run very slowly or very quickly by using small or large increments with the **SetTime()** member function.

Because arbitrary values can be sent to the **SetTime()** member function, animations can be stopped, started, sped up, slowed down, and even played in reverse.

ANIMATION OPTIONS

The **GetOptions()** and **SetOptions()** member functions are used to specify an animation's behavior. These options include:

- linear vs. spline animation

- open vs. closed animation

- use position

- use scale and rotation

Using *linear animation* means that the Animation interface will animate objects between key frames by calculating the shortest distance between keys. *Spline-based* animation uses curves to calculate an object's position, providing a more rounded, flowing movement.

The open/close option determines how the Animation object interprets out-of-range time values used with the **SetTime()** function. In a closed animation, time values wrap around. That is, an out-of-range time value is subtracted by the greatest key value, so closed animations repeat themselves even when the time setting keeps increasing. Open animations ignore out-of-range time settings. This setting is purely for convenience, because an open animation can be repeated by re-starting the animation's time value.

The *use position* setting activates the animation's position keys. With this setting disabled, the position keys have no effect. Deactivating the position keys can be useful if you want an animation to control an object's scale and rotation, but not its position.

The *use scale and rotation* setting activates the animation's scale and rotation keys. When this setting is disabled, the scale and rotation keys have no effect. Deactivating this setting allow you to control an object's scale and rotation while the object's position is controlled by the animation object.

DIRECT3DRMANIMATIONSET: THE ANIMATION SET INTERFACE

An animation set is a collection of animation objects and is useful for representing entire animated scenes. Typically an animation set is created by importing an animated scene from an animation package such as 3D Studio. Each object in the scene is represented by an animation object, and all of the animation objects make up the animation set.

The **Direct3DRMAnimationSet** interface is used to control animation sets and is created with the **Direct3DRM CreateAnimationSet()** member function.

LOADING ANIMATION SETS

Animation sets are loaded using the **Direct3DRMAnimationSet Load()** member function. The file name used with the **Load()** function must refer to a file that contains a complete animation scene. Like other file loading member functions in Direct3D, the Load member function can read from files, program resources, or memory.

Individual Animation objects can be added and removed from an **AnimationSet** object using the **AddAnimation()** and **DeleteAnimation()** member functions.

SETTING TIME IN ANIMATION SETS

Like the **Direct3DRMAnimation** interface, the **Direct3DRMAnimationSet** interface provides a **SetTime()** member function. In the case of the **AnimationSet**, the **SetTime()** member function sets the time for each animation contained in the animation set.

DIRECT3D DATA TYPES

Direct3D defines a number of data types sure to be used again and again in your programs. We'll discuss these data types in this section.

D3DVALUE

D3DVALUE is the most fundamental Direct3D data type. **D3DVALUE** is declared to be of the type **float** and is used throughout Direct3D to represent vertex coordinates, light intensities, rotation speeds, and so on.

In 32-bit C++ environments, such as Visual C++, numbers not explicitly assigned a type are assumed to be of type **int** (if no decimal point is used) or **double** (if a decimal point is used). In other words, if you use unspecified floating point values in your programs, the compiler will represent the values with eight bytes (for a double) instead of four (for a float). For this reason, along with the fact that code that uses the **D3DVALUE** type explicitly is more likely to be portable, the **D3DVALUE** type is used extensively in Direct3D programs. If you are sure that your program will not need to be ported to a different platform, and you detest the abundance of **D3DVALUE** casts in your code (quite understandable), you can use an 'f' suffix to indicate the data type to the compiler (you must use a decimal point with this technique). Some examples are shown below:

```
d3dfunction( D3DVALUE( 3 ) )   // typical and safe
d3dfunction( D3DVALUE(3.0) )   // typical and safe
d3dfunction( 3 )     // assumed to be int--causes compiler warning
d3dfunction( 3.0 )   // assumed to be double--causes compiler warning
d3dfunction( 3.0f )  // ok but possibly not portable
d3dfunction( 3f )    // not legal--decimal point must be used
```

D3DVECTOR

The **D3DVECTOR** structure is defined this way:

```
typedef struct _D3DVECTOR {
    union {
        D3DVALUE x;
        D3DVALUE dvX;
    };
    union {
        D3DVALUE y;
        D3DVALUE dvY;
    };
    union {
        D3DVALUE z;
        D3DVALUE dvZ;
    };
} D3DVECTOR, *LPD3DVECTOR;
```

The union keyword is used to allow the tags x and dvX (for example) to be used interchangeably. The **D3DVECTOR** structure is used throughout Direct3D to express not only vectors but also points.

D3DCOLOR

Direct3D uses the **D3DCOLOR** type to represent colors. A color has a red, green, blue, and an alpha component. Each of these components can vary in value from zero to one—zero being none or off, and one being full or on.

Actually, it's a little more complicated than that. **D3DCOLOR** is of type **DWORD**, so it can't store four floating point values. The values are stored by multiplying each color component by 255 and shifting them into the

DWORD. Direct3D supplies macros for this purpose. A **D3DCOLOR** type can be assigned with the **D3DRGB** or **D3DRGBA** macros. For example:

```
D3DCOLOR color=D3DRGB(1,1,1);      // creates a white D3DCOLOR
// or ...
D3DCOLOR color=D3DRGBA(1,1,1,0);  // create a white D3DCOLOR with a
                                   // zero alpha value
```

The values that are passed to **D3DRGB** and **D3DRGBA** should range from zero to one. The macros handle the multiplication and conversion of the values. Also, it isn't necessary to cast the values with **D3DVALUE**, since the color creation macros also supply casts.

Individual color components can be extracted from **D3DCOLOR** values with the **D3DRMColorGetRed()**, **D3DRMColorGetGreen()**, **D3DRM-ColorGetBlue()**, and **D3DRMColorGetAlpha()** functions.

D3DRMBOX

Direct3D uses the **D3DRMBOX** structure to describe an object's size. Both the **Direct3DRMMesh** and the **Direct3DRMMeshBuilder** interfaces provide **GetBox()** member functions that can be used to retrieve an object's dimensions. **D3DRMBOX** contains two **D3DVECTOR** structures:

```
typedef struct _D3DRMBOX
{
    D3DVECTOR min, max;
} D3DRMBOX;
```

Although the **D3DVECTOR** structure type is used, the data contained in a vector structure is a point and not a vector. The min and max structures are used to indicate opposite corners of the smallest possible box that could contain the object in question.

D3DRMVERTEX

Direct3D uses **D3DRMVERTEX** structure to describe the vertices in a mesh and is defined like this:

```
typedef struct _D3DRMVERTEX{
    D3DVECTOR position;
    D3DVECTOR normal;
```

```
    D3DVALUE  tu, tv;
    D3DCOLOR  color;
} D3DRMVERTEX;
```

The **position** vector structure describes the vertex location. The **normal** vector describes either a vertex normal (in Gouraud mode) or a face vector (in flat mode). The **tu** and **tv** values determine the coordinate within a texture that is to be mapped to the vertex. The color entry determines the vertex color.

The **D3DRMVERTEX** structure is accepted by the **Direct3DRMMesh GetVertices()** and **SetVertices()** member functions. **GetVertices()** fills an array of **D3DRMVERTEX** structures with the values used by specified vertices. These values can be modified and then passed to **SetVertices()**, thereby modifying the mesh characteristics. Animation techniques, such as vertex animation and texture animation, can be achieved in this way. Also, a program can override the default normals face or vertex normals with **GetVertices()** and **SetVertices()** functions.

D3DRMQUATERNION

Quaternions describe rotation. In Chapter 2 we used a vector and a rotation value to describe a rotation. The vector describes the axis of rotation, and the rotation value describes the amount of rotation. Quaternions encapsulate the vector and the rotation value into one structure:

```
typedef struct _D3DRMQUATERNION {
    D3DVALUE   s;
    D3DVECTOR  v;
}D3DRMQUATERNION;
typedef D3DRMQUATERNION, *LPD3DRMQUATERNION;
```

Quaternions can be initialized with the **D3DRMQuaternionFromRotation()** function. The function takes a vector and a rotation value and creates a quaternion.

Quaternions are useful for calculating intermediate rotation values. The **D3DRMQuaternionSlerp()** function, for example, accepts two quaternions and a slerp value as arguments. The function calculates an intermediate quaternion between two vectors. The slerp value determines where the new quaternion should be between the two input quaternions. Using a slerp value of 0.5, for example, creates a quaternion that is exactly between the two input quaternions.

HRESULT

The vast majority of DirectX member functions return the **HRESULT** type as an error code. **HRESULT** is a 32-bit value that indicates a function's return status. Direct3D supplies a number of constants that should be used to evaluate these return values. Ideally, functions return the **D3DRM_OK** constant, indicating that the function call was successful. If the function fails, a value indicating the nature of the failure will be returned.

X FILES

The X file format is Direct3D's native file format. X files can store multiple meshes, frame hierarchies, and complete animations. Textures cannot be stored in X files.

In DirectX 2, Direct3D supports only text versions of X files. DirectX 3 and above supports both text and binary formats.

Text-based X files are typically larger and take longer to load than their binary counterparts, but they can be viewed and edited easily.

X files can be created either with the CONV3DS utility or with a Direct3D program via the **Direct3DRMMeshbuilder Save**() member function. The **Save**() function produces only X files that contain meshes.

Meshbuilder limitations

If you add a frame hierarchy to a meshbuilder and call the **Save**() function, the resulting X file will contain all of the objects in the hierarchy, but they will all be part of a single mesh, and the hierarchy will not be present.

CONV3DS

Direct3D includes the CONV3DS utility for the creation of X files. CONV3DS converts 3D Studio files (.3DS) to X files. CONV3DS supplies a

Option	Explanation
m	Produce single mesh instead of frame hierarchy.
t	Produce text X files.
A	Include animation data (if animation data is present).
f	Don't import frame translation data.

OPTIONS FOR THE CONV3DS UTILITY.

Table 3.1

number of command-line options. Some of the more useful options are listed in Table 3.1.

CONCLUSION

Now that you know what the Direct3D interfaces look like and what they do, we can get to the fun part—the code. In Chapter 4 we will discuss the code in a Direct3D application.

Chapter

4

THE CODE

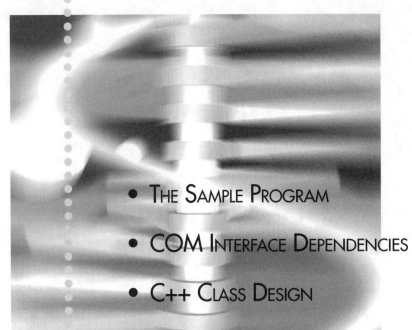

- The Sample Program

- COM Interface Dependencies

- C++ Class Design

- Initializing Direct3D

- Constructing Scenes

- Maintaining Scenes

- Shutting Down Direct3D

- Convenience Functions

4

THE CODE

It's time to get to work. We can talk about graphics terminology and programming models all we want, but nothing is going to get done unless we start programming.

In this chapter, we'll talk about the structure of a Direct3D program. We'll discuss the sequence of events that must take place in order to initialize and maintain the Direct3D interfaces. After that, we will talk about class design and the functions that do the work.

THE DIRECT3D APPWIZARD

Chapter 3 introduced the Direct3D AppWizard. For review, the Direct3D AppWizard is a custom Visual C++ tool that you can use to create complete Direct3D applications. The AppWizard presents a number of dialog boxes that you can use to specify options for the new application. You can decide which object the application will display, what light sources will be used, and even what the class names will be.

The code that the AppWizard generates is the subject of this chapter. We'll create an application with the AppWizard and use the resulting code throughout the chapter. All of the book's demos were started with the Direct3D AppWizard, so they share the same general structure. Understanding the discussion in this chapter means that you will have a strong understanding of all of the demos.

THE SAMPLE APPLICATION

We will use the Direct3D AppWizard to create a project called Sample. Chapter 1 outlines the steps required to create a new project, so we won't repeat them here. We will accept the AppWizard defaults in every dialog, but with one exception: Instead of using the default directional light source, we will specify an animated spotlight. The AppWizard's Lighting dialog box appears in Figure 4.1.

Deselect the Directional checkbox, check the Spotlight checkbox, then check the Animate spotlight checkbox. The figure appears with the settings we will use.

Accept the default settings on the remaining dialogs. The AppWizard will create a project that is ready to compile.

DIRECT3D COM INTERFACE DEPENDENCIES

In Chapter 3, we discussed the Direct3D COM interfaces and the functionalities that they support. During the discussion, we learned that some of the interfaces cannot be created without others. The interfaces

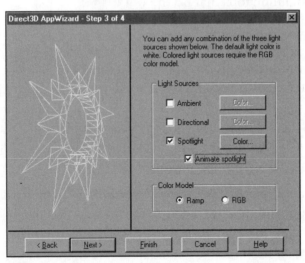

Figure 4.1
The Direct3D AppWizard light selection dialog box.

must be created in a specific order. In this section, we'll talk about these dependencies and how they affect our programs.

DEPENDENCY TREES

The easiest way to analyze dependencies is with a dependency tree. A dependency tree illustrates each interface's reliance on other interfaces by representing each interface as a node in a tree. A tree root node represents an interface that does not depend on the existence of other interfaces. Subsequent nodes represent interfaces that depend on the root interface either directly or indirectly. Figure 4.2 is a dependency tree for the Direct3D interfaces.

The nodes in the figure contain both the interface name (in bold) and the variable name that we will use to identify each interface.

The figure shows that the only interface that does not depend on other interfaces is the **Direct3DRM** interface. The lines that travel from **Direct3DRM** to the **DirectDrawClipper** and **Direct3DRMFrame** nodes indicate that these interfaces depend on the existence of the **Direct3DRM** interface.

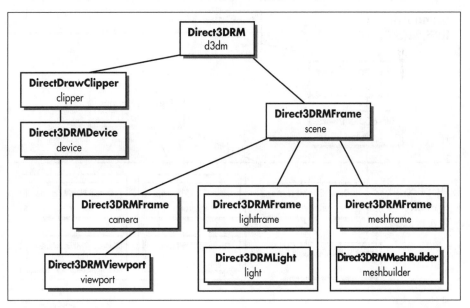

Figure 4.2
A dependency tree for the Direct3D interfaces.

The system of nodes extents from the root node to the **Direct3DRMViewport**, **Direct3DRMLight**, and **Direct3DRMMeshBuilder** interface nodes. These interfaces depend indirectly on all of the other interfaces in the tree. Notice that the **Direct3DRMViewport** interface depends directly on two interfaces.

GROWING YOUR OWN DEPENDENCY TREES

The dependency tree shown in Figure 4.2 can be divided into two parts. The nodes near the root of the tree represent interfaces that are present in all Direct3D programs, while the remaining nodes represent interfaces vary from one application to the next. We'll call the first group the *standard interfaces* and the second *application specific interfaces*. Figure 4.3 shows the tree as it appears once this distinction has been made.

The figure illustrates that the interfaces that make up the scene itself are application defined. This distinction will play an important role later when we talk about class design. Our goal will be to automate the creation of the standard interfaces while allowing the application specific interfaces to be created and modified according to the demands of the application.

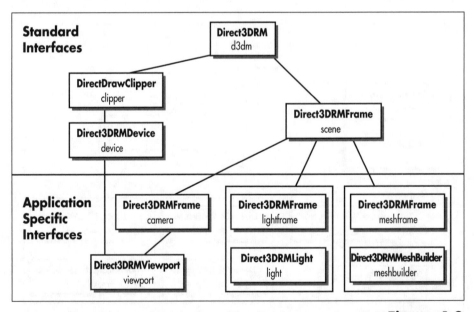

Figure 4.3

Separating standard interfaces from application specific interfaces.

SEQUENCE OF EVENTS

Dependency trees imply creation order. For example, the **Direct3DRM** object appears at the top of the tree, so all other objects in the tree depend on its existence. This means that the **Direct3DRM** object must be created first. After it has been created, either the scene frame or the clipper object can be created. This continues until all of the objects on the branches have been created. Figure 4.4 shows a creation order that complies with the demands of the dependency tree.

The figure shows that the standard interfaces are created first, and then the application specific interfaces are created. This is not the only possible order because some interface pairs, such as the **meshbuilder** and **meshframe** interfaces, can be switched, but the code that we will look at later uses this order.

CLASS DESIGN

Now, let's move away from Direct3D COM interfaces and talk about C++ classes. We'll be using C++ classes to manage the complexity of our programs.

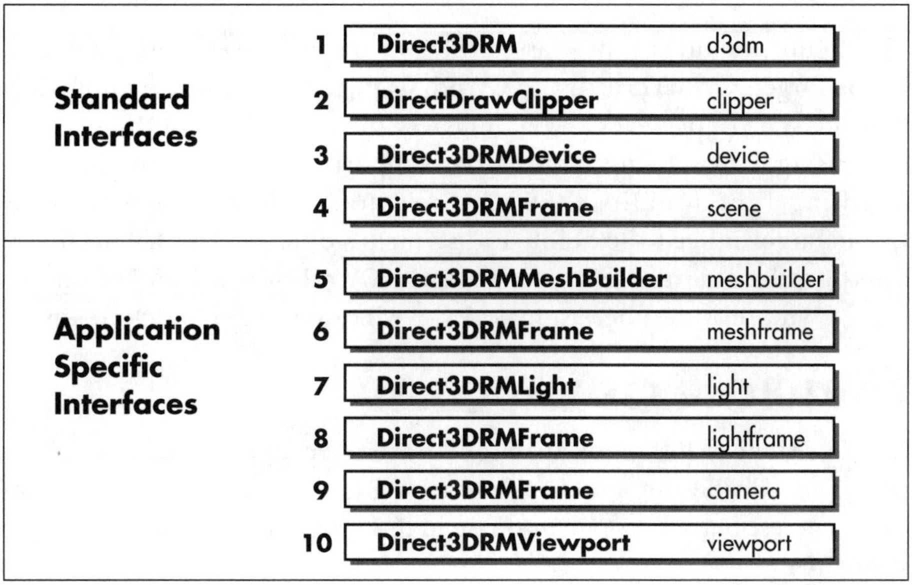

Standard Interfaces	1	Direct3DRM	d3dm
	2	DirectDrawClipper	clipper
	3	Direct3DRMDevice	device
	4	Direct3DRMFrame	scene
Application Specific Interfaces	5	Direct3DRMMeshBuilder	meshbuilder
	6	Direct3DRMFrame	meshframe
	7	Direct3DRMLight	light
	8	Direct3DRMFrame	lightframe
	9	Direct3DRMFrame	camera
	10	Direct3DRMViewport	viewport

Figure 4.4
Interface creation order.

These classes are not substitutes for the Direct3D interfaces. The C++ classes will contain and manage the Direct3D interfaces.

The code in this book uses MFC. The strategy is to use MFC's functionality without using the MFC Document/View architecture. We will use two MFC classes: **CWinApp** and **CFrameWnd**. **CWinApp** represents a Windows application, and **CFrameWnd** represents an actual window. We'll use **CWinApp** as the base class for a Direct3D specific application class and **CFrameWnd** as a base class for a Direct3D specific window class. We'll name the **CWinApp** derived class **RMApp** (RM for Retained Mode) and the **CFrameWnd** derived class **RMWin**.

We won't, however, put all of an application's functionality in these two classes. Instead, we will put only the standard Direct3D functionality—the functionality that remains the same from one application to another—into these classes. Then, we'll create two more classes where we'll put the application specific code. The names of these last two classes is up to you (the AppWizard makes recommendations, but you can override them). We created the Sample application for this chapter using the suggested class names: **SampleApp** and **SampleWin**. Figure 4.5 is an inheritance tree for the classes that we'll be using.

The figure includes four classes that we haven't discussed: **CObject**, **CCmdTarget**, **CWinThread**, and **CWnd**. **CObject** is the fundamental MFC base class. Almost every MFC class is derived from **CObject**. The **CCmdTarget** (command target) class supports the bulk of the message handling functionality that MFC provides. Classes derived from **CCmdTarget** inherit the ability to use message maps. The **CWinThread** class provides multithreading support. The **CWnd** class is the MFC window class. **CWnd** provides the vast majority of window-specific functionality.

DIVISION OF LABOR

Before we take a closer look at any of the member functions that we will be using, let's divide the member functions into four categories. Each category corresponds to a stage or phase in the program execution. The four stages are:

1. Initializing Direct3D

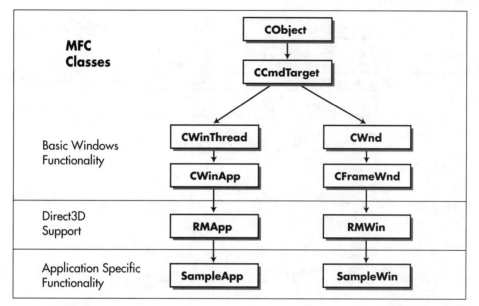

Figure 4.5
Class functionality and inheritance.

2. Creating a scene

3. Maintaining a scene

4. Shutting down

Most of our discussion in this chapter focuses on the first stage, because it is the most complicated step (for now anyway). Once Direct3D has been initialized, it is pretty easy to use. Stages 2 and 3 are covered in detail in the next five chapters. Stage 4 is just a matter of releasing any interfaces that we've created.

INITIALIZING DIRECT3D

Earlier in this chapter, we determined that there is a specific order in which Direct3D interfaces should be created. Figure 4.4 illustrated the order and which steps were standard steps and which were application specific.

Now that we've introduced the classes that we'll be using, it is a good time to revisit the interface creation order, this time with classes and member

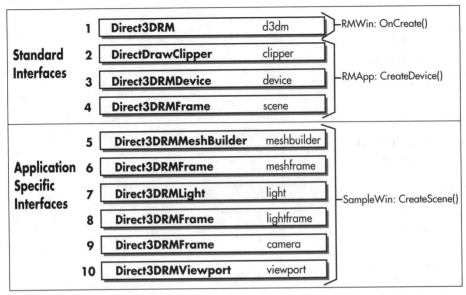

Figure 4.6

Interface creation order with regard to interface categories.

functions in mind. Figure 4.6 is just like Figure 4.4 except that it lists the member functions that are responsible for the step.

As promised, the **RMWin** class creates the standard objects, and the **SampleWin** class creates application objects.

Now, let's look at all of the functions involved in program initialization in the order that they are invoked.

THE INITINSTANCE() MEMBER FUNCTION

The **InitInstance**() member function is a **CWinApp** virtual member function that is overridden in order to perform initialization tasks. Both **RMApp** and **SampleApp** provide versions of **InitInstance**().

The **SampleApp** version of **InitInstance**() is responsible for the creation of the window object. Several settings can also be specified at this time. The **SampleApp::InitInstance**() function looks like this:

```
BOOL SampleApp::InitInstance()
{
```

```
#ifdef _DEBUG
    afxTraceEnabled=FALSE;
#endif
    SampleWin* win=new SampleWin;
    if (!win->Create( "Sample Application", IDI_ICON, IDR_MAINMENU ))
        return FALSE;
    win->SetColorModel( D3DCOLOR_MONO );
    m_pMainWnd=win;
    return RMApp::InitInstance();
}
```

The first three lines of the function initialize the **TRACE** MFC functionality. **TRACE** macros are handy for displaying diagnostic messages during program execution. By default, **TRACE** macros are enabled, but **TRACE** macros are slow. If you use them frequently, they can visibly affect the performance of your application (especially if you use them in functions that are called for each screen update). The **afxTraceEnabled** variable can be used to activate and deactivate **TRACE** macros. Setting this variable to **FALSE** disables the **TRACE** functionality. Notice that the variable assignment is placed inside a conditional compilation block. This is because **TRACE** functionality is only available in programs that are compiled in DEBUG mode. In release mode, the **afxTraceEnabled** function doesn't exist, so a check is made to insure that the **afxTraceEnabled** variable is assigned only in DEBUG mode.

Next, an instance of the **SampleWin** class is created. The **Create()** member function is then called to initialize the window. The **Create()** function takes three arguments. The first is a string that will appear on the title bar of the window. The second argument is a resource identifier for the icon that is to be used for the program. The third argument is a resource identifier that identifies the program's menu.

After the **Create()** member function is called (and checked for success), the **SetColorModel()** member function is called. The **D3DCOLOR_MONO** constant is used to indicate that we will be using the Ramp or monochrome lighting model instead of the RGB model. The default color model is Ramp, so this function call isn't necessary, but it is included here to indicate the proper point to specify the color model. Calling the **SetColorModel()** member function later in the program's execution will have no effect.

Finally the **CWnd::m_pMainWnd** data member is assigned to point to the new window. This is an important step, because MFC uses this data member to access the window.

The **SampleApp::InitInstance()** function terminates by calling the **RMApp::InitInstance()** function, which looks like this:

```
BOOL RMApp::InitInstance()
{
    ASSERT(m_pMainWnd);
    m_pMainWnd->ShowWindow( SW_SHOWNORMAL );
    m_pMainWnd->UpdateWindow();
    return TRUE;
}
```

The first thing that the function does is check to make sure that the **m_pMainWnd** data member has been assigned. The **ASSERT** macro will terminate the program with a message box if the data member is **NULL**.

Next, the **ShowWindow()** and **UpdateWindow()** member functions are called. These functions are inherited from the **CWnd** class and are required for window initialization.

Finally, **TRUE** is returned. Should an error occur in the **InitInstance()** function, the function should return **FALSE** to notify MFC that the application was unable to perform its initialization.

THE ONCREATE() MEMBER FUNCTION

The **OnCreate()** function is inherited by **RMWin** from the **CWnd** class. The function is called during window creation (after the window has been created but before the window is displayed) and provides a good place to initialize Direct3D. The code looks like this:

```
int RMWin::OnCreate(LPCREATESTRUCT lpCreateStruct)
{
    HRESULT r;
    r = Direct3DRMCreate( &d3drm );
    if (r!=D3DRM_OK)
    {
        TRACE("failed to create D3DRM object\n");
        return -1;
    }
```

```
    return 0;
}
```

The function uses the **Direct3DRMCreate()** function to initialize a pointer to the **Direct3DRM** interface. The **d3drm** data member is used throughout the program to invoke various **Direct3DRM** interface functions.

The value returned by **Direct3DRMCreate()** is then checked. Any value other than **D3DRM_OK** indicates an error. If an error is detected, a diagnostic message is displayed, and the function returns with a return value of –1. This signals MFC to abort the window creation. If all goes well, then 0 is returned.

Using the TRACE macros
If (or when) you run into trouble while programming with the code on the CD-ROM, make sure that the TRACE macros are enabled and that you are using the debug version of DirectX. Both the code on the CD-ROM and the debug version of DirectX will display error messages when compiled in DEBUG mode and executed from Visual C++.

THE CREATEDEVICE() FUNCTION

The **CreateDevice()** member function is responsible for creating the standard Direct3D interfaces, the most important of which is the **Direct3DRMDevice** interface. **CreateDevice()** is a private member function, so it performs its task outside of the knowledge of classes that are derived from **RMWin**. The function is shown in Listing 4.1.

Listing 4.1   The RMWin::CreateDevice() function.

```
BOOL RMWin::CreateDevice()
{
    HRESULT r;

    r = DirectDrawCreateClipper( 0, &clipper, NULL );
    if (r!=D3DRM_OK)
    {
        TRACE("failed to create D3D clipper\n");
        return FALSE;
    }
```

```
r = clipper->SetHWnd( NULL, m_hWnd );
if (r!=DD_OK)
{
    TRACE("failed in SetHWnd call\n");
    return FALSE;
}

RECT rect;
::GetClientRect( m_hWnd, &rect );

r = d3drm->CreateDeviceFromClipper( clipper, GetGUID(),
        rect.right, rect.bottom,
        &device );
if (r!=D3DRM_OK)
{
    TRACE("CreateDeviceFromClipper failed\n");
    return FALSE;
}

device->SetQuality( D3DRMRENDER_GOURAUD );

HDC hdc = ::GetDC( m_hWnd );
int bpp = ::GetDeviceCaps( hdc, BITSPIXEL );
::ReleaseDC( m_hWnd, hdc );

switch ( bpp )
{
case 8:
    device->SetDither( FALSE );
    break;
case 16:
    device->SetShades( 32 );
    d3drm->SetDefaultTextureColors( 64 );
    d3drm->SetDefaultTextureShades( 32 );
    device->SetDither( FALSE );
    break;
case 24:
case 32:
    device->SetShades( 256 );
    d3drm->SetDefaultTextureColors( 64 );
    d3drm->SetDefaultTextureShades( 256 );
    device->SetDither( FALSE );
    break;
}
```

```
r = d3drm->CreateFrame( NULL, &scene );
if (r!=D3DRM_OK)
{
    TRACE("CreateFrame(&scene) failed\n");
    return FALSE;
}

if (CreateScene()==FALSE)
{
    AfxMessageBox("CreateScene() failed");
    return FALSE;
}
ASSERT( camera );
ASSERT( viewport );
return TRUE;
}
```

The first thing that you should know about the **CreateDevice()** function is
that it assigns values to three **RMWin** data members: **clipper**, **device**, and **scene**.
These values are protected members of **RMWin**, so they can be accessed
by the **SampleWin** class members. This allows **SampleWin** to use the interfaces that **RMWin** creates.

The first data member to be assigned is the **clipper** member. The
DirectDrawCreateClipper() function is used to retrieve a pointer to a
DirectDrawClipper interface. A clipper is a DirectDraw construct that
manages window updates. Clippers allow DirectDraw and Direct3D applications to behave properly in windowed environments. The clipper object
gets its name from the fact that overlapping windows must be drawn according to which portions of the window are visible. This rectangular clipping is handled by Windows, and the clipper object represents this
functionality.

After the clipper has been created, the **DirectDrawClipper SetHWnd()**
member function is called. This introduces the clipper to the window that
it will be managing. The **m_hWnd** data member that is used as an argument is a window handle that is initialized by MFC.

Next, the **GetClientRect()** and **CreateDeviceFromClipper()** functions are
called. **GetClientRect()** is a Win32 function that retrieves the dimensions
of the client area of the window (the client area is the inner portion of the

window and does not include the window frame and menu). The **CreateDeviceFromClipper()** member function is a **Direct3DRM** function that is used to create a pointer to the **Direct3DRMDevice** interface.

The **CreateDeviceFromClipper()** function takes several arguments and deserves a closer look. The function call appears as it does in the **CreateDevice()** function:

```
r = d3drm->CreateDeviceFromClipper( clipper, GetGUID(),
        rect.right, rect.bottom,
        &device );
```

The first **CreateDeviceFromClipper()** argument is a pointer to the **DirectDrawClipper** interface. The second argument is the return value from the **GetGUID()** member function. We'll look at the **GetGUID()** function after we finish looking at the **CreateDevice()** function.

The third and fourth arguments are the width and height of the client area. This causes **CreateDeviceFromClipper()** to create a device that will fit nicely in the window.

Window resizing

Direct3D devices cannot be resized. If a window is resized, the existing device must be destroyed and replaced with a device that has been created according to the window's new size. You'll see how this is done when we talk about the **RMWin::OnSize()** member function.

The address of the device data member is passed as the last argument, allowing the pointer to be modified to point to the new device.

After the device has been created, it is configured to use Gouraud shading with the **SetQuality()** member function:

```
device->SetQuality( D3DRMRENDER_GOURAUD );
```

When a device is first created, it defaults to flat shading. We are changing this setting so that our programs use Gouraud shading by default. This setting can be overridden (again) later, when we are creating the application specific interfaces.

The next thing that **CreateDevice()** does is retrieve the pixel depth of the current video mode:

```
HDC hdc = ::GetDC( m_hWnd );
int bpp = ::GetDeviceCaps( hdc, BITSPIXEL );
::ReleaseDC( m_hWnd, hdc );
```

The **GetDeviceCaps()** function is used to assign the number of bits used to represent each pixel to the **bpp** variable. This value determines the maximum number of colors that a video mode can display at any given time. The **bpp** value is then used in a switch statement to assign settings to both the **Direct3DRMDevice** and the **Direct3DRM** objects. Optimum settings differ from one application to the next. The values used in **CreateDevice()** are good general purpose settings, but only experimentation will yield the best results for your application.

Next, the root frame for the scene is created with the **Direct3DRM CreateFrame()** member function:

```
r = d3drm->CreateFrame( NULL, &scene );
```

Technically, the root frame is part of the scene and should be created by the application specific code. Practically speaking, however, all scenes have a root frame, so its creation here is justified.

Next, the **CreateScene()** function is called:

```
if (CreateScene()==FALSE)
{
    AfxMessageBox("CreateScene() failed");
    return FALSE;
}
```

The **CreateScene()** member function is the function that the **SampleWin** class overrides to allow the creation of application specific scenes. The **CreateScene()** function can be used to create any kind of scene you want, but there is one requirement. You must initialize the **camera** and **viewport** data members. We'll look at **CreateScene()** soon.

The last four lines of the **CreateDevice()** function appear as follows:

```
CreateScene();
ASSERT( camera );
ASSERT( viewport );
return TRUE;
```

The **ASSERT** macro checks if the **camera** and **viewport** data members have been initialized and terminates the application with a message box if they haven't.

Finally, **CreateDevice()** returns **TRUE**. If you look back at listing 4.1, you'll see that if any of the functions fail, a **TRACE** macro message is displayed and **FALSE** is returned. Returning **FALSE** notifies the **RMWin** class to terminate the application.

THE GETGUID() FUNCTION

The **GetGUID()** member function is used to retrieve a GUID (globally unique identifier) that identifies the device that is to be created by the **CreateDeviceFromClipper()** function. If instead of using **GetGUID()** we use **NULL**, **CreateDeviceFromClipper()** will choose a Ramp color model device automatically. We use **GetGUID()** so that we can specify either Ramp or RGB color model. The **GetGUID()** function appears in Listing 4.2.

Listing 4.2   The GetGUID() function.
```
GUID* RMWin::GetGUID()
{
    static GUID* lpguid;
    HRESULT r;

    D3DFINDDEVICESEARCH searchdata;
    memset(&searchdata, 0, sizeof searchdata);
    searchdata.dwSize = sizeof searchdata;
    searchdata.dwFlags = D3DFDS_COLORMODEL;
    searchdata.dcmColorModel = colormodel;

    static D3DFINDDEVICERESULT resultdata;
    memset( &resultdata, 0, sizeof resultdata );
    resultdata.dwSize = sizeof resultdata;

    LPDIRECTDRAW ddraw;
    r = DirectDrawCreate( NULL, &ddraw, NULL );
```

```
    if (r!=DD_OK)
    {
        TRACE("DirectDrawCreate failed\n");
        return NULL;
    }

    LPDIRECT3D d3d;
    r = ddraw->QueryInterface( IID_IDirect3D, (void**)&d3d );
    if ( r != D3DRM_OK )
    {
        TRACE("d3drm->QueryInterface failed\n");
        ddraw->Release();
        return NULL;
    }

    r=d3d->FindDevice( &searchdata, &resultdata );
    if ( r==D3D_OK )
        lpguid = &resultdata.guid;
    else
    {
        TRACE("FindDevice failure\n");
        lpguid=NULL;
    }

    d3d->Release();
    ddraw->Release();

    return lpguid;
}
```

Before we go on, we should talk about why the **GetGUID**() function is as complicated as it is. Our goal is to acquire a GUID for a specific Direct3D device. It would seem that the **Direct3DRM** interface would supply a member function that we could use for this purpose. Perhaps Direct3D could have been designed this way, but it wasn't.

We are using the Retained Mode portion of Direct3D, and Retained Mode programs rely internally on the Immediate Mode portion to do the actual rendering. The bottom line is that a Direct3D device is an Immediate Mode construct, so we'll have to use an Immediate Mode interface to locate the device we want. Immediate Mode functionality is accessed through the **Direct3D** COM interface.

We can acquire a pointer to a **Direct3D** interface by creating a **DirectDraw** interface and then using the **QueryInterface()** member function. This works because the **DirectDraw** object provided in DirectX version 2 and up supports the **Direct3D** interface. The **QueryInterface()** call would fail if we were using DirectX 1.

Let's look at the **GetGUID()** function (Listing 4.2) from the beginning. The first thing that the function does is prepare two structures that will be used to store information about the device. The **searchdata** structure is used to indicate the color model that we are requesting, and the **resultdata** structure will be used to store the result of the search. These structures are created and initialized as shown:

```
D3DFINDDEVICESEARCH searchdata;
memset(&searchdata, 0, sizeof searchdata);
searchdata.dwSize = sizeof searchdata;
searchdata.dwFlags = D3DFDS_COLORMODEL;
searchdata.dcmColorModel = colormodel;

static D3DFINDDEVICERESULT resultdata;
memset( &resultdata, 0, sizeof resultdata );
resultdata.dwSize = sizeof resultdata;
```

The fields in each of the structures are set to zero with the **memset()** function, then the **dwSize** field is assigned to the size of the structure.

The dwSize field

It might seem silly to require that a field in a structure contain the size of the structure, but this is done to allow future functionality to be added without forcing older programs to be modified. Microsoft can increase the size of the structure in a future version of Direct3D, and programs written now will still work, because Direct3D can determine what version of the structure is being used based on the value in the **dwSize** field.

The **dwFlags** field is assigned to the **D3DFDS_COLORMODEL** constant, indicating that the only criterion that we are specifying is the device's color model. The **dcmColorModel** field is then assigned to the **colormodel** data member. The **colormodel** data member defaults to **D3DCOLOR_MONO** but can be changed with the **SetColorModel()** function (refer back to the **InitInstance()** function).

The next step that **GetGUID()** performs is the creation of a **DirectDraw** interface:

```
LPDIRECTDRAW ddraw;
r = DirectDrawCreate( NULL, &ddraw, NULL );
if (r!=DD_OK)
{
    TRACE("DirectDrawCreate failed\n");
    return NULL;
}
```

The **DirectDrawCreate()** function is used to retrieve a pointer to the **DirectDraw** interface. If this function fails, a **TRACE** message is displayed and **NULL** is returned.

Once a pointer to the **DirectDraw** interface has been acquired, the object can be queried for the **Direct3D** interface:

```
LPDIRECT3D d3d;
r = ddraw->QueryInterface( IID_IDirect3D, (void**)&d3d );
if ( r != D3DRM_OK )
{
    TRACE("d3drm->QueryInterface failed\n");
    ddraw->Release();
    return NULL;
}
```

The **IID_IDirect3D** constant is the GUID for the **Direct3D** interface and is used to indicate to **QueryInterface()** which interface we are seeking. If the function succeeds, the **d3d** pointer will point to an instance of the Direct3D interface. If the query fails, a **TRACE** message is displayed and the function returns **NULL** after releasing the **DirectDraw** interface.

Now we can perform the actual search for the device GUID:

```
r=d3d->FindDevice( &searchdata, &resultdata );
if ( r==D3D_OK )
    lpguid = &resultdata.guid;
```

```
else
{
    TRACE("FindDevice failure\n");
    lpguid=NULL;
}
```

The **Direct3D FindDevice**() member function takes pointers to the two structures that we prepared earlier as arguments. If the function returns **D3D_OK**, then a GUID was found and the **lpguid** variable assigned to point to the GUID.

Notice that both the **resultdata** and the **lpguid** variables are declared static. This is because the GUID itself is a 128-bit value. By declaring these data members as static, we can return a pointer to the GUID instead of making a copy.

The last thing that the **GetGUID**() function does before returning is release the **DirectDraw** and **Direct3D** interfaces.

CONSTRUCTING SCENES

At this point, we've initialized the standard Direct3D interfaces. The steps we've discussed are performed by **RMApp** and **RMWin**. The next step is to create a scene.

THE CREATESCENE() FUNCTION

When we were looking at the **CreateDevice**() function, we learned that one of the last things that **CreateDevice**() does is call the **CreateScene**() function. The **CreateScene**() function is declared as a pure virtual member function in the **RMWin** class. This means that classes derived from **RMWin** must provide a version of **CreateScene**(). The **CreateScene**() member is responsible for the creation of any meshes, light sources, and frame hierarchies that the application will display.

Before we present the **CreateScene**() function, we should mention that the **SampleWin** class inherits several important data members from the **RMWin** class. The **CreateScene**() function has access to these data members because they are declared as protected data members. These data members are:

- **d3drm**: This is the pointer to the **Direct3DRM** interface that was created in the **RMWin::OnCreate()** function. We will use this pointer to create meshbuilders, lights, frames and other Direct3D objects.

- **device**: This is a pointer to the **Direct3DRMDevice** interface. It can be used to specify device settings, such as the maximum rendering quality. The **device** pointer is also used for creating a viewport.

- **scene**: The **scene** data member is a pointer to the **Direct3DRMFrame** interface and serves as the root frame for our scene. The objects we create will be attached to the scene frame.

- **camera**: The **camera** data member is also a pointer to the **Direct3DRMFrame** interface. Unlike the **d3drm**, **device**, and **scene** data members, **camera** is not initialized by the **RMWin** class. It is up to us to create the camera frame. The orientation and location that we give to the camera frame will determine the orientation and location from which the scene is viewed.

- **viewport**: The **viewport** data member is a pointer to the **Direct3DRMViewport** interface. This pointer, like the **camera** pointer, is uninitialized. We will initialize it using the **Direct3DRM CreateViewport()** function.

Listing 4.3 is the **CreateScene()** function from our sample application.

Listing 4.3   The SampleWin::CreateScene() function.

```
BOOL SampleWin::CreateScene()
{
    HRESULT r;
    // ------MESH--------
    d3drm->CreateMeshBuilder( &meshbuilder );
    r=meshbuilder->Load( meshname, NULL, D3DRMLOAD_FROMFILE,
            NULL, NULL );
    if (r!=D3DRM_OK)
    {
        CString msg;
        msg.Format( "Failed to load file '%s'\n", meshname );
        AfxMessageBox( msg );
        return FALSE;
    }
    ScaleMesh( meshbuilder, D3DVALUE(25) );
```

```
LPDIRECT3DRMFRAME meshframe;
d3drm->CreateFrame( scene, &meshframe );
meshframe->AddVisual( meshbuilder );
meshframe->SetRotation( scene,
        D3DVALUE(0), D3DVALUE(1), D3DVALUE(0),
        D3DVALUE(.1) );
meshframe->Release();
meshframe=0;

// --------SPOT LIGHT--------
LPDIRECT3DRMLIGHT slight;
d3drm->CreateLightRGB( D3DRMLIGHT_SPOT,
        D3DVALUE(1.00), D3DVALUE(1.00), D3DVALUE(1.00),
        &slight);

LPDIRECT3DRMFRAME slightframe;
d3drm->CreateFrame( scene, &slightframe );
slightframe->AddLight( slight );
slightframe->SetPosition ( scene,
        D3DVALUE(0),D3DVALUE(20),D3DVALUE(-20) );
slightframe->SetOrientation( scene,
        D3DVALUE(0), D3DVALUE(-20), D3DVALUE(20),
        D3DVALUE(0), D3DVALUE(1), D3DVALUE(0));
slightframe->AddMoveCallback( MoveLight, NULL );
slight->Release();
slight=0;
slightframe->Release();
slightframe=0;

//------ CAMERA----------
d3drm->CreateFrame( scene, &camera );
camera->SetPosition( scene, D3DVALUE(0), D3DVALUE(0), D3DVALUE(-50));
d3drm->CreateViewport( device, camera, 0, 0,
        device->GetWidth(), device->GetHeight(),
        &viewport);

return TRUE;
}
```

The **CreateScene()** function shown in Listing 4.3 performs three steps:

1. Creates and configures a mesh

2. Creates and configures a spotlight

3. Creates and configures a viewport

CREATING A MESH

The first step requires that a pointer to the **Direct3DRMMeshBuilder** interface is created. The **Direct3DRMMeshBuilder Load()** member function is used to load a mesh from a file. If the **Load()** function fails (if the file doesn't exist or if it is not a valid file), a message box is displayed and the function returns **FALSE**, signaling the application to terminate. Let's take another look at this code:

```
d3drm->CreateMeshBuilder( &meshbuilder );
r=meshbuilder->Load( meshname, NULL, D3DRMLOAD_FROMFILE, NULL, NULL );
if (r!=D3DRM_OK)
{
    CString msg;
    msg.Format( "Failed to load file '%s'\n", meshname );
    AfxMessageBox( msg );
    return FALSE;
}
ScaleMesh( meshbuilder, D3DVALUE(25) );
```

If the mesh loads successfully, the **meshbuilder** is scaled with the **ScaleMesh()** function. **ScaleMesh()** is a convenience function provided by the **RMWin** class. We use it here to scale the mesh to insure that it appears properly, regardless of the mesh's original dimensions. We'll look at the **ScaleMesh()** function later in this chapter.

Next, the **meshbuilder** is added to a frame. This portion of code appears as follows:

```
LPDIRECT3DRMFRAME meshframe;
d3drm->CreateFrame( scene, &meshframe );
meshframe->AddVisual( meshbuilder );
meshframe->SetRotation( scene,
        D3DVALUE(0), D3DVALUE(1), D3DVALUE(0),
        D3DVALUE(0.1) );
meshframe->Release();
meshframe=0;
```

The **Direct3DRM CreateFrame()** function is used to initialize a pointer called **meshframe**. Notice that that first argument used with the **CreateFrame()** function is the **scene** frame. This means that the new frame (**meshframe**) is a child frame of the **scene** frame.

Next, the **meshbuilder** is attached to the new frame with the frame's **AddVisual()** member function. Multiple meshes can be added to single frames, but typically, only one mesh is attached to a frame.

The next function call assigns a rotation attribute to the frame. The **SetRotation()** member function takes a vector and a rotation value as arguments. In this case, a vector aligned with the Y axis and a rotation value of 0.1 is specified. Our mesh, because it is attached to the frame that we are assigning a rotation to, will rotate 0.1 radians around the Y axis between each screen update.

After the rotation has been assigned, the frame's **Release()** member function is called. Remember that **Release()** does not necessarily destroy an object. **Release()** decrements the object's internal reference count. **Release()** should be called whenever a pointer to an interface is no longer needed. The object will decide when to destroy itself. We called **Release()** here because we no longer need a pointer to this interface.

CREATING A SPOTLIGHT

The second step in the **CreateScene()** function is the creation of a spotlight:

```
LPDIRECT3DRMLIGHT slight;
d3drm->CreateLightRGB( D3DRMLIGHT_SPOT,
      D3DVALUE(1.00), D3DVALUE(1.00), D3DVALUE(1.00),
      &slight);
```

The **Direct3DRM CreateLightRGB()** function is used to create a light named **slight** (s for spotlight). The **D3DRMLIGHT_SPOT** constant is used to specify the type of the light source that is to be created. Other flags include **D3DRMLIGHT_AMBIENT**, **D3DRMLIGHT_DIRECTIONAL**, **D3DRMLIGHT_ PARALLELPOINT,** and **D3DRMLIGHT_POINT**.

Next, a frame called **slightframe** is created:

```
LPDIRECT3DRMFRAME slightframe;
d3drm->CreateFrame( scene, &slightframe );
```

This frame, like the frame for the meshbuilder, uses the **scene** frame as a parent. The new frame is then assigned a position with the **SetPosition()** member function:

```
slightframe->SetPosition ( scene,
        D3DVALUE(0),D3DVALUE(20),D3DVALUE(-20) );
```

The first argument is called the reference frame, and the following arguments indicate the frame's new position. The **SetPosition**() function uses the reference frame to determine how the frame's new position should be decided. In this example, we are using the scene's root frame as a reference frame, so the position values indicate an absolute position. The root frame is located at the origin, so we are placing our spotlight 20 units above the origin and 20 units behind the origin. If, for example, we used these same values but used a reference frame that was located at <0, 100, 0>, then the frame's new position would be <0, 120, –20>.

Next, the **SetOrientation**() function is used to assign an orientation to the **slightframe** frame:

```
slightframe->SetOrientation( scene,
        D3DVALUE(0), D3DVALUE(-20), D3DVALUE(20),
        D3DVALUE(0), D3DVALUE(1), D3DVALUE(0));
```

Like **SetPosition**(), the **SetOrientation**() function takes a reference frame as the first argument, however, **SetOrientation**() expects six additional arguments. The six values specify two vectors that indicate the frame's new orientation. The first vector indicates the direction that the frame should face. By default, frames are aligned with the Z axis, facing away from the viewer. For this reason, this first vector is called the Z axis vector. The second vector is called the Y axis vector, because by default, it is aligned with the Y axis.

It is perhaps more intuitive to call these vectors the *forward* and *up* vectors. The forward vector indicates the direction that the frame is to face. The up vector indicates the direction that is above the frame (this vector is sometimes called the sky vector).

In our code, we are using <0, –20, 20> as the forward vector. This means that the frame is facing in the direction of the point <0, –20, 20>, so our frame will be facing down 20 units and forward 20 units (from the origin). The up vector that we are using is <0, 1, 0>, which is the default up vector. We'll study frames and frame orientation in more detail in Chapter 7.

The remainder of the spotlight creation/configuration code from the **CreateScene()** function looks like this:

```
slightframe->AddLight( slight );
slightframe->AddMoveCallback( MoveLight, NULL );
slight->Release();
slight=0;
slightframe->Release();
slightframe=0;
```

The **AddLight()** member function is used to attach the spotlight to the frame that we just finished configuring.

Next, the **AddMoveCallback()** function is called. **AddMoveCallback()** is used to install callback functions that can be used to adjust a frame's position and orientation during a program's execution. We'll talk about callbacks and the **AddMoveCallback()** function later in this chapter.

Finally, the **slight** and **slightframe** pointers are released to notify the objects that the pointers will not longer be used (they will go out of scope at the end of the **CreateScene()** function).

CREATING A VIEWPORT

The third and final step in the **CreateScene()** function is the creation of a viewport. The code looks like this:

```
d3drm->CreateFrame( scene, &camera );
camera->SetPosition( scene, D3DVALUE(0), D3DVALUE(0), D3DVALUE(-50));
d3drm->CreateViewport( device, camera, 0, 0,
        device->GetWidth(), device->GetHeight(),
        &viewport);
```

Before the viewport can be created, we need to create a frame that will be used to describe the viewport's position and orientation. The **Direct3DRM CreateFrame()** function is used to initialize the **camera** pointer. Recall that the **camera** pointer is provided by the **RMWin** class, so it is not declared in the **CreateScene()** function.

The **camera** frame is positioned with **SetPosition()**. The position and orientation of the camera frame determines where the scene will be viewed from. Recall that when we created the mesh and attached it to a frame, we did not reposition the frame. This means that the mesh will be displayed at the origin, <0, 0, 0>. If we expect to see the mesh through our new viewport, we need to pull the camera frame away from the origin. The **SetPosition()** function is used to place the camera frame 50 units behind the origin.

The viewport is created with the **CreateViewport()** function. The first argument is the **device** that was created with the **CreateDevice()** function. The second argument is the **camera** frame that we just created. The next four arguments specify the position and dimensions of the viewport. The position is 0, 0, (the top/left corner of the device) and the dimensions are the same as the device dimensions (recall when the device was created, we used the window client area dimensions). The last argument is the address of the pointer that will point to the new viewport.

Finally, the **CreateScene()** function returns **TRUE** to indicate to the **RMWin** class that the scene has been created successfully.

MAINTAINING SCENES

So far, we've followed our sample program through the initialization of Direct3D and the creation of a complete scene. Let's turn our attention now to what happens during program execution.

THE ONIDLE() FUNCTION

The **Direct3DRM** interface provides a **Tick()** member function that can be used to signal Direct3D to update all of the objects in a scene and then render and display a new image based on the results. The **Tick()** function drives Direct3D applications.

Our program uses the **OnIdle()** function to call **Tick()**. The **OnIdle()** function is called by MFC whenever there are no messages to be processed. Calling **Tick()** from an **OnIdle()** function means that system updates are performed as often as possible. The **OnIdle()** function looks like this:

```
BOOL RMApp::OnIdle(LONG)
{
    ASSERT( RMWin::d3drm );
    RMWin::d3drm->Tick( D3DVALUE(1) );
    return TRUE;
}
```

The function first insures that the **RMWin::d3drm** data member has been initialized. If so, the **Tick()** function is called. The function returns **TRUE** to notify MFC that further **OnIdle()** invocations are expected (returning **FALSE** causes MFC to stop calling **OnIdle()**).

The **Tick()** function can be used to control an application's speed in two ways. First, as mentioned previously, the more often **Tick()** is called, the more often Direct3D updates itself. There is, of course, a limit to how often the **Tick()** function can be called. If your program is running on a slow machine, the time it takes for the **Tick()** function to execute will increase.

The second way to control a program's speed is with the argument that the **Tick()** function expects. Using an argument of 1.0 means that the system will do a full update and display the results. Sending a reduced value causes Direct3D to update the animation in a scene according to the argument's value.

For example, if we construct a scene that contains an object that rotates one quarter turn on each update and use a **Tick()** argument of 0.5, the object's rotation is cut in half. Two system updates will be required to rotate the object a quarter turn. Likewise, if you use 2 as an argument, the animation in a scene will run at double speed.

The ability to slow and speed the application's internal update rate means that programs can be written so that they perform animation at the exact same speed on any system, regardless of the number of screen updates. On a slow machine, the program can use large **Tick()** arguments to compensate for the lack of screen updates. On a fast system, small **Tick()** values can be used to control the application speed while letting the screen update speed run as fast as possible.

Practically speaking, if a computer is capable of fewer than 10 or 15 screen updates per second, the application will be irritating despite the fact that the animation speed is correct.

THE ONACTIVATE() FUNCTION

In general, Direct3D is pretty cooperative and does what you tell it to do. It does, however, make a few demands. One of these demands is that you tell it whenever your application receives a **WM_ACTIVATE** message. Direct3D provides a **HandleActivate()** function for this purpose. The only problem is that the **HandleActivate()** function is part of the **Direct3DRMWinDevice** interface, and we don't have such an interface in our program.

The **Direct3DRMWinDevice** interface is supported by the same object that supports the **Direct3DRMDevice** interface, so we can solve our problem by using the existing **Direct3DRMDevice** interface to acquire the **Direct3DRMWinDevice** interface.

The **RMWin::OnActivate()** function is charged with the responsibility of acquiring the **WinDevice** interface and calling the **HandleActivate()** member function:

```
void RMWin::OnActivate(UINT state, CWnd* other, BOOL minimize)
{
    LPDIRECT3DRMWINDEVICE windev;
    if (device)
    {
        if (device->QueryInterface( IID_IDirect3DRMWinDevice,
          (void**)&windev)==0 )
        {
            if (windev->HandleActivate((unsigned short)
              MAKELONG((WORD)state,(WORD)0))!=0)
                AfxMessageBox("windev->HandleActivate() failure");
            windev->Release();
        }
        else
            AfxMessageBox("device->QueryInterface(WinDevice) failure");
    }
    CFrameWnd::OnActivate(state, other, minimize);
}
```

We use the **IID_IDirect3DRMWinDevice** GUID to indicate to the **QueryInterface()** function that we are seeking a pointer to a **Direct3DRMWinDevice** interface. Once we have a pointer to the interface, we can call the **HandleActivate()** function. Both **QueryInterface()** and **HandleActivate()** return zero if successful.

THE ONPAINT() FUNCTION

Direct3D also expects to be notified when an application receives a **WM_PAINT** message. The **Direct3DRMWinDevice** interface supports a

HandlePaint() member function for this purpose, so the **OnPaint()** function looks similar to the **OnActivate()** function. The major difference is that we use the **OnPaint()** function to invoke the **CreateDevice()** function the first time that **OnPaint()** is called. The **OnPaint()** function appears like this:

```
void RMWin::OnPaint()
{
    static BOOL first = TRUE;
    if (first)
    {
        first = FALSE;
        BOOL ok=CreateDevice();
        if (!ok)
            PostQuitMessage(0);
    }

    if (GetUpdateRect(NULL, FALSE)==FALSE)
        return;

    if (device)
    {
        LPDIRECT3DRMWINDEVICE windev;
        PAINTSTRUCT ps;
        BeginPaint(&ps);
        if (device->QueryInterface(IID_IDirect3DRMWinDevice,
          (void**)&windev)==0)
        {
            if (windev->HandlePaint(ps.hdc)!=0)
                AfxMessageBox("windev->HandlePaint() failure");
            windev->Release();
        }
        else
            AfxMessageBox("Failed to create Windows device to handle
              WM_PAINT");
        EndPaint(&ps);
    }
}
```

A static flag is used to determine when the **OnPaint()** function is first called. If the **CreateDevice()** function returns **FALSE**, the program is terminated. The flag is set to **TRUE** so that the **CreateDevice()** function is only called once.

The **GetUpdateRect()** function is used to determine if a repaint is necessary. If the **GetUpdateRect()** function returns **FALSE**, then no portion of the window needs redrawing, and the function returns.

The remainder of the function is similar to the **OnActivate()** function. The **QueryInterface()** function is used to retrieve the **Direct3DRMWinDevice** interface pointer, and the pointer is used to call the **HandlePaint()** function.

THE ONSIZE() FUNCTION

The **OnSize()** function is called by MFC whenever a **WM_SIZE** message is received. The message indicates that the user has resized the window. The **RMWin** class provides an **OnSize()** function to reconfigure the device and the viewport to reflect the window's new dimensions.

Direct3D devices cannot be resized. This means that when a window is resized, the existing device must be destroyed and replaced with a new device. If it is necessary to destroy the existing device, the **OnSize()** function stores the current device settings and uses them to configure the new device. The **OnSize()** function looks like this:

```
void RMWin::OnSize(UINT type, int cx, int cy)
{
    CFrameWnd::OnSize(type, cx, cy);

    if (!device)
        return;

    int width = cx;
    int height = cy;
    if (width && height)
    {
        int view_width = viewport->GetWidth();
        int view_height = viewport->GetHeight();
        int dev_width = device->GetWidth();
        int dev_height = device->GetHeight();

        if (view_width == width && view_height == height)
            return;

        int old_dither = device->GetDither();
        D3DRMRENDERQUALITY old_quality = device->GetQuality();
        int old_shades = device->GetShades();
```

```
        viewport->Release();
        device->Release();
        d3drm->CreateDeviceFromClipper( clipper, GetGUID(), width,
           height, &device );

        device->SetDither(old_dither);
        device->SetQuality(old_quality);
        device->SetShades(old_shades);

        width = device->GetWidth();
        height = device->GetHeight();
        d3drm->CreateViewport(device, camera, 0, 0, width, height,
           &viewport);
    }
}
```

The function minimizes the number of cases in which the existing device must be destroyed. This is done by checking to make sure that the new window dimensions are valid and that the window size has, in fact, changed.

If a new device must be created, the **CreateDeviceFromClipper()** function is used just as it was in the **CreateDevice()** function. After the new device has been created and configured, a new viewport is created as well.

THE ONERASEBKGND() FUNCTION

Direct3D allows you to specify background colors with the **Direct3DRMFrame SetSceneBackground()** function, but when a window is resized, Windows erases the contents of the client area without regard for the Direct3D background color. By default, Windows uses white to erase the client area.

MFC provides the **CWnd::OnEraseBkgnd()** function to override the default Windows behavior. The **RMWin** class provides a version of **OnEraseBkgnd()** that uses the current Direct3D background color to erase the client area. The code looks like this:

```
BOOL RMWin::OnEraseBkgnd( CDC* pDC )
{
    COLORREF bgcolor;
    if (scene)
    {
        D3DCOLOR scenecolor=scene->GetSceneBackground();
        bgcolor=D3DCOLOR_2_COLORREF(scenecolor);
    }
```

```
    else
        bgcolor=RGB(0,0,0);

    CBrush br( bgcolor );
    CRect rc;
    GetClientRect(&rc);
    pDC->FillRect(&rc, &br);
    return TRUE;
}
```

The function declares an instance of the **COLORREF** type and assigns it to the current Direct3D background color. The **D3DCOLOR_2_COLORREF()** function converts the **D3DCOLOR** type to the **COLORREF** type. We'll look at this function later. If the scene frame has not yet been created, black is used.

The **COLORREF** instance is then used to create a **CBrush** object, and the dimensions of the client area are retrieved. The **CDC::FillRect()** function is used to color the client area of the window, and the function returns **TRUE** to notify MFC that the function was successful.

USING CALLBACK FUNCTIONS

Early in this chapter, when we were using the Direct3D AppWizard to create the Sample application, we specified that we wanted an animated spotlight. The AppWizard added code to the project that updates the spotlight's orientation during the execution of the program.

This updating is accomplished with a callback function. Callback functions are functions that Direct3D calls whenever it is about to perform a system update. These functions can be used to adjust program settings at runtime.

When we were creating the spotlight in the **CreateScene()** function, we installed a callback function named **MoveLight()**. The callback installation looks like this:

```
slightframe->AddMoveCallback( MoveLight, NULL );
```

The **AddMoveCallback()** function is a **Direct3DRMFrame** member function. The first argument is a pointer to the function that is to be called on each update. The second parameter is a pointer to data that will be passed to the callback function. This extra data is optional, so we are sending **NULL**.

The **MoveLight()** function adjusts the spotlight's orientation. The code appears as follows:

```
void SampleWin::MoveLight(LPDIRECT3DRMFRAME lightframe, void*, D3DVALUE)
{
    // move the spotlight over the meshes
    static const D3DVALUE lim = D3DVALUE(0.3);
    static D3DVALUE xi = D3DVALUE(0.01);
    static D3DVALUE yi = D3DVALUE(0.005);
    static D3DVALUE x, y;
    if (x<-LIM || x>lim)
        xi=-xi;
    if (y<-LIM || y>lim)
        yi=-yi;
    x+=xi;
    y+=yi;
    lightframe->SetOrientation( NULL,
        x, y-1, D3DVALUE(1),
        D3DVALUE(0), D3DVALUE(1), D3DVALUE(0));
}
```

The function uses a simple "bouncing ball" algorithm to calculate a new orientation for the spotlight on each invocation. The spotlight's movement is limited by the **lim** constant and is incremented with the **xi** and **yi** values. After a new orientation has been calculated, it is assigned to the frame with the **SetOrientation()** function.

Callback functions are always declared static, as shown:

```
class SampleWin : public RMWin
{
// ...
private:
    static void MoveLight(LPDIRECT3DRMFRAME frame, void* arg,
        D3DVALUE delta);
// ...
};
```

This is required, because regular member functions require an implicit class pointer. Declaring the function as static removes this dependency but means that the callback function cannot access the classes' member functions. It is for this reason that the **AddMoveCallback()** function provides a way to supply the callback with extra data.

Callbacks installed with **AddMoveCallback()** are required to have three parameters. The first is a pointer to the frame interface that installed the callback. The second parameter is the pointer that is optionally used to supply extra data to the callback. The third parameter is the value that was passed to the **Tick()** function. Recall that the **Tick()** function can be used to slow and speed a program's animation rate. If you always pass 1.0 to the **Tick()** function, then it is safe to ignore this parameter.

SHUTTING THINGS DOWN

Initializing Direct3D, creating scenes, and performing runtime animation is so much fun that it seems a shame to terminate a program, but it happens nevertheless.

THE ONDESTROY() FUNCTION

Before an MFC application terminates, the **OnDestroy()** function is called. This is a good place to release the references that we have created. **RMWin** provides a version of **OnDestroy()** that releases the standard Direct3D interfaces. The function looks like this:

```
void RMWin::OnDestroy()
{
    if (scene)
    {
        scene->Release();
        scene=0;
    }

    if (device)
    {
        device->Release();
        device=0;
    }

    if (d3drm)
    {
        d3drm->Release();
```

```
        d3drm=0;
    }

    if (clipper)
    {
        clipper->Release();
        clipper=0;
    }
}
```

HELPER FUNCTIONS

Some of the functions that we've looked at use functions that are not Win32, MFC, or Direct3D functions. These functions are convenience functions that the **RMWin** class provides. We'll look at these functions next.

THE SCALEMESH() FUNCTION

In the **CreateScene()** function, after the **meshbuilder** had been created and loaded, the **ScaleMesh()** function was used to insure that the mesh was a certain size. This code appears, again:

```
d3drm->CreateMeshBuilder( &meshbuilder );
r=meshbuilder->Load( meshname, NULL, D3DRMLOAD_FROMFILE, NULL, NULL );
if (r!=D3DRM_OK)
{
    CString msg;
    msg.Format( "Failed to load file '%s'\n", meshname );
    AfxMessageBox( msg );
    return FALSE;
}
ScaleMesh( meshbuilder, D3DVALUE(25) );
```

The **ScaleMesh()** function takes two arguments: a pointer to the **meshbuilder** and a size value. The size value is not a scale factor but rather an ideal size for the object. The **ScaleMesh()** function calculates a scale factor that will bring the largest dimension of the object as near as possible to the size limit. In the code above, **ScaleMesh()** scales the object so that its longest side is 25 units in length. The **ScaleMesh()** function looks like this:

```
void RMWin::ScaleMesh( LPDIRECT3DRMMESHBUILDER mesh, D3DVALUE dim)
{
    D3DRMBOX box;
```

```
mesh->GetBox( &box );
D3DVALUE sizex = box.max.x - box.min.x;
D3DVALUE sizey = box.max.y - box.min.y;
D3DVALUE sizez = box.max.z - box.min.z;
D3DVALUE largedim=D3DVALUE(0);
if (sizex>largedim)
    largedim=sizex;
if (sizey>largedim)
    largedim=sizey;
if (sizez>largedim)
    largedim=sizez;
D3DVALUE scalefactor = dim/largedim;
mesh->Scale( scalefactor, scalefactor, scalefactor );
}
```

The function uses the **Direct3DRMMeshBuilder GetBox()** function to retrieve the dimensions of the mesh. It uses this data to determine which dimension of the mesh is the longest and calculates a scale factor that will scale the object to the prescribed size. The last function call performs the scaling.

THE GETMOUSE() FUNCTIONS

The mouse is a fundamental part of Windows and users expect mouse support as much as they expect keyboard support. The **GetMouseX()** and **GetMouseY()** functions are supplied by the **RMWin** class so that your code can determine the current mouse location at any time. Both functions return the mouse position in pixel units. These functions are declared as static so that they can be used by callback functions.

COLORREF AND D3DCOLOR CONVERSIONS

Windows uses the **COLORREF** type to express colors. Direct3D uses the **D3DCOLOR** type. The two types are not compatible, so the **RMWin** class provides conversion functions. The **COLORREF_2_D3DCOLOR()** function converts the Windows color type to the Direct3D color type. The **D3DCOLOR_2_COLORREF()** function performs the opposite conversion. The code for both functions appears as shown:

```
inline D3DCOLOR RMWin::COLORREF_2_D3DCOLOR(COLORREF cref)
{
    D3DVALUE r=D3DVALUE(GetRValue(cref))/D3DVALUE(255);
```

```
    D3DVALUE g=D3DVALUE(GetGValue(cref))/D3DVALUE(255);
    D3DVALUE b=D3DVALUE(GetBValue(cref))/D3DVALUE(255);
    return D3DRMCreateColorRGB( r, g, b );
}

inline COLORREF RMWin::D3DCOLOR_2_COLORREF(D3DCOLOR d3dclr)
{
    D3DVALUE red=D3DVALUE(255)*D3DRMColorGetRed(d3dclr);
    D3DVALUE green=D3DVALUE(255)*D3DRMColorGetGreen( d3dclr );
    D3DVALUE blue=D3DVALUE(255)*D3DRMColorGetBlue( d3dclr );
    return RGB((int)red,(int)green,(int)blue);
}
```

Both functions are declared inline in order to minimize the performance impact.

Performance issues

In general, worrying about performance while using a package like Direct3D is like rearranging deck chairs on the Titanic. Ninety-nine percent of the work that a Direct3D program does is done by Direct3D. The application code is a very small part of the big picture and would have to be poorly written indeed before a performance hit could be detected.

EXPERIMENTAL LEARNING

There is no greater learning tool than experimentation. One of the great things about software development is that experimentation is easy and free. If we were architects or nuclear engineers, our mistakes could cause serious damage and the loss of millions of dollars. A software developer's mistakes usually don't cause anything more serious than a reboot.

Experiment with the code in the Sample example. Experiment with the demos on the CD-ROM. Try adding multiple meshes to a scene. Experiment with colored lighting (don't forget to use the RGB color model).

When you are finished experimenting, it'll be time to read Chapter 5, where you'll learn about textures and texture mapping.

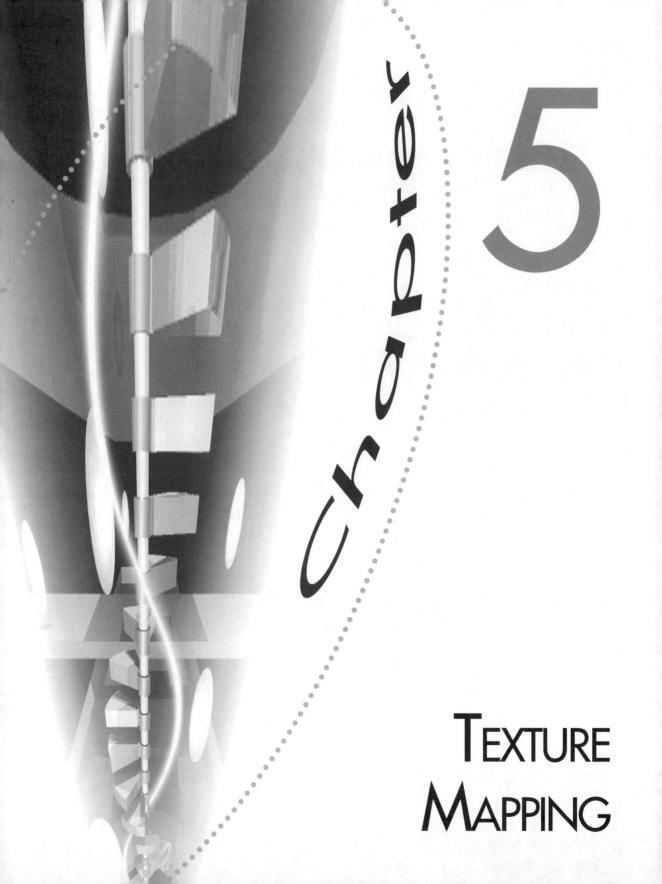

Chapter

5

TEXTURE
MAPPING

- APPLYING TEXTURES

- TEXTURE WRAPS

- DECALS

- TRANSPARENCY

- TEXTURE ANIMATION

CHAPTER 5

TEXTURE MAPPING

This chapter is the first of six that focus on specific Direct3D techniques. As much as possible, each technique is covered with discussion and a demo. For you impatient types (like myself), the demos we'll be looking at in this chapter are:

- Jade
- Wraps
- Decal
- OrbStar
- TextureDrift
- ShowRoom

The demos in this chapter, along with all of the demos on the CD-ROM, were started with the Direct3D AppWizard, so they all share the same general structure. This allows us to discuss only the portions of each demo that are unique. Chapter 4 documents the overall structure of programs created with the AppWizard.

TEXTURE MAPPING TESTBED

Before we look at any code, let's talk about our goal. We are going to be mapping textures onto objects. One way to do this is with a texture wrap. A texture wrap is not a visible object, but a method that determines how a texture is applied to a mesh. Direct3D supports three types of texture wraps: flat, cylindrical, and spherical.

One way to experiment with texture wrapping methods is with Xpose, the X file viewer on the CD-ROM. You can use Xpose to rotate and spin a mesh, change its settings, and save the mesh when you are done. Xpose is shown in Figure 5.1.

Xpose allows you to apply textures to a mesh. Apply a new texture by selecting the Load option from the Texture menu. You will be presented with an Open File dialog box. You can specify either BMP or PPM files, but the dimensions of the texture must be a power of 2 (16, 32, 64, 128...).

By default, Xpose uses a spherical texture wrap to map textures, but this can be changed with the Texture Wrap Settings dialog. This dialog can be accessed with the Texture|Wrap Settings menu option. The Texture Wrap Settings dialog box appears in Figure 5.2.

Figure 5.1

Xpose.

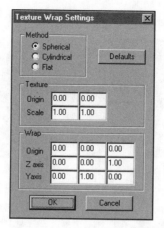

Figure 5.2
The Texture Wrap Settings dialog box.

You can adjust any of the texture wrap settings by making changes to the dialog box and pressing the OK button.

Xpose is useful for experimenting with Direct3D features other than texture mapping.

APPLYING A TEXTURE TO A MESH

The first order of business is applying a texture to an object. Our strategy is to take a demo that is very much like the default project that the Direct3D AppWizard creates and apply a texture to the object that the demo displays.

THE JADE DEMO

The Jade demo displays a mesh that forms the letters "D3D" and applies a jade texture to the mesh. For visual effect, and so that you can see the mesh from different angles, the mesh is animated. The Jade demo appears in Figure 5.3.

The Jade demo uses a flat texture wrap to apply the jade texture to the mesh. This means that the texture is applied straight on the mesh, with no curving or wrapping of the texture. For this reason, when the mesh is viewed

Figure 5.3
The Jade demo.

from the same direction that the texture was applied, the texture appears much as it does when viewed in a paint program. The texture used in the Jade demo is shown in Figure 5.4.

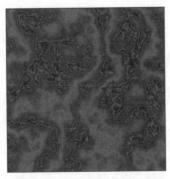

Figure 5.4
The texture used by the Jade demo.

The Jade demo demonstrates the following techniques:

- Loading meshes and textures from a program's resources. Most of the demos on the CD-ROM require that meshes and/or textures be loaded at runtime. Rather than risk the possibility that these files won't be available, each demo stores the required files as resources. If you want to modify the demos to use files instead of resources, refer to the Sample demo in Chapter 4 or examine the code that the Direct3D AppWizard creates.

- Using the **Direct3DRMWrap** interface to map a texture onto a mesh.

- Using menu options to change the mesh render settings at runtime.

- Using a callback function to perform animation.

THE JADEWIN CLASS

Most the Jade demo's functionality is provided by the **JadeWin** class. The **JadeWin** class inherits its basic Direct3D functionality from the **RMWin** class that is documented in Chapter 4. The **JadeWin** class definition looks like this:

```
class JadeWin : public RMWin
{
public:
    JadeWin();
    BOOL CreateScene();
    static void MoveFrame(LPDIRECT3DRMFRAME frame, void*, D3DVALUE);
protected:
    //{{AFX_MSG(JadeWin)
    afx_msg void OnRenderWireframe();
    afx_msg void OnRenderFlat();
    afx_msg void OnRenderGouraud();
    afx_msg void OnUpdateRenderFlat(CCmdUI* pCmdUI);
    afx_msg void OnUpdateRenderGouraud(CCmdUI* pCmdUI);
    afx_msg void OnUpdateRenderWireframe(CCmdUI* pCmdUI);
    //}}AFX_MSG
    DECLARE_MESSAGE_MAP()
private:
    LPDIRECT3DRMMESHBUILDER meshbuilder;
};
```

Three public member functions are declared: a constructor, the **CreateScene()** function, and a callback function called **MoveFrame()**. The constructor is used to initialize the class's single data member:

```
JadeWin::JadeWin()
{
    meshbuilder=0;
}
```

The **CreateScene()** function creates and configures the objects that will be used in the scene. The **MoveFrame()** function is declared **static** so that it can be installed as a callback by the **CreateScene()** function. **MoveFrame()** will be used to alter the orientation of the frame to which the demo's mesh is attached. This will cause the mesh to appear at a different orientation for each screen update.

The six protected member functions are message handling functions that support the Jade demo's Render menu functionality.

THE JADEWIN::CREATESCENE() FUNCTION

The Jade demo **CreateScene()** function is shown in Listing 5.1.

Listing 5.1   The JadeWin::CreateScene() function.

```
BOOL JadeWin::CreateScene()
{
    HRESULT r;
    //------- BACKGROUND --------
    scene->SetSceneBackgroundRGB( D3DVALUE(.2), D3DVALUE(.2),
        D3DVALUE(.2) );

    //------- MESH --------
    D3DRMLOADRESOURCE resinfo;
    resinfo.hModule=NULL;
    resinfo.lpName=MAKEINTRESOURCE( IDR_D3DMESH );
    resinfo.lpType="MESH";
    d3drm->CreateMeshBuilder( &meshbuilder );
    meshbuilder->SetPerspective( TRUE );
    r=meshbuilder->Load( &resinfo, NULL, D3DRMLOAD_FROMRESOURCE, NULL,
        NULL );
    if (r!=D3DRM_OK)
    {
        TRACE("meshbuilder->Load() failed\n");
        return FALSE;
    }
    ScaleMesh( meshbuilder, D3DVALUE(35) );
```

```
//-------- TEXTURE --------
LPDIRECT3DRMTEXTURE texture;
HRSRC texture_id = FindResource( NULL,
    MAKEINTRESOURCE(IDR_JADETEXTURE), "TEXTURE" );
r = d3drm->LoadTextureFromResource( texture_id, &texture );
if (r!=D3DRM_OK)
{
    TRACE("d3drm->LoadTextureFromResource() failed\n");
    return FALSE;
}
meshbuilder->SetTexture( texture );
texture->Release();
texture=0;

//-------- WRAP --------
D3DRMBOX box;
meshbuilder->GetBox( &box );
D3DVALUE w=box.max.x-box.min.x;
D3DVALUE h=box.max.y-box.min.y;

LPDIRECT3DRMWRAP wrap;
d3drm->CreateWrap(D3DRMWRAP_FLAT, scene,
    D3DVALUE(0.0), D3DVALUE(0.0), D3DVALUE(0.0),  // wrap origin
    D3DVALUE(0.0), D3DVALUE(0.0), D3DVALUE(1.0),  // z axis of wrap
    D3DVALUE(0.0), D3DVALUE(1.0), D3DVALUE(0.0),  // y axis of wrap
    D3DVALUE(0.5), D3DVALUE(0.5),                 // texture origin
    D3DDivide(1,w), D3DDivide(1,h),               // texture scale
    &wrap);
wrap->Apply( meshbuilder );
wrap->Release();
wrap=0;

//------- MESH FRAME ----------
LPDIRECT3DRMFRAME meshframe;
d3drm->CreateFrame( scene, &meshframe );
meshframe->AddVisual( meshbuilder );
meshframe->AddMoveCallback( MoveFrame, NULL );
meshframe->Release();

//---------- LIGHT -----------
LPDIRECT3DRMLIGHT light;
d3drm->CreateLightRGB( D3DRMLIGHT_AMBIENT,
        D3DVALUE(1),D3DVALUE(1), D3DVALUE(1),
        &light );
scene->AddLight( light );
```

```
light->Release();
light=0;

//---------- CAMERA -----------
d3drm->CreateFrame( scene, &camera );
camera->SetPosition( scene,
        D3DVALUE(0.0), D3DVALUE(0.0), D3DVALUE(-50.0) );
d3drm->CreateViewport( device, camera, 0, 0,
        device->GetWidth(), device->GetHeight(),
        &viewport );

return TRUE;
}
```

The **CreateScene()** function performs seven steps:

1. The scene's background color is changed.

2. The mesh is loaded.

3. The jade texture is loaded.

4. A texture wrap is created and applied.

5. A frame is created for placement of the mesh.

6. An ambient light source is created.

7. A viewport is created.

Let's examine this function one step at a time. The first thing that **CreateScene()** does is change the scene's background color using the **SetSceneBackgroundRGB()** function:

```
scene->SetSceneBackgroundRGB( D3DVALUE(.2), D3DVALUE(.2), D3DVALUE(.2) );
```

The **SetSceneBackgroundRGB()** function takes three arguments that describe the red, green, and blue components of the new background color. In this case, we are using a dark gray.

Next, the **Direct3DRMMeshBuilder** interface is used to load and configure the mesh:

```
D3DRMLOADRESOURCE resinfo;
resinfo.hModule=NULL;
```

```
resinfo.lpName=MAKEINTRESOURCE( IDR_D3DMESH );
resinfo.lpType="MESH";
d3drm->CreateMeshBuilder( &meshbuilder );
meshbuilder->SetPerspective( TRUE );
r=meshbuilder->Load( &resinfo, NULL, D3DRMLOAD_FROMRESOURCE, NULL,
    NULL);
if (r!=D3DRM_OK)
{
   TRACE("meshbuilder->Load() failed\n");
    return FALSE;
}
ScaleMesh( meshbuilder, D3DVALUE(35) );
```

In order to load meshes from resources, a **D3DRMLOADRESOURCE** structure must be prepared. The **D3DRMLOADRESOURCE** structure contains
three fields: **hModule**, **lpName**, and **lpType**. The **hModule** field identifies
the module that contains the resource. This is useful if resources must be
loaded from executables other than the calling executable, but for our
purposes, we can use **NULL** to indicate that the resources are located in
the calling program. The **lpName** field is used to store a value that identifies the resource that we are seeking. The **lpType** field is used to indicate
what type of resource is to be located.

The MESH resource type

There is nothing magic about the **MESH** resource type (Visual
C++ doesn't have any knowledge of Direct3D meshes).
The demos in this book store meshes in resource sections,
labeled **MESH**, to separate the mesh resources from other
resources.

Once the **D3DRMLOADRESOURCE** structure has been prepared, the
meshbuilder pointer is initialized with the **Direct3DRM CreateMeshBuilder()**
function. Perspective correction is enabled for the new mesh with the
SetPerspective() function. Perspective correction will prevent the texture
that we apply to the mesh from drifting during animation (comment this
line out and compile the demo to see this effect).

Next, the **Load()** member function is called using a pointer to the
D3DRMLOADRESOURCE structure as the first argument. The third

Load() argument (the **D3DRMLOAD_FROMRESOURCE** flag) indicates to Direct3D that we are loading a file from a resource and not from disk. The **Load()** return value is then checked for success. The **CreateScene()** function returns **FALSE** if the **Load()** function fails.

Checking return values

Most of the Direct3D functions return an **HRESULT** value that indicates the function's status. As a rule, it isn't necessary to check the return value of every function, but it is a good idea to check functions that perform operations that may fail for practical reasons. For example, functions that load files often fail because the file cannot be located. In this case it is unlikely that the **Load()** function will fail because the mesh that is being loaded is part of the program's EXE file.

Finally, the **ScaleMesh()** function is used to indicate an ideal size for the mesh. The first **ScaleMesh()** argument is the **Direct3DRMMeshBuilder** that is to be scaled. The second is a value indicating the desired size for the mesh.

The next step (Step 3) is to load the texture. Loading textures from a program's resources is a little different than loading meshes. With meshes, the **Load()** function is used regardless of whether the mesh is located in a file or in the program's resources. With textures, separate functions are used to load from files and resources. We will use the **LoadTextureFromResource()** function (instead of the **LoadTexture()** function):

```
LPDIRECT3DRMTEXTURE texture;
HRSRC texture_id = FindResource( NULL,
    MAKEINTRESOURCE(IDR_JADETEXTURE), "TEXTURE" );
r = d3drm->LoadTextureFromResource( texture_id, &texture );
if (r!=D3DRM_OK)
{
    TRACE("d3drm->LoadTextureFromResource() failed\n");
    return FALSE;
}
meshbuilder->SetTexture( texture );
texture->Release();
texture=0;
```

The **LoadTextureFromResource()** function takes two arguments: an instance of the **HRSRC** structure and the address of a pointer to the **Direct3DRMTexture** interface. The **HRSRC** structure is a Win32 structure that is similar to the **D3DRMLOADRESOURCE** structure that we used with the **Meshbuilder Load()** function. The **HRSRC** structure is initialized with the **FindResource()** function. The three arguments that **FindResource()** expects identify the resource that we are attempting to load. The first argument is a module handle. Because the texture that we are loading is located in the same executable as the **CreateScene()** function, we can use **NULL**. The second argument is a value that identifies the resource to be loaded. The third argument identifies the type of resource.

Once the **HRSRC** structure is initialized, the **LoadTextureFromResource()** function is called. If the **LoadTextureFromResource()** fails, **CreateScene()** returns **FALSE** (after displaying a message with the **TRACE** macro). If the function succeeds, the texture is associated with the previously loaded mesh using the **Direct3DRMMeshBuilder SetTexture()** function. Finally, the **texture** pointer is released because it is no longer needed. The pointer is assigned a value of zero after it is released.

Avoid dangling pointers

It is a good idea to avoid dangling pointers by assigning them to zero after they have been released. Getting into this habit will save you trouble later if a released pointer is inadvertently used.

The **SetTexture()** function does not indicate how the texture is to be applied, only that the texture is to be applied. We must use a texture wrap to specify how a texture is to be applied. In Step 4, we'll be creating and applying a flat texture wrap, which means that the texture will not be curved or warped but applied straight onto the mesh. Our goal is to scale the texture so that it is the same size as the mesh. In order to do this, we need to know the size of the mesh. The code below appears in the **CreateScene()** function before the texture wrap is created:

```
D3DRMBOX box;
meshbuilder->GetBox( &box );
```

```
D3DVALUE w = box.max.x-box.min.x;
D3DVALUE h = box.max.y-box.min.y;
```

The **GetBox()** function is used to fill a **D3DRMBOX** structure with the dimensions of the mesh. We then use these values to calculate the width and height of the mesh. Notice that we are calculating only the width and height of the mesh, and not the depth. This is because textures are two-dimensional; the mesh's depth is extraneous information.

Now, we can create and apply the texture wrap:

```
LPDIRECT3DRMWRAP wrap;
d3drm->CreateWrap( D3DRMWRAP_FLAT, scene,
        D3DVALUE(0.0), D3DVALUE(0.0), D3DVALUE(0.0),   // wrap origin
        D3DVALUE(0.0), D3DVALUE(0.0), D3DVALUE(1.0),   // z axis
        D3DVALUE(0.0), D3DVALUE(1.0), D3DVALUE(0.0),   // y axis
        D3DVALUE(0.5), D3DVALUE(0.5),                  // texture origin
        D3DDivide(1,w), D3DDivide(1,h),                // texture scale
        &wrap );
wrap->Apply( meshbuilder );
wrap->Release();
wrap=0;
```

We use the **Direct3DRM CreateWrap()** function to create the wrap. The **CreateWrap()** function takes 16 arguments. The first argument is the wrap method. We are using the **D3DRMWRAP_FLAT** constant to indicate a flat texture wrap. The second argument is a reference frame. We are using the scene's root frame to indicate that the values that we are using in the remaining arguments are to be treated as absolute values. If we used another frame, the remaining argument would be interpreted as relative to the supplied frame.

Specifying absolute values

There are two ways to indicate to Direct3D that the values you are specifying are to be treated as absolute, and not relative, values. The first is to use the root frame as a reference frame (as shown in this code). The second is to specify **NULL** as the reference frame.

THE WRAP SETTINGS FOR THE JADE DEMO.

Parameter	Values
wrap origin	<0.0, 0.0, 0.0>
wrap Z axis	<0.0, 0.0, 1.0>
wrap Y axis	<0.0, 1.0, 0.0>

Table 5.1

The following nine **CreateWrap()** arguments specify the location and orientation of the wrap. The values used in the **CreateScene()** function appear in Table 5.1.

The first three arguments indicate the location of the wrap origin. By using <0.0, 0.0, 0.0>, we are indicating that the wrap is to be placed on the mesh's local axis (the mesh's private origin; usually the center of the mesh).

The second three arguments define a vector that indicates the facing direction for the wrap. In this example, we are using a vector that is aligned with the Z axis, pointing away from the viewer. The third set of three arguments is a vector that indicates what direction is up for the wrap. We are using a vector that is aligned with the Y axis, pointing up.

The following four **CreateWrap()** arguments specify the origin and scale for the texture. The settings used in the **CreateScene()** function appear in Table 5.2.

The texture origin settings determine the location in the texture that will be mapped to the texture wrap origin. We are using 0.5 for both the X and Y texture origin settings in order to center the texture on the wrap origin (the value 0.5 indicates the center of the texture, 0.0 indicates the top or left edge of the texture, and 1.0 indicates the right or bottom edge of the texture).

THE TEXTURE SETTINGS FOR THE JADE DEMO.

Parameter	Values
texture origin	<0.5, 0.5>
texture scale	< D3DDivide(1,w), D3DDivide(1,h) >

Table 5.2

The texture scale settings determine the texture's size in proportion to the texture wrap. Recall that we intend to scale the texture so that it fits snugly over the mesh. We've already centered the texture by using texture origin settings of 0.5. Now, we scale the texture to fit the mesh by using the mesh's width and height. Direct3D provides the **D3DDivide** macro as a convenience. The macro casts the arguments to the **D3DVALUE** type and divides the first argument by the second. This gives us a scale factor that scales the texture to fit over the mesh.

The final **CreateWrap()** argument is the address of a pointer that is to be initialized to point to the new **Direct3DRMWrap** interface. Once the wrap has been created, it is applied to the mesh with the **Direct3DRMWrap Apply()** function:

```
wrap->Apply( meshbuilder );
```

The **Apply()** function calculates the manner in which the texture will be applied to each face in the mesh. After the **Apply()** function is called, the **wrap** pointer is released.

Step 5 is the creation of a frame for the mesh:

```
LPDIRECT3DRMFRAME meshframe;
d3drm->CreateFrame( scene, &meshframe );
meshframe->AddVisual( meshbuilder );
meshframe->AddMoveCallback( MoveFrame, NULL );
meshframe->Release();
meshframe=0;
```

The **Direct3DRM CreateFrame()** function is used to create a frame named **meshframe**. The meshbuilder is attached to the new frame with the **AddVisual()** function. Next the **MoveFrame()** callback function is installed with the **AddMoveCallback()** function. Finally, the **meshframe** pointer is released.

Step 6 is the creation of an ambient light source:

```
LPDIRECT3DRMLIGHT light;
d3drm->CreateLightRGB( D3DRMLIGHT_AMBIENT,
        D3DVALUE(1),D3DVALUE(1), D3DVALUE(1),
        &light );
```

```
scene->AddLight( light );
light->Release();
light=0;
```

An ambient light source is used in this demo because of its ease of use. We'll talk about light sources in detail in Chapter 6.

The seventh and final step that the **CreateScene()** function performs is the creation of a viewport:

```
d3drm->CreateFrame( scene, &camera );
camera->SetPosition( scene,
        D3DVALUE(0.0), D3DVALUE(0.0), D3DVALUE(-50.0) );
d3drm->CreateViewport( device, camera, 0, 0,
        device->GetWidth(), device->GetHeight(),
        &viewport );
```

The **camera** and **viewport** data members are inherited from the **RMWin** class and must be initialized by the **CreateScene()** function. The **camera** data member is a pointer to the **Direct3DRMFrame** interface as is initialized with the **Direct3DRM CreateFrame()** function. The new frame is positioned fifty units away from the origin with the **SetPosition()** function. Finally the **viewport** pointer is initialized with the **Direct3DRM CreateViewport()** function.

The **CreateScene()** returns **TRUE** to indicate that the scene has been successfully created. Returning **FALSE** from the **CreateScene()** function causes the application to terminate with a message box.

THE JADEWIN::MOVEFRAME() FUNCTION

The **MoveFrame()** function is a callback function that manages the mesh's animation. The function appears below:

```
void JadeWin::MoveFrame(LPDIRECT3DRMFRAME frame, void*, D3DVALUE)
{
    static int x;
    static int y;
    static int xi=7;
    static int yi=13;
    if (x<-31 || x>31)
        xi=-xi;
```

```
if (y<-35 || y>35)
    yi=-yi;
x+=xi;
y+=yi;
frame->SetOrientation( NULL,
        D3DVALUE(x), D3DVALUE(y), D3DVALUE(50),
        D3DVALUE(0), D3DVALUE(1), D3DVALUE(0) );
}
```

The **MoveFrame()** function uses a simple "bouncing ball" algorithm to reorient the frame that the mesh is attached to for each screen update. The static integers are used to track the frame's position, and calculate new positions. Once a new position has been calculated, it is assigned to the frame with the **Direct3DRMFrame SetOrientation()** function.

THE JADEWIN RENDER FUNCTIONS

The Jade demo (like most of the demos on the CD-ROM) allows the mesh's render method to be changed during the program's execution. This functionality is provided by the **OnRenderWireframe()**, **OnRenderFlat()**, and **OnRenderGouraud()** functions are invoked by MFC when the Render menu entries are selected. These three functions look like this:

```
void JadeWin::OnRenderWireframe()
{
    if (meshbuilder)
        meshbuilder->SetQuality( D3DRMRENDER_WIREFRAME );
}

void JadeWin::OnRenderFlat()
{
    if (meshbuilder)
        meshbuilder->SetQuality( D3DRMRENDER_FLAT );
}

void JadeWin::OnRenderGouraud()
{
    if (meshbuilder)
        meshbuilder->SetQuality( D3DRMRENDER_GOURAUD );
}
```

Each function uses the **Direct3DRMMeshBuilder SetQuality()** to specify a rendering method. Three more functions are required to properly enable and disable the check marks that appear to the left of the currently active rendering method on the Render menu. The **OnUpdateRenderFlat()**, **OnUpdateRenderGouraud()**, and **OnUpdateRenderWireframe()** functions look this way:

```
void JadeWin::OnUpdateRenderWireframe(CCmdUI* pCmdUI)
{
    if (meshbuilder)
    {
        D3DRMRENDERQUALITY meshquality = meshbuilder->GetQuality();
        pCmdUI->SetCheck( meshquality==D3DRMRENDER_WIREFRAME );
    }
}

void JadeWin::OnUpdateRenderFlat(CCmdUI* pCmdUI)
{
    if (meshbuilder)
    {
        D3DRMRENDERQUALITY meshquality = meshbuilder->GetQuality();
        pCmdUI->SetCheck( meshquality==D3DRMRENDER_FLAT );
    }
}

void JadeWin::OnUpdateRenderGouraud(CCmdUI* pCmdUI)
{
    if (meshbuilder)
    {
        D3DRMRENDERQUALITY meshquality = meshbuilder->GetQuality();
        pCmdUI->SetCheck( meshquality==D3DRMRENDER_GOURAUD );
    }
}
```

MFC calls all three of these functions whenever it is about to display the Render menu. Each function checks the mesh's current settings and indicates to MFC whether the check mark for a particular menu entry should be enabled.

Almost all of the demos on the CD-ROM support menus such as the Render menu. Menu support functions such as these can be added and removed from projects with the Visual C++ ClassWizard.

TEXTURE WRAPS

The Jade demo uses a flat texture wrap. Direct3D supports two additional wrap methods: cylindrical and spherical. A cylindrical texture wrap method attempts to bend the texture in one direction, bringing two opposite edges of the texture together. A spherical texture wrap method attempts to bend a texture in such a way that the texture forms a sphere. The use of the word "attempt" is appropriate here because, as you will see, these wrapping methods are only approximations.

THE WRAPS DEMO

The Wraps demo displays three meshes: a cube, a cylinder, and a sphere. A single texture is applied to each mesh, but the texture wrapping method is adjustable. By default, a flat wrap is used on the cube, a cylindrical wrap is used on the cylinder, and a spherical wrap is used on the sphere. The demo provides menu options that let you specify which wrap type is used on the meshes. The Wraps demo is shown in Figure 5.5.

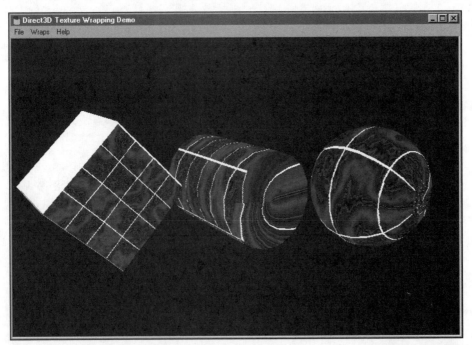

Figure 5.5
The Wraps demo.

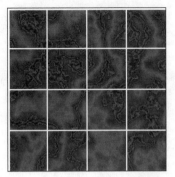

Figure 5.6
The texture used by the Wraps demo.

The Wraps demo uses a modified version of the texture used by the Jade demo. Lines have been drawn across the texture to illustrate the manner in which the texture has been applied. The modified texture is shown in Figure 5.6.

The Wraps demo demonstrates the following techniques:

- Loading and displaying multiple meshes.

- Applying arbitrary wraps to a mesh at runtime. The Wraps menu lets you change the texture wrapping method for the objects during the program's execution.

THE WRAPSWIN CLASS

The bulk to the Wraps demo's functionality is provided by the **WrapsWin** class. The class definition look like this:

```
class WrapsWin : public RMWin
{
public:
    WrapsWin();
    BOOL CreateScene();
protected:
    //{{AFX_MSG(WrapsWin)
    afx_msg void OnWrapsFlat();
    afx_msg void OnWrapsCylinder();
    afx_msg void OnWrapsSphere();
    afx_msg void OnWrapsReset();
    //}}AFX_MSG
    DECLARE_MESSAGE_MAP()
```

```
private:
    BOOL LoadMeshes();
    BOOL LoadTexture();
    void ApplyWraps();
    void ApplyFlat( LPDIRECT3DRMMESHBUILDER );
    void ApplyCylinder( LPDIRECT3DRMMESHBUILDER );
    void ApplySphere( LPDIRECT3DRMMESHBUILDER );
private:
    LPDIRECT3DRMMESHBUILDER box;
    LPDIRECT3DRMMESHBUILDER cyl;
    LPDIRECT3DRMMESHBUILDER sphere;
    D3DRMWRAPTYPE boxwraptype;
    D3DRMWRAPTYPE cylwraptype;
    D3DRMWRAPTYPE spherewraptype;
};
```

Like the **JadeWin** class, the **WrapsWin** class provides two public member functions: a constructor and a **CreateScene()** function. The constructor is used to initialize the class's data members. The **CreateScene()** function constructs the demo's scene. We'll look at the **CreateScene()** function soon.

The Wraps demo doesn't support a Render menu, but it does support a Wraps menu. The Wraps menu lets the user select what type of texture wrap methods that are to be used. Four protected member functions are declared by the **WrapsWin** class to support the Wraps menu functionality: **OnWrapsFlat()**, **OnWrapsCylinder()**, **OnWrapsSphere()**, and **OnWrapsReset()**.

Six private member functions are declared. The **LoadMeshes()** and **LoadTexture()** functions are used to simplify the **CreateScene()** function. The remaining four functions are used to change the texture wrap settings during the demo's execution.

Finally six private data members are declared. The **box**, **cyl**, and **sphere** data members are pointers to the **Direct3DRMMeshBuilder** interface. They will be used to access the three meshes in the scene. The remaining three data members are used to indicate which texture wrap method is to be used on each of the three meshes.

THE WRAPSWIN::CREATESCENE() FUNCTION

Let's look at the code for the Wraps demo. As with all the demos in this book, the demo uses the **RMWin** class as a base class and adds functionality by overriding the **CreateScene**() function. The Wraps demo declares the **WrapsWin** class, and the **CreateScene**() function is responsible for loading the three meshes that appear in the demo. Because this demo is a little more complicated than the code we've looked at previously, **CreateScene**() doles out much is its work to "helper" functions. The **CreateScene**() function for the Wraps demo appears below.

```
BOOL WrapsWin::CreateScene()
{
    //-------- MESHES AND TEXTURES --------
    if (LoadMeshes()==FALSE)
        return FALSE;

    if (LoadWrapsTexture()==FALSE)
        return FALSE;

    OnWrapsReset();

    //--------- LIGHT ----------
    LPDIRECT3DRMFRAME lightframe;
    LPDIRECT3DRMLIGHT light;
    d3drm->CreateLightRGB(D3DRMLIGHT_AMBIENT,
            D3DVALUE(1),D3DVALUE(1), D3DVALUE(1),
            &light);
    d3drm->CreateFrame( scene, &lightframe );
    lightframe->AddLight( light );
    lightframe->Release();
    lightframe=0;
    light->Release();
    light=0;

    //---------- CAMERA ------------
    d3drm->CreateFrame( scene, &camera );
    camera->SetPosition(scene,
            D3DVALUE(0.0), D3DVALUE(0.0), D3DVALUE(-50));
    d3drm->CreateViewport( device, camera, 0, 0,
            device->GetWidth(), device->GetHeight(),
            &viewport );

    return TRUE;
}
```

The **CreateScene()** function performs three steps:

1. Creation and configuration of the meshes, textures, and texture wraps

2. Creation and configuration of a light source

3. Creation and placement of the program's viewport

The **CreateScene()** function creates and initializes the meshes, textures, and texture wraps by calling the **LoadMeshes()**, **LoadWrapsTexture()**, and **OnWrapsReset()** functions. As the name implies, the **LoadMeshes()** function loads the three meshes that the demo uses. **LoadMeshes()** is also responsible for the creation and placement of the frames to which the meshes will be attached. The **LoadWrapsTexture()** function loads the texture that will be applied to all three meshes.

The **OnWrapsReset()** function serves two purposes. It is used here in the **CreateScene()** function to initialize the program's settings, and it is an event handler that gets called whenever you select the Reset option from the Wraps menu.

The **LoadMeshes()**, **LoadWrapsTexture()**, and **OnWrapsReset()** functions do most of the work for the Wraps demo and deserve a closer look.

THE WRAPSWIN::LOADMESHES() FUNCTION

The **LoadMeshes()** function creates three meshes and attaches each mesh to a frame. The frames are positioned apart from each other and given identical rotation attributes. The **LoadMeshes()** function appears as Listing 5.2.

Listing 5.2   The WrapsWin::LoadMeshes() function.

```
BOOL WrapsWin::LoadMeshes()
{
    HRESULT r;

    const D3DVALUE meshscale=D3DVALUE(13);
    const D3DVALUE meshspacing=D3DVALUE(15);

    D3DRMLOADRESOURCE resinfo;
    resinfo.hModule=NULL;
    resinfo.lpName=MAKEINTRESOURCE( IDR_BOXMESH );
    resinfo.lpType="MESH";
```

```
d3drm->CreateMeshBuilder( &box );
r=box->Load( &resinfo, NULL, D3DRMLOAD_FROMRESOURCE, NULL, NULL);
if (r!=D3DRM_OK)
{
    TRACE("failed to load internal box mesh\n");
    return FALSE;
}
box->SetPerspective(TRUE);
ScaleMesh( box, meshscale-D3DVALUE(2) );

LPDIRECT3DRMFRAME boxframe;
d3drm->CreateFrame( scene, &boxframe );
boxframe->SetPosition(scene,
        -meshspacing, D3DVALUE(0), D3DVALUE(0) );
boxframe->SetRotation( scene,
        D3DVALUE(0), D3DVALUE(1), D3DVALUE(1),
        D3DVALUE(.1) );
boxframe->AddVisual( box );

resinfo.hModule=NULL;
resinfo.lpName=MAKEINTRESOURCE( IDR_CYLMESH );
resinfo.lpType="MESH";

d3drm->CreateMeshBuilder( &cyl );
cyl->Load( &resinfo, NULL, D3DRMLOAD_FROMRESOURCE, NULL, NULL );
if (r!=D3DRM_OK)
{
    TRACE("failed to load internal cylinder mesh\n");
    return FALSE;
}
cyl->SetPerspective( TRUE );
ScaleMesh( cyl, meshscale );

LPDIRECT3DRMFRAME cylframe;
d3drm->CreateFrame( scene, &cylframe );
cylframe->SetRotation( scene,
        D3DVALUE(0), D3DVALUE(1), D3DVALUE(1),
        D3DVALUE(.1) );
cylframe->AddVisual( cyl );

resinfo.hModule=NULL;
resinfo.lpName=MAKEINTRESOURCE( IDR_SPHEREMESH );
resinfo.lpType="MESH";

d3drm->CreateMeshBuilder( &sphere );
sphere->Load( &resinfo, NULL, D3DRMLOAD_FROMRESOURCE, NULL, NULL);
```

```
if (r!=D3DRM_OK)
{
    TRACE("failed to load internal sphere mesh\n");
    return FALSE;
}
sphere->SetPerspective( TRUE );
ScaleMesh( sphere, meshscale );

LPDIRECT3DRMFRAME sphereframe;
d3drm->CreateFrame( scene, &sphereframe );
sphereframe->SetPosition( scene,
        D3DVALUE(meshspacing), D3DVALUE(0), D3DVALUE(0) );
sphereframe->SetRotation( scene,
        D3DVALUE(0), D3DVALUE(1), D3DVALUE(1),
        D3DVALUE(.1) );
sphereframe->AddVisual( sphere );

return TRUE;
}
```

The function declares some constant values that are used in the code to position and scale the meshes, and then initializes a pointer to the **Direct3DRMMeshBuilder** interface. The cube mesh is loaded from the program's resources with the **Load()** function.

Next, the **SetPerspective()** function is used to enable perspective correction. If you have installed the demos on your computer, you are encouraged to comment out this function call and recompile the Wraps demo. Perspective correction is especially discernible in the case of the cube mesh because of the large faces.

The mesh is then scaled with the **ScaleMesh()** function. We discussed the **ScaleMesh()** function in Chapter 4. **ScaleMesh()** is provided by the **RMWin** class as a convenient way to scale a mesh to a specific size. The constant used to determine the cube's size is adjusted a bit because cube shaped meshes tend to appear larger than other meshes (because they allow maximum volume in minimum space).

After the mesh has been scaled, the **LoadMeshes()** function creates a frame and positions it according to the **meshspacing** constant. The cube mesh appears to the left of the other meshes, so it is given a negative X axis value. The frame is then given a rotation attribute with the **SetRotation()**

function. Finally, the mesh is attached to the frame with the **Frame AddVisual**() function.

THE WRAPSWIN::LOADWRAPSTEXTURE() FUNCTION

The **LoadWrapsTexture**() function loads the texture shown in Figure 5.6 and associates it with the three meshes loaded previously by the **LoadMeshes**() function. The **LoadWrapsTexture**() function appears below:

```
BOOL WrapsWin::LoadWrapsTexture()
{
    HRSRC texture_id = FindResource( NULL, MAKEINTRESOURCE(
        IDR_JADETEXTURE), "TEXTURE" );
    LPDIRECT3DRMTEXTURE texture;
    d3drm->LoadTextureFromResource( texture_id, &texture );
    box->SetTexture( texture );
    cyl->SetTexture( texture );
    sphere->SetTexture( texture );
    texture->Release();
    texture=0;
    return TRUE;
}
```

The **LoadWrapsTexture**() function uses the Win32 **FindResource**() function to initialize an instance of the **HRSRC** structure. The **HRSRC** structure identifies the texture that we are attempting to load and is used as an argument to the **LoadTextureFromResource**() function. The new texture is then associated with the three meshes with the **Direct3DRMMeshBuilder SetTexture**() member function. The pointer to the texture is then released and **TRUE** is returned to indicate success.

THE WRAPSWIN::ONWRAPSRESET() FUNCTION

Recall that the Wraps demo **CreateScene**() function called three functions before creating a light source and a viewport: **LoadMeshes**(), **LoadWraps-Texture**(), and **OnWrapsReset**(). The **OnWrapsReset**() function assigns data members in the **WrapsWin** class so that a flat texture wrap is applied to the cube mesh, a cylindrical wrap is assigned to the cylinder mesh, and a spherical wrap is assigned to the sphere mesh. The **OnWrapsReset**() function looks like this:

```
void WrapsWin::OnWrapsReset()
{
    boxwraptype=D3DRMWRAP_FLAT;
    cylwraptype=D3DRMWRAP_CYLINDER;
    spherewraptype=D3DRMWRAP_SPHERE;

    ApplyWraps();
}
```

The **boxwraptype**, **cylwraptype**, and **spherewraptype** variables are **WrapsWin**
data members that are of the Direct3D **D3DRMWRAPTYPE** type. The
OnWrapReset() function assigns each of these data members using constants that are also supplied by Direct3D. We'll talk about the **ApplyWraps()**
function next.

THE WRAPSWIN::APPLYWRAPS() FUNCTION

The **ApplyWraps()** function is responsible for assigning the correct texture wrap type to each mesh depending on the values of the **WrapsWin**
data members. The **ApplyWraps()** function looks like this:

```
void WrapsWin::ApplyWraps()
{
    if ( boxwraptype==D3DRMWRAP_FLAT )
        ApplyFlat( box );
    else if ( boxwraptype==D3DRMWRAP_CYLINDER )
        ApplyCylinder( box );
    else
        ApplySphere( box );

    if ( cylwraptype==D3DRMWRAP_FLAT )
        ApplyFlat( cyl );
    else if ( cylwraptype==D3DRMWRAP_CYLINDER )
        ApplyCylinder( cyl );
    else
        ApplySphere( cyl );

    if ( spherewraptype==D3DRMWRAP_FLAT )
        ApplyFlat( sphere );
    else if ( spherewraptype==D3DRMWRAP_CYLINDER )
        ApplyCylinder( sphere );
    else
        ApplySphere( sphere );
}
```

The **ApplyWraps()** function determines the type of wrap that is to be used for each mesh and calls the appropriate function to perform the actual application of the texture wrap. We won't look at each of these functions because they are all quite similar. The **ApplyFlat()** function appears below:

```
void WrapsWin::ApplyFlat( LPDIRECT3DRMMESHBUILDER meshbuilder )
{
    D3DRMBOX box;
    meshbuilder->GetBox( &box );
    D3DVALUE width=box.max.x-box.min.x;
    D3DVALUE height=box.max.y-box.min.y;

    LPDIRECT3DRMWRAP wrap;
    d3drm->CreateWrap( D3DRMWRAP_FLAT, NULL,
            D3DVALUE(0.0), D3DVALUE(0.0), D3DVALUE(0.0), // wrap origin
            D3DVALUE(0.0), D3DVALUE(0.0), D3DVALUE(1.0), // z axis
            D3DVALUE(0.0), D3DVALUE(1.0), D3DVALUE(0.0), // y axis
            D3DVALUE(0.5), D3DVALUE(0.5),                // texture origin
            D3DDivide(1,width), D3DDivide(1,height),     // texture scale
            &wrap );
    wrap->Apply( meshbuilder );
    wrap->Release();
    wrap=0;
}
```

The **ApplyFlat()** function first calculates the width and height of the mesh that is to be texture mapped. The **Direct3DRMMeshBuilder GetBox()** function is used to initialize a **D3DRMBOX** structure with the dimensions of the mesh. Then, an instance of the **Direct3DRMWrap** interface is created with the **Direct3DRM CreateWrap()** function. The new wrap is applied to the mesh with the **Direct3DRMWrap Apply()** function. Finally, the **wrap** pointer is released.

There are three more **WrapsWin** member functions: **OnWrapsFlat()**, **OnWrapsCylinder()**, and **OnWrapsSphere()**. These functions serve as event handlers for the Wraps menu and are similar to the **OnWrapsReset()** function, except that they each assign the same type of texture wrap to the three meshes. The **OnWrapsFlat()** function is shown below:

```
void WrapsWin::OnWrapsFlat()
{
    boxwraptype=D3DRMWRAP_FLAT;
```

```
cylwraptype=D3DRMWRAP_FLAT;
spherewraptype=D3DRMWRAP_FLAT;

ApplyWraps();
}
```

DECALS

The demos we've looked at so far apply textures to the **Direct3DRMMesh-Builder** interface, and the meshbuilder is then attached to a frame with the **Direct3DRMFrame AddVisual**() function.

In this section, we introduce and discuss decals. A decal is a texture that is added directly to a scene. Decals appear in the scene just like they do in a paint program; they cannot be wrapped around objects in the scene. Decals can be moved and scaled, but they cannot be rotated; decals always face the camera. This fact limits the usefulness of decals, but they are still useful for adding 2D elements to a scene. Explosions, for instance, are often represented using decals because representing an explosion with faces and meshes is too demanding for most applications.

About decals
Although some of the **Direct3DRMTexture** member functions use the word "decal," decals are implemented with the **Direct3DRMTexture** interface. There is no **Direct3DRM-Decal** interface.

THE DECAL DEMO

Direct3D's decal support is showcased in the Decal demo. The Decal demo animates two decals by moving them around the screen. The Decal demo is shown in Figure 5.7.

The Decal demo demonstrates the following techniques:

- Direct3D's decal support

- The use of "dummy" frames to animate objects

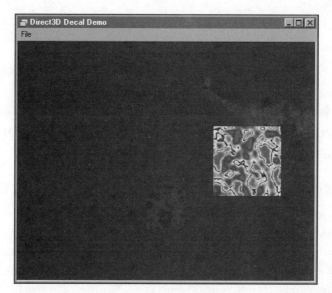

Figure 5.7
The Decal demo.

Before we look at the code for the Decal demo, we need to talk about dummy frames. A dummy frame is a frame used solely to animate other frames. Dummy frames are not attached to any visual objects such as meshes and decals. They are used as parents for frames that are attached to visual objects.

The Decal demo animates two decals in an orbit around the origin. This is accomplished by placing two dummy frames at the origin and assigning a different rotation attribute to each frame. The decals are attached to two separate (non-dummy) frames. Each of the non-dummy frames is a child of one of the dummy frames and is positioned away from the origin. Because child frames imitate the motions of parent frames, the non-dummy frames travel in an orbit around their parent frames.

THE DECALWIN CLASS

The Decal demo provides its functionality in the **DecalWin** class:

```
class DecalWin : public RMWin
{
public:
    BOOL CreateScene();
```

```
protected:
    //{{AFX_MSG(DecalWin)
    //}}AFX_MSG
    DECLARE_MESSAGE_MAP()
};
```

The **DecalWin** class is simple. It declares only one function: **CreateScene()**.
The **protected** portion of the class contains ClassWizard code that is necessary if message handlers are to be added later.

THE DECALWIN::CREATESCENE() FUNCTION

In contrast to the Wraps demo, all of the Decal demo functionality is provided
in the **CreateScene()** function. The **CreateScene()** function creates and
configures the decals, a light source, and a viewport. Because the animation in
the Decal demo is accomplished with motion attributes, no callback functions are necessary. The **CreateScene()** function appears as Listing 5.3.

Listing 5.3   The DecalWin::CreateScene() function.

```
BOOL DecalWin::CreateScene()
{
    //------ DECALS --------
    LPDIRECT3DRMTEXTURE texture1, texture2;
    HRSRC texture_id;
    texture_id=FindResource( NULL, MAKEINTRESOURCE(IDR_TEXTURE1),
        "TEXTURE" );
    d3drm->LoadTextureFromResource( texture_id, &texture1 );
    texture1->SetDecalOrigin( 64, 64 );

    texture_id=FindResource( NULL, MAKEINTRESOURCE(IDR_TEXTURE2),
        "TEXTURE" );
    d3drm->LoadTextureFromResource( texture_id, &texture2 );
    texture2->SetDecalOrigin( 64, 64 );

    //-------- FRAMES --------
    LPDIRECT3DRMFRAME dummyframe1;
    d3drm->CreateFrame( scene, &dummyframe1 );
    dummyframe1->SetRotation( scene,
            D3DVALUE(0), D3DVALUE(1), D3DVALUE(0),
            D3DVALUE(0.05) );

    LPDIRECT3DRMFRAME dummyframe2;
    d3drm->CreateFrame( scene, &dummyframe2 );
```

```
dummyframe2->SetRotation(scene,
        D3DVALUE(1), D3DVALUE(0), D3DVALUE(0),
        D3DVALUE(-0.05) );

LPDIRECT3DRMFRAME orbitframe1;
d3drm->CreateFrame( dummyframe1, &orbitframe1 );
orbitframe1->SetPosition( dummyframe1,
        D3DVALUE(2), D3DVALUE(0), D3DVALUE(0) );
orbitframe1->AddVisual( texture1 );

LPDIRECT3DRMFRAME orbitframe2;
d3drm->CreateFrame( dummyframe2, &orbitframe2 );
orbitframe2->SetPosition( dummyframe2,
        D3DVALUE(0), D3DVALUE(-2), D3DVALUE(0) );
orbitframe2->AddVisual( texture2 );

texture1->Release();
texture1=0;
texture2->Release();
texture2=0;
dummyframe1->Release();
dummyframe1=0;
dummyframe2->Release();
dummyframe2=0;
orbitframe1->Release();
orbitframe1=0;
orbitframe2->Release();
orbitframe2=0;

//--------- LIGHT --------
LPDIRECT3DRMLIGHT light;
d3drm->CreateLightRGB( D3DRMLIGHT_AMBIENT,
        D3DVALUE(1.0),D3DVALUE(1.0), D3DVALUE(1.0),
        &light );
scene->AddLight( light );
light->Release();
light=0;

//--------- VIEWPORT --------
d3drm->CreateFrame( scene, &camera );
camera->SetPosition( scene,
        D3DVALUE(0.0), D3DVALUE(0.0), D3DVALUE(-6.0) );
d3drm->CreateViewport( device, camera,
        0, 0,
        device->GetWidth(), device->GetHeight(),
        &viewport );
```

```
    return TRUE;
}
```

The **CreateScene()** function performs four steps:

1. Create the two textures that will be used as decals

2. Create frames for the two textures

3. Create a light source

4. Create a viewport

The first step is loading two textures. As with most of the demos, the textures are stored as resources in the demo's EXE file:

```
LPDIRECT3DRMTEXTURE texture1, texture2;
HRSRC texture_id;
texture_id=FindResource( NULL, MAKEINTRESOURCE(IDR_TEXTURE1),
    "TEXTURE" );
d3drm->LoadTextureFromResource( texture_id, &texture1 );
texture1->SetDecalOrigin( 64, 64 );

texture_id=FindResource( NULL, MAKEINTRESOURCE(IDR_TEXTURE2),
    "TEXTURE" );
d3drm->LoadTextureFromResource( texture_id, &texture2 );
texture2->SetDecalOrigin( 64, 64 );
```

After the each texture is loaded, the **SetDecalOrigin()** function is called. The **SetDecalOrigin()** function is used to determine the location within the texture that will serve as the texture's origin. By default, a texture's upper-left-hand corner is the origin (x=0, y=0), meaning that when a texture is attached to a frame, the upper-left-hand corner of the texture appears at the frame's location. The size of the two textures that the Decal demo uses is 128 by 128. Using the value 64 as arguments to the **SetDecalOrigin()** function places the texture's origin in the center of the texture.

Next, the demo's frames (both dummy and non-dummy) are created:

```
LPDIRECT3DRMFRAME dummyframe1;
d3drm->CreateFrame( scene, &dummyframe1 );
dummyframe1->SetRotation( scene,
        D3DVALUE(0), D3DVALUE(1), D3DVALUE(0),
        D3DVALUE(0.05) );
```

```
LPDIRECT3DRMFRAME dummyframe2;
d3drm->CreateFrame( scene, &dummyframe2 );
dummyframe2->SetRotation(scene,
        D3DVALUE(1), D3DVALUE(0), D3DVALUE(0),
        D3DVALUE(-0.05) );

LPDIRECT3DRMFRAME orbitframe1;
d3drm->CreateFrame( dummyframe1, &orbitframe1 );
orbitframe1->SetPosition( dummyframe1,
        D3DVALUE(2), D3DVALUE(0), D3DVALUE(0) );
orbitframe1->AddVisual( texture1 );

LPDIRECT3DRMFRAME orbitframe2;
d3drm->CreateFrame( dummyframe2, &orbitframe2 );
orbitframe2->SetPosition( dummyframe2,
        D3DVALUE(0), D3DVALUE(-2), D3DVALUE(0) );
orbitframe2->AddVisual( texture2 );
```

Each dummy frame is given a rotation with the **SetRotation()** function but is not moved from its original location (the origin). The orbiting frames are positioned away from the dummy frames with the **SetPosition**() function. Notice that the dummy frames are children of the **scene** frame (the root of the frame hierarchy), and the orbiting frames are children of the dummy frames. The previously created textures are attached to the orbiting frames with the **AddVisual()** function. The fact that the textures are attached directly to the frames is what makes them decals.

Steps 3 and 4 create a light source and viewport for the Decal demo. The code is very similar to the code that we saw in the Jade demo. You'll learn more about light sources and viewports later in this book.

TRANSPARENCY

The **Direct3DRMTexture** interface lets you specify a color within a texture that is to be treated as transparent by Direct3D. Portions of a texture that are transparent allow meshes and textures that would normally be hidden by the texture to be visible.

By default, a texture's transparency is disabled. The **Direct3DRMTexture SetDecalTransparency()** function can be used to enable and disable transparency. When transparency is enabled, any black pixels within the texture are transparent. The transparent color can be specified with the **SetDecalTransparencyColor()** function.

THE ORBSTAR DEMO

The OrbStar demo uses transparency to animate a star within a sphere. The star mesh and the sphere mesh are both placed at the origin. The sphere is scaled to be larger than the star, so the star wouldn't be visible if the texture used on the sphere wasn't partially transparent. The OrbStar demo is shown in Figure 5.8.

The texture that is applied to the sphere in the demo is shown in Figure 5.9.

The OrbStar demo demonstrates the following techniques:

- Using transparent textures

- Using multiple callback functions

- Using the **D3DRMVectorRandom()** function to generate random vectors

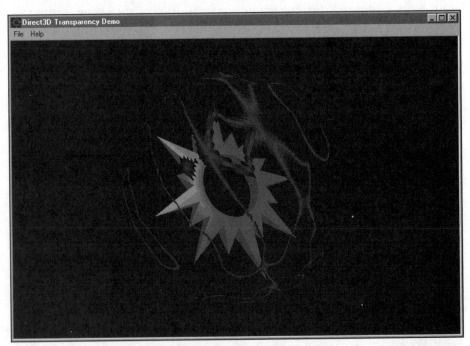

Figure 5.8
The OrbStar demo.

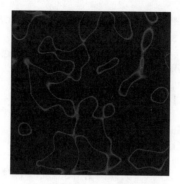

Figure 5.9
The texture used in the OrbStar demo.

THE ORBSTARWIN CLASS

The **OrbStarWin** class provides most of the OrbStar demo's functionality. The class definition looks like this:

```
class OrbStarWin : public RMWin
{
public:
    BOOL CreateScene();
    static void MoveSphere(LPDIRECT3DRMFRAME frame, void* arg,
        D3DVALUE delta);
    static void MoveStar(LPDIRECT3DRMFRAME frame, void* arg,
        D3DVALUE delta);
protected:
    //{{AFX_MSG(OrbStarWin)
    //}}AFX_MSG
    DECLARE_MESSAGE_MAP()
};
```

The class declares three functions: **CreateScene()**, **MoveSphere()**, and **MoveStar()**. The **CreateScene()** function constructs the demo's scene. The **MoveSphere()** and **MoveStar()** functions are callback functions that we will use to animate the two meshes in the scene.

THE ORBSTARWIN::CREATESCENE() FUNCTION

The **CreateScene()** function for the OrbStar demo creates the star and sphere meshes, the texture that is to be applied to the sphere, two light sources, and a viewport. The **CreateScene()** function is shown as Listing 5.4.

Listing 5.4   The OrbStarWin::CreateScene() function.

```
BOOL OrbStarWin::CreateScene()
{
    //-------- STAR MESH --------
    D3DRMLOADRESOURCE resinfo;
    resinfo.hModule=NULL;
    resinfo.lpName=MAKEINTRESOURCE( IDR_STARMESH );
    resinfo.lpType="MESH";
    LPDIRECT3DRMMESHBUILDER starbuilder;
    d3drm->CreateMeshBuilder( &starbuilder );
    starbuilder->Load( &resinfo, NULL, D3DRMLOAD_FROMRESOURCE,
        NULL, NULL );
    starbuilder->SetColorRGB( D3DVALUE(1.0), D3DVALUE(0.0),
        D3DVALUE(0.0) );
    ScaleMesh( starbuilder, D3DVALUE(20) );

    //--------- STAR FRAME --------
    LPDIRECT3DRMFRAME starframe;
    d3drm->CreateFrame( scene, &starframe );
    starframe->SetRotation( scene,
            D3DVALUE(1.0), D3DVALUE(0.0),D3DVALUE(0.0),
            D3DVALUE(0.1) );
    starframe->AddVisual( starbuilder );
    starframe->AddMoveCallback( MoveStar, NULL );
    starframe->Release();
    starframe=0;
    starbuilder->Release();
    starbuilder=0;

    //--------- SPHERE MESH --------
    resinfo.hModule=NULL;
    resinfo.lpName=MAKEINTRESOURCE( IDR_SPHEREMESH );
    resinfo.lpType="MESH";
    LPDIRECT3DRMMESHBUILDER spherebuilder;
    d3drm->CreateMeshBuilder( &spherebuilder );
    spherebuilder->Load( &resinfo, NULL, D3DRMLOAD_FROMRESOURCE,
        NULL, NULL );
    spherebuilder->SetPerspective( TRUE );
    ScaleMesh( spherebuilder, D3DVALUE(25) );

    //--------- SPHERE TEXTURE ------
    LPDIRECT3DRMTEXTURE texture;
    HRSRC texture_id = FindResource( NULL, MAKEINTRESOURCE(
        IDR_TRANSTEXTURE), "TEXTURE" );
    d3drm->LoadTextureFromResource( texture_id, &texture );
```

```
texture->SetDecalTransparency( TRUE );
spherebuilder->SetTexture( texture );
texture->Release();
texture=0;

//---------- SPHERE WRAP --------
D3DRMBOX box;
spherebuilder->GetBox( &box );
D3DVALUE width=box.max.x-box.min.x;
D3DVALUE height=box.max.y-box.min.y;

LPDIRECT3DRMWRAP wrap;
d3drm->CreateWrap( D3DRMWRAP_FLAT, NULL,
        D3DVALUE(0.0), D3DVALUE(0.0), D3DVALUE(0.0),   // origin
        D3DVALUE(0.0), D3DVALUE(1.0), D3DVALUE(0.0),   // z axis
        D3DVALUE(0.0), D3DVALUE(0.0), D3DVALUE(1.0),   // y axis
        D3DVALUE(0.5), D3DVALUE(0.5),                  // origin
        D3DDivide(1,width), D3DDivide(1,height),       // scale
        &wrap );
wrap->Apply( spherebuilder );
wrap->Release(); wrap=0;

//-------- SPHERE FRAME ----------
LPDIRECT3DRMFRAME sphereframe;
d3drm->CreateFrame( scene, &sphereframe );
sphereframe->SetRotation( scene,
        D3DVALUE(0), D3DVALUE(1), D3DVALUE(0),
        D3DVALUE(.1) );
sphereframe->AddVisual( spherebuilder );
sphereframe->AddMoveCallback( MoveSphere, NULL );
sphereframe->Release();
sphereframe=0;
spherebuilder->Release();
spherebuilder=0;

//---------- LIGHT --------
LPDIRECT3DRMLIGHT light1, light2;
d3drm->CreateLightRGB( D3DRMLIGHT_AMBIENT,
        D3DVALUE(0.8),D3DVALUE(0.8), D3DVALUE(0.8),
        &light1 );
d3drm->CreateLightRGB( D3DRMLIGHT_DIRECTIONAL,
        D3DVALUE(0.9), D3DVALUE(0.9), D3DVALUE(0.9),
        &light2 );

LPDIRECT3DRMFRAME lightframe;
d3drm->CreateFrame( scene, &lightframe );
```

```
lightframe->SetOrientation( scene,
        D3DVALUE(-1), D3DVALUE(-1), D3DVALUE(1),
        D3DVALUE(0), D3DVALUE(1), D3DVALUE(0) );

lightframe->AddLight( light1 );
lightframe->AddLight( light2 );

lightframe->Release();
lightframe=0;
light1->Release();
lightframe=0;
light2->Release();
lightframe=0;

//----------- VIEWPORT --------
d3drm->CreateFrame( scene, &camera );
camera->SetPosition( scene,
        D3DVALUE(0.0), D3DVALUE(0.0), D3DVALUE(-50) );
d3drm->CreateViewport( device, camera, 0, 0,
            device->GetWidth(), device->GetHeight(),
            &viewport );

return TRUE;
}
```

The **CreateScene()** function performs eight steps:

1. Creation of the star mesh
2. Creation of the star frame
3. Creation of the sphere mesh
4. Creation of a partially transparent texture
5. Creation of a texture wrap for the sphere mesh
6. Creation of a frame for the sphere
7. Creation of a light source
8. Creation of a viewport

The star mesh is created first:

```
D3DRMLOADRESOURCE resinfo;
resinfo.hModule=NULL;
```

```
resinfo.lpName=MAKEINTRESOURCE( IDR_STARMESH );
resinfo.lpType="MESH";
LPDIRECT3DRMMESHBUILDER starbuilder;
d3drm->CreateMeshBuilder( &starbuilder );
starbuilder->Load( &resinfo, NULL, D3DRMLOAD_FROMRESOURCE,
    NULL, NULL );
starbuilder->SetColorRGB( D3DVALUE(1.0), D3DVALUE(0.0),
    D3DVALUE(0.0) );
ScaleMesh( starbuilder, D3DVALUE(20) );
```

As with the other demos we've seen, the **Direct3DRMMeshBuilder Load()**
member function is used to load the mesh from the program's resources.
Once the mesh has been loaded, **SetColorRGB()** function is used to assign
the mesh's color to red. The **ScaleMesh()** function is used to scale to mesh
to a specific size.

Next, a frame (called **starframe**) is created and given a rotation attribute:

```
LPDIRECT3DRMFRAME starframe;
d3drm->CreateFrame( scene, &starframe );
starframe->SetRotation( scene,
        D3DVALUE(1.0), D3DVALUE(0.0),D3DVALUE(0.0),
        D3DVALUE(0.1) );
starframe->AddVisual( starbuilder );
starframe->AddMoveCallback( MoveStar, NULL );
starframe->Release();
starframe=0;
starbuilder->Release();
starbuilder=0;
```

The new frame is given a rotation attribute around the X axis. As you'll
see, this attribute is only temporary because we will be using callback functions to change the frame's rotation attribute during the demo's execution. The previously created meshbuilder is attached to the new frame
with the **AddVisual()** function. Before the **starframe** and **starbuilder** pointers are released, the **MoveStar()** callback function is installed. We'll look
at the **MoveStar()** function later. The **starframe** and **starbuilder** pointers
are then released.

Next, the sphere mesh is created and loaded:

```
resinfo.hModule=NULL;
resinfo.lpName=MAKEINTRESOURCE( IDR_SPHEREMESH );
```

```
resinfo.lpType="MESH";
LPDIRECT3DRMMESHBUILDER spherebuilder;
d3drm->CreateMeshBuilder( &spherebuilder );
spherebuilder->Load( &resinfo, NULL, D3DRMLOAD_FROMRESOURCE, NULL, NULL );
spherebuilder->SetPerspective( TRUE );
ScaleMesh( spherebuilder, D3DVALUE(25) );
```

After the mesh is loaded, the **SetPerspective()** function is used to enable perspective correction for the sphere mesh. This wasn't done for the star mesh because no texture will be applied to the star mesh. The sphere mesh is then scaled to be slightly larger than the star mesh.

Step 4 is the creation of the sphere texture:

```
LPDIRECT3DRMTEXTURE texture;
HRSRC texture_id = FindResource( NULL, MAKEINTRESOURCE(
    IDR_TRANSTEXTURE), "TEXTURE" );
d3drm->LoadTextureFromResource( texture_id, &texture );
texture->SetDecalTransparency( TRUE );
spherebuilder->SetTexture( texture );
texture->Release();
texture=0;
```

As with the other demos, the **LoadTextureFromResource()** is used to create the texture. Next, the **SetDecalTransparency()** function is used to enable transparency. We are not specifying a transparency color, so black is used by default. The texture is associated with the sphere mesh using the **Direct3DRMMeshBuilder SetTexture()** function. The **texture** pointer is then released.

Next, a texture wrap is created that is used to apply the new texture to the sphere mesh:

```
D3DRMBOX box;
spherebuilder->GetBox( &box );
D3DVALUE width=box.max.x-box.min.x;
D3DVALUE height=box.max.y-box.min.y;

LPDIRECT3DRMWRAP wrap;
d3drm->CreateWrap( D3DRMWRAP_FLAT, NULL,
        D3DVALUE(0.0), D3DVALUE(0.0), D3DVALUE(0.0),  // origin
        D3DVALUE(0.0), D3DVALUE(1.0), D3DVALUE(0.0),  // z axis
        D3DVALUE(0.0), D3DVALUE(0.0), D3DVALUE(1.0),  // y axis
```

```
        D3DVALUE(0.5), D3DVALUE(0.5),              // origin
        D3DDivide(1,width), D3DDivide(1,height),   // scale
        &wrap );
wrap->Apply( spherebuilder );
wrap->Release(); wrap=0;
```

A flat texture wrap is used, and the dimensions of the mesh are used to size the wrap to the fit the mesh. The texture wrap is applied to the sphere mesh with the **Direct3DRMWrap Apply()** function.

Step 6 is the creation of a frame for the sphere mesh:

```
LPDIRECT3DRMFRAME sphereframe;
d3drm->CreateFrame( scene, &sphereframe );
sphereframe->SetRotation( scene,
        D3DVALUE(0), D3DVALUE(1), D3DVALUE(0),
        D3DVALUE(.1) );
sphereframe->AddVisual( spherebuilder );
sphereframe->AddMoveCallback( MoveSphere, NULL );
sphereframe->Release();
sphereframe=0;
spherebuilder->Release();
spherebuilder=0;
```

The new frame is given a rotation attribute, but, like the frame that we created in Step 2, a callback function will be used to change this rotation attribute. The frame is attached to the sphere mesh with the **AddVisual()** function, and the **MoveSphere()** callback is installed. The **sphereframe** and **spherebuilder** pointers are then released.

Steps 7 and 8 create the light sources and viewport for the scene. The code is very similar to the code that appears in the Jade demo. You'll learn more about light sources and viewports later in this book.

THE ORBSTAR CALLBACK FUNCTIONS

The **OrbStar CreateScene()** function installs two callback functions: one for the frame to which the star mesh is attached and another for the sphere mesh frame. These functions periodically assign a random rotation attribute to each frame, causing the meshes in the demo to change their rotation speed and direction. The **MoveStar()** and **MoveSphere()** callback functions are virtually identical, so only the **MoveStar()** function is shown.

```
void OrbStarWin::MoveStar(LPDIRECT3DRMFRAME frame, void*, D3DVALUE)
{
    static UINT delay;
    if (++delay<11)
        return;
    delay=0;

    LPDIRECT3DRMFRAME scene;
    frame->GetScene( &scene );

    D3DVECTOR spinvect;
    D3DRMVectorRandom( &spinvect );
    D3DVALUE spin=D3DDivide(rand()%100+1,200);
    frame->SetRotation( scene,
            spinvect.x, spinvect.y, spinvect.z,
            spin );
}
```

The **MoveStar()** function uses a **static** counter variable to regulate the frequency that adjusts the frame's rotation attribute. In this case, the counter must reach 11 before an adjustment is made.

Once it is determined that a new rotation attribute will be calculated, a pointer to the scene's root frame is retrieved with the **Direct3DRMFrame GetScene()** function. Remember that callback functions must be declared as **static** because of the fact that regular member functions require a class pointer in order to be invoked. Static member functions don't have access to their class's data members (unless the data members are also declared **static**). If the **MoveStar()** function was non-static, we would be able to use the **RMWin::scene** data member, just as we did in the **CreateScene()** function. Luckily, Direct3D passes a pointer to the callback's frame as the first parameter to the callback function and supplies the **GetScene()** function. We will need a pointer to the scene frame as the reference pointer to the **SetRotation()** function later in the function.

The **MoveStar()** function calculates a new rotation attribute randomly. A random vector is retrieved with the **D3DRMVectorRandom()** function, and a rotation speed is calculated with the **rand()** function. The frame's new rotation attribute is installed with the **SetRotation()** function.

TEXTURE ANIMATION

In this chapter, you've learned how to apply textures to meshes using texture wrapping methods. You've learned about decals and about transparency. Now, we will look at texture animation.

There are two forms of texture animation. One form animates a single texture by changing the way that the texture is applied. The second form uses multiple textures, applying one at a time to produce a sort of texture movie. We'll talk about both forms in this section, starting with animating a single texture.

There are a number of ways to animate a single texture. The texture's scale, origin, wrap method, and even transparency settings can be adjusted to modify the way that a texture is applied to a mesh. Probably, the most straightforward way is to move a texture across a mesh by changing the texture origin.

THE TEXTUREDRIFT DEMO

The TextureDrift demo uses a single mesh and a single texture. The texture is applied to the mesh using a slightly different texture origin on each screen update, causing the texture to travel, or drift, across the mesh. The TextureDrift demo is shown in Figure 5.10 (but you'll have to run the TextureDrift demo if you want to see any texture animation).

The TextureDrift demo demonstrates the following techniques:

- Animating a single texture by altering the manner in which the texture is applied to a mesh

- Using the **Direct3DRMMesh** interface to avoid the extra overhead of using the **Direct3DRMMeshBuilder** interface

- Using the **Direct3DRMFrame GetVisuals()** function to retrieve pointers to objects attached to the frame

The TextureDrift demo uses a slightly different technique than the other demos that we've looked at. The previous demos used the **Direct3DRMMeshBuilder** interface to create and display meshes (except for the Decal demo which did not use meshes at all). The TextureDrift demo uses the **Direct3DRMMesh-Builder** interface for mesh creation but not for mesh display. Instead, the

Figure 5.10
The TextureDrift demo.

Direct3DRMMeshBuilder interface is used to create an instance of the **Direct3DRMMesh** interface. This is done for performance reasons. In Chapter 3, we talked about the fact that instances of the **Direct3DRMMeshBuilder** interface must create internal instances of the **Direct3DRMMesh** interface whenever a change is made to the mesh. We use the **Direct3DRMMesh** interface directly in the TextureDrift demo to avoid this extra overhead.

This does not mean that we made bad design decisions for the previous demos. The **Direct3DRMMeshBuilder** interface offers good performance as long as the mesh properties do not change frequently during program execution. We are using the **Direct3DRMMesh** interface for the TextureDrift demo because the mesh characteristics will be changing for every screen update.

THE TEXTUREDRIFTWIN CLASS

The TextureDrift demo provides its functionality in the **TextureDriftWin** class. The class is defined as follows:

```
class TextureDriftWin : public RMWin
{
public:
    BOOL CreateScene();
    static void MoveTexture(LPDIRECT3DRMFRAME frame,
        void* arg, D3DVALUE delta);
protected:
    //{{AFX_MSG(TextureDriftWin)
    //}}AFX_MSG
    DECLARE_MESSAGE_MAP()
};
```

The class declares two functions: **CreateScene**() and **MoveTexture**(). The **CreateScene**() constructs the demo's scene, and the **MoveTexture**() function is a callback function that is used to perform the texture animation.

The **protected** portion of the class is present in case you want to add message handlers with ClassWizard.

THE TEXTUREDRIFTWIN::CREATESCENE() FUNCTION

The **TextureDriftWin::CreateScene**() function creates one mesh and a texture. The texture is associated with the mesh, but no texture wrap is supplied. A callback function is used to generate a texture wrap for each screen update. The **CreateScene**() function appears as Listing 5.5.

Listing 5.5   The TextureDriftWin::CreateScene() function.

```
BOOL TextureDriftWin::CreateScene()
{
    //------ MESHBUILDER ------
    D3DRMLOADRESOURCE resinfo;
    resinfo.hModule=NULL;
    resinfo.lpName=MAKEINTRESOURCE( IDR_D3DMESH );
    resinfo.lpType="MESH";
    LPDIRECT3DRMMESHBUILDER meshbuilder;
    d3drm->CreateMeshBuilder( &meshbuilder );
    meshbuilder->Load( &resinfo, NULL, D3DRMLOAD_FROMRESOURCE, NULL,
        NULL );
    meshbuilder->Scale( D3DVALUE(1), D3DVALUE(1), D3DVALUE(.5) );
    ScaleMesh( meshbuilder, D3DVALUE(35) );
    meshbuilder->SetPerspective( TRUE );
```

```
//------- TEXTURE ------
HRSRC texture_id = FindResource( NULL, MAKEINTRESOURCE(
    IDR_TEXTURE), "TEXTURE" );
LPDIRECT3DRMTEXTURE texture;
d3drm->LoadTextureFromResource( texture_id, &texture );
meshbuilder->SetTexture( texture );
texture->Release();
texture=0;

//-------- MESH --------
LPDIRECT3DRMMESH mesh;
meshbuilder->CreateMesh( &mesh );
meshbuilder->Release();
meshbuilder=0;

//-------- MESH FRAME --------
LPDIRECT3DRMFRAME meshframe;
d3drm->CreateFrame( scene, &meshframe );
meshframe->SetOrientation( scene,
        D3DVALUE(0), D3DVALUE(-1), D3DVALUE(1),
        D3DVALUE(0), D3DVALUE(1), D3DVALUE(0));
meshframe->AddVisual( mesh );
meshframe->AddMoveCallback( MoveTexture, NULL );
meshframe->Release();
meshframe=0;
mesh->Release();
mesh=0;

//-------- LIGHTS ----------
LPDIRECT3DRMLIGHT light;
d3drm->CreateLightRGB( D3DRMLIGHT_AMBIENT,
        D3DVALUE(1),D3DVALUE(1), D3DVALUE(1),
        &light );
scene->AddLight( light );
light->Release();
light=0;

//-------- VIEWPORT ----------
d3drm->CreateFrame( scene, &camera );
camera->SetPosition( scene,
        D3DVALUE(0.0), D3DVALUE(0.0), D3DVALUE(-50.0));
d3drm->CreateViewport( device, camera, 0, 0,
        device->GetWidth(), device->GetHeight(),
        &viewport );

return TRUE;
}
```

The **CreateScene()** function performs six steps:

1. Creation of the mesh using the **Direct3DRMMeshBuilder** interface

2. Creation of a texture for the mesh

3. Creation of the **Direct3DRMMesh** interface

4. Creation of a frame for the mesh

5. Creation of a light source

6. Creation of a viewport

First, the **Direct3DRMMeshBuilder** interface is used to load a mesh from the demo's resources:

```
D3DRMLOADRESOURCE resinfo;
resinfo.hModule=NULL;
resinfo.lpName=MAKEINTRESOURCE( IDR_D3DMESH );
resinfo.lpType="MESH";
LPDIRECT3DRMMESHBUILDER meshbuilder;
d3drm->CreateMeshBuilder( &meshbuilder );
meshbuilder->Load( &resinfo, NULL, D3DRMLOAD_FROMRESOURCE,
    NULL, NULL );
meshbuilder->Scale( D3DVALUE(1), D3DVALUE(1), D3DVALUE(.5) );
ScaleMesh( meshbuilder, D3DVALUE(35) );
meshbuilder->SetPerspective( TRUE );
```

Notice that after the mesh is loaded, we are using the **Direct3DRMMeshBuilder Scale()** function to reduce the Z dimension of the mesh. Using the value 0.5 for the Z argument of the **Scale()** function cuts the size of the mesh along the Z axis in half. After the **Scale()** function is called, the **ScaleMesh()** function is used to specify that the mesh should be scaled so that its longest dimension is equal to 35. The **SetPerspective()** function is called to enable perspective correction.

Next, the texture is created:

```
HRSRC texture_id = FindResource( NULL, MAKEINTRESOURCE(IDR_TEXTURE),
    "TEXTURE" );
LPDIRECT3DRMTEXTURE texture;
d3drm->LoadTextureFromResource( texture_id, &texture );
meshbuilder->SetTexture( texture );
```

```
texture->Release();
texture=0;
```

The new texture is associated with the previously created meshbuilder with
the **SetTexture()** function, but no texture wrap is created. Next, an instance of
the **Direct3DRMMesh** interface is created using the existing meshbuilder:

```
LPDIRECT3DRMMESH mesh;
meshbuilder->CreateMesh( &mesh );
meshbuilder->Release();
meshbuilder=0;
```

After the **CreateMesh()** function is called, the meshbuilder is no longer
needed, so it is released.

Next, a new frame is created, and the mesh is attached:

```
LPDIRECT3DRMFRAME meshframe;
d3drm->CreateFrame( scene, &meshframe );
meshframe->SetOrientation( scene,
        D3DVALUE(0), D3DVALUE(-1), D3DVALUE(1),
        D3DVALUE(0), D3DVALUE(1), D3DVALUE(0));
meshframe->AddVisual( mesh );
meshframe->AddMoveCallback( MoveTexture, NULL );
meshframe->Release();
meshframe=0;
mesh->Release();
mesh=0;
```

The new frame is oriented so that the mesh will appear at a 45 degree
angle to the viewport, and the **AddVisual()** function is used to attach the
mesh to the frame. The **MoveTexture()** callback function that will animate
the texture is installed with the **AddMoveCallback()** function.

Notice that the **mesh** pointer is released. We released the **meshbuilder** and
texture pointers earlier in the function, so this means that we no longer
have pointers to any graphical objects. This would make it difficult to apply new texture wrap settings if there wasn't a way to retrieve a frame's
visual objects. We'll see how this is done when we look at the **MoveTexture()**
callback function.

Steps 5 and 6 create a light source and a viewport for the scene.

THE TEXTUREDRIFTWIN::MOVETEXTURE() FUNCTION

MoveTexture() is a callback function that creates and applies a texture wrap that differs for each invocation. First, however, the **Direct3DRMMesh** interface that was added to the frame by the **CreateScene**() function must be retrieved. The **MoveTexture**() callback function appears as Listing 5.6.

Listing 5.6   The TextureDriftWin::MoveTexture() function.

```
void TextureDriftWin::MoveTexture(LPDIRECT3DRMFRAME frame,
    void*, D3DVALUE)
{
    static D3DVALUE xtex;
    xtex+=D3DVALUE(.02);

    LPDIRECT3DRMVISUALARRAY visualarray;
    frame->GetVisuals( &visualarray );
    int nvisuals = visualarray->GetSize();
    for ( int i = 0; i < nvisuals; i++ )
    {
        LPDIRECT3DRMVISUAL visual;
        visualarray->GetElement( i, &visual );
        LPDIRECT3DRMMESH mesh;
        if (visual->QueryInterface( IID_IDirect3DRMMesh,
            (void**)&mesh) == 0)
        {
            D3DRMBOX box;
            mesh->GetBox( &box );
            D3DVALUE w=box.max.x-box.min.x;
            D3DVALUE h=box.max.y-box.min.y;

            LPDIRECT3DRMWRAP wrap;
            d3drm->CreateWrap( D3DRMWRAP_FLAT, NULL,
                    D3DVALUE(0.0), D3DVALUE(0.0), D3DVALUE(0.0),
                    D3DVALUE(0.0), D3DVALUE(0.0), D3DVALUE(1.0),
                    D3DVALUE(0.0), D3DVALUE(1.0), D3DVALUE(0.0),
                    xtex, D3DVALUE(0.5),                // texture origin
                    D3DDivide(1,w), D3DDivide(1,h),  // texture scale
                    &wrap );
            wrap->Apply( mesh );
            wrap->Release();
            wrap=0;
            mesh->Release();
            mesh=0;
        }
```

```
        visual->Release();
        visual=0;
    }
    visualarray->Release();
    visualarray=0;
}
```

The **MoveTexture()** function first declares a static **D3DVALUE** that it increments on each invocation. This value is used as the texture's X origin value,
so incrementing the value causes the texture to drift across in the mesh.

Next, the **Direct3DRMFrame GetVisuals()** function is used to retrieve an
array of visual objects that are attached to the frame (the **frame** pointer is
passed to the callback function by Direct3D as the function's first parameter).

The **GetVisuals()** function initializes a pointer to the **Direct3DRMVisualArray**
interface. **Direct3DRMVisualArray** is an interface that supports only two
member functions: **GetSize()** and **GetElement()**.

A loop is used to iterate through the array of visual objects. The number of
items in the array is determined with the **GetSize()** function, and each
item in the array is retrieved with the **GetElement()** function. The pointers retrieved from the array are pointers to the **Direct3DRMVisual** interface (which provides no member functions). The **QueryInterface()** is used
to inquire as to whether the object supports the **Direct3DRMMesh** interface. We know that one, and only one, of the objects retrieved by
GetElement() will support the **Direct3DRMMesh** interface because we created and attached the mesh to this frame in the **CreateScene()** function.

Once a pointer to the **Direct3DRMMesh** interface has been acquired, a
Direct3DRMWrap interface is created and applied to the mesh.

THE SHOWROOM DEMO

The ShowRoom demo performs texture animation by using multiple textures on a single mesh, one at a time. The mesh used in the ShowRoom
demo is a simple box. The textures are rendered images of a car facing
different directions. A different texture is used for each screen update, so
the car appears to be animated. The mesh that the textures are applied to
is rotating, so both the mesh and the texture are animated. The ShowRoom
demo appears in Figure 5.11.

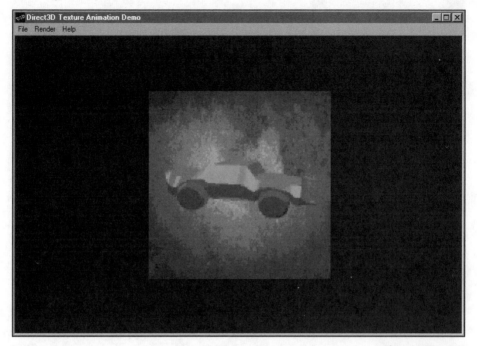

Figure 5.11
The ShowRoom demo.

The ShowRoom demo demonstrates the following techniques:

- Performing texture animation with multiple textures

- Using the **Direct3DRMMesh** interface

- Animation with rotation attributes

Like the TextureDrift demo, the ShowRoom demo used the **Direct3DRMMesh** interface to avoid the extra overhead of the **Direct3DRMMeshBuilder** interface.

THE SHOWROOMWIN CLASS

The ShowRoom demo's functionality is provided in the **ShowRoomWin** class. The class is defined like this:

```
class ShowRoomWin : public RMWin
{
public:
```

```
    BOOL CreateScene();
    static void UpdateTexture(LPDIRECT3DRMFRAME frame, void*, D3DVALUE);
protected:
    //{{AFX_MSG(ShowRoomWin)
    //}}AFX_MSG
    DECLARE_MESSAGE_MAP()
private:
    static LPDIRECT3DRMMESH mesh;
    static LPDIRECT3DRMTEXTURE texture[15];
};
```

Two public member functions are declared: **CreateScene()** and **Update-Texture()**. The **CreateScene()** function is used to construct the scene and the **UpdateTexture()** function is a callback function that is used to change the texture that is currently applied the to demo's mesh.

Two private data members are declared: **mesh** and **texture**. The mesh data member is a pointer to the **Direct3DRMMesh** interface and will be used to access the mesh on which our animated texture will appear. The **texture** data member is an array of textures that will each appear on the mesh.

THE SHOWROOM::CREATESCENE() FUNCTION

In order to construct the ShowRoom demo scene, the **CreateScene()** function loads 15 textures, each an image of the car rendered from a different angle. A mesh and a flat texture wrap are created, and the first texture is applied to the mesh. A callback function is used to apply subsequent textures to the mesh. Listing 5.7 is the **CreateScene()** function for the ShowRoom demo.

Listing 5.7   The ShowRoomWin::CreateScene() function.

```
BOOL ShowRoomWin::CreateScene()
{
    //-------- TEXTURES --------
    HRSRC texture_id;
    int t=0;
    texture_id=FindResource( NULL, MAKEINTRESOURCE(IDR_TEXTURE01),
        "TEXTURE" );
    d3drm->LoadTextureFromResource( texture_id, &texture[t++]);
    texture_id=FindResource( NULL, MAKEINTRESOURCE(IDR_TEXTURE02),
        "TEXTURE" );
    d3drm->LoadTextureFromResource( texture_id, &texture[t++]);
    texture_id=FindResource( NULL, MAKEINTRESOURCE(IDR_TEXTURE03),
        "TEXTURE" );
```

```
d3drm->LoadTextureFromResource( texture_id, &texture[t++]);
texture_id=FindResource( NULL, MAKEINTRESOURCE(IDR_TEXTURE04),
    "TEXTURE" );
d3drm->LoadTextureFromResource( texture_id, &texture[t++]);
texture_id=FindResource( NULL, MAKEINTRESOURCE(IDR_TEXTURE05),
    "TEXTURE" );
d3drm->LoadTextureFromResource( texture_id, &texture[t++]);
texture_id=FindResource( NULL, MAKEINTRESOURCE(IDR_TEXTURE06),
    "TEXTURE" );
d3drm->LoadTextureFromResource( texture_id, &texture[t++]);
texture_id=FindResource( NULL, MAKEINTRESOURCE(IDR_TEXTURE07),
    "TEXTURE" );
d3drm->LoadTextureFromResource( texture_id, &texture[t++]);
texture_id=FindResource( NULL, MAKEINTRESOURCE(IDR_TEXTURE08),
    "TEXTURE" );
d3drm->LoadTextureFromResource( texture_id, &texture[t++]);
texture_id=FindResource( NULL, MAKEINTRESOURCE(IDR_TEXTURE09),
    "TEXTURE" );
d3drm->LoadTextureFromResource( texture_id, &texture[t++]);
texture_id=FindResource( NULL, MAKEINTRESOURCE(IDR_TEXTURE10),
    "TEXTURE" );
d3drm->LoadTextureFromResource( texture_id, &texture[t++]);
texture_id=FindResource( NULL, MAKEINTRESOURCE(IDR_TEXTURE11),
    "TEXTURE" );
d3drm->LoadTextureFromResource( texture_id, &texture[t++]);
texture_id=FindResource( NULL, MAKEINTRESOURCE(IDR_TEXTURE12),
    "TEXTURE" );
d3drm->LoadTextureFromResource( texture_id, &texture[t++]);
texture_id=FindResource( NULL, MAKEINTRESOURCE(IDR_TEXTURE13),
    "TEXTURE" );
d3drm->LoadTextureFromResource( texture_id, &texture[t++]);
texture_id=FindResource( NULL, MAKEINTRESOURCE(IDR_TEXTURE14),
    "TEXTURE" );
d3drm->LoadTextureFromResource( texture_id, &texture[t++]);
texture_id=FindResource( NULL, MAKEINTRESOURCE(IDR_TEXTURE15),
    "TEXTURE" );
d3drm->LoadTextureFromResource( texture_id, &texture[t++]);

// ------- MESH BUILDER --------
D3DRMLOADRESOURCE resinfo;
resinfo.hModule=NULL;
resinfo.lpName=MAKEINTRESOURCE( IDR_BOXMESH );
resinfo.lpType="MESH";
LPDIRECT3DRMMESHBUILDER meshbuilder;
d3drm->CreateMeshBuilder( &meshbuilder );
```

```
meshbuilder->Load( &resinfo, NULL, D3DRMLOAD_FROMRESOURCE,
    NULL, NULL );
meshbuilder->Scale( D3DVALUE(1), D3DVALUE(1), D3DVALUE(.1) );
ScaleMesh( meshbuilder, D3DVALUE(20) );
meshbuilder->SetPerspective( TRUE );
meshbuilder->SetQuality( D3DRMRENDER_FLAT );
meshbuilder->SetTexture( texture[0] );


//--------- WRAP --------
D3DRMBOX box;
meshbuilder->GetBox(&box);
D3DVALUE width=box.max.x-box.min.x;
D3DVALUE height=box.max.y-box.min.y;


LPDIRECT3DRMWRAP wrap;
d3drm->CreateWrap( D3DRMWRAP_FLAT, NULL,
        D3DVALUE(0.0), D3DVALUE(0.0), D3DVALUE(0.0),   // wrap origin
        D3DVALUE(0.0), D3DVALUE(0.0), D3DVALUE(1.0),   // z axis
        D3DVALUE(0.0), D3DVALUE(1.0), D3DVALUE(0.0),   // y axis
        D3DVALUE(0.5), D3DVALUE(0.5),                  // origin
        D3DDivide(1,width),D3DDivide(1,height),        // scale
        &wrap );
wrap->Apply( meshbuilder );
wrap->Release();
wrap=0;


//------- MESH ------
meshbuilder->CreateMesh( &mesh );
meshbuilder->Release();
meshbuilder=0;


//------- FRAME --------
LPDIRECT3DRMFRAME meshframe;
d3drm->CreateFrame( scene, &meshframe );
meshframe->AddVisual( mesh );
meshframe->SetRotation( scene,
        D3DVALUE(0), D3DVALUE(1), D3DVALUE(0),
        D3DVALUE(0.05) );
meshframe->AddMoveCallback( UpdateTexture, NULL );
meshframe->Release();
meshframe=0;


//-------- LIGHTS --------
LPDIRECT3DRMLIGHT dlight, alight;
```

```
d3drm->CreateLightRGB( D3DRMLIGHT_DIRECTIONAL,
        D3DVALUE(1.0), D3DVALUE(1.0), D3DVALUE(1.0),
        &dlight );
d3drm->CreateLightRGB( D3DRMLIGHT_AMBIENT,
        D3DVALUE(1.0), D3DVALUE(1.0), D3DVALUE(1.0),
        &alight );

LPDIRECT3DRMFRAME lightframe;
d3drm->CreateFrame( scene, &lightframe );
lightframe->SetOrientation( scene,
        D3DVALUE(0), D3DVALUE(-1), D3DVALUE(1),
        D3DVALUE(0), D3DVALUE(1), D3DVALUE(0));
lightframe->AddLight( dlight );
lightframe->AddLight( alight );
lightframe->Release();
lightframe=0;
dlight->Release();
dlight=0;
alight->Release();
alight=0;

//------ CAMERA ----------
d3drm->CreateFrame( scene, &camera );
camera->SetPosition( scene, D3DVALUE(0), D3DVALUE(0), D3DVALUE(-50));
d3drm->CreateViewport( device, camera, 0, 0,
        device->GetWidth(), device->GetHeight(),
        &viewport );

return TRUE;
}
```

The **CreateScene()** function performs seven steps:

1. Creation of 15 textures

2. Creation and configuration of a meshbuilder

3. Creation and application of a flat texture wrap

4. Creation of the **Direct3DRMMesh** interface

5. Creation of a frame for the mesh

6. Creation of a light source

7. Creation of a viewport

The first portion of the **CreateScene()** function is straightforward (and tedious). The 15 textures are loaded, and a pointer to each texture is stored in the **texture** array.

Next, a cube mesh is loaded using the **Direct3DRMMeshBuilder** interface. The cube is scaled using the **Scale()** function:

```
D3DRMLOADRESOURCE resinfo;
resinfo.hModule=NULL;
resinfo.lpName=MAKEINTRESOURCE( IDR_BOXMESH );
resinfo.lpType="MESH";
LPDIRECT3DRMMESHBUILDER meshbuilder;
d3drm->CreateMeshBuilder( &meshbuilder );
meshbuilder->Load( &resinfo, NULL, D3DRMLOAD_FROMRESOURCE,
    NULL, NULL );
meshbuilder->Scale( D3DVALUE(1), D3DVALUE(1), D3DVALUE(.1) );
ScaleMesh( meshbuilder, D3DVALUE(20) );
meshbuilder->SetPerspective( TRUE );
meshbuilder->SetQuality( D3DRMRENDER_FLAT );
meshbuilder->SetTexture( texture[0] );
```

This is done because we want a nearly flat rectangular mesh to which we can apply the textures. Rather than create a rectangular mesh, we can use a cube with its Z dimension scaled to one-tenth its original size. The new mesh is then configured to use perspective correction and the flat rendering mode. The first texture in the **texture** array is associated with the new mesh.

Step 3 is the creation and application of a texture wrap:

```
D3DRMBOX box;
meshbuilder->GetBox(&box);
D3DVALUE width=box.max.x-box.min.x;
D3DVALUE height=box.max.y-box.min.y;

LPDIRECT3DRMWRAP wrap;
d3drm->CreateWrap( D3DRMWRAP_FLAT, NULL,
        D3DVALUE(0.0), D3DVALUE(0.0), D3DVALUE(0.0),   // wrap origin
        D3DVALUE(0.0), D3DVALUE(0.0), D3DVALUE(1.0),   // z axis
        D3DVALUE(0.0), D3DVALUE(1.0), D3DVALUE(0.0),   // y axis
        D3DVALUE(0.5), D3DVALUE(0.5),                  // origin
        D3DDivide(1,width),D3DDivide(1,height),        // scale
        &wrap );
```

Chapter 5
TEXTURE MAPPING 185

```
wrap->Apply( meshbuilder );
wrap->Release();
wrap=0;
```

A flat texture wrap is created that sizes the texture to fit snugly on the mesh. The texture wrap is applied to the meshbuilder with the **Apply()** function.

Next, the previously loaded meshbuilder is used to initialize a pointer to the **Direct3DRMMesh** interface:

```
meshbuilder->CreateMesh( &mesh );
meshbuilder->Release();
meshbuilder=0;
```

The new mesh is created with all of the settings of the meshbuilder.

Next, a frame is created and the mesh is attached:

```
LPDIRECT3DRMFRAME meshframe;
d3drm->CreateFrame( scene, &meshframe );
meshframe->AddVisual( mesh );
meshframe->SetRotation( scene,
        D3DVALUE(0), D3DVALUE(1), D3DVALUE(0),
        D3DVALUE(0.05) );
meshframe->AddMoveCallback( UpdateTexture, NULL );
meshframe->Release();
meshframe=0;
```

The new frame is given a rotation attribute around the Y axis. Also, the **UpdateTexture()** callback function is installed.

THE SHOWROOM::UPDATETEXTURE() FUNCTION

The **UpdateTexture()** callback function is responsible for installing a new texture for each screen update. The **UpdateTexture()** function looks like this:

```
void ShowRoomWin::UpdateTexture(LPDIRECT3DRMFRAME frame,
    void*, D3DVALUE)
{
    static UINT count;
    int curtex=count%15;
    frame->DeleteVisual( mesh );
```

```
      mesh->SetGroupTexture( 0, texture[curtex] );
      frame->AddVisual( mesh );
      count++;
}
```

A **static** counter variable is used to determine which texture is to be applied to the mesh. The new texture is applied with the **Direct3DRMMesh
SetGroupTexture()** function, but the meshbuilder must be removed from
the frame and added after the **SetGroupTexture()** function is called. This
is because the **SetGroupTexture()** function has no effect once a
meshbuilder has been added to a frame.

The **Direct3DRMMesh SetGroupTexture()** function is similar to the
Direct3DRMMeshBuilder SetTexture() function that we used in the previous demos. The difference is that the **Direct3DRMMesh** interface supports
groups, and the **Direct3DRMMeshBuilder** interface does not. A group is a
set of faces than can be manipulated as a single entity. We'll talk about the
Direct3DRMMesh interface in more detail in Chapter 8.

CONCLUSION

The ShowRoom demo concludes our discussion of texture mapping. As usual,
you are strongly encouraged to experiment with the demos—that's what
they're for. When you are finished experimenting, you'll be ready to move
on to the next chapter and learn all about light sources and shadows.

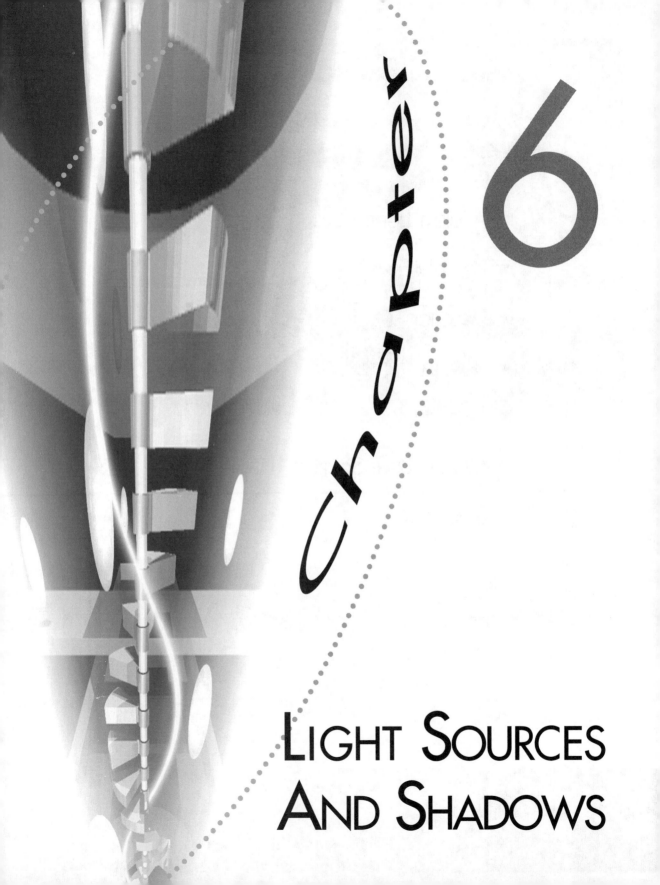

Chapter

6

LIGHT SOURCES
AND SHADOWS

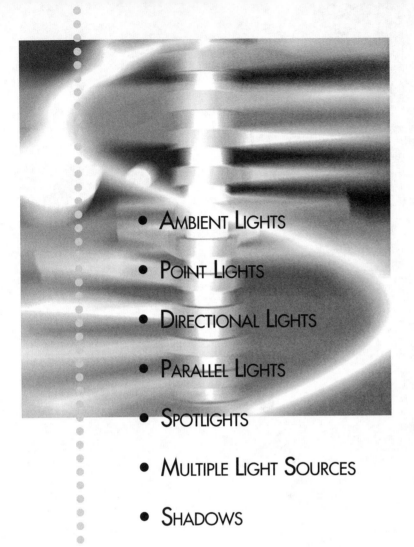

- Ambient Lights

- Point Lights

- Directional Lights

- Parallel Lights

- Spotlights

- Multiple Light Sources

- Shadows

6

LIGHT SOURCES AND SHADOWS

You learned a little about light sources in Chapters 4 and 5. In this chapter, we'll engage in a more detailed discussion about each type of light source that Direct3D supports. We'll also talk about shadows.

For most of the topics, we'll be using demos from the CD-ROM. The demos we'll study in this chapter are:

• Firefly

• SpaceStation

• SpaceDonut

• Spotlight

• Fork

RENDERING METHODS AND COLOR MODELS

Before we talk about specific light source types, we should review the distinction between rendering methods and color models, and talk about how they affect light sources.

A rendering method (wireframe, flat, Gouraud, etc.) is the technique that is used to produce a program's final output. Rendering methods are sometimes called lighting or shading methods.

Color models (RGB versus Ramp), are independent from the rendering method. The RGB color model supports colored lighting, and the Ramp model does not. The Ramp model typically outperforms the RGB model.

Rendering methods and color models are independent; any rendering method can be used with any color model. However, both rendering methods and color models affect the way light sources are interpreted. The differences are as follows:

• The Ramp color model does not support colored lighting. This doesn't mean that colored lights are ignored; it means that a light's color settings are converted to grayscale in the Ramp color model.

• Light sources have no effect with wireframe and unlit rendering methods. Both of these methods use only the color of the face and the color of any texture that is applied to the face. Light sources are ignored.

• The flat and Gouraud rendering methods both take light sources into consideration, but each does so differently. The flat rendering method uses the light sources in the scene to determine a single color for each face. Gouraud rendering uses light sources to determine colors for each vertex. The vertex colors are then used to calculate the colors that will be used to represent each face.

Many of the demos on the CD-ROM provide menu options that allow the rendering method to be changed at runtime, so the difference between rendering methods is easy to evaluate.

Most of the demos on the CD-ROM use the Ramp color model for the performance advantage. We will, however, use the RGB color model in this chapter to demonstrate colored lighting.

AMBIENT LIGHTS

In the real world, ambient light is indirect light. Ambient light is light that has been reflected and diffused. In the evening, for example, ambient light allows us to see even though the sun has gone down. The sun's rays are scattered by the atmosphere and provide an even, low-intensity light that has no single direction and no single origin.

Light that truly has no direction and no origin doesn't exist in the real world. The sun's light being diffused and scattered by the atmosphere is an approximation of ambient light—the sun's light still travels in specific directions and has an indirect origin (the sun). In Direct3D, ambient light has no direction and no origin.

Technically, an ambient light looks like any other light source. It is represented by the **Direct3DRMLight** interface and must be attached to a frame to be visible. An ambient light, however, ignores the location and orientation of the frame to which it is attached.

DEMONSTRATING AMBIENT LIGHT

Frankly, ambient light is pretty boring. It is useful, especially when combined with other light types, but by itself, ambient lighting is not very impressive. After several unsatisfactory attempts at a demo that used only ambient light, I gave up and decided that ambient light didn't deserve its own demo. Instead, we'll use the Direct3D AppWizard to create an application that uses ambient lighting to illuminate an object of your choice.

From the Visual C++ Developer Studio, select the File|New menu option. The New window will appear. Select Project Workspace. The New Project Workspace window will appear. Select the Direct3D AppWizard in the Type listbox, and enter a name for the project, such as "AmbientLight," then press the Create button.

The introductory Direct3D AppWizard dialog box will appear. Press the Next button. The dialog box that appears next allows you to choose the object that will be displayed by the new application. By default, the Swirl object is used. Select the "Let me choose an object" radio button, and enter the name of an object in the Object edit box, or use the Browse button to invoke a file selection dialog. The Object Selection dialog box appears in Figure 6.1 with the DirectX SDK sphere1.x file selected.

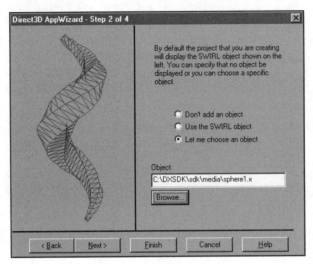

Figure 6.1

The Direct3D AppWizard object selection dialog box.

X file contents

Remember that you must select an X file that contains a single mesh. X files containing animations or frame hierarchies will not display correctly. The majority of the X files on the CD-ROM contain single meshes.

Once you have selected the mesh that is to be displayed, press the Next button.

The dialog that appears allows you to specify the types of light sources that will be in the project. The light source selection dialog box appears in Figure 6.2.

A directional light source is used by default. Deselect the Directional checkbox, and select the Ambient checkbox. Also, change the Color Model from Ramp to RGB. This will allow us to use colored lighting. Figure 6.2 shows the Light Selection dialog as it appears with the new settings.

Accept the default settings on the following dialog, and press the Finish button. The AppWizard will then display a confirmation dialog. Press the OK button. Developer Studio will now create a new application according

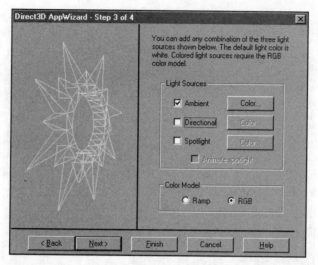

Figure 6.2

The Direct3D AppWizard light source selection dialog box.

to the settings you have specified. When Developer Studio is finished (it doesn't take long), compile and run the new application. The new application will look like the one in Figure 6.3 (particularly if you choose the sphere1.x file).

Dependency warnings

Visual C++ often displays a number of warnings when a new project is first compiled or when Update All Dependencies is selected from the Build menu. This is because Visual tries to locate all H files that are used with the **#include** directive, and a message is displayed whenever an H file cannot be found. Unfortunately, Visual does not preprocess files prior to searching for the names of H files. This means that H files that are not used by a project because of an **#ifdef** conditional are searched for along with the H files that are used by the project. These warnings can safely be ignored.

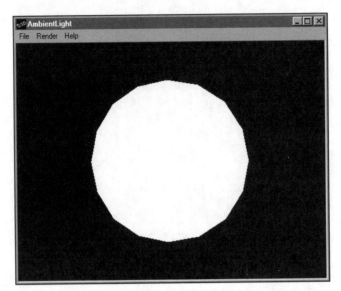

Figure 6.3
The application created by the Direct3D AppWizard.

No matter what object you selected, it probably doesn't look very good. This is because the ambient light source illuminates each part of the mesh with the same intensity. The result is a silhouette of the object. If you apply a texture to the mesh, it will look a little better, but it will still appear dull and flat.

We will use the project that we have just created to demonstrate the following techniques:

- Using an ambient light source

- Using the **Direct3DRMMeshBuilder** interface

- Changing a mesh's rendering method at runtime

THE AMBIENTLIGHTWIN CLASS

The majority of the functionality in our new project is supplied by the **AmbientLightWin** class. The class is defined like this:

```
class AmbientLightWin : public RMWin
{
public:
    AmbientLightWin();
    BOOL CreateScene();
```

```
protected:
    //{{AFX_MSG(AmbientLightWin)
    afx_msg void OnRenderWireframe();
    afx_msg void OnRenderFlat();
    afx_msg void OnRenderGouraud();
    afx_msg void OnUpdateRenderFlat(CCmdUI* pCmdUI);
    afx_msg void OnUpdateRenderGouraud(CCmdUI* pCmdUI);
    afx_msg void OnUpdateRenderWireframe(CCmdUI* pCmdUI);
    //}}AFX_MSG
    DECLARE_MESSAGE_MAP()
private:
    LPDIRECT3DRMMESHBUILDER meshbuilder;
};
```

The **AmbientLightWin** class is derived from the **RMWin** class. It declares two public functions: a constructor and a **CreateScene()** function. The constructor initializes the class's only data member:

```
AmbientLightWin::AmbientLightWin()
{
    meshbuilder=0;
}
```

The **meshbuilder** data member is a pointer to the **Direct3DRMMeshBuilder** interface and will be used to point to the mesh in the application. The **meshbuilder** pointer is initialized by the **CreateScene()** function, which we will look at soon.

The class declares six protected member functions that serve as message handlers. The first three functions, **OnRenderWireframe()**, **OnRenderFlat()**, and **OnRenderGouraud()**, are called when one of the Render menu items is selected. The last three functions are called by MFC just before a menu is displayed. These functions are used to activate the check mark that appears next to the currently active menu entry method. We'll look at these functions later.

THE AMBIENTLIGHTWIN::CREATESCENE() FUNCTION

The scene is constructed by the **CreateScene()** function. If you named your project "AmbientLight", the **CreateScene()** function will look similar to Listing 6.1.

Listing 6.1   The AmbientLightWin::CreateScene() function.

```
BOOL AmbientLightWin::CreateScene()
{
    HRESULT r;
    // ------MESH--------
    d3drm->CreateMeshBuilder( &meshbuilder );
    r=meshbuilder->Load( meshname, NULL, D3DRMLOAD_FROMFILE,
            NULL, NULL );
    if (r!=D3DRM_OK)
    {
        CString msg;
        msg.Format( "Failed to load file '%s'\n", meshname );
        AfxMessageBox( msg );
        return FALSE;
    }
    ScaleMesh( meshbuilder, D3DVALUE(25) );


    //------- MESH FRAME --------
    LPDIRECT3DRMFRAME meshframe;
    d3drm->CreateFrame( scene, &meshframe );
    meshframe->AddVisual( meshbuilder );
    meshframe->SetRotation( scene,
            D3DVALUE(0), D3DVALUE(1), D3DVALUE(0),
            D3DVALUE(.1) );
    meshframe->Release();
    meshframe=0;


    // --------AMBIENT LIGHT--------
    LPDIRECT3DRMLIGHT alight;
    d3drm->CreateLightRGB( D3DRMLIGHT_AMBIENT,
            D3DVALUE(1.00), D3DVALUE(1.00), D3DVALUE(1.00),
            &alight );
    scene->AddLight( alight );
    alight->Release();
    alight=0;


    //------ CAMERA----------
    d3drm->CreateFrame( scene, &camera );
    camera->SetPosition( scene,
            D3DVALUE(0), D3DVALUE(0), D3DVALUE(-50) );
    d3drm->CreateViewport( device, camera, 0, 0,
            device->GetWidth(), device->GetHeight(),
            &viewport );


    return TRUE;
}
```

The **CreateScene()** function performs these steps:

1. Creates and loads a mesh

2. Creates a frame for the mesh

3. Creates an ambient light source

4. Creates a viewport

The first step uses the **Direct3DRMMeshBuilder** interface to load a mesh from a file. Let's take a closer look:

```
d3drm->CreateMeshBuilder( &meshbuilder );
r=meshbuilder->Load( meshname, NULL, D3DRMLOAD_FROMFILE, NULL, NULL );
if (r!=D3DRM_OK)
{
    CString msg;
    msg.Format( "Failed to load file '%s'\n", meshname );
    AfxMessageBox( msg );
    return FALSE;
}
ScaleMesh( meshbuilder, D3DVALUE(25) );
```

First, the **meshbuilder** data member is initialized with the **Direct3DRM CreateMeshBuilder()** function. The **Load()** function is then used to load the mesh file from disk (the **meshname** variable identifies the mesh file that you selected with the AppWizard). If the **Load()** function fails, a message box is displayed and **FALSE** is returned. If the **Load()** function succeeds, the **ScaleMesh()** function is used to determine an ideal size for the mesh.

The second step of the **CreateScene()** function is the creation of a frame to which the mesh will be attached. The code looks like this:

```
LPDIRECT3DRMFRAME meshframe;
d3drm->CreateFrame( scene, &meshframe );
meshframe->AddVisual( meshbuilder );
meshframe->SetRotation( scene,
        D3DVALUE(0), D3DVALUE(1), D3DVALUE(0),
        D3DVALUE(.1) );
meshframe->Release();
meshframe=0;
```

The **meshframe** pointer is declared as a pointer to the **Direct3DRMFrame** interface. The **Direct3DRM CreateFrame()** function is then used to create the new frame. The **meshbuilder** that was created in Step 1 is attached to the new frame with the **AddVisual()** function.

The **SetRotation()** function is then used to assign a rotation attribute to the frame. The frame is instructed to rotate around the Y axis (indicated by the first three numeric arguments). The final **SetRotation()** argument indicates that the frame is to rotate 0.1 radians per system update.

The third step of the **CreateScene()** function is the creation of the ambient light source:

```
LPDIRECT3DRMLIGHT alight;
d3drm->CreateLightRGB( D3DRMLIGHT_AMBIENT,
        D3DVALUE(1.00), D3DVALUE(1.00), D3DVALUE(1.00),
         &alight );
scene->AddLight( alight );
alight->Release();
alight=0;
```

The **alight** pointer is declared as a pointer to the **Direct3DRMLight** interface. The **CreateLightRGB()** function is used to create the light source and initialize the **alight** pointer. The first argument that the **CreateLightRGB()** function expects is a constant that indicates the type of light source that is to be created. The **D3DRMLIGHT_AMBIENT** constant is one of five that can be used. These five constants are:

- D3DRMLIGHT_AMBIENT
- D3DRMLIGHT_POINT
- D3DRMLIGHT_SPOT
- D3DRMLIGHT_DIRECTIONAL
- D3DRMLIGHT_PARALLELPOINT

The three numeric **CreateLightRGB()** arguments indicate the color of the light source. The values that appear (1, 1, 1) indicate a white light source because the red, green, and blue components are all assigned their maximum values. Some alternatives to white light are shown below.

```
d3drm->CreateLightRGB( D3DRMLIGHT_AMBIENT,
        D3DVALUE(1.00), D3DVALUE(0.00), D3DVALUE(0.00),
        &alight );  // creates a red light
```

```
d3drm->CreateLightRGB( D3DRMLIGHT_AMBIENT,
        D3DVALUE(0.00), D3DVALUE(1.00), D3DVALUE(0.00),
        &alight );  // creates a green light

d3drm->CreateLightRGB( D3DRMLIGHT_AMBIENT,
        D3DVALUE(0.00), D3DVALUE(0.00), D3DVALUE(1.00),
        &alight );  // creates a blue light

d3drm->CreateLightRGB( D3DRMLIGHT_AMBIENT,
        D3DVALUE(1.00), D3DVALUE(0.00), D3DVALUE(1.00),
        &alight );  // create a purple light

d3drm->CreateLightRGB( D3DRMLIGHT_AMBIENT,
        D3DVALUE(0.30), D3DVALUE(0.30), D3DVALUE(0.30),
        &alight );  // creates a dark gray light
```

If only one ambient light source is present in a scene (as is true in this scene), all of the faces in the scene will be rendered using the color of the light source. The final argument to the **CreateLightRGB**() function is the address of the **alight** pointer.

Next, the new light is attached to the scene frame:

```
scene->AddLight( alight );
```

As you'll see later in this chapter when we discuss other light source types, we don't add most light sources directly to a scene's root frame. Ambient lights can be attached to the root frame because ambient lights are not affected by a frame's location and orientation. In fact, ambient light sources can be added to any frame in a scene, and the result will be the same.

Finally, the **alight** pointer is released and assigned to zero:

```
alight->Release();
alight=0;
```

Remember, we are releasing a pointer when we call **Release**(), not the object itself. The object will be destroyed only if this turns out to be the only pointer that points to the object. In this case, the light will not be destroyed because it has been added to the scene.

The fourth and final step that the **CreateScene**() function performs is the creation of a viewport:

```
d3drm->CreateFrame( scene, &camera );
camera->SetPosition( scene,
        D3DVALUE(0), D3DVALUE(0), D3DVALUE(-50) );
d3drm->CreateViewport( device, camera, 0, 0,
        device->GetWidth(), device->GetHeight(),
        &viewport );
```

This portion of code initializes two pointers: **camera** and **viewport**. Recall from Chapter 4 that these pointers are data members belonging to the **RMWin** class. Our **CreateScene()** function must initialize these pointers. If we fail to do so, the application will terminate with an error message.

The **camera** pointer is a pointer to the **Direct3DRMFrame** interface and is initialized with the **Direct3DRM CreateFrame()** function. The new frame is then positioned 50 units away from the origin. This is because the mesh that we created in Step 1 was placed at the origin (by default). We are pulling the camera away from the origin so that the object will appear in the viewport. Finally, the **Direct3DRM CreateViewport()** function is used to initialize the **viewport** pointer.

The last thing that the **CreateScene()** function does is return **TRUE** to indicate that all is well. If **FALSE** is returned from a **CreateScene()** function, the application will terminate with an error message.

THE AMBIENTLIGHT DEMO RENDER FUNCTIONS

One of the features that the Direct3D AppWizard puts into a project (whether you ask for it or not) is a Render menu that allows the mesh's rendering method to be changed during the program's execution. When we looked at the **AmbientLightWin** class definition, we saw declarations for the six member functions that provide this functionality. The **OnRenderWireframe()**, **OnRenderFlat()**, and **OnRenderGouraud()** functions are message handlers that are called when one of the Render menu entries are selected. The functions look like this:

```
void AmbientLightWin::OnRenderWireframe()
{
    if (meshbuilder)
        meshbuilder->SetQuality( D3DRMRENDER_WIREFRAME );
}
```

```
void AmbientLightWin::OnRenderFlat()
{
    if (meshbuilder)
        meshbuilder->SetQuality( D3DRMRENDER_FLAT );
}

void AmbientLightWin::OnRenderGouraud()
{
    if (meshbuilder)
        meshbuilder->SetQuality( D3DRMRENDER_GOURAUD );
}
```

The value of the **meshbuilder** pointer is checked in case the **meshbuilder** pointer has not been initialized. If it has, the **Direct3DRMMeshBuilder SetQuality()** function changes the render method (or quality) of the mesh.

The remaining three member functions, **OnUpdateRenderFlat()**, **OnUpdateRenderGouraud()**, and **OnUpdateRenderWireframe()**, are called whenever Windows is about to display the Render menu. These functions are used to activate the check mark that appears to the left of the currently active menu entry. The functions look like this:

```
void AmbientLightWin::OnUpdateRenderWireframe(CCmdUI* pCmdUI)
{
    if (meshbuilder)
    {
        D3DRMRENDERQUALITY meshquality = meshbuilder->GetQuality();
        pCmdUI->SetCheck( meshquality==D3DRMRENDER_WIREFRAME );
    }
}

void AmbientLightWin::OnUpdateRenderFlat(CCmdUI* pCmdUI)
{
    if (meshbuilder)
    {
        D3DRMRENDERQUALITY meshquality = meshbuilder->GetQuality();
        pCmdUI->SetCheck( meshquality==D3DRMRENDER_FLAT );
    }
}

void AmbientLightWin::OnUpdateRenderGouraud(CCmdUI* pCmdUI)
{
    if (meshbuilder)
    {
```

```
D3DRMRENDERQUALITY meshquality = meshbuilder->GetQuality();
pCmdUI->SetCheck( meshquality==D3DRMRENDER_GOURAUD );
    }
}
```

Each of these three functions uses the **Direct3DRMMeshBuilder GetQuality()** function to retrieve the mesh's current rendering methods. The rendering method is then used to determine if the menu selection's check mark should be enabled. Using a comparison that is **TRUE** as an argument to the **SetCheck()** function enables the check mark.

These six member functions are present, in some form, in most of the demos on the CD-ROM.

POINT LIGHTS

A point light is a light source that emits light in all directions from a single location. Point lights are similar to the light sources that we are accustomed to in the real world, such as light bulbs. The familiar behavior of point lights make them a natural choice for many situations. Point lights are affected by their location but ignore orientation (a point light's orientation is meaningless because light is cast in all directions).

Unfortunately, the point light's ease of use and familiar behavior is offset by a performance hit. Because point lights cast light in every conceivable direction, more calculation is necessary to render scenes that contain point lights.

THE FIREFLY DEMO

The Firefly demo uses a point light to illuminate a chalice. The chalice is placed at the origin, and the point light is animated around the chalice. For visual effect, a small spherical mesh is animated along with the light source, creating the illusion that the sphere (the firefly) is emitting light and illuminating the chalice. Remember that the sphere is added only for visual effect. You cannot see a point light (or any other light source)—you can only see the light that it emits. The Firefly demo appears in Figure 6.4.

If you run the Firefly demo, you'll be able to see that the light's position affects the way that the chalice is illuminated. Use the Render menu to

Figure 6.4
The Firefly demo.

change the rendering method. Notice that in wireframe mode, the light has no effect.

The Firefly demo demonstrates the following techniques:

- Using a point light

- Representing a light source with a mesh

- Using multiple rendering methods in the same scene

- Performing animation with dummy frames

We'll talk about each of these techniques as we walk through the Firefly code.

THE FIREFLYWIN CLASS

The majority of the Firefly demo's functionality is provided by the **FireflyWin** class. The **FireflyWin** class is derived from the **RMWin** class and is defined as follows:

```
class FireflyWin : public RMWin
{
public:
    FireflyWin();
    BOOL CreateScene();
protected:
    //{{AFX_MSG(FireflyWin)
    afx_msg void OnRenderWireframe();
    afx_msg void OnRenderFlat();
    afx_msg void OnRenderGouraud();
    afx_msg void OnUpdateRenderFlat(CCmdUI* pCmdUI);
    afx_msg void OnUpdateRenderGouraud(CCmdUI* pCmdUI);
    afx_msg void OnUpdateRenderWireframe(CCmdUI* pCmdUI);
    //}}AFX_MSG
    DECLARE_MESSAGE_MAP()
private:
    LPDIRECT3DRMMESHBUILDER chalicebuilder;
};
```

The **FireflyWin** class declared two public member functions: a constructor and the **CreateScene()** function. The constructor assigns zero to the **chalicebuilder** data member:

```
FireflyWin::FireflyWin()
{
    chalicebuilder=0;
}
```

The six protected member functions provide support for the Firefly demo's Render menu.

THE FIREFLYWIN::CREATESCENE() FUNCTION

The Firefly demo constructs its scene with the **CreateScene()** function. The function is responsible for creating two meshes: one for the chalice and one for the firefly. One point light and one viewport is created. The light source and the spherical mesh are animated using dummy frames. Refer to the Decal demo in Chapter 5 for a discussion of dummy frames. The Firefly demo **CreateScene()** function appears in Listing 6.2.

Listing 6.2   The FireflyWin::CreateScene() function.
```
BOOL FireflyWin::CreateScene()
{
```

```
//-------- CHALICE MESH --------
D3DRMLOADRESOURCE resinfo;
resinfo.hModule=NULL;
resinfo.lpName=MAKEINTRESOURCE( IDR_CHALICEMESH );
resinfo.lpType="MESH";
d3drm->CreateMeshBuilder( &chalicebuilder );
chalicebuilder->Load( &resinfo, NULL, D3DRMLOAD_FROMRESOURCE,
        NULL, NULL );
ScaleMesh( chalicebuilder, D3DVALUE(25) );

//------- CHALICE FRAME ------
LPDIRECT3DRMFRAME chaliceframe;
d3drm->CreateFrame( scene, &chaliceframe );
chaliceframe->AddVisual( chalicebuilder );

chaliceframe->Release();
chaliceframe=0;

//-------- POINT LIGHT --------
LPDIRECT3DRMLIGHT pointlight;
d3drm->CreateLightRGB( D3DRMLIGHT_POINT,
        D3DVALUE(1.0),D3DVALUE(1.0), D3DVALUE(1.0),
        &pointlight );

//-------- FLY MESH ------
resinfo.hModule=NULL;
resinfo.lpName=MAKEINTRESOURCE( IDR_SPHEREMESH );
resinfo.lpType="MESH";
LPDIRECT3DRMMESHBUILDER flybuilder;
d3drm->CreateMeshBuilder( &flybuilder );
flybuilder->Load( &resinfo, NULL, D3DRMLOAD_FROMRESOURCE,
        NULL, NULL );
flybuilder->SetQuality( D3DRMRENDER_WIREFRAME );
ScaleMesh( flybuilder, D3DVALUE(0.3) );

//-------- LIGHT FRAMES --------
LPDIRECT3DRMFRAME dummyframe;
d3drm->CreateFrame( scene, &dummyframe );
dummyframe->SetRotation( scene,
        D3DVALUE(0), D3DVALUE(1), D3DVALUE(0),
        D3DVALUE(.08) );

LPDIRECT3DRMFRAME lightframe;
d3drm->CreateFrame( dummyframe, &lightframe );
lightframe->SetPosition( dummyframe,
        D3DVAL(15), D3DVAL(6), D3DVAL(0) );
```

```
lightframe->AddLight( pointlight );
lightframe->AddVisual( flybuilder );

flybuilder->Release();
flybuilder=0;
lightframe->Release();
lightframe=0;
dummyframe->Release();
dummyframe=0;
pointlight->Release();
pointlight=0;

//-------- VIEWPORT ------------
d3drm->CreateFrame( scene, &camera );
camera->SetPosition( scene,
        D3DVALUE(0.0), D3DVALUE(20.0), D3DVALUE(-50.0) );
camera->SetOrientation( scene,
        D3DVALUE(0), D3DVALUE(-20), D3DVALUE(50),
        D3DVALUE(0), D3DVALUE(1), D3DVALUE(0) );
d3drm->CreateViewport( device, camera, 0, 0,
        device->GetWidth(), device->GetHeight(),
        &viewport );

return TRUE;
}
```

The **CreateScene**() function performs six steps:

1. Creates and loads the chalice mesh

2. Creates a frame for the chalice mesh

3. Creates the point light

4. Creates a mesh to represent the firefly

5. Creates the frames for the light and the firefly mesh

6. Creates a viewport

The first step is the creation of the chalice mesh:

```
D3DRMLOADRESOURCE resinfo;
resinfo.hModule=NULL;
resinfo.lpName=MAKEINTRESOURCE( IDR_CHALICEMESH );
resinfo.lpType="MESH";
```

```
d3drm->CreateMeshBuilder( &chalicebuilder );
chalicebuilder->Load( &resinfo, NULL, D3DRMLOAD_FROMRESOURCE,
        NULL, NULL );
ScaleMesh( chalicebuilder, D3DVALUE(25) );
```

The **Direct3DRMMeshBuilder** interface is used to load the mesh from the program's resources. Then, the **ScaleMesh()** function is used to resize the mesh.

The new mesh is then attached to a frame called **chaliceframe**:

```
LPDIRECT3DRMFRAME chaliceframe;
d3drm->CreateFrame( scene, &chaliceframe );
chaliceframe->AddVisual( chalicebuilder );

chaliceframe->Release();
chaliceframe=0;
```

The chalice mesh is attached to the new frame with the **AddVisual()** function. The frame is not repositioned, so the mesh will appear at the origin. Notice that the **chalicebuilder** pointer is not declared in the **CreateScene()** function. The **chalicebuilder** pointer is a **FireflyWin** data member. This is done so that the rendering method can be changed from the Render menu. Notice, also, that the **chalicebuilder** pointer is not released in the **CreateScene()** function. If we did release the **chalicebuilder** pointer, we would have no way to change the render method during the program's execution.

The next step is the creation of the point light. First, the **Direct3DRM CreateLightRGB()** function is used to create the light source:

```
LPDIRECT3DRMLIGHT pointlight;
d3drm->CreateLightRGB( D3DRMLIGHT_POINT,
        D3DVALUE(1.0), D3DVALUE(1.0), D3DVALUE(1.0),
        &pointlight );
```

The **D3DRMLIGHT_POINT** constant is used to indicate the type of light source that we are creating. The following three numeric arguments indicate that we are creating a light source that will emit white light. The final argument is the address of the pointer that is to point to the new **Direct3DRMLight** interface.

Next, the mesh that represents the firefly is created:

```
resinfo.hModule=NULL;
resinfo.lpName=MAKEINTRESOURCE( IDR_SPHEREMESH );
resinfo.lpType="MESH";
LPDIRECT3DRMMESHBUILDER flybuilder;
d3drm->CreateMeshBuilder( &flybuilder );
flybuilder->Load( &resinfo, NULL, D3DRMLOAD_FROMRESOURCE,
        NULL, NULL );
flybuilder->SetQuality( D3DRMRENDER_WIREFRAME );
ScaleMesh( flybuilder, D3DVALUE(0.3) );
```

There is no actual firefly mesh, a spherical mesh is used to represent the fire-fly. The sphere mesh resource identifier is used to prepare the **resinfo** struc-ture. The **meshbuilder** is created with the **Direct3DRM CreateMeshBuilder()** function, and the mesh is loaded with the **Direct3DRMMeshBuilder Load()** function. The **SetQuality()** function is then used to specify the wireframe rendering method. This is done so that the mesh will appear distinctly in the scene. Remember that the wireframe rendering method uses the mesh color to draw the mesh and ignores any light sources in the scene. Using the wireframe method causes the mesh to appear in the exact color of the mesh and not a calculated color. Finally, the **meshbuilder** is scaled with the **ScaleMesh()** function.

The fifth step is the creation of two frames that we will use to animate the light source and the spherical mesh:

```
LPDIRECT3DRMFRAME dummyframe;
d3drm->CreateFrame( scene, &dummyframe );
dummyframe->SetRotation( scene,
        D3DVALUE(0), D3DVALUE(1), D3DVALUE(0),
        D3DVALUE(.08) );

LPDIRECT3DRMFRAME lightframe;
d3drm->CreateFrame( dummyframe, &lightframe );
lightframe->SetPosition( dummyframe,
        D3DVAL(15), D3DVAL(6), D3DVAL(0) );

lightframe->AddLight( pointlight );
lightframe->AddVisual( flybuilder );

flybuilder->Release();
flybuilder=0;
```

```
lightframe->Release();
lightframe=0;
dummyframe->Release();
dummyframe=0;
pointlight->Release();
pointlight=0;
```

The **dummyframe** pointer is initialized with the **Direct3DRM CreateFrame()** function and is a child of the scene's root frame (**scene**). The new frame is given a rotation around the Y axis. This will cause any child frames (such as the frame that is created next) to rotate around the Y axis.

The second frame (**lightframe**) is created as a child of **dummyframe**. Then, the **SetPosition()** function is used to move the frame away from the origin. If we didn't move this frame away from the origin, the frame would rotate in place instead of orbiting the dummy frame.

Next, both the fly mesh and the point light are attached to the **lightframe** frame. This ensures that both the firefly mesh and the point light will be in the same location at all times.

Finally, all four of the pointers (two frame pointers, the **flybuilder** pointer, and the **pointlight** pointer) are released and assigned zero.

The remainder of the **FireflyWin::CreateScene()** function (Listing 6.2) creates the demo's viewport. We'll study viewports in detail in Chapter 9.

DIRECTIONAL LIGHTS

Directional lights are the opposite of point lights. While a point light has a location but no orientation, a directional light has orientation but no location. Directional lights produce light rays that are parallel, so there is no single point where the light originates.

Directional lights are useful for representing distant light sources such as the sun. Because all of the rays in a directional light are parallel, less calculation is necessary to render scenes that contain directional lights. Directional lights are more efficient than point lights because all of the light rays travel in the same direction.

THE SPACESTATION DEMO

Because directional lights are best suited for representing distant light sources, we'll use space as the setting for our next demo. The SpaceStation demo displays a space station and illuminates it with a directional light. The SpaceStation demo appears in Figure 6.5.

The SpaceStation demo demonstrates the following techniques:

- Using a directional light source

- Animation using rotation attributes

- Changing the rendering quality of a mesh at runtime

- Altering a camera's up or sky vector to "roll" the camera

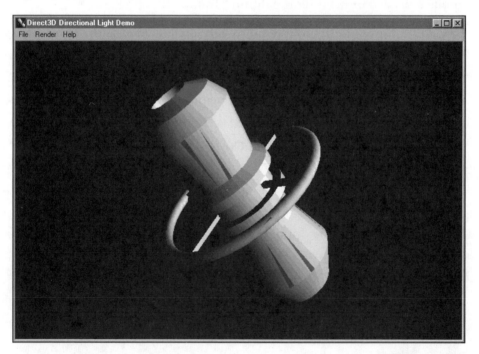

Figure 6.5
The SpaceStation demo.

THE SPACESTATIONWIN CLASS

The bulk of the SpaceStation demo's functionality is provided by the
SpaceStationWin class. The class definition looks like this:

```
class SpaceStationWin : public RMWin
{
public:
    SpaceStationWin();
    BOOL CreateScene();
protected:
    //{{AFX_MSG(SpaceStationWin)
    afx_msg void OnRenderWireframe();
    afx_msg void OnRenderFlat();
    afx_msg void OnRenderGouraud();
    afx_msg void OnUpdateRenderFlat(CCmdUI* pCmdUI);
    afx_msg void OnUpdateRenderGouraud(CCmdUI* pCmdUI);
    afx_msg void OnUpdateRenderWireframe(CCmdUI* pCmdUI);
    //}}AFX_MSG
    DECLARE_MESSAGE_MAP()
private:
    LPDIRECT3DRMMESHBUILDER meshbuilder;
};
```

The **SpaceStationWin** class declares two public member functions: a constructor and the **CreateScene()** function. The constructor assigns zero to
the **meshbuilder** data member:

```
SpaceStationWin::SpaceStationWin()
{
    meshbuilder=0;
}
```

The six protected member functions provide support for the SpaceStation
demo's Render menu. The private **meshbuilder** pointer is used by the protected member functions to modify the mesh's settings.

THE SPACESTATIONWIN::CREATESCENE() FUNCTION

The SpaceStation demo is one of the simplest demos on the CD-ROM.
The demo uses one mesh and one light source, and uses no callbacks or

textures. The SpaceStation scene is constructed with the **SpaceStationWin:: CreateScene()** function, as shown in Listing 6.3.

Listing 6.3   The SpaceStationWin::CreateScene() function.

```
BOOL SpaceStationWin::CreateScene()
{
    // ------- MESH --------
    D3DRMLOADRESOURCE resinfo;
    resinfo.hModule=NULL;
    resinfo.lpName=MAKEINTRESOURCE( IDR_STATIONMESH );
    resinfo.lpType="MESH";
    d3drm->CreateMeshBuilder( &meshbuilder );
    meshbuilder->Load( &resinfo, NULL, D3DRMLOAD_FROMRESOURCE,
            NULL, NULL );
    ScaleMesh( meshbuilder, D3DVALUE(32) );

    // ------ MESH FRAME --------
    LPDIRECT3DRMFRAME meshframe;
    d3drm->CreateFrame( scene, &meshframe );
    meshframe->AddVisual( meshbuilder );
    meshframe->SetRotation( scene,
            D3DVALUE(0), D3DVALUE(1), D3DVALUE(0),
            D3DVALUE(.05) );
    meshframe->Release();
    meshframe=0;

    // --------- LIGHT AND FRAME --------
    LPDIRECT3DRMLIGHT light;
    d3drm->CreateLightRGB( D3DRMLIGHT_DIRECTIONAL,
            D3DVALUE(1.00), D3DVALUE(1.00), D3DVALUE(1.00),
            &light );

    LPDIRECT3DRMFRAME lightframe;
    d3drm->CreateFrame( scene, &lightframe );
    lightframe->AddLight( light );
    lightframe->SetOrientation( scene,
            D3DVALUE(-1), D3DVALUE(0), D3DVALUE(1),
            D3DVALUE(0), D3DVALUE(1), D3DVALUE(0) );
    light->Release();
    light=0;
    lightframe->Release();
    lightframe=0;

    //------ CAMERA----------
    d3drm->CreateFrame( scene, &camera );
```

```
camera->SetPosition( scene,
        D3DVALUE(0), D3DVALUE(25), D3DVALUE(-50) );
camera->SetOrientation( scene,
        D3DVALUE(0), D3DVALUE(-23), D3DVALUE(50),
        D3DVALUE(0.7), D3DVALUE(1), D3DVALUE(0) );
d3drm->CreateViewport( device, camera, 0, 0,
        device->GetWidth(), device->GetHeight(),
        &viewport );

    return TRUE;
}
```

The **CreateScene()** function performs four steps:

1. Creates the space station mesh

2. Creates a frame for the space station mesh

3. Creates the directional light source and frame

4. Creates a viewport

The code that performs the first step looks like this:

```
D3DRMLOADRESOURCE resinfo;
resinfo.hModule=NULL;
resinfo.lpName=MAKEINTRESOURCE( IDR_STATIONMESH );
resinfo.lpType="MESH";
d3drm->CreateMeshBuilder( &meshbuilder );
meshbuilder->Load( &resinfo, NULL, D3DRMLOAD_FROMRESOURCE,
        NULL, NULL );
ScaleMesh( meshbuilder, D3DVALUE(32) );
```

First, an instance of the **D3DRMLOADRESOURCE** structure is declared and used to store the location of the space station mesh in the program's resources. Then, the **Direct3DRM CreateMeshBuilder()** function is used to initialize the **meshbuilder** pointer. The **meshbuilder** pointer is a data member of the **SpaceStationWin** class, so it isn't declared in the **CreateScene()** function. Next, the **Direct3DRMMeshBuilder Load()** function is used to load the space station mesh. No error checking is provided here because the mesh is part of the program's EXE file. Once the program has been tested (as this demo has), the **Load()** function's success is virtually guaranteed. Once the **Load()** function returns, the **ScaleMesh()** function is used to specify an ideal size for the mesh.

The next step (Step 2) is the creation of a frame for the space station mesh:

```
LPDIRECT3DRMFRAME meshframe;
d3drm->CreateFrame( scene, &meshframe );
meshframe->AddVisual( meshbuilder );
meshframe->SetRotation( scene,
        D3DVALUE(0), D3DVALUE(1), D3DVALUE(0),
        D3DVALUE(.05) );
meshframe->Release();
meshframe=0;
```

Once the frame has been created, the space station **meshbuilder** (**meshframe**) is attached to the new frame with the **Direct3DRMFrame AddVisual()** function. The frame is then given a rotation attribute with the **SetRotation()** function. The arguments used with **SetRotation()** will cause the mesh to rotate around the Y axis by .05 radians per screen update. Finally, the **meshframe** pointer is released and assigned to zero.

Next, **CreateScene()** creates and configures the directional light source, and attaches it to a frame:

```
LPDIRECT3DRMLIGHT light;
d3drm->CreateLightRGB( D3DRMLIGHT_DIRECTIONAL,
        D3DVALUE(1.00), D3DVALUE(1.00), D3DVALUE(1.00),
        &light );

LPDIRECT3DRMFRAME lightframe;
d3drm->CreateFrame( scene, &lightframe );
lightframe->AddLight( light );
lightframe->SetOrientation( scene,
        D3DVALUE(-1), D3DVALUE(0), D3DVALUE(1),
        D3DVALUE(0), D3DVALUE(1), D3DVALUE(0) );
light->Release();
light=0;
lightframe->Release();
lightframe=0;
```

A pointer to the **Direct3DRMLight** interface called **light** is declared and then initialized with the **Direct3DRM CreateLightRGB()** function. The **D3DRMLIGHT_DIRECTIONAL** constant is used to indicate the desired type of light source. The following three arguments indicate a white light color, and the final argument is the address of the **light** pointer.

Next, a frame for the light source is created. The **lightframe** pointer is initialized with the **CreateFrame()** function, and the light is attached to the new frame with the **Direct3DRMFrame AddLight()** function.

The **SetOrientation()** function is used to orient the light source. Notice that the forward vector (the vector defined by the first three numeric arguments) defines a vector that points away from the origin along both the X and Z axes. The negative X axis value indicates that the light will travel from left to right (from the viewer's point of view), and the positive Z axis value indicates that the light will travel away from the viewer. Figure 6.6 illustrates the light's direction in relation to the space station mesh (as viewed from above).

After the light has been oriented, both the **light** and the **lightframe** pointers are released.

The fourth and final portion of the **SpaceStationWin::CreateScene()** function creates and configures a viewport. Take another look at the SpaceStation demo (Figure 6.5). Notice that the space station mesh is tilted.

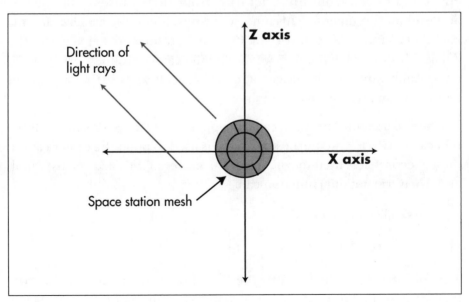

Figure 6.6
The SpaceStation scene, as seen from above.

This isn't because we tilted the frame to which the space station mesh is attached. In fact, all we did to the mesh frame is assign a rotation attribute on the Y axis. Yet, if you run the SpaceStation demo, the station is tilted, and it rotates in the same direction as the tilt.

This is because rather than tilting both the mesh and rotation vector, we tilted the viewport. The **viewport** creation code looks like this:

```
d3drm->CreateFrame( scene, &camera );
camera->SetPosition( scene,
        D3DVALUE(0), D3DVALUE(25), D3DVALUE(-50) );
camera->SetOrientation( scene,
        D3DVALUE(0), D3DVALUE(-23), D3DVALUE(50),
        D3DVALUE(0.7), D3DVALUE(1), D3DVALUE(0) );
d3drm->CreateViewport( device, camera, 0, 0,
        device->GetWidth(), device->GetHeight(),
        &viewport );
```

This portion of code differs from the other demos that we've looked at. First, the **camera** frame is positioned differently. Usually, we pull the camera straight back from the origin by using the values <0, 0, –50> as **SetPosition()** arguments. This time, we've positioned the **camera** 50 units back and 25 units above the origin. By default, frames are aligned with the Z axis. This means that unless we modify the **camera** frame's orientation, we probably won't see the space station mesh at all because the camera will be viewing an area above the mesh.

The **SetOrientation()** function call that appears after the **SetPosition()** function call is used for two purposes. First, it is used to point the **camera** at the mesh. Second, it is used to roll, or tilt the **camera**. Let's take a closer look at the **SetOrientation()** function call:

```
camera->SetOrientation( scene,
        D3DVALUE(0), D3DVALUE(-23), D3DVALUE(50),
        D3DVALUE(0.7), D3DVALUE(1), D3DVALUE(0) );
```

The forward vector (defined by the first three numeric arguments) defines a vector that travels from the origin to a point that is 23 units below and 50 units behind the origin. Notice that this vector is almost exactly the opposite of the vector that defines the **camera**'s position. This is no coincidence. In fact, you can always get a **camera** to point at the origin by using a forward vector that is the opposite of the **camera**'s positioning vector. The forward vector for the **camera** has been adjusted a bit for visual effect (via trial and error), so the vectors are not exactly opposite.

Now let's look at the up or sky vector (defined by the last three numeric **SetOrientation**() arguments). In the other demos, we've used the values <0, 1, 0> to specify a vector aligned with the Y axis and pointing up (hence the vector's name). This time we are using the values <0.7, 1, 0>. By using a vector that points almost as far to the right as it does up, the **camera** is tilted or rolled to the right.

The last function call in the **CreateScene**() function is the **Direct3DRM CreateViewport**() function. This function call is the same in the other demos.

PARALLEL POINT LIGHTS

Parallel point lights are similar to directional lights, but parallel point lights cast light in two directions. Parallel point lights are affected by both location and orientation. In regard to performance, parallel point lights are similar to directional lights.

THE SPACEDONUT DEMO

The SpaceDonut demo places a parallel point light between two raspberry (possibly blueberry) frosted donuts. The SpaceDonut demo appears in Figure 6.7.

The SpaceDonut demo demonstrates the following techniques:

* Using a parallel point light source

* Using rotation attributes to perform animation

* Using the **Direct3DRMMeshBuilder SetColorRGB**() function

* Attaching a single mesh to multiple frames

* Using menu options to change rendering settings at runtime

THE SPACEDONUTWIN CLASS

The SpaceDonut demo provides the bulk of its functionality in the **SpaceDonutWin** class. The class is defined as follows:

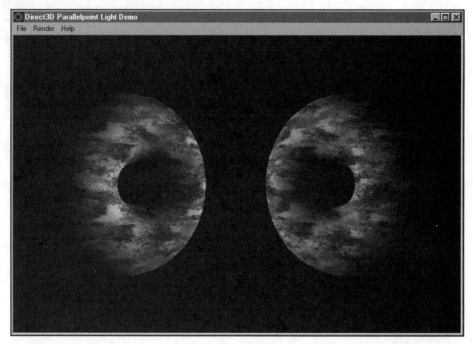

Figure 6.7
The SpaceDonut demo.

```
class SpaceDonutWin : public RMWin
{
public:
    SpaceDonutWin();
    BOOL CreateScene();
protected:
    //{{AFX_MSG(SpaceDonutWin)
    afx_msg void OnRenderWireframe();
    afx_msg void OnRenderFlat();
    afx_msg void OnRenderGouraud();
    afx_msg void OnUpdateRenderFlat(CCmdUI* pCmdUI);
    afx_msg void OnUpdateRenderGouraud(CCmdUI* pCmdUI);
    afx_msg void OnUpdateRenderWireframe(CCmdUI* pCmdUI);
    //}}AFX_MSG
    DECLARE_MESSAGE_MAP()
private:
    LPDIRECT3DRMMESHBUILDER meshbuilder;
};
```

Like all of the demos on the CD-ROM, the SpaceDonut demo derives its window class from the **RMWin** class. The **SpaceDonutWin** class provides two public member functions: a constructor and the **CreateScene()** function. The constructor is responsible for initializing any data members that the class defines (one, in this case). The **CreateScene()** function constructs the application's scene.

The six protected member functions provide support for the demo's Render menu. These functions use the **meshbuilder** data member to modify the mesh's settings.

THE SPACEDONUTWIN::CREATESCENE() FUNCTION

The SpaceDonut demo's scene is constructed by the **CreateScene()** function, as shown in Listing 6.4.

Listing 6.4   The SpaceDonutWin::CreateScene() function.

```
BOOL SpaceDonutWin::CreateScene()
{
    // ------- DONUT MESH --------
    D3DRMLOADRESOURCE resinfo;
    resinfo.hModule=NULL;
    resinfo.lpName=MAKEINTRESOURCE( IDR_DONUTMESH );
    resinfo.lpType="MESH";
    d3drm->CreateMeshBuilder( &meshbuilder );
    meshbuilder->Load( &resinfo, NULL, D3DRMLOAD_FROMRESOURCE,
            NULL, NULL );
    meshbuilder->SetPerspective( TRUE );
    meshbuilder->SetColorRGB( D3DVALUE(1), D3DVALUE(1), D3DVALUE(1) );
    ScaleMesh( meshbuilder, D3DVALUE(20) );

    //------ FROSTING TEXTURE --------
    LPDIRECT3DRMTEXTURE texture;
    HRSRC texture_id = FindResource( NULL,
            MAKEINTRESOURCE(IDR_FROSTINGTEXTURE),
            "TEXTURE" );
    d3drm->LoadTextureFromResource( texture_id, &texture );
    meshbuilder->SetTexture( texture );
    texture->Release();
    texture=0;
```

```
//------- WRAP ----------
D3DRMBOX box;
meshbuilder->GetBox( &box );
D3DVALUE w=box.max.x-box.min.x;
D3DVALUE h=box.max.y-box.min.y;

LPDIRECT3DRMWRAP wrap;
d3drm->CreateWrap( D3DRMWRAP_FLAT, scene,
        D3DVALUE(0.0), D3DVALUE(0.0), D3DVALUE(0.0), // wrap origin
        D3DVALUE(0.0), D3DVALUE(1.0), D3DVALUE(0.0), // wrap z axis
        D3DVALUE(0.0), D3DVALUE(0.0), D3DVALUE(1.0), // wrap y axis
        D3DVALUE(0.5), D3DVALUE(0.5),                // texture origin
        D3DDivide(1,w), D3DDivide(1,h),              // texture scale
        &wrap );
wrap->Apply( meshbuilder );
wrap->Release();
wrap=0;


//------- DONUT FRAMES --------
LPDIRECT3DRMFRAME leftframe;
d3drm->CreateFrame( scene, &leftframe );
leftframe->SetPosition( scene,
        D3DVALUE(-12), D3DVALUE(0), D3DVALUE(0) );
leftframe->SetOrientation( scene,
        D3DVALUE(0), D3DVALUE(1), D3DVALUE(0),
        D3DVALUE(0), D3DVALUE(0), D3DVALUE(1) );
leftframe->SetRotation( scene,
        D3DVALUE(0), D3DVALUE(1), D3DVALUE(0),
        D3DVALUE(0.1) );
leftframe->AddVisual( meshbuilder );
leftframe->Release();
leftframe=0;


LPDIRECT3DRMFRAME rightframe;
d3drm->CreateFrame( scene, &rightframe );
rightframe->SetPosition( scene,
        D3DVALUE(12), D3DVALUE(0), D3DVALUE(0) );
rightframe->SetOrientation( scene,
        D3DVALUE(0), D3DVALUE(1), D3DVALUE(0),
        D3DVALUE(0), D3DVALUE(0), D3DVALUE(1) );
rightframe->SetRotation( scene,
        D3DVALUE(0), D3DVALUE(1), D3DVALUE(0),
        D3DVALUE(-0.1) );
rightframe->AddVisual( meshbuilder );
rightframe->Release();
rightframe=0;
```

```
// --------- PARALLELPOINT LIGHT --------
LPDIRECT3DRMLIGHT light;
d3drm->CreateLightRGB( D3DRMLIGHT_PARALLELPOINT,
        D3DVALUE(1.0), D3DVALUE(1.0), D3DVALUE(1.0),
        &light );

LPDIRECT3DRMFRAME lightframe;
d3drm->CreateFrame( scene, &lightframe );
lightframe->AddLight( light );

lightframe->Release();
lightframe=0;
light->Release();
light=0;

//------ CAMERA ----------
d3drm->CreateFrame( scene, &camera );
camera->SetPosition( scene,
    D3DVALUE(0), D3DVALUE(0), D3DVALUE(-50) );
d3drm->CreateViewport( device, camera, 0, 0,
        device->GetWidth(), device->GetHeight(),
        &viewport );

return TRUE;
}
```

The **CreateScene()** function performs these six steps:

1. Creates the donut mesh

2. Creates and loads the donut frosting texture

3. Applies the frosting texture to the donut mesh

4. Creates two frames and places one on each side of the origin, attaching the donut mesh to each frame

5. Creates a parallel point light and a frame

6. Creates a viewport

Let's examine the code for each of these steps. We'll start with the first step: creating and loading the donut mesh:

```
D3DRMLOADRESOURCE resinfo;
resinfo.hModule=NULL;
```

```
resinfo.lpName=MAKEINTRESOURCE( IDR_DONUTMESH );
resinfo.lpType="MESH";
d3drm->CreateMeshBuilder( &meshbuilder );
meshbuilder->Load( &resinfo, NULL, D3DRMLOAD_FROMRESOURCE,
        NULL, NULL );
meshbuilder->SetPerspective( TRUE );
meshbuilder->SetColorRGB( D3DVALUE(1), D3DVALUE(1), D3DVALUE(1) );
ScaleMesh( meshbuilder, D3DVALUE(20) );
```

This code is similar to the **meshbuilder** code in the other demos. The mesh that is to be loaded is identified by the **resinfo** structure. The **IDR_ DONUTMESH** constant is the resource identifier for a mesh file that has been imported into the project. The **"MESH"** string identifies the resource category. The **meshbuilder** pointer is initialized with the **Direct3DRM CreateMeshBuilder()** function, then the **Load()** function is used to load the mesh. Texture correction is enabled with the **SetPerspective()** function. This is optional and is used to improve the appearance of the mesh once the texture is applied.

Next, the **Direct3DRMMeshBuilder SetColorRGB()** function is used to set the mesh's color to white. This is done because the donut mesh used by this demo has multicolored faces. We can set the color of all of the faces in the mesh with the **SetColorRGB()** function. Finally, the **ScaleMesh()** function is used to dictate the size of the mesh.

Step 2, creating and loading the donut frosting texture, looks like this:

```
LPDIRECT3DRMTEXTURE texture;
HRSRC texture_id = FindResource( NULL,
        MAKEINTRESOURCE(IDR_FROSTINGTEXTURE),
        "TEXTURE" );
d3drm->LoadTextureFromResource( texture_id, &texture );
meshbuilder->SetTexture( texture );
texture->Release();
texture=0;
```

The texture that is to be loaded is identified with the **texture_id** variable. The **FindResource()** function is used to specify the resource identifier (**IDR_FROSTINGTEXTURE**) and the resource type (**"TEXTURE"**).

The **texture** pointer is initialized with the **LoadTextureFromResource()** function. The new texture is associated with the **meshbuilder** using the **SetTexture()** function. Finally, the **texture** pointer is released.

The third step that the **SpaceDonutWin::CreateScene()** function performs is the creation and application of a texture wrap. The code looks like this:

```
D3DRMBOX box;
meshbuilder->GetBox( &box );
D3DVALUE w=box.max.x-box.min.x;
D3DVALUE h=box.max.y-box.min.y;

LPDIRECT3DRMWRAP wrap;
d3drm->CreateWrap( D3DRMWRAP_FLAT, scene,
      D3DVALUE(0.0), D3DVALUE(0.0), D3DVALUE(0.0), // wrap origin
      D3DVALUE(0.0), D3DVALUE(1.0), D3DVALUE(0.0), // wrap z axis
      D3DVALUE(0.0), D3DVALUE(0.0), D3DVALUE(1.0), // wrap y axis
      D3DVALUE(0.5), D3DVALUE(0.5),                // texture origin
      D3DDivide(1,w), D3DDivide(1,h),              // texture scale
      &wrap );
wrap->Apply( meshbuilder );
wrap->Release();
wrap=0;
```

The **Direct3DRM CreateWrap()** function is documented in Chapter 5 (see the Wraps demo), so we won't worry about this code here. In short, a flat texture wrap is created that stretches the texture to fit on the mesh. The texture is then applied to the mesh with the **Direct3DRMWrap Apply()** function.

The fourth step is the creation and placement of two frames. The **CreateScene()** function uses the **leftframe** and **rightframe** variables to identify these two frames. The code for the **leftframe** pointer is shown here.

```
LPDIRECT3DRMFRAME leftframe;
d3drm->CreateFrame( scene, &leftframe );
leftframe->SetPosition( scene,
      D3DVALUE(-12), D3DVALUE(0), D3DVALUE(0) );
leftframe->SetOrientation( scene,
      D3DVALUE(0), D3DVALUE(1), D3DVALUE(0),
      D3DVALUE(0), D3DVALUE(0), D3DVALUE(1) );
leftframe->SetRotation( scene,
      D3DVALUE(0), D3DVALUE(1), D3DVALUE(0),
      D3DVALUE(0.1) );
leftframe->AddVisual( meshbuilder );
leftframe->Release();
leftframe=0;
```

The **leftframe** pointer is initialized with the **CreateFrame()** function. The **SetPosition()** function is used to move the frame away from its default location (the origin). The frame is moved 12 units to the left.

The next function call, **SetOrientation()**, is necessary because of the way the donut mesh is oriented within the mesh file. The mesh file defines the donut as being aligned with the Y axis (the donut is lying down). We want to orient the donut to be aligned with the Z axis (to stand the donut up on its side). To accomplish this, we need know what the donut's forward and up vectors are.

An object's default forward vector is <0, 0, 1>, meaning that the object faces the positive Z axis. The default up vector is <0, 1, 0>. This means that to get the donut oriented the way we want, all we have to do is swap the forward and up vectors. This makes the donut face in the direction that was previously up and treats the direction that it was previously facing as up.

Next, a rotation attribute is assigned to the frame. The rotation is around the Y axis, and the rotation amount is 0.1 radians per update. Finally, the donut mesh is attached to the frame with the **AddVisual()** function, and the frame pointer is released.

The code to create and configure the **rightframe** pointer is similar to the **leftframe** code. The differences are:

- The **rightframe** frame is positioned to the right of the origin.

- The rotation amount is negative, causing the two frames to spin in opposite directions.

Notice that this demo attaches a single meshbuilder to multiple frames. This is a useful technique for displaying and animating objects. Bear in mind, however, that although multiple objects appear in the scene, only one object exists. If you change the texture or color of the meshbuilder, any and all instances of the object will reflect the change. In fact, if you run the SpaceDonut demo and change the rendering settings with the Render menu, you'll notice that both instances of the mesh change in appearance.

The fifth step that the **CreateScene()** function performs is the creation of the parallel point light source and a frame for placing the light source.

The code looks like this:

```
LPDIRECT3DRMLIGHT light;
d3drm->CreateLightRGB( D3DRMLIGHT_PARALLELPOINT,
        D3DVALUE(1.0), D3DVALUE(1.0), D3DVALUE(1.0),
        &light );

LPDIRECT3DRMFRAME lightframe;
d3drm->CreateFrame( scene, &lightframe );
lightframe->AddLight( light );

lightframe->Release();
lightframe=0;
light->Release();
light=0;
```

The **Direct3DRM CreateLightRGB**() function is used to initialize the **light** pointer. The **D3DRMLIGHT_PARALLELPOINT** constant indicates the light type, and the three numeric values specify the red, green, and blue components of the light's color (we are creating a white light).

Next, the **lightframe** pointer is initialized with the **Direct3DRM CreateFrame**() function. The light is then attached to the new frame with the **AddLight**() function. Finally, both the **light** and the **lightframe** pointers are released.

The sixth and final step that **CreateScene**() performs is the creation and placement of the viewport:

```
d3drm->CreateFrame( scene, &camera );
camera->SetPosition( scene,
        D3DVALUE(0), D3DVALUE(0), D3DVALUE(-50) );
d3drm->CreateViewport( device, camera, 0, 0,
        device->GetWidth(), device->GetHeight(),
        &viewport );
```

As with the other demos, the **camera** frame is initialized and placed. In this case, we are moving the camera 50 units behind the origin. The **viewport** pointer is then initialized with the **Direct3DRM CreateViewport**() function.

SPOTLIGHTS

Spotlights produce light in the shape of a cone. The light's position decides the location of the tip of the cone, and the light's orientation decides the location of the base of the cone.

Actually, the light that a spotlight produces is better described in terms of two cones: an outer cone and an inner cone. The outer cone determines the area that the spotlight is capable of illuminating. No light falls outside of the outer cone. The inner cone determines the area that receives the light's full illumination. The area between these two cones experiences a gradually fading illumination—from full illumination near the inner cone, to no illumination near the outer cone.

The inner cone is called the umbra cone. The umbra cone size is determined by the umbra angle. The outer cone is called the penumbra cone. The penumbra cone size is determined by the penumbra angle. The umbra and penumbra cones are illustrated in Figure 6.8.

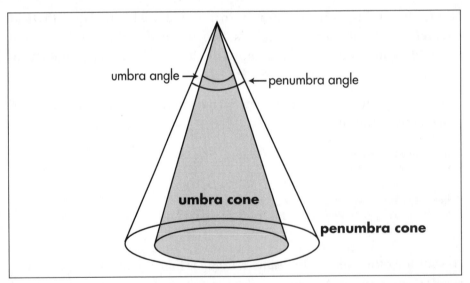

Figure 6.8
The anatomy of a spotlight.

The **Direct3DRMLight** interface provides these member functions for the adjustment and inspection of the umbra and penumbra angles:

- GetPenumbra()

- GetUmbra()

- SetPenumbra()

- SetUmbra()

THE SPOTLIGHT DEMO

The Spotlight demo animates a spotlight over three spherical meshes. The spotlight's umbra and penumbra angles can be adjusted with the Spotlight demo's Beam menu. The Spotlight demo appears in Figure 6.9.

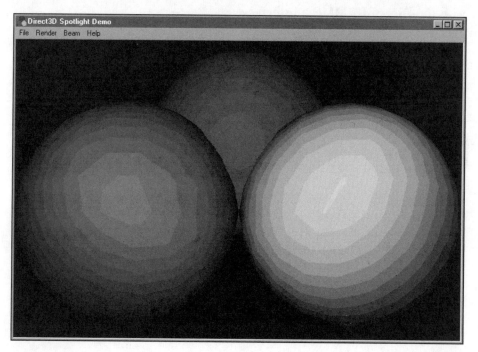

Figure 6.9
The Spotlight demo.

The Spotlight demo demonstrates the following techniques:

- Using the spotlight light source type

- Using a callback to animate a light source

- Using the **Direct3DRMMesh** interface to avoid extra overhead associated with the **Direct3DRMMeshBuilder** interface

- Changing **Direct3DRMMesh** rendering quality settings at runtime

- Changing spotlight umbra and penumbra settings at runtime

The Spotlight demo uses the **Direct3DRMMesh** interface instead of the **Direct3DRMMeshBuilder** interface to demonstrate alternatives to the way that the other demos are written. There is nothing exceptional about the Spotlight demo that requires the added performance benefits that come with the **Direct3DRMMesh** interface.

THE SPOTLIGHTWIN CLASS

The Spotlight demo uses the **RMWin** class as a base class for its **SpotlightWin** class:

```
class SpotlightWin : public RMWin
{
public:
    SpotlightWin();
    BOOL CreateScene();
protected:
    //{{AFX_MSG(SpotlightWin)
    afx_msg void OnRenderWireframe();
    afx_msg void OnRenderFlat();
    afx_msg void OnRenderGouraud();
    afx_msg void OnUpdateRenderFlat(CCmdUI* pCmdUI);
    afx_msg void OnUpdateRenderGouraud(CCmdUI* pCmdUI);
    afx_msg void OnUpdateRenderWireframe(CCmdUI* pCmdUI);
    afx_msg void OnBeamNormal();
    afx_msg void OnBeamNarrow();
    afx_msg void OnBeamWide();
    afx_msg void OnUpdateBeamNormal(CCmdUI* pCmdUI);
    afx_msg void OnUpdateBeamNarrow(CCmdUI* pCmdUI);
    afx_msg void OnUpdateBeamWide(CCmdUI* pCmdUI);
    //}}AFX_MSG
    DECLARE_MESSAGE_MAP()
```

```
private:
    static void MoveLight(LPDIRECT3DRMFRAME frame, void* arg,
        D3DVALUE delta);
private:
    LPDIRECT3DRMMESH mesh1, mesh2, mesh3;
    LPDIRECT3DRMLIGHT spotlight;
    int beamwidth;
};
```

The **SpotlightWin** class definition looks quite a bit different than the class definitions for the other demos that we've looked at in this chapter. The first and most obvious difference is that there are more protected member functions. The first six protected functions are familiar from the other demos and are used to implement the demo's Render menu. The new functions are used to implement the demo's Beam menu. We'll look at these functions later.

Another difference is the presence of the **MoveLight()** function declaration. **MoveLight()** is a callback function that we will use to animate the spotlight.

The class's data members are also different. The previous class definitions used a single **Direct3DRMMeshBuilder** pointer. The **SpotlightWin** class declares three pointers to the **Direct3DRMMesh** interface. These pointers are used to access the three sphere meshes used in the demo.

The class also declares a **Direct3DRMLight** pointer. This pointer is used by the member functions that implement the Beam menu. These functions also use the **beamwidth** data member to store the current spotlight settings.

THE SPOTLIGHTWIN::CREATESCENE() FUNCTION

The Spotlight demo's **CreateScene()** function is responsible for creating the meshes, the spotlight, and installing a callback function that animates the spotlight. The **SpotlightWin::CreateScene()** function appears in Listing 6.5.

Listing 6.5   The SpotlightWin::CreateScene() function.

```
BOOL SpotlightWin::CreateScene()
{
    //----- MESHES --------
    D3DRMLOADRESOURCE resinfo;
```

```
resinfo.hModule=NULL;
resinfo.lpName=MAKEINTRESOURCE( IDR_SPHEREMESH );
resinfo.lpType="MESH";
LPDIRECT3DRMMESHBUILDER builder;
d3drm->CreateMeshBuilder( &builder );
builder->Load( &resinfo, NULL, D3DRMLOAD_FROMRESOURCE,
        NULL, NULL );
builder->SetColorRGB(D3DVALUE(1.0), D3DVALUE(0.0), D3DVALUE(0.0) );
builder->CreateMesh( &mesh1 );
builder->SetColorRGB(D3DVALUE(0.0), D3DVALUE(1.0), D3DVALUE(0.0) );
builder->CreateMesh( &mesh2 );
builder->SetColorRGB(D3DVALUE(0.0), D3DVALUE(0.0), D3DVALUE(1.0) );
builder->CreateMesh( &mesh3 );
builder->Release();
builder=0;


//----- MESH FRAMES --------
LPDIRECT3DRMFRAME frame1;
d3drm->CreateFrame( scene, &frame1 );
frame1->SetPosition( scene,
        D3DVALUE(-2), D3DVALUE(0), D3DVALUE(0) );
frame1->AddVisual( mesh1 );
frame1->Release();
frame1=0;


LPDIRECT3DRMFRAME frame2;
d3drm->CreateFrame( scene, &frame2 );
frame2->SetPosition(scene,
        D3DVALUE(2), D3DVALUE(0), D3DVALUE(0) );
frame2->AddVisual( mesh2 );
frame2->Release();
frame2=0;


LPDIRECT3DRMFRAME frame3;
d3drm->CreateFrame( scene, &frame3 );
frame3->SetPosition(scene,
        D3DVALUE(0), D3DVALUE(0), D3DVALUE(2) );
frame3->AddVisual( mesh3 );
frame3->Release();
frame3=0;


//------- SPOTLIGHT ------
d3drm->CreateLightRGB( D3DRMLIGHT_SPOT,
        D3DVALUE(0.8), D3DVALUE(0.8), D3DVALUE(0.8),
        &spotlight );
OnBeamNormal();
```

```
//------ SPOTLIGHT FRAME --------
LPDIRECT3DRMFRAME lightframe;
d3drm->CreateFrame( scene, &lightframe );
lightframe->SetPosition( scene,
        D3DVALUE(0), D3DVALUE(10), D3DVALUE(-10) );
lightframe->SetOrientation( scene,
        D3DVALUE(0), D3DVALUE(-1), D3DVALUE(1),
        D3DVALUE(0), D3DVALUE(1), D3DVALUE(0) );

lightframe->AddLight( spotlight );
lightframe->AddMoveCallback( MoveLight, NULL );

lightframe->Release();
lightframe=0;

//------ CAMERA ------
d3drm->CreateFrame( scene, &camera );
camera->SetPosition( scene,
        D3DVALUE(0), D3DVALUE(6), D3DVALUE(-6) );
camera->SetOrientation( scene,
        D3DVALUE(0), D3DVALUE(-1), D3DVALUE(1.1),
        D3DVALUE(0), D3DVALUE(1), D3DVALUE(0) );
d3drm->CreateViewport( device, camera, 0, 0,
        device->GetWidth(), device->GetHeight(),
        &viewport );

return TRUE;
}
```

The **CreateScene()** function performs five steps:

1. Uses the **Direct3DRMMeshBuilder** interface to load a spherical mesh and creates three pointers to the **Direct3DRMMesh** interface

2. Creates and positions a frame for each of the three meshes

3. Creates and configures a spotlight

4. Creates a frame for the spotlight

5. Creates and configures a viewport

Let's look at the first step:

```
D3DRMLOADRESOURCE resinfo;
resinfo.hModule=NULL;
```

```
resinfo.lpName=MAKEINTRESOURCE( IDR_SPHEREMESH );
resinfo.lpType="MESH";
LPDIRECT3DRMMESHBUILDER builder;
d3drm->CreateMeshBuilder( &builder );
builder->Load( &resinfo, NULL, D3DRMLOAD_FROMRESOURCE,
        NULL, NULL );
builder->SetColorRGB(D3DVALUE(1.0), D3DVALUE(0.0), D3DVALUE(0.0) );
builder->CreateMesh( &mesh1 );
builder->SetColorRGB(D3DVALUE(0.0), D3DVALUE(1.0), D3DVALUE(0.0) );
builder->CreateMesh( &mesh2 );
builder->SetColorRGB(D3DVALUE(0.0), D3DVALUE(0.0), D3DVALUE(1.0) );
builder->CreateMesh( &mesh3 );
builder->Release();
builder=0;
```

First, an instance of the **D3DRMLOADRESOURCE** structure is declared and initialized. The **resinfo** structure identifies the spherical mesh that we will be using.

A pointer to the **Direct3DRMMeshBuilder** interface called **builder** is then declared. The **Direct3DRM CreateMeshBuilder()** function is used to initialize the **builder** pointer. The **Load()** function is used to load the mesh. The address of the previously prepared **resinfo** structure is used as the first argument to the **Load()** function.

Next, the three pointers to the **Direct3DRMMesh** interface are initialized. Each is initialized with the **Direct3DRMMeshBuilder CreateMesh()** function. The **meshbuilder** is assigned a different color setting before each invocation of **CreateMesh()**. This creates three meshes, each represented by the **Direct3DRMMesh** interface and each a different color. Once the third mesh has been created, the **builder** pointer is released.

The second step that the **CreateScene()** function performs is the creation and positioning of three frames, one for each mesh:

```
LPDIRECT3DRMFRAME frame1;
d3drm->CreateFrame( scene, &frame1 );
frame1->SetPosition(scene,
        D3DVALUE(-2), D3DVALUE(0), D3DVALUE(0) );
frame1->AddVisual( mesh1 );
frame1->Release();
frame1=0;
```

```
LPDIRECT3DRMFRAME frame2;
d3drm->CreateFrame( scene, &frame2 );
frame2->SetPosition(scene,
        D3DVALUE(2), D3DVALUE(0), D3DVALUE(0) );
frame2->AddVisual( mesh2 );
frame2->Release();
frame2=0;

LPDIRECT3DRMFRAME frame3;
d3drm->CreateFrame( scene, &frame3 );
frame3->SetPosition(scene,
        D3DVALUE(0), D3DVALUE(0), D3DVALUE(2) );
frame3->AddVisual( mesh3 );
frame3->Release();
frame3=0;
```

Each frame is created with the **Direct3DRM CreateFrame**() function and then positioned in a different location. The third frame is placed behind the first two. Each of the previously created meshes is attached to one of the frames with the **AddVisual**() function. Each frame pointer is released once a mesh has been attached.

Step 3 is the creation of the spotlight. The code looks like this:

```
d3drm->CreateLightRGB( D3DRMLIGHT_SPOT,
        D3DVALUE(0.8), D3DVALUE(0.8), D3DVALUE(0.8),
        &spotlight );
OnBeamNormal();
```

First, the **Direct3DRM CreateLightRGB**() function is used to initialize the **spotlight** pointer. The **D3DRMLIGHT_SPOT** constant is used to indicate that we are creating a spotlight. We are using 0.8 for the light's red, green, and blue color components, indicating a light that is bright gray in color.

Next, the **OnBeamNormal**() function is called. The **OnBeamNormal**() function is a message handler for the Beam|Normal menu selection. We invoke it here to assign the spotlight umbra and penumbra angles. We'll look at the **OnBeamNormal**() function soon.

Step 4 is the creation of the frame to which we will attach the spotlight:

```
LPDIRECT3DRMFRAME lightframe;
d3drm->CreateFrame( scene, &lightframe );
```

```
lightframe->SetPosition( scene,
        D3DVALUE(0), D3DVALUE(10), D3DVALUE(-10) );
lightframe->SetOrientation( scene,
        D3DVALUE(0), D3DVALUE(-1), D3DVALUE(1),
        D3DVALUE(0), D3DVALUE(1), D3DVALUE(0) );

lightframe->AddLight( spotlight );
lightframe->AddMoveCallback( MoveLight, NULL );

lightframe->Release();
lightframe=0;
```

The **lightframe** pointer is initialized with the **Direct3DRM CreateFrame()** function. The **SetPosition()** function is then used to position the frame 10 units above and 10 units behind the origin. The **SetOrientation()** function is used to point the light at the origin.

Next, the previously created spotlight is attached to the new frame with the **AddLight()** function. Also, the **MoveLight()** callback function is installed with the **AddMoveCallback()** function. Lastly, the **lightframe** pointer is released.

The fifth and final step that the **CreateScene()** function performs is the creation of a viewport:

```
d3drm->CreateFrame( scene, &camera );
camera->SetPosition( scene,
        D3DVALUE(0), D3DVALUE(6), D3DVALUE(-6) );
camera->SetOrientation( scene,
        D3DVALUE(0), D3DVALUE(-1), D3DVALUE(1.1),
        D3DVALUE(0), D3DVALUE(1), D3DVALUE(0) );
d3drm->CreateViewport( device, camera, 0, 0,
        device->GetWidth(), device->GetHeight(),
        &viewport );
```

First, the **camera** frame is initialized. Then, the frame is positioned six units above and six units behind the origin. The **SetOrientation()** function is used to point the **camera** frame toward the origin. Finally, the **Direct3DRM CreateViewport()** function is used to initialize the **viewport** pointer.

THE SPOTLIGHTWIN::MOVELIGHT() FUNCTION

The Spotlight demo's **CreateScene()** function installs the **MoveLight()** callback function. **MoveLight()** calculates a new orientation for the spotlight frame for each scene update. The **MoveLight()** function looks like this:

```
void SpotlightWin::MoveLight(LPDIRECT3DRMFRAME frame, void*, D3DVALUE)
{
    static const D3DVALUE LIM = D3DVALUE(0.3);
    static D3DVALUE xi = D3DVALUE(0.03);
    static D3DVALUE yi = D3DVALUE(0.04);
    static D3DVALUE x, y;
    if (x<-LIM || x>LIM)
        xi=-xi;
    if (y<-LIM || y>LIM)
        yi=-yi;
    x+=xi;
    y+=yi;
    frame->SetOrientation( NULL,
        x, y-1, D3DVALUE(1),
        D3DVALUE(0), D3DVALUE(1), D3DVALUE(0) );
}
```

Like the Jade demo in Chapter 5, the Spotlight demo uses a simple "bouncing ball" algorithm to perform animation (we'll study more sophisticated animation techniques in Chapter 7). The static values that are declared in the **MoveLight()** function are used to track and limit the frame's orientation. Once a new orientation is calculated, it is installed with the **SetOrientation()** function.

THE SPOTLIGHT DEMO RENDER FUNCTIONS

Early in this chapter, when we studied ambient light by creating the AmbientLight project, we looked at the six member functions that implemented the demo's Render menu. These functions used the **Direct3DRMMeshBuilder GetQuality()** and **SetQuality()** functions. This strategy won't work with the Spotlight demo because we are using the **Direct3DRMMesh** interface.

The **Direct3DRMMesh** interface is almost entirely dedicated to the manipulation of groups. Groups are sets of faces within a mesh that can be modified as a single entity. The **Direct3DRMMesh** interface provides **GetGroupColor()** and **SetGroupColor()** member functions that allow the color of a group of faces to be inspected and assigned. The only trouble is that these functions expect identifiers that indicate which group of faces within the mesh we are interested in.

These group identifiers are important when you are using a mesh that has multiple groups, as you will see in Chapter 8. For now, however, all of the faces in each of our three meshes belong to the same group. Luckily for us, meshes that use only one group use zero as the group identifier. This default group identifier is used in the following Spotlight demo functions:

```
void SpotlightWin::OnRenderWireframe()
{
    mesh1->SetGroupQuality( 0, D3DRMRENDER_WIREFRAME );
    mesh2->SetGroupQuality( 0, D3DRMRENDER_WIREFRAME );
    mesh3->SetGroupQuality( 0, D3DRMRENDER_WIREFRAME );
}

void SpotlightWin::OnRenderFlat()
{
    mesh1->SetGroupQuality( 0, D3DRMRENDER_FLAT );
    mesh2->SetGroupQuality( 0, D3DRMRENDER_FLAT );
    mesh3->SetGroupQuality( 0, D3DRMRENDER_FLAT );
}

void SpotlightWin::OnRenderGouraud()
{
    mesh1->SetGroupQuality( 0, D3DRMRENDER_GOURAUD );
    mesh2->SetGroupQuality( 0, D3DRMRENDER_GOURAUD );
    mesh3->SetGroupQuality( 0, D3DRMRENDER_GOURAUD );
}

void SpotlightWin::OnUpdateRenderWireframe(CCmdUI* pCmdUI)
{
    D3DRMRENDERQUALITY quality=mesh1->GetGroupQuality( 0 );
    pCmdUI->SetCheck( quality==D3DRMRENDER_WIREFRAME );
}

void SpotlightWin::OnUpdateRenderFlat(CCmdUI* pCmdUI)
{
    D3DRMRENDERQUALITY quality=mesh1->GetGroupQuality( 0 );
    pCmdUI->SetCheck( quality==D3DRMRENDER_FLAT );
}

void SpotlightWin::OnUpdateRenderGouraud(CCmdUI* pCmdUI)
{
    D3DRMRENDERQUALITY quality=mesh1->GetGroupQuality( 0 );
    pCmdUI->SetCheck( quality==D3DRMRENDER_GOURAUD );
}
```

The first three functions are called when the user selects the menu options from the demo's Render menu. The **SetGroupQuality()** function is used to change the rendering method for the meshes. The second three functions are called by MFC before the Render menu is displayed. The **SetCheck()** function is used to activate the check mark that appears to the left of the current menu item.

THE SPOTLIGHT DEMO BEAM FUNCTIONS

The Spotlight demo provides a Beam menu which allows the spotlight's umbra and penumbra angles to be modified. The six member functions that provide this functionality follow:

```
void SpotlightWin::OnBeamNormal()
{
    spotlight->SetUmbra( D3DVALUE(0.2) );
    spotlight->SetPenumbra( D3DVALUE(0.4) );
    beamwidth=BEAM_NORMAL;
}

void SpotlightWin::OnBeamNarrow()
{
    spotlight->SetUmbra( D3DVALUE(0.1) );
    spotlight->SetPenumbra( D3DVALUE(0.2) );
    beamwidth=BEAM_NARROW;
}

void SpotlightWin::OnBeamWide()
{
    spotlight->SetUmbra( D3DVALUE(0.4) );
    spotlight->SetPenumbra( D3DVALUE(0.8) );
    beamwidth=BEAM_WIDE;
}

void SpotlightWin::OnUpdateBeamNormal(CCmdUI* pCmdUI)
{
    pCmdUI->SetCheck( beamwidth==BEAM_NORMAL );
}

void SpotlightWin::OnUpdateBeamNarrow(CCmdUI* pCmdUI)
{
    pCmdUI->SetCheck( beamwidth==BEAM_NARROW );
}
```

```
void SpotlightWin::OnUpdateBeamWide(CCmdUI* pCmdUI)
{
    pCmdUI->SetCheck( beamwidth==BEAM_WIDE );
}
```

One of the first three member functions is called when an entry on the Beam menu is selected. The **SetUmbra()** and **SetPenumbra()** functions are used to modify the spotlight's characteristics. Also, the **beamwidth** data member is assigned according to which set of spotlight settings is currently in effect. This data member is used by the second three member functions to activate a check mark for the current spotlight settings.

MULTIPLE LIGHT SOURCES

The demos that we've looked at so far in this chapter are each intended to familiarize you with a specific light source type. Each demo uses one light source to clearly illustrate the light source's qualities.

This does not mean, however, that you can't use more than one light source in your programs. Light sources can be used in any combination, and programs can use multiple instances of the same light source type as well.

SHADOWS

This chapter is titled *Light Sources And Shadows*, and we've talked about the five light source types that Direct3D supports, so it's time to talk about shadows.

Before we begin, however, it should be pointed out that in Direct3D, light sources and shadows have little to do with each other. In Direct3D, a shadow is an object that can be inserted into a scene to approximate the behavior of a real shadow.

THE SHADOW DEMO

The Shadow demo creates a scene where a fork is hovering above a rectangular platform. A light source illuminates the fork and the platform, and the fork's shadow is cast onto the platform (or seems to be). The Shadow demo appears in Figure 6.10.

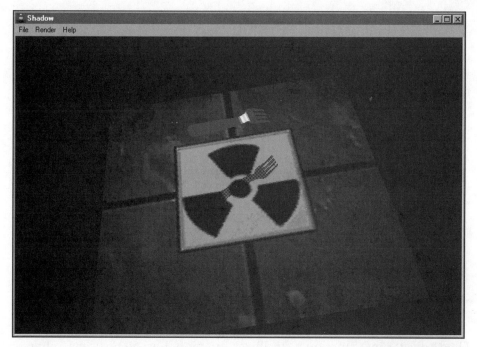

Figure 6.10
The Shadow demo.

The Shadow demo demonstrates the following techniques:

- Using the **Direct3DRMShadow** interface

- Using a callback function to modify the characteristics of an animation during program execution

- Generating random vectors with the **D3DRMVectorRandom()** function

THE SHADOWWIN CLASS

The bulk of the Shadow demo's functionality is provided by the **ShadowWin** class:

```
class ShadowWin : public RMWin
{
public:
    ShadowWin();
    BOOL CreateScene();
```

```
protected:
    //{{AFX_MSG(ShadowWin)
    afx_msg void OnRenderWireframe();
    afx_msg void OnRenderFlat();
    afx_msg void OnRenderGouraud();
    afx_msg void OnUpdateRenderFlat(CCmdUI* pCmdUI);
    afx_msg void OnUpdateRenderGouraud(CCmdUI* pCmdUI);
    afx_msg void OnUpdateRenderWireframe(CCmdUI* pCmdUI);
    //}}AFX_MSG
    DECLARE_MESSAGE_MAP()
private:
    static void AdjustSpin(LPDIRECT3DRMFRAME frame, void*, D3DVALUE);
private:
    LPDIRECT3DRMMESHBUILDER floorbuilder;
    LPDIRECT3DRMMESHBUILDER forkbuilder;
};
```

The class provides two public member functions: a constructor and the **CreateScene()** function. It also declares the six Render menu functions that appear in the other demos.

The **AdjustSpin()** function is a callback function that will be used to change the fork's movement as the demo executes. The callback function is installed by the **CreateScene()** function.

Finally, two data members are declared. Both data members are pointers to the **Direct3DRMMeshBuilder** interface. The pointers will be used during scene creation and by the Render menu message handler functions.

THE SHADOWWIN::CREATESCENE() FUNCTION

The scene is created by the **CreateScene()** function, which appears in Listing 6.6.

Listing 6.6   The ShadowWin::CreateScene() function.

```
//------------ FLOOR MESH --------
D3DRMLOADRESOURCE resinfo;resinfo.hModule=NULL;
resinfo.lpName=MAKEINTRESOURCE( IDR_CUBEMESH );
resinfo.lpType="MESH";
d3drm->CreateMeshBuilder( &floorbuilder );
floorbuilder->Load( &resinfo, NULL, D3DRMLOAD_FROMRESOURCE,
        NULL, NULL );
floorbuilder->Scale( D3DVALUE(5), D3DVALUE(.05), D3DVALUE(5) );
```

```
floorbuilder->SetPerspective( TRUE );
floorbuilder->SetQuality( D3DRMRENDER_FLAT );

//------------ FLOOR TEXTURE --------------
LPDIRECT3DRMTEXTURE texture;
HRSRC texture_id = FindResource( NULL,
        MAKEINTRESOURCE(IDR_FLOORTEXTURE), "TEXTURE" );
d3drm->LoadTextureFromResource( texture_id, &texture );
floorbuilder->SetTexture( texture );
texture->Release();
texture=0;

//------------ FLOOR WRAP ------------
D3DRMBOX box;
floorbuilder->GetBox( &box );
D3DVALUE w=box.max.x-box.min.x;
D3DVALUE h=box.max.z-box.min.z;

LPDIRECT3DRMWRAP wrap;
d3drm->CreateWrap( D3DRMWRAP_FLAT, NULL,
        D3DVALUE(0.0), D3DVALUE(0.0), D3DVALUE(0.0), // wrap origin
        D3DVALUE(0.0), D3DVALUE(1.0), D3DVALUE(0.0), // wrap z axis
        D3DVALUE(0.0), D3DVALUE(0.0), D3DVALUE(1.0), // wrap y axis
        D3DVALUE(.5) ,D3DVALUE(0.5),                 // texture origin
        D3DDivide(1,w), D3DDivide(1,h),              // texture scale
        &wrap );
wrap->Apply( floorbuilder );
wrap->Release();
wrap=0;

//------------- FLOOR FRAME ----------
LPDIRECT3DRMFRAME floorframe;
d3drm->CreateFrame( scene, &floorframe );
floorframe->AddVisual( floorbuilder );
floorframe->Release();
floorframe=0;

//---------------- FORK MESH --------
resinfo.hModule=NULL;
resinfo.lpName=MAKEINTRESOURCE( IDR_FORKMESH );
resinfo.lpType="MESH";
d3drm->CreateMeshBuilder( &forkbuilder );
forkbuilder->Load( &resinfo, NULL, D3DRMLOAD_FROMRESOURCE,
        NULL, NULL );
forkbuilder->SetQuality( D3DRMRENDER_FLAT );
```

```
//--------------- FORK FRAME ----------
LPDIRECT3DRMFRAME forkframe;
d3drm->CreateFrame( scene, &forkframe );
forkframe->SetRotation( scene,
        D3DVALUE(1), D3DVALUE(1), D3DVALUE(1),
        D3DVALUE(0.4) );
forkframe->SetPosition( scene,
        D3DVALUE(0), D3DVALUE(6), D3DVALUE(0) );
forkframe->AddVisual( forkbuilder );
forkframe->AddMoveCallback( AdjustSpin, NULL );

//-------------- AMBIENT LIGHT --------
LPDIRECT3DRMLIGHT ambientlight;
d3drm->CreateLightRGB( D3DRMLIGHT_AMBIENT,
        D3DVALUE(1),D3DVALUE(1), D3DVALUE(1),
        &ambientlight );
scene->AddLight( ambientlight );
ambientlight->Release();
ambientlight=0;

//-------------- POINT LIGHT ----------
LPDIRECT3DRMLIGHT pointlight;
d3drm->CreateLightRGB( D3DRMLIGHT_POINT,
        D3DVALUE(1),D3DVALUE(1), D3DVALUE(1),
        &pointlight );

LPDIRECT3DRMFRAME lightframe;
d3drm->CreateFrame( scene, &lightframe );
lightframe->SetPosition( scene,
        D3DVALUE(0), D3DVALUE(30), D3DVALUE(0) );
lightframe->AddLight( pointlight );
lightframe->Release();
lightframe=0;

//-------------- SHADOW ----------
LPDIRECT3DRMVISUAL shadow;
d3drm->CreateShadow( forkbuilder, pointlight,
        D3DVALUE(0), box.max.y+D3DVALUE(0.1), D3DVALUE(0),
        D3DVALUE(0), box.max.y+D3DVALUE(1.0), D3DVALUE(0),
        (LPDIRECT3DRMVISUAL*)&shadow );
forkframe->AddVisual( shadow );

shadow->Release();
shadow=0;
forkframe->Release();
forkframe=0;
```

```
pointlight->Release();
pointlight=0;

//------------ VIEWPORT --------
d3drm->CreateFrame( scene, &camera );
camera->SetPosition( scene,
        D3DVALUE(0.0), D3DVALUE(25.0), D3DVALUE(-20.0) );
camera->SetOrientation( scene,
        D3DVALUE(0), D3DVALUE(-25), D3DVALUE(20),
        D3DVALUE(.1), D3DVALUE(1), D3DVALUE(0) );
d3drm->CreateViewport( device, camera,
        0, 0,
        device->GetWidth(), device->GetHeight(),
        &viewport );

return TRUE;
}
```

The **CreateScene()** function constructs the scene in 10 short steps:

1. Creates the mesh that will represent the platform or floor

2. Creates a texture for the floor mesh

3. Creates and applies a texture wrap for the floor mesh

4. Positions the floor mesh with a frame

5. Creates the fork mesh

6. Positions the fork mesh with a frame

7. Creates an ambient light

8. Creates a point light

9. Creates the shadow

10. Creates a viewport

Let's start with Step 1, creating the floor mesh:

```
D3DRMLOADRESOURCE resinfo;
resinfo.hModule=NULL;
resinfo.lpName=MAKEINTRESOURCE( IDR_CUBEMESH );
resinfo.lpType="MESH";
d3drm->CreateMeshBuilder( &floorbuilder );
```

```
floorbuilder->Load( &resinfo, NULL, D3DRMLOAD_FROMRESOURCE,
        NULL, NULL );
floorbuilder->Scale( D3DVALUE(5), D3DVALUE(.05), D3DVALUE(5) );
floorbuilder->SetPerspective( TRUE );
floorbuilder->SetQuality( D3DRMRENDER_FLAT );
```

A cube shaped mesh is used to represent the floor. The mesh is loaded
with the **Direct3DRMMeshBuilder Load()** function, and then the mesh is
flattened out with the **Scale()** function. Perspective correction is enabled
for the mesh, and the mesh's rendering method is specified as flat.

The next step is the loading of a texture that will be applied to the floor mesh:

```
LPDIRECT3DRMTEXTURE texture;
HRSRC texture_id = FindResource( NULL,
        MAKEINTRESOURCE(IDR_FLOORTEXTURE), "TEXTURE" );
d3drm->LoadTextureFromResource( texture_id, &texture );
floorbuilder->SetTexture( texture );
texture->Release();
texture=0;
```

A value that identifies the mesh is created with the Win32 **FindResource()**
function. The texture is then loaded with the **LoadTextureFromResource()**
function and associated with the previously created **meshbuilder** using the
SetTexture() function. The **texture** pointer is released after it has been used.

Step 3 is the creation and application of a texture wrap for the floor mesh:

```
D3DRMBOX box;
floorbuilder->GetBox( &box );
D3DVALUE w=box.max.x-box.min.x;
D3DVALUE h=box.max.z-box.min.z;

LPDIRECT3DRMWRAP wrap;
d3drm->CreateWrap( D3DRMWRAP_FLAT, NULL,
        D3DVALUE(0.0), D3DVALUE(0.0), D3DVALUE(0.0), // wrap origin
        D3DVALUE(0.0), D3DVALUE(1.0), D3DVALUE(0.0), // wrap z axis
        D3DVALUE(0.0), D3DVALUE(0.0), D3DVALUE(1.0), // wrap y axis
        D3DVALUE(.5) ,D3DVALUE(0.5),                 // texture origin
        D3DDivide(1,w), D3DDivide(1,h),              // texture scale
        &wrap );
wrap->Apply( floorbuilder );
wrap->Release();
wrap=0;
```

The **Direct3DRMMeshBuilder GetBox()** function is used to retrieved the floor mesh's dimensions. The mesh dimensions (along with plenty of other values) are used to create a flat texture wrap. The texture wrap is used to apply the previously associated texture on the floor mesh using the **Direct3DRMWrap Apply()** function. The **wrap** pointer is then released. See the Wraps demo in Chapter 5 for a discussion of the **CreateWrap()** function.

Next, a frame is created for the floor meshbuilder:

```
LPDIRECT3DRMFRAME floorframe;
d3drm->CreateFrame( scene, &floorframe );
floorframe->AddVisual( floorbuilder );
floorframe->Release();
floorframe=0;
```

The frame is created with the **Direct3DRM CreateFrame()** function. The **AddVisual()** function is used to attach the meshbuilder to the new frame. The **floorframe** pointer is released because it is no longer needed.

Step 5 is the creation of the fork mesh:

```
resinfo.hModule=NULL;
resinfo.lpName=MAKEINTRESOURCE( IDR_FORKMESH );
resinfo.lpType="MESH";
d3drm->CreateMeshBuilder( &forkbuilder );
forkbuilder->Load( &resinfo, NULL, D3DRMLOAD_FROMRESOURCE,
        NULL, NULL );
forkbuilder->SetQuality( D3DRMRENDER_FLAT );
```

The fork mesh file is part of the program's resources (like the floor mesh and the floor texture). The mesh is loaded with the **Direct3DRMMeshBuilder Load()** function. A flat rendering method is specified for the mesh. Notice that we are not enabling perspective correction because no texture will be applied to the fork mesh.

Next, a frame for the fork mesh is created and configured:

```
LPDIRECT3DRMFRAME forkframe;
d3drm->CreateFrame( scene, &forkframe );
forkframe->SetRotation( scene,
        D3DVALUE(1), D3DVALUE(1), D3DVALUE(1),
        D3DVALUE(0.4) );
```

```
forkframe->SetPosition( scene,
        D3DVALUE(0), D3DVALUE(6), D3DVALUE(0) );
forkframe->AddVisual( forkbuilder );
forkframe->AddMoveCallback( AdjustSpin, NULL );
```

The new frame is given a rotation attribute, but this assignment is temporary because the **AdjustSpin()** callback function will override this setting after a few system updates. The fork frame is positioned six units above the origin (the floor mesh is placed at the origin).

The fork mesh is attached to the fork frame with the **AddVisual()** function. Lastly, the **AdjustSpin()** callback function is installed using the **Direct3DRMFrame AddMoveCallback()** function.

Step 7 is the creation of an ambient light source:

```
LPDIRECT3DRMLIGHT ambientlight;
d3drm->CreateLightRGB( D3DRMLIGHT_AMBIENT,
        D3DVALUE(1),D3DVALUE(1), D3DVALUE(1),
        &ambientlight );
scene->AddLight( ambientlight );
ambientlight->Release();
ambientlight=0;
```

Early in this chapter, when we learned how to use ambient lights, we attached the light source directly to the scene's root frame. Here too, we are saving ourselves the trouble of creating a frame by using the root frame (**scene**) frame.

Step 8 is the creation of a point light. This is the light source that will cast the shadow of the fork mesh. The code looks like this:

```
LPDIRECT3DRMLIGHT pointlight;
d3drm->CreateLightRGB( D3DRMLIGHT_POINT,
        D3DVALUE(1),D3DVALUE(1), D3DVALUE(1),
        &pointlight );

LPDIRECT3DRMFRAME lightframe;
d3drm->CreateFrame( scene, &lightframe );
lightframe->SetPosition( scene,
        D3DVALUE(0), D3DVALUE(30), D3DVALUE(0) );
lightframe->AddLight( pointlight );
lightframe->Release();
lightframe=0;
```

Once the light has been created, a frame is created to position the light. The frame is positioned 30 units above the origin. The light source is attached to the new frame with the **AddLight**() function.

The next step is the creation of the **Direct3DRMShadow** object:

```
LPDIRECT3DRMSHADOW shadow;
d3drm->CreateShadow( forkbuilder, pointlight,
        D3DVALUE(0), box.max.y+D3DVALUE(0.1), D3DVALUE(0),
        D3DVALUE(0), box.max.y+D3DVALUE(1.0), D3DVALUE(0),
        (LPDIRECT3DRMVISUAL*)&shadow );
forkframe->AddVisual( shadow );

shadow->Release();
shadow=0;
forkframe->Release();
forkframe=0;
pointlight->Release();
pointlight=0;
```

The shadow is created with the **Direct3DRM CreateShadow**() function, which expects nine arguments. The first argument is a pointer to the visual object that is to cast the shadow. The second argument is a pointer to the light source that is to be used when calculating the shadow's shape. The next six arguments define the plane on which the shadow is to appear (the first three arguments indicate a point on the plane, and the following three arguments specify a vector that is perpendicular to the plane). The last argument expected by the **Direct3DRM CreateShadow**() function is the address of the pointer that is to be initialized. For inexplicable reasons, the **CreateShadow**() subject expects a pointer to the **Direct3DRMVisual** interface instead of the **Direct3DRMShadow** interface for its final argument. A cast is required to get the compiler to accept the pointer's address.

The tenth and final step of the **CreateScene**() function is the creation of the viewport:

```
d3drm->CreateFrame( scene, &camera );
camera->SetPosition( scene,
        D3DVALUE(0.0), D3DVALUE(25.0), D3DVALUE(-20.0) );
camera->SetOrientation( scene,
        D3DVALUE(0), D3DVALUE(-25), D3DVALUE(20),
        D3DVALUE(.1), D3DVALUE(1), D3DVALUE(0) );
```

```
d3drm->CreateViewport( device, camera,
        0, 0,
        device->GetWidth(), device->GetHeight(),
        &viewport );
```

The **camera** frame is initialized with the **Direct3DRM CreateFrame()** function, and positioned above and in front of the origin, pointing at the origin. The **CreateViewport()** function is used to initialized the **viewport** pointer.

The last thing that the **CreateScene()** function does is return **TRUE** to indicate that the scene has been created successfully.

THE SHADOWWIN::ADJUSTSPIN() FUNCTION

The **AdjustSpin()** function is a callback function that changes the fork frame's rotation attribute periodically. The function uses the **D3DRMVectorRandom()** function to generate random vectors.

```
void ShadowWin::AdjustSpin(LPDIRECT3DRMFRAME frame, void*, D3DVALUE)
{
static UINT delay;
    if (++delay<11)
        return;
    delay=0;

    LPDIRECT3DRMFRAME scene;
    frame->GetScene( &scene );

    D3DVECTOR spinvect;
    D3DRMVectorRandom( &spinvect );
    D3DVALUE spin=D3DDivide( rand()%100+1, 200 );
    frame->SetRotation( scene,
            spinvect.x, spinvect.y, spinvect.z,
            spin );
}
```

This function appears (with a different name) in the OrbStar demo. See Chapter 5 for an explanation.

THE SHADOW DEMO RENDER FUNCTIONS

One final note on the Shadow demo. In order to implement the Render menu, the message handlers must modify the settings of two meshbuilders instead of just one. The code for the Render|Wireframe menu selection looks like this:

```
void ShadowWin::OnRenderWireframe()
{
    if (floorbuilder)
        floorbuilder->SetQuality( D3DRMRENDER_WIREFRAME );
    if (forkbuilder)
        forkbuilder->SetQuality( D3DRMRENDER_WIREFRAME );
}
```

CONCLUSION

Hopefully, you now know all you want to know about Direct3D light sources and shadows. Probably, you now know *more* than you want to know!

In Chapter 7, we'll get away from using simple animation (i.e., rotation attributes), as we study frame hierarchies, key-framing, animation sets, and animating cameras.

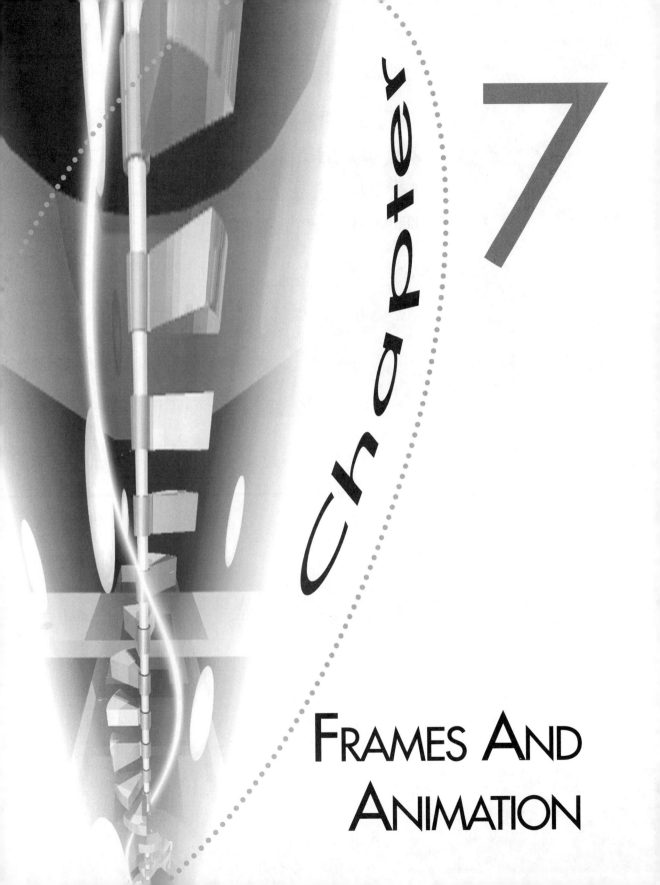

Chapter 7

7

FRAMES AND
ANIMATION

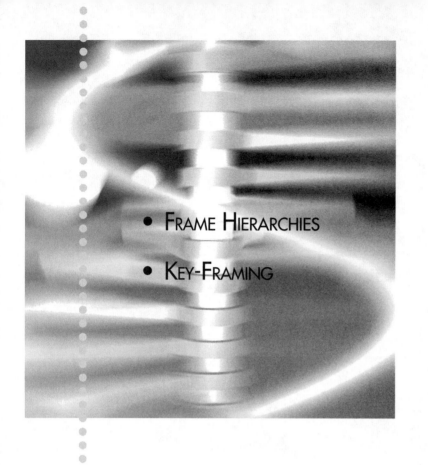

- FRAME HIERARCHIES

- KEY-FRAMING

CHAPTER
7

FRAMES AND ANIMATION

The subject of this chapter is animation. In particular, we are interested in animation techniques supported by Direct3D. As it turns out, Direct3D provides strong general-purpose animation support.

We've already seen some of Direct3D's animation support. Some of the demos in chapters 5 and 6 used the **Direct3DRMFrame** interface to animate meshes. The Decal demo (Chapter 5) and the Firefly demo (Chapter 6) use dummy frames and rotation attributes to perform animation. Other demos use callback functions to adjust a frame's position and/or orientation. Frames provide a powerful animation tool, especially when organized in hierarchies. We'll look at frame hierarchies in this chapter.

We will also explore Direct3D's key-framing support. Key-framing support is provided by the **Direct3DRMAnimation** interface and provides flexible, general purpose animation capabilities.

We'll study these demos in this chapter:

• Molecule

• Rocket

• Target

We'll use the Molecule demo to study frame hierarchies. The Rocket and Target demos provide examples of key-framing. The Target demo uses several animation techniques in addition to key-framing.

(253)

FRAME HIERARCHIES

All Direct3D scenes are constructed using frame hierarchies. The demos that we've looked at so far use simple hierarchies consisting of a single root frame and any number of child frames. Although we have been using frame hierarchies all along, it hasn't been very obvious because the hierarchies have been very simple. Figure 7.1 shows a simple frame hierarchy, typical of those used by previous demos.

The frames in Figure 7.1 are named to suggest their purpose. The hierarchy shown might appear in any application that uses two meshes, a light source, and a camera.

We have seen demos with more complicated frame hierarchies in previous chapters. The Decal and Firefly demos use dummy frames, so the frame hierarchy is slightly more complicated. The frame hierarchy used by these two demos looks like the hierarchy that appears in Figure 7.2.

In the hierarchy shown in Figure 7.2, the second mesh frame (mesh2frame) is attached to a dummy frame instead of the scene's root frame. This allows the second mesh frame to be animated either by moving the mesh2frame or the dummy frame. You may want to review the Decal and Firefly demos if you are unclear on dummy frames.

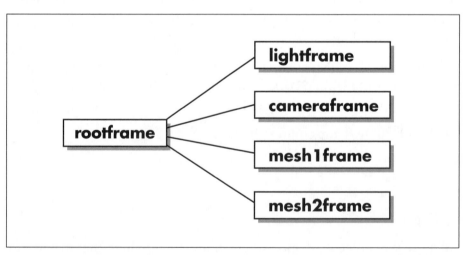

Figure 7.1
A simple frame hierarchy.

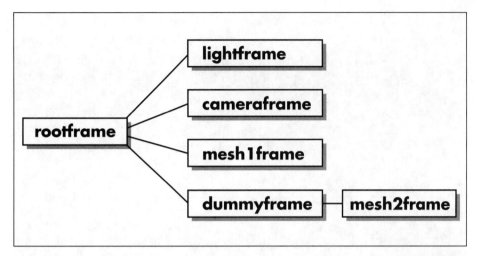

Figure 7.2
A slightly more complex frame hierarchy.

THE MOLECULE DEMO

The Molecule demo uses frame hierarchies to model theoretical molecular structures. The demo constructs a frame hierarchy and attaches spherical meshes to each frame in the hierarchy. The size and color of the attached mesh depends on the frame's location within the hierarchy. The Molecule demo provides menu commands that allow the complexity of the molecule to be adjusted. The Molecule demo appears in Figure 7.3.

The demo's Depth menu allows the depth of the frame hierarchy to be adjusted. The menu allows depths ranging from one through six. A setting of one means that the molecule will consist of just one sphere. A setting of six means that the frame hierarchy has six levels of child frames.

The Children menu allows you to specify the number of child frames. By default, each frame in the hierarchy has two children. The Children menu allows one, two, three, or four children to be specified.

These two menus allow the Molecule's frame hierarchy to be modified considerably. A depth setting of one, for example, creates a frame hierarchy with only one frame. The default setting (depth=4, children=2) produces 15 frames. The maximum setting (depth=6, children=4) produces a hierarchy with 1,365 frames.

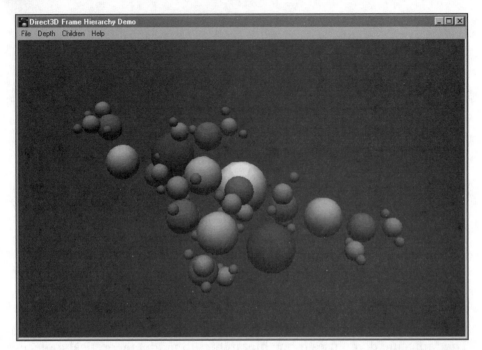

Figure 7.3
The Molecule demo.

The Molecule demo demonstrates the following techniques:

- Using the **Direct3DRMFrame** interface and recursive functions to create frame hierarchies

- Using mesh instances

- Using menu commands to adjust the frame hierarchy settings

THE MOLECULEWIN CLASS

The Molecule demo provides its functionality with the **MoleculeWin** class:

```
class MoleculeWin : public RMWin
{
public:
    MoleculeWin();
    BOOL CreateScene();
protected:
    //{{AFX_MSG(MoleculeWin)
    afx_msg void OnDepth1();
```

```
    afx_msg void OnDepth2();
    afx_msg void OnDepth3();
    afx_msg void OnDepth4();
    afx_msg void OnDepth5();
    afx_msg void OnDepth6();
    afx_msg void OnChildren1();
    afx_msg void OnChildren2();
    afx_msg void OnChildren3();
    afx_msg void OnChildren4();
    afx_msg void OnUpdateChildren1(CCmdUI* pCmdUI);
    afx_msg void OnUpdateChildren2(CCmdUI* pCmdUI);
    afx_msg void OnUpdateChildren3(CCmdUI* pCmdUI);
    afx_msg void OnUpdateChildren4(CCmdUI* pCmdUI);
    afx_msg void OnUpdateDepth1(CCmdUI* pCmdUI);
    afx_msg void OnUpdateDepth2(CCmdUI* pCmdUI);
    afx_msg void OnUpdateDepth3(CCmdUI* pCmdUI);
    afx_msg void OnUpdateDepth4(CCmdUI* pCmdUI);
    afx_msg void OnUpdateDepth5(CCmdUI* pCmdUI);
    afx_msg void OnUpdateDepth6(CCmdUI* pCmdUI);
    //}}AFX_MSG
    DECLARE_MESSAGE_MAP()
private:
    BOOL CreateHierarchy();
    BOOL CreateChildren(LPDIRECT3DRMFRAME frame, int depth);
private:
    LPDIRECT3DRMMESH mesh[MAXDEPTH];
    int curdepth;
    int numchildren;
    int framecount;
};
```

The class declares two public functions: a constructor and the **CreateScene()** function. The constructor is used to initialize the class's data members. The **CreateScene()** function constructs the demo's initial scene. We'll look at **CreateScene()** soon.

Twenty protected message-handling functions have been installed using ClassWizard. These functions provide functionality for the demo's Depth and Children menus.

Two private member functions are declared: **CreateHierarchy()** and **CreateChildren()**. The **CreateHierarchy()** function is responsible for the construction of frame hierarchies given the demo's current settings. This function is called at program startup and whenever one of the hierarchy settings is changed.

The **CreateHierarchy()** function uses the **CreateChildren()** function to create hierarchies. The **CreateChildren()** function is a recursive function that adds child frames to an existing frame.

Finally, three data members are declared:

```
LPDIRECT3DRMMESH mesh[MAXDEPTH];
int curdepth;
int numchildren;
```

The **mesh** data member is an array of pointers to the **Direct3DRMMesh** interface. We'll use this array to store a mesh for each frame depth. The demo creates six meshes—one for each possible depth. Multiple instances of each mesh are displayed when a mesh is attached to multiple frames.

The **curdepth** and **numchildren** data members store the demo's current hierarchy settings. These data members are modified by the Depth and Children menu command handler functions, and are used by the **CreateHierarchy()** and **CreateChildren()** functions. These data members are initialized by the **MoleculeWin** constructor as shown:

```
MoleculeWin::MoleculeWin()
{
    curdepth=4;
    numchildren=2;
}
```

THE MOLECULEWIN::CREATESCENE() FUNCTION

The Molecule demo's initial scene is constructed by the **CreateScene()** function. The function appears in Listing 7.1.

Listing 7.1   The MoleculeWin::CreateScene() function.

```
BOOL MoleculeWin::CreateScene()
{
    // ------- SRAND --------
    srand((unsigned)time(NULL));

    // ------- MESH --------
    D3DRMLOADRESOURCE resinfo;
    resinfo.hModule=NULL;
    resinfo.lpName=MAKEINTRESOURCE( IDR_SPHEREMESH );
```

```
resinfo.lpType="MESH";
LPDIRECT3DRMMESHBUILDER meshbuilder;
d3drm->CreateMeshBuilder( &meshbuilder );
meshbuilder->Load( &resinfo, NULL, D3DRMLOAD_FROMRESOURCE,
        NULL, NULL );

for (int i=0;i<MAXDEPTH;i++)
{
    ScaleMesh( meshbuilder, D3DVALUE(MAXDEPTH-i) );
    D3DCOLOR clr=meshcolor[i];
    D3DVALUE r=D3DRMColorGetRed( clr );
    D3DVALUE g=D3DRMColorGetGreen( clr );
    D3DVALUE b=D3DRMColorGetBlue( clr );
    meshbuilder->SetColorRGB( r, g, b );
    LPDIRECT3DRMMESH m;
    meshbuilder->CreateMesh( &m );
    mesh[i]=m;
}

meshbuilder->Release();
meshbuilder=0;

// -------- FRAME HIERARCHY ------
CreateHierarchy();

// --------DIRECTIONAL LIGHT--------
LPDIRECT3DRMLIGHT dlight;
d3drm->CreateLightRGB( D3DRMLIGHT_DIRECTIONAL,
        D3DVALUE(1.00), D3DVALUE(1.00), D3DVALUE(1.00),
        &dlight);

LPDIRECT3DRMFRAME dlightframe;
d3drm->CreateFrame( scene, &dlightframe );
dlightframe->AddLight( dlight );
dlightframe->SetOrientation( scene,
        D3DVALUE(0), D3DVALUE(-1), D3DVALUE(1),
        D3DVALUE(0), D3DVALUE(1), D3DVALUE(0));
dlight->Release();
dlight=0;
dlightframe->Release();
dlightframe=0;

//------ CAMERA----------
d3drm->CreateFrame( scene, &camera );
camera->SetPosition( scene,
        D3DVALUE(0), D3DVALUE(0), D3DVALUE(-50) );
```

```
d3drm->CreateViewport( device, camera, 0, 0,
        device->GetWidth(), device->GetHeight(),
        &viewport);

    return TRUE;
}
```

The **CreateScene()** function performs five steps:

1. Initializes a random number generator

2. Creates six meshes

3. Creates the frame hierarchy, complete with attached meshes

4. Creates a light source

5. Creates a viewport

First, the **srand()** function is called using the return value from the **time()** function as an argument. This is done to initialize the random number generator. The Molecule demo uses the **rand()** function to add random characteristics to the frame hierarchies. Because we are initializing the random generator with a value that changes each time the demo is executed, the frame hierarchy attributes (such as rotation axes and velocities) differ with each invocation of the demo.

Step 2 is the creation of six meshes. First, a spherical mesh is loaded:

```
D3DRMLOADRESOURCE resinfo;
resinfo.hModule=NULL;
resinfo.lpName=MAKEINTRESOURCE( IDR_SPHEREMESH );
resinfo.lpType="MESH";
LPDIRECT3DRMMESHBUILDER meshbuilder;
d3drm->CreateMeshBuilder( &meshbuilder );
meshbuilder->Load( &resinfo, NULL, D3DRMLOAD_FROMRESOURCE,
        NULL, NULL );
```

An instance of **Direct3DRMMeshBuilder** is used to load the mesh from the program's resources. The **meshbuilder** pointer will be used to access the new mesh. Next, six instances of **Direct3DRMMesh** are created:

```
for (int i=0;i<MAXDEPTH;i++)
{
    ScaleMesh( meshbuilder, D3DVALUE(MAXDEPTH-i) );
```

```
    D3DCOLOR clr=meshcolor[i];
    D3DVALUE r=D3DRMColorGetRed( clr );
    D3DVALUE g=D3DRMColorGetGreen( clr );
    D3DVALUE b=D3DRMColorGetBlue( clr );
    meshbuilder->SetColorRGB( r, g, b );
    meshbuilder->CreateMesh( &mesh[i] );
}
```

A loop is used to create the meshes. The scale and color of the mesh depends on the iteration of the loop. The **meshcolor** array contains the colors that are to be used for each mesh. Once the color has been assigned, an instance of the **Direct3DRMMesh** interface is created using the **Direct3DRMMeshBuilder CreateMesh()** function.

Step 3 is the creation of the frame hierarchy:

```
CreateHierarchy();
```

The **CreateHierarchy()** function constructs a frame hierarchy based on the **curdepth** and **numchildren** data members. These two data members are given default settings by the **MoleculeWin** constructor but can be modified from the Depth and Children menus.

Steps 4 and 5 create a light source and a viewport. We'll omit discussion of these steps because light sources are covered in Chapter 6 and the viewport creation step is described in Chapters 4 and 9.

THE MOLECULEWIN::CREATEHIERARCHY() FUNCTION

The **CreateHierarchy()** function is responsible for creating the frame hierarchy. The function looks like this:

```
BOOL MoleculeWin::CreateHierarchy()
{
    static LPDIRECT3DRMFRAME mainframe;
    if (mainframe)
    {
        scene->DeleteChild( mainframe );
        mainframe->Release();
    }
    d3drm->CreateFrame( scene, &mainframe );
```

```
    for (int i=0;i<numchildren;i++)
        CreateChildren( mainframe, curdepth );

    return TRUE;
}
```

The function uses a static frame pointer (**mainframe**) to access the root frame of the frame hierarchy. This frame should not be confused with the scene's root frame (**scene**). The **scene** frame is the root for the entire scene. The **mainframe** frame is the root of the frame hierarchy.

If it has been initialized, the **mainframe** pointer is removed from the scene with the **Direct3DRMFrame DeleteChild()** function. This is done to remove previous frame hierarchies from the scene. The **mainframe** pointer is initialized using the **Direct3DRM CreateFrame()** function. The **scene** pointer is used as the first **CreateFrame()** argument, indicating the new frame is a child of the **scene** frame.

A loop is then used to invoke the **CreateChildren()** function. The number of loop iterations depends on the **numchildren** data member. The **CreateChildren()** function takes two arguments: a pointer to the frame that is to be given child frames, and an integer indicating the desired depth of the frame hierarchy. This integer is important because it determines at which point the recursive **CreateChildren()** function will cease to invoke itself.

THE MOLECULEWIN::CREATECHILDREN() FUNCTION

The **CreateChildren()** function assigns rotation attributes, attaches meshes, and creates child frames:

```
BOOL MoleculeWin::CreateChildren(LPDIRECT3DRMFRAME frame, int depth)
{
    LPDIRECT3DRMFRAME parent;
    frame->GetParent( &parent );

    D3DVECTOR vector;
    D3DRMVectorRandom( &vector );
    frame->SetRotation( parent,
            vector.x, vector.y, vector.z ,
            D3DVALUE(rand()%100)/D3DVALUE(1000)+D3DVALUE(.1) );
    frame->AddVisual( mesh[curdepth-depth] );
```

```
    if (depth>1)
    {
        LPDIRECT3DRMFRAME child;
        d3drm->CreateFrame( frame, &child );

        static int count;
        count++;
        D3DVALUE trans=distance[curdepth-depth];
        D3DVALUE smalltrans=trans/D3DVALUE(2);
        D3DVALUE xtrans=(count%2) ? trans : -trans;
        D3DVALUE ytrans=(rand()%2) ? smalltrans : -smalltrans;
        D3DVALUE ztrans=(rand()%2) ? smalltrans : -smalltrans;
        child->SetPosition( frame, xtrans, ytrans, ztrans );

        for (int i=0;i<numchildren;i++)
            CreateChildren( child, depth-1 );
    }
    return TRUE;
}
```

The **CreateChildren()** function first assigns a rotation attribute to the supplied frame. In order for such an attribute to be assigned, a pointer to the frame's parent frame must be retrieved. The **Direct3DRMFrame GetParent()** function is used for this purpose. Once the frame's parent is known, a rotation attribute is calculated and applied:

```
D3DVECTOR vector;
D3DRMVectorRandom( &vector );
frame->SetRotation( parent,
        vector.x, vector.y, vector.z ,
        D3DVALUE(rand()%100)/D3DVALUE(1000)+D3DVALUE(.1) );
```

Notice that the **parent** frame is used as the first argument to the **SetRotation()** function. First, however, the **D3DRMVectorRandom()** function is used to calculate a random vector. The vector is used to supply three of the **SetRotation()** function arguments. The last **SetRotation()** argument, which indicates the rotation velocity, is calculated with the **rand()** function. The equation used to calculate the velocity assures a randomly selected, slow-to-medium rotation speed.

Next, the appropriate mesh is attached to the frame:

```
frame->AddVisual( mesh[curdepth-depth] );
```

The mesh is selected based on the depth of the current frame. The remainder of the **CreateChildren()** function looks like this:

```
if (depth>1)
{
    LPDIRECT3DRMFRAME child;
    d3drm->CreateFrame( frame, &child );

    static int count;
    count++;
    D3DVALUE trans=distance[curdepth-depth];
    D3DVALUE smalltrans=trans/D3DVALUE(2);
    D3DVALUE xtrans=(count%2) ? trans : -trans;
    D3DVALUE ytrans=(rand()%2) ? smalltrans : -smalltrans;
    D3DVALUE ztrans=(rand()%2) ? smalltrans : -smalltrans;
    child->SetPosition( frame, xtrans, ytrans, ztrans );

    for (int i=0;i<numchildren;i++)
        CreateChildren( child, depth-1 );
}
```

Execution of this portion of the function depends on the **depth** parameter. If **depth** is greater than one, the code is executed. The code creates a new child frame with the **Direct3DRM CreateFrame()** function. The new frame is positioned on a semi-random basis. A static counter variable is used to further discourage predictable results. The newly calculated position is applied using the **SetPosition()** function.

Finally, the **CreateChildren()** function calls itself. A loop is used to invoke the function based on the number of child frames that should be attached. Notice that the second **CreateChildren()** argument is **depth**–1. Once the **depth** parameter reaches one, no further child frames are created. Failure to subtract 1 from the depth argument would result in a function that calls itself indefinitely.

THE MOLECULEWIN DEPTH FUNCTIONS

The Molecule demo's Depth menu offers six different depth settings. Each setting is implemented with two functions. The functions for the first depth setting (depth=1) look like this:

```
void MoleculeWin::OnDepth1()
{
```

```
    curdepth=1;
    CreateHierarchy();
}

void MoleculeWin::OnUpdateDepth1(CCmdUI* pCmdUI)
{
    pCmdUI->SetCheck( curdepth==1 );
}
```

The first function, **OnDepth1()**, is called when the first Depth menu entry is selected. It assigns 1 to the **curdepth** data member and rebuilds the frame hierarchy with a call to the **CreateHierarchy()** function.

The second function, **OnUpdateDepth1()**, is called by MFC before the Depth menu is displayed. The **SetCheck()** function is used to indicate if a check mark should appear next to the menu entry.

The remaining 10 Depth menu functions are virtually identical to the these functions. The only difference is the value used to manipulate the **curdepth** data member.

THE MOLECULEWIN CHILDREN FUNCTIONS

The Children menu offers four settings, ranging from one to four. Like the Depth menu functions, each menu entry is implemented with two functions. The functions for the first Children menu entry (children=1) look like this:

```
void MoleculeWin::OnChildren1()
{
    numchildren=1;
    CreateHierarchy();
}

void MoleculeWin::OnUpdateChildren1(CCmdUI* pCmdUI)
{
    pCmdUI->SetCheck( numchildren==1 );
}
```

These functions look similar to the Depth menu functions. The only difference is that the **numchildren** data member is used instead of the **curdepth** data member.

KEY-FRAMING

Key-framing is an animation technique where an animation sequence is defined in terms of keys. Each key represents a position and orientation that will be applied to a given object at a specific time within the animation. The position and orientation of the object is determined throughout the animation sequence based on these keys.

It is perhaps unfortunate that Direct3D uses the term *frame*. Frames in Direct3D refer to the **Direct3DRMFrame** interface. Key-framing uses the term frame in the traditional sense (as in a "frame" of animation). Bear in mind that these two uses are entirely different. Key-framing theory is discussed in Chapter 2.

Direct3D supports key-framing with the **Direct3DRMAnimation** interface. The interface allows animation sequences to be defined and controlled using these member functions:

- AddPositionKey()

- AddRotateKey()

- AddScaleKey()

- SetTime()

The **AddPositionKey()**, **AddRotateKey()**, and **AddScaleKey()** functions are used to add key frames to the animation. These three functions all take a time index as the first argument. The time index indicates the time within the animation sequence where the given key will take effect. The **SetTime()** function is used to specify the current time within the animation sequence.

The **Direct3DRMAnimation** interface determines an object's location throughout the animation sequence by interpolating between key frames. This calculation can be performed on a linear or spline basis. Linear animation means that the shortest possible path between two key frames is used. Spline-based animation uses splines, or curves, to calculate animation paths. Spline-based animation is usually more realistic than linear animation.

The **Direct3DRMAnimation** interface is designed primarily to animate **Direct3DRMFrame** instances. It is not difficult, however, to use the interface for general purpose animation. In Chapter 8, you will learn how **Direct3DRMAnimation** can be used to perform vertex animation. In Chapter 9, viewport settings are animated using **Direct3DRMAnimation**. In this chapter, however, we will be using the animation interface to animate frames.

THE ROCKET DEMO

The Rocket demo uses key-framing to animate a rocket. The animation sequence is defined with just a few key frames, and the remainder of the sequence is calculated by an instance of the **Direct3DRMAnimation** interface. The demo provides an Animation menu that allows the animation settings to be adjusted at run-time. The menu supports two commands: Linear and Spline. A Speed menu is also provided. The Speed menu allows the speed of the animation sequence to be adjusted.

The Rocket demo appears in Figure 7.4.

Figure 7.4
The Rocket demo.

The Rocket demo demonstrates the following techniques:

- Using the **Direct3DRMAnimation** interface to create and execute key-framed animation sequences

- Applying a texture to a mesh using the mesh's texture setting (instead of using a texture wrap)

- Using a callback function to update an animation sequence

THE ROCKETWIN CLASS

The Rocket demo provides its functionality with the **RocketWin** class:

```
class RocketWin : public RMWin
{
public:
    RocketWin();
    BOOL CreateScene();
protected:
    //{{AFX_MSG(RocketWin)
    afx_msg void OnRenderWireframe();
    afx_msg void OnRenderFlat();
    afx_msg void OnRenderGouraud();
    afx_msg void OnUpdateRenderFlat(CCmdUI* pCmdUI);
    afx_msg void OnUpdateRenderGouraud(CCmdUI* pCmdUI);
    afx_msg void OnUpdateRenderWireframe(CCmdUI* pCmdUI);
    afx_msg void OnAnimationLinear();
    afx_msg void OnAnimationSpline();
    afx_msg void OnUpdateAnimationLinear(CCmdUI* pCmdUI);
    afx_msg void OnUpdateAnimationSpline(CCmdUI* pCmdUI);
    afx_msg void OnSpeedFast();
    afx_msg void OnSpeedMedium();
    afx_msg void OnSpeedSlow();
    afx_msg void OnUpdateSpeedFast(CCmdUI* pCmdUI);
    afx_msg void OnUpdateSpeedMedium(CCmdUI* pCmdUI);
    afx_msg void OnUpdateSpeedSlow(CCmdUI* pCmdUI);
    //}}AFX_MSG
    DECLARE_MESSAGE_MAP()
private:
    static void UpdateScene(LPDIRECT3DRMFRAME, void*, D3DVALUE);
    static HRESULT LoadTexture(char*, void*, LPDIRECT3DRMTEXTURE*);
private:
    LPDIRECT3DRMMESHBUILDER meshbuilder;
    LPDIRECT3DRMANIMATION animation;
    static D3DVALUE speed;
};
```

Two public member functions are declared: a constructor and **CreateScene**(). The constructor initializes the class's data members to zero. The **CreateScene**() function constructs the demo's scene, including the animation sequence.

Sixteen protected message handling functions are declared. The first six provide the demo's Render menu functionality. The following four functions provide the demo's Animation menu support. The last six functions provide support for the Speed menu.

Two private member functions are declared: **UpdateScene**() and **LoadTexture**(). Both of these functions are callback functions. The **UpdateScene**() function is used to update the animation sequence. The **LoadTexture**() function is used to load and attach a texture to the rocket mesh.

Three data members are declared:

```
LPDIRECT3DRMMESHBUILDER meshbuilder;
LPDIRECT3DRMANIMATION animation;
static D3DVALUE speed;
```

The **meshbuilder** pointer is used to load and modify the rocket mesh. This pointer is used by the **CreateScene**() function and the Render menu functions. The **animation** pointer is used to manipulate the **Direct3DRMAnimation** object. The **speed** data member is used to control the rate that the animation sequence is executed.

THE ROCKETWIN::CREATESCENE() FUNCTION

The Rocket demo **CreateScene**() function appears in Listing 7.2.

Listing 7.2   The RocketWin::CreateScene() function.

```
BOOL RocketWin::CreateScene()
{
    //-------- MESH ----------
    D3DRMLOADRESOURCE resinfo;
    resinfo.hModule=NULL;
    resinfo.lpName=MAKEINTRESOURCE( IDR_ROCKETMESH );
    resinfo.lpType="MESH";
    d3drm->CreateMeshBuilder( &meshbuilder );
```

```
meshbuilder->Load( &resinfo, NULL, D3DRMLOAD_FROMRESOURCE,
        LoadTexture, NULL );
ScaleMesh( meshbuilder, D3DVALUE(10) );

//-------- ANIMATION --------
d3drm->CreateAnimation( &animation );
for (int i=0; i<11; i++)
{
    D3DRMQUATERNION    quat;
    D3DRMQuaternionFromRotation( &quat, &vect[i], rot[i] );
    animation->AddRotateKey( D3DVALUE(i), &quat );
    animation->AddPositionKey( D3DVALUE(i),
            trans[i].x, trans[i].y, trans[i].z  );
}
OnAnimationLinear();

//-------- MESH FRAME ------
LPDIRECT3DRMFRAME meshframe;
d3drm->CreateFrame( scene, &meshframe );
meshframe->AddVisual( meshbuilder );
meshframe->AddMoveCallback( UpdateScene, animation );
animation->SetFrame( meshframe );
meshframe->Release();
meshframe=0;

//-------- LIGHTS --------
LPDIRECT3DRMLIGHT dlight;
LPDIRECT3DRMLIGHT alight;
d3drm->CreateLightRGB(D3DRMLIGHT_AMBIENT,
        D3DVALUE(0.5),D3DVALUE(0.5), D3DVALUE(0.5),
        &alight);
d3drm->CreateLightRGB(D3DRMLIGHT_DIRECTIONAL,
        D3DVALUE(1.0),D3DVALUE(1.0), D3DVALUE(1.0),
        &dlight);

LPDIRECT3DRMFRAME lightframe;
d3drm->CreateFrame( scene, &lightframe );
lightframe->SetOrientation( scene,
        D3DVALUE(0), D3DVALUE(-2), D3DVALUE(1),
        D3DVALUE(0), D3DVALUE(1), D3DVALUE(0) );
lightframe->AddLight( dlight );
lightframe->AddLight( alight );

dlight->Release();
dlight=0;
alight->Release();
```

```
alight=0;
lightframe->Release();
lightframe=0;

//-------- VIEWPORT --------
d3drm->CreateFrame( scene, &camera );
camera->SetPosition(scene,
        D3DVALUE(0), D3DVALUE(0), D3DVALUE(-50.0));
d3drm->CreateViewport(device, camera,
        0, 0,
        device->GetWidth(), device->GetHeight(),
        &viewport);

return TRUE;
}
```

The **CreateScene()** function performs five steps:

1. Creates a mesh

2. Creates an animation sequence

3. Creates a frame for mesh placement and installs an update callback

4. Creates two light sources

5. Creates a viewport

The first step is the creation of a mesh:

```
D3DRMLOADRESOURCE resinfo;
resinfo.hModule=NULL;
resinfo.lpName=MAKEINTRESOURCE( IDR_ROCKETMESH );
resinfo.lpType="MESH";
d3drm->CreateMeshBuilder( &meshbuilder );
meshbuilder->Load( &resinfo, NULL, D3DRMLOAD_FROMRESOURCE,
    LoadTexture, NULL );
ScaleMesh( meshbuilder, D3DVALUE(10) );
```

The mesh is loaded from the program's resources using the
Direct3DRMMeshBuilder interface. With one exception, this code looks
like the mesh loading code in all of the other demos. The difference is
that we are using a callback function to apply a texture to the mesh. The
fourth **Direct3DRMMeshBuilder Load()** argument is a pointer to an optional callback function for loading textures. Normally, we use zero for this

argument, but, in the interest of variety, we will use the **LoadTexture()** function as a callback. The **LoadTexture()** function looks like this:

```
HRESULT RocketWin::LoadTexture(char*, void*,
                            LPDIRECT3DRMTEXTURE* texture)
{
    HRSRC id = FindResource( NULL, MAKEINTRESOURCE(IDR_ROCKETTEXTURE),
            "TEXTURE" );
    RMWin::d3drm->LoadTextureFromResource( id, texture );
    return D3DRM_OK;
}
```

The function is provided with a pointer to the **Direct3DRMTexture** interface. All we have to do is create the texture using the supplied pointer. Direct3D will apply the texture to the mesh automatically. Notice that we are not using a texture wrap to apply the texture. This is because we are using the texture mapping data that is saved in the mesh file.

 Texture mapping the easy way

Texture mapping data can be stored in mesh files by applying texture mapping attributes to a mesh with a modeling tool, such as 3D Studio. By default, texture mapping data is imported by the DirectX CONV3DS utility. This technique is an alternative to the methods discussed in Chapter 5.

Notice also that the first callback parameter is a string pointer. This pointer indicates the name of the texture that is stored in the mesh file. This parameter is useful because it allows the same callback function to be used for multiple meshes. In our case, we are not using the texture name because we have only one texture to apply.

Returning to the **CreateScene()** function, Step 2 is the creation of an animation sequence:

```
d3drm->CreateAnimation( &animation );
for (int i=0; i<11; i++)
{
    D3DRMQUATERNION quat;
    D3DRMQuaternionFromRotation( &quat, &vect[i], rot[i] );
```

```
    animation->AddRotateKey( D3DVALUE(i), &quat );
    animation->AddPositionKey( D3DVALUE(i),
            trans[i].x, trans[i].y, trans[i].z   );
}
OnAnimationLinear();
```

First, the **Direct3DRM CreateAnimation()** function is used to initialize an instance of the **Direct3DRMAnimation** interface. A loop is then used to add keys to the animation. Two types of keys are added for each loop iteration: a rotate key and a position key. The rotate keys specify how our animated rocket will be oriented throughout the animation sequence. The position keys indicate where the rocket will be located. In order to understand the purpose of these keys, we will need to look at the key data.

The rotation key data is stored in two arrays: **vect** and **rot**. The **vect** array contains vectors that indicate the axis of rotation, and the **rot** array indicates rotation amounts (in radians). The two arrays are initialized as follows:

```
D3DVECTOR vect[]=    // rotation vector for each key frame
{
  { D3DVALUE(1), D3DVALUE(0), D3DVALUE(0) },
  { D3DVALUE(1), D3DVALUE(0), D3DVALUE(0) },
  { D3DVALUE(1), D3DVALUE(0), D3DVALUE(0) },
  { D3DVALUE(1), D3DVALUE(0), D3DVALUE(0) },
  { D3DVALUE(0), D3DVALUE(1), D3DVALUE(0) },
  { D3DVALUE(1), D3DVALUE(0), D3DVALUE(0) },
  { D3DVALUE(0), D3DVALUE(1), D3DVALUE(0) },
  { D3DVALUE(1), D3DVALUE(0), D3DVALUE(0) },
  { D3DVALUE(0), D3DVALUE(1), D3DVALUE(0) },
  { D3DVALUE(1), D3DVALUE(0), D3DVALUE(0) },
  { D3DVALUE(1), D3DVALUE(0), D3DVALUE(0) },
};

const D3DVALUE rot[]= // object rotation at each key frame
{
    PI/2,
    PI,
    -(PI/2),
    PI,
    PI/2,
    PI,
    -(PI/2),
    -PI,
```

```
    PI/2,
    PI,
    PI/2,
};
```

The **vect** array is initialized with sets of X, Y, and Z values. The three values form a vector that determines an axis of rotation. The **rot** array uses the **PI** constant to indicate how much the object should be rotated around the given axis. A rotation of PI/2 is equivalent to 180 degrees. Using PI rotates by 90 degrees. The rotation direction is reversed with negative values.

Let's look again at the loop contents:

```
D3DRMQUATERNION quat;
D3DRMQuaternionFromRotation( &quat, &vect[i], rot[i] );
animation->AddRotateKey( D3DVALUE(i), &quat );
animation->AddPositionKey( D3DVALUE(i),
        trans[i].x, trans[i].y, trans[i].z  );
```

The **Direct3DRMAnimation AddRotateKey()** function accepts quaternions. A *quaternion* is a structure that stores both a rotation vector and a rotation velocity. We use the **D3DRMQuaternionFromRotation()** function to convert our vector and rotation velocity into a quaternion. The address of the new quaternion is then used as the second argument to the **AddRotateKey()**. The first **AddRotateKey()** argument is a time index for the new key.

The **AddPositionKey()** function is a little easier to use. Four arguments are expected: a time index, and three values that indicate a position. Our code uses the **trans** array to indicate the animation sequence positions. The **trans** array is defined like this:

```
const D3DVECTOR trans[]=  // object location for each key frame
{
    { D3DVALUE(0), D3DVALUE(0), FARLIM },
    { XOUTLIM,     D3DVALUE(0), CLOSELIM },
    { D3DVALUE(0), D3DVALUE(0), FARLIM },
    { -XOUTLIM,    D3DVALUE(0), CLOSELIM },
    { D3DVALUE(0), D3DVALUE(0), FARLIM },
    { D3DVALUE(0), -YOUTLIM,    CLOSELIM },
    { D3DVALUE(0), D3DVALUE(0), FARLIM },
    { D3DVALUE(0), YOUTLIM,     CLOSELIM },
    { D3DVALUE(0), D3DVALUE(0), FARLIM },
```

```
      { D3DVALUE(0), D3DVALUE(0), CLOSELIM-3 },
      { D3DVALUE(0), D3DVALUE(0), FARLIM },
};
```

The **XOUTLIM, YOUTLIM, FARLIM,** and **CLOSELIM** constants indicate values that were arrived at via trial and error. The **XOUTLIM** constant indicates how far to the left and right the rocket travels. The **YOUTLIM** constant controls the rocket's vertical limits. The **FARLIM** and **CLOSELIM** constants control the rocket's Z axis movement.

Step 3 of the **CreateScene()** function is the creation of a frame for the rocket mesh:

```
LPDIRECT3DRMFRAME meshframe;
d3drm->CreateFrame( scene, &meshframe );
meshframe->AddVisual( meshbuilder );
meshframe->AddMoveCallback( UpdateScene, animation );
animation->SetFrame( meshframe );
meshframe->Release();
meshframe=0;
```

A new frame is created with the **Direct3DRM CreateFrame()** function. The previously created rocket mesh is attached to the frame using the **Direct3DRMFrame AddVisual()** function.

The **UpdateScene()** callback function is installed with the **AddMoveCallback()** function. The callback will be used to update the animation sequence during the demo's operation. Notice that the **animation** pointer is used as the second argument. Any value used as the second **AddMoveCallback()** argument is passed to the callback function each time the callback function is invoked. Sending a pointer to the animation object will allow our callback function to control the animation sequence (remember, callback functions are **static,** so they do not enjoy automatic access to data members).

Next, the **Direct3DRMAnimation SetFrame()** function is used to attach the frame to the **Direct3DRMAnimation** object that was initialized in Step 2. Now the frame's location, rotation, and scale will be controlled by the animation object.

In steps 4 and 5, **CreateScene()** creates light sources and a viewport. We'll skip discussion of these steps so that we can study the **UpdateScene()** callback function.

THE ROCKETWIN::UPDATESCENE() FUNCTION

The **UpdateScene()** callback function is responsible for updating the animation sequence. The function is defined like this:

```
void RocketWin::UpdateScene(LPDIRECT3DRMFRAME, void* p, D3DVALUE)
{
    LPDIRECT3DRMANIMATION animation=(LPDIRECT3DRMANIMATION)p;
    static D3DVALUE time;
    time+=speed;
    animation->SetTime( time );
}
```

First, the function initializes a pointer to the **Direct3DRMAnimation** interface. Recall that the animation pointer was passed to the **AddMoveCallback()** function. This means that Direct3D is passing the pointer's value to our callback function, so the **UpdateScene()** function's second parameter has the same value as the pointer. Before we can use it, however, we must cast it to the correct type. The local **animation** pointer is initialized using the function's second parameter and a type cast.

Next, a static counter variable, **time,** is incremented. The increment value is stored in the static **speed** variable. As you'll see later, the speed value can be changed from the demo's Speed menu. This allows the speed of the animation sequence to be changed easily.

The **Direct3DRMAnimation SetTime()** function is used to install a new time index. The time index controls the current state of the animation sequence. This function call causes the animation object to calculate a new position and rotation based on the new time index. The frame attached to the animation sequence is then repositioned according to the results. Because our rocket mesh is attached to the frame, the **SetTime()** function call repositions the rocket mesh.

THE ROCKETWIN ANIMATION FUNCTIONS

The Rocket demo's Animation menu supports two commands: Linear and Spline. Each of these commands is implemented with two functions. The four functions that implement the Animation menu commands look like this:

```
void RocketWin::OnAnimationLinear()
{
    animation->SetOptions( D3DRMANIMATION_LINEARPOSITION |
            D3DRMANIMATION_CLOSED |
            D3DRMANIMATION_POSITION |
            D3DRMANIMATION_SCALEANDROTATION );
}

void RocketWin::OnAnimationSpline()
{
    animation->SetOptions( D3DRMANIMATION_SPLINEPOSITION |
            D3DRMANIMATION_CLOSED |
            D3DRMANIMATION_POSITION |
            D3DRMANIMATION_SCALEANDROTATION );
}

void RocketWin::OnUpdateAnimationLinear(CCmdUI* pCmdUI)
{
    D3DRMANIMATIONOPTIONS options;
    options = animation->GetOptions();
    pCmdUI->SetCheck( options & D3DRMANIMATION_LINEARPOSITION );
}

void RocketWin::OnUpdateAnimationSpline(CCmdUI* pCmdUI)
{
    D3DRMANIMATIONOPTIONS options;
    options = animation->GetOptions();
    pCmdUI->SetCheck( options & D3DRMANIMATION_SPLINEPOSITION );
}
```

The first two functions, **OnAnimationLinear()** and **OnAnimationSpline()**, use the **Direct3DRMAnimation SetOptions()** function to specify a set of flags. The flags used by the two functions differ by one. The **OnAnimationLinear()** function uses the **D3DRMANIMATION_LINEARPOSITION** flag, and the **OnAnimationSpline()** function uses the **D3DRMANIMATION_SPLINE-POSITION** flag.

The **D3DRMANIMATION_CLOSED** flag indicates a closed animation sequence (as opposed to an open animation sequence). A closed animation sequence means we can use a continuously increasing time index value with the **SetTime()** function. As the time index increases, the animation sequence is executed repeatedly.

The **D3DRMANIMATION_POSITION** flag indicates that we are interested in the animation's positional output. The **D3DRMANIMATION_SCALE-ANDROTATION** flag indicates that we want scale and rotational output as well.

The **OnUpdateAnimationLinear()** and **OnUpdateAnimationSpline()** functions use the **Direct3DRMAnimation GetOptions()** function to retrieve the animation's current settings. The **GetOptions()** return value is used to check if the particular animation mode is in effect. If so, the menu check-mark is enabled.

THE ROCKETWIN SPEED FUNCTIONS

The Rocket demo provides a Speed menu that allows three speed settings: Fast, Medium, and Slow. The two functions that implement the Speed|Fast menu command look like this:

```
void RocketWin::OnSpeedFast()
{
    speed=fastspeed;
}

void RocketWin::OnUpdateSpeedFast(CCmdUI* pCmdUI)
{
    pCmdUI->SetCheck( speed==fastspeed);
}
```

These functions simply use the **fastspeed** constant to assign and inspect the **speed** data member. The Speed menu functions use these constants to control the animation sequence speed:

```
const D3DVALUE fastspeed=D3DVALUE(0.026);
const D3DVALUE mediumspeed=D3DVALUE(0.013);
const D3DVALUE slowspeed=D3DVALUE(0.007);
```

The larger the increment, the faster the animation sequence appears. The **slowspeed** constant indicates a very small value, resulting in slow, smooth animation.

MORE ANIMATION

As I mentioned at the beginning of this chapter, animation is a large topic. We'll close this chapter by presenting one more demo. The Target demo, unlike the other demos in this book, is not designed to showcase any one particular technique or functionality. The Target demo uses three forms of animation.

THE TARGET DEMO

The Target demo creates a scene in which a bay of rockets or missiles follow a target. The target's movement is dictated by an animation sequence, much in the same way that the rocket mesh in the Rocket demo is animated. Each missile is animated. The missiles follow the target's movement throughout the animation sequence. The Target demo also uses an animated camera. The camera orbits the scene, always looking toward the missiles. The Target demo appears in Figure 7.5.

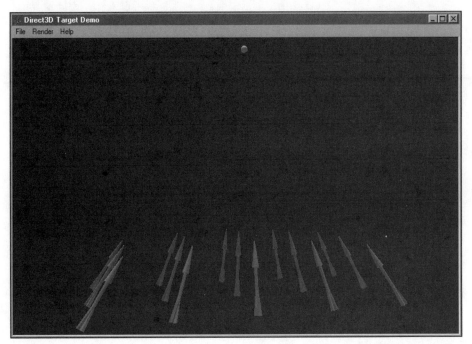

Figure 7.5
The Target demo.

The Target demo demonstrates the following techniques:

- Using the **Direct3DRMFrame LookAt()** function to adjust frame orientation

- Using the **Direct3DRMAnimation** interface to create and execute an animation sequence

- Animating a camera with a dummy frame

- Using mesh instances

We'll talk about each of these techniques as we talk about the Target demo code.

THE TARGETWIN CLASS

The Target demo provides its functionality with the **TargetWin** class:

```
class TargetWin : public RMWin
{
public:
    TargetWin();
    BOOL CreateScene();
protected:
    //{{AFX_MSG(TargetWin)
    afx_msg void OnRenderWireframe();
    afx_msg void OnRenderFlat();
    afx_msg void OnRenderGouraud();
    afx_msg void OnUpdateRenderFlat(CCmdUI* pCmdUI);
    afx_msg void OnUpdateRenderGouraud(CCmdUI* pCmdUI);
    afx_msg void OnUpdateRenderWireframe(CCmdUI* pCmdUI);
    //}}AFX_MSG
    DECLARE_MESSAGE_MAP()
private:
    static void OrientFrame(LPDIRECT3DRMFRAME frame, void*, D3DVALUE);
    static void MoveTarget(LPDIRECT3DRMFRAME frame, void*, D3DVALUE);
private:
    LPDIRECT3DRMMESHBUILDER meshbuilder;
};
```

Two public member functions are declared: a constructor and **CreateScene()**. The constructor initializes the class's single data member. The **CreateScene()** function constructs the demo's scene.

Six protected member functions are declared. These functions provide support for the demo's Render menu.

Two private callback functions are declared: **OrientFrame**() and **MoveTarget**(). The **OrientFrame**() function is used to position each missile to point toward the target. The **MoveTarget**() function is used to updated the target's position.

Finally, a single private data member is declared. The **meshbuilder** pointer is used to load the mesh that represents the demo's missiles. This data member is used both by the **CreateScene**() function and the Render menu functions.

THE TARGETWIN::CREATESCENE() FUNCTION

The Target demo **CreateScene**() function appears in Listing 7.3.

Listing 7.3   The TargetWin::CreateScene() function.

```
BOOL TargetWin::CreateScene()
{
    // ------- TARGET MESH --------
    D3DRMLOADRESOURCE resinfo;
    resinfo.hModule=NULL;
    resinfo.lpName=MAKEINTRESOURCE( IDR_SPHEREMESH );
    resinfo.lpType="MESH";
    LPDIRECT3DRMMESHBUILDER targetbuilder;
    d3drm->CreateMeshBuilder( &targetbuilder );
    targetbuilder->Load( &resinfo, NULL, D3DRMLOAD_FROMRESOURCE,
            NULL, NULL );
    ScaleMesh( targetbuilder, D3DVALUE(.75) );

    // --------- TARGET ANIMATION ----------
    LPDIRECT3DRMANIMATION animation;
    d3drm->CreateAnimation( &animation );
    animation->SetOptions(  D3DRMANIMATION_SPLINEPOSITION |
            D3DRMANIMATION_CLOSED |
            D3DRMANIMATION_POSITION );
    animation->AddPositionKey( D3DVALUE(0),
            D3DVALUE(-20), D3DVALUE(0), D3DVALUE(-20) );
    animation->AddPositionKey( D3DVALUE(12),
            D3DVALUE(0), D3DVALUE(15), D3DVALUE(0) );
    animation->AddPositionKey( D3DVALUE(24),
            D3DVALUE(20), D3DVALUE(0), D3DVALUE(-20) );
    animation->AddPositionKey( D3DVALUE(35),
            D3DVALUE(0), D3DVALUE(0), D3DVALUE(0) );
```

```
animation->AddPositionKey( D3DVALUE(49),
        D3DVALUE(20), D3DVALUE(0), D3DVALUE(20) );
animation->AddPositionKey( D3DVALUE(65),
        D3DVALUE(0), D3DVALUE(15), D3DVALUE(0) );
animation->AddPositionKey( D3DVALUE(74),
        D3DVALUE(-20), D3DVALUE(0), D3DVALUE(20) );
animation->AddPositionKey( D3DVALUE(85),
        D3DVALUE(0), D3DVALUE(0), D3DVALUE(0) );
animation->AddPositionKey( D3DVALUE(99),
        D3DVALUE(-20), D3DVALUE(0), D3DVALUE(-20) );

// ---------- TARGET FRAME --------
LPDIRECT3DRMFRAME targetframe;
d3drm->CreateFrame( scene, &targetframe );
animation->SetFrame( targetframe );
targetframe->AddVisual( targetbuilder );
targetframe->AddMoveCallback( MoveTarget, animation );

targetbuilder->Release();
targetbuilder=0;

// ------- MISSILE MESH --------
resinfo.hModule=NULL;
resinfo.lpName=MAKEINTRESOURCE( IDR_MISSLEMESH );
resinfo.lpType="MESH";
d3drm->CreateMeshBuilder( &meshbuilder );
meshbuilder->Load( &resinfo, NULL, D3DRMLOAD_FROMRESOURCE,
        NULL, NULL );
meshbuilder->SetColorRGB(
        D3DVALUE(.67), D3DVALUE(.82), D3DVALUE(.94) );
meshbuilder->SetQuality( D3DRMRENDER_FLAT );
ScaleMesh( meshbuilder, D3DVALUE(7) );

// ------- MISSILE FRAMES ------
for (int i=0;i<5;i++)
{
    for (int j=0;j<3;j++)
    {
        LPDIRECT3DRMFRAME meshframe;
        d3drm->CreateFrame( scene, &meshframe );

        meshframe->SetPosition( scene,
                D3DVALUE((i-2)*8),
                D3DVALUE(-12),
                D3DVALUE((j-1)*8) );
        meshframe->AddVisual( meshbuilder );
```

```
        meshframe->AddMoveCallback( OrientFrame, targetframe );

        meshframe->Release();
        meshframe=0;
    }
}

// --------DIRECTIONAL LIGHT--------
LPDIRECT3DRMLIGHT dlight;
d3drm->CreateLightRGB( D3DRMLIGHT_DIRECTIONAL,
        D3DVALUE(1.00), D3DVALUE(1.00), D3DVALUE(1.00),
        &dlight );
LPDIRECT3DRMLIGHT alight;
d3drm->CreateLightRGB( D3DRMLIGHT_AMBIENT,
        D3DVALUE(0.50), D3DVALUE(0.50), D3DVALUE(0.50),
        &alight );


LPDIRECT3DRMFRAME lightframe;
d3drm->CreateFrame( scene, &lightframe );
lightframe->AddLight( dlight );
lightframe->AddLight( alight );
lightframe->SetOrientation( scene,
        D3DVALUE(0), D3DVALUE(-1), D3DVALUE(0),
        D3DVALUE(0), D3DVALUE(0), D3DVALUE(1));
alight->Release();
alight=0;
dlight->Release();
dlight=0;
lightframe->Release();
lightframe=0;


//------ CAMERA----------
LPDIRECT3DRMFRAME cameradummy;
d3drm->CreateFrame( scene, &cameradummy );
cameradummy->SetRotation( scene,
        D3DVALUE(0), D3DVALUE(1), D3DVALUE(0),
        D3DVALUE(.01) );

d3drm->CreateFrame( cameradummy, &camera );
camera->SetPosition( scene,
        D3DVALUE(0), D3DVALUE(0), D3DVALUE(-50));
d3drm->CreateViewport( device, camera, 0, 0,
        device->GetWidth(), device->GetHeight(),
        &viewport);

    return TRUE;

}
```

The **CreateScene()** function performs seven steps:

1. Loads a spherical mesh for representation of the missile target

2. Creates an animation sequence for the target mesh

3. Creates a frame for the target mesh and installs a callback function for animation sequence updates

4. Loads the missile mesh

5. Creates 15 frames and attaches the missile mesh to each

6. Creates two light sources

7. Creates a viewport

The first step is the creation of a target mesh:

```
D3DRMLOADRESOURCE resinfo;
resinfo.hModule=NULL;
resinfo.lpName=MAKEINTRESOURCE( IDR_SPHEREMESH );
resinfo.lpType="MESH";
LPDIRECT3DRMMESHBUILDER targetbuilder;
d3drm->CreateMeshBuilder( &targetbuilder );
targetbuilder->Load( &resinfo, NULL, D3DRMLOAD_FROMRESOURCE,
        NULL, NULL );
ScaleMesh( targetbuilder, D3DVALUE(.75) );
```

The mesh is loaded from the program's resources. The **resinfo** structure identifies the resource entry where the mesh is stored. **The Direct3DRM-MeshBuilder Load()** function is used to load the mesh. The mesh is then scaled using the **RMWin::ScaleMesh()** function.

In Step 2, an animation sequence is created that will be used to animate the target mesh:

```
LPDIRECT3DRMANIMATION animation;
d3drm->CreateAnimation( &animation );
animation->SetOptions( D3DRMANIMATION_SPLINEPOSITION |
        D3DRMANIMATION_CLOSED |
        D3DRMANIMATION_POSITION );
animation->AddPositionKey( D3DVALUE(0),
        D3DVALUE(-20), D3DVALUE(0), D3DVALUE(-20) );
```

```
animation->AddPositionKey( D3DVALUE(12),
        D3DVALUE(0), D3DVALUE(15), D3DVALUE(0) );
animation->AddPositionKey( D3DVALUE(24),
        D3DVALUE(20), D3DVALUE(0), D3DVALUE(-20) );
animation->AddPositionKey( D3DVALUE(35),
        D3DVALUE(0), D3DVALUE(0), D3DVALUE(0) );
animation->AddPositionKey( D3DVALUE(49),
        D3DVALUE(20), D3DVALUE(0), D3DVALUE(20) );
animation->AddPositionKey( D3DVALUE(65),
        D3DVALUE(0), D3DVALUE(15), D3DVALUE(0) );
animation->AddPositionKey( D3DVALUE(74),
        D3DVALUE(-20), D3DVALUE(0), D3DVALUE(20) );
animation->AddPositionKey( D3DVALUE(85),
        D3DVALUE(0), D3DVALUE(0), D3DVALUE(0) );
animation->AddPositionKey( D3DVALUE(99),
        D3DVALUE(-20), D3DVALUE(0), D3DVALUE(-20) );
```

First, the **Direct3DRM CreateAnimation()** function is used to initialize an instance of the **Direct3DRMAnimation** interface. Next, the **Direct3DRM-Animation SetOptions()** function is called. We are using three flags with the **SetOptions()** function. The **D3DRMANIMATION_SPLINEPOSITION** flag indicates that we want the animation sequence to be calculated using splines. The **D3DRMANIMATION_CLOSED** flag allows us to use a continuously incrementing time index to execute the animation sequence repeatedly. The **D3DRMANIMATION_POSITION** flag indicates to the animation object that we are interested in the animation sequence's positional output. Notice that the **D3DRMANIMATION_SCALEAND-ROTATION** flag is absent (this flag is used by the Rocket demo, but not the Target demo). Omitting this flag allows the animation object to skip any scaling or rotational calculation, allowing the animation sequence to execute with less overhead.

The remainder of Step 2 consists of several calls to the **Direct3DRMAnimation AddPositionKey()** function. When we created the animation sequence in the Rocket demo, we used a loop to add keys that were defined by array entries. With the Target demo, we aren't using arrays or a loop. Each key is added with a separate call to the **AddPositionKey()** function. As with the Rocket demo, the positions used in the animation sequence were arrived at by experimentation.

Step 3 is the creation of a frame for placement and animation of the target mesh:

```
LPDIRECT3DRMFRAME targetframe;
d3drm->CreateFrame( scene, &targetframe );
animation->SetFrame( targetframe );
targetframe->AddVisual( targetbuilder );
targetframe->AddMoveCallback( MoveTarget, animation );

targetbuilder->Release();
targetbuilder=0;
```

First, the **Direct3DRM CreateFrame()** function is used to initialize the local **targetframe** pointer. The new frame pointer is then used as an argument to the **Direct3DRMAnimation SetFrame()** function. This function call associates the frame with the animation sequence. The frame's position is now controlled by the animation object.

The **Direct3DRMFrame AddVisual()** function is used to attach the target mesh to the frame. The **MoveTarget()** callback function is then installed with the **Direct3DRMFrame AddMoveCallback()** function. Notice that the **animation** pointer is used as the second **AddMoveCallback()** argument. This will give the callback function access to the animation object. Finally, the **targetbuilder** pointer (which was initialized in Step 1) is released.

Broken COM promises

Normally, local pointers to Direct3D interfaces are released before the end of the function. In the Target demo, there are two exceptions to this rule. The **animation** and **targetframe** pointers are not released because they are used by callback functions. Releasing these pointers would cause COM to destroy the objects, and the callback functions would crash the program.

Another solution would be to continue calling **Release()**, but only after a call to the **AddRef()** member function. This notifies COM that an extra reference to the object has been created. According to the COM specification, this second method is preferable. We'll use the first method to keep the code as simple as possible.

In Step 4, the mesh that represents the missiles is loaded:

```
resinfo.hModule=NULL;
resinfo.lpName=MAKEINTRESOURCE( IDR_MISSLEMESH );
resinfo.lpType="MESH";
d3drm->CreateMeshBuilder( &meshbuilder );
meshbuilder->Load( &resinfo, NULL, D3DRMLOAD_FROMRESOURCE,
        NULL, NULL );
meshbuilder->SetColorRGB(
        D3DVALUE(.67), D3DVALUE(.82), D3DVALUE(.94) );
meshbuilder->SetQuality( D3DRMRENDER_FLAT );
ScaleMesh( meshbuilder, D3DVALUE(7) );
```

Like the target mesh, the missile mesh is stored in the program's resources. After the mesh is loaded, the **Direct3DRMMeshBuilder SetColorRGB()** function is used to give the mesh a light blue color. The **SetQuality()** function is used to indicate to Direct3D that the mesh should be rendered with flat shading. This setting can be changed from the demo's Render menu. Lastly, the **ScaleMesh()** function is used to scale the mesh to seven units.

Step 5 uses a nested loop to create 15 frames and attach the missile mesh to each. The code also installs a callback function for each frame:

```
for (int i=0;i<5;i++)
{
    for (int j=0;j<3;j++)
    {
        LPDIRECT3DRMFRAME meshframe;
        d3drm->CreateFrame( scene, &meshframe );
        meshframe->SetPosition( scene,
                D3DVALUE((i-2)*8),
                D3DVALUE(-12),
                D3DVALUE((j-1)*8) );
        meshframe->AddVisual( meshbuilder );
        meshframe->AddMoveCallback( OrientFrame, targetframe );
        meshframe->Release();
        meshframe=0;
    }
}
```

The **meshframe** pointer is used to initialize each frame. New frames are positioned according to the current iteration of the two loops. The **Direct3DRMFrame AddVisual()** function is used to attach the missile mesh to each frame. The **AddMoveCallback()** function is used to install the **OrientFrame()** callback function. Notice that the **targetframe** pointer is used as the second **AddMoveCallback()** argument. This gives the callback function access to the frame that will be followed by the missile. The **meshframe** pointer is released after the **AddMoveCallback()** function is called.

Steps 6 and 7 create light sources and a viewport. We'll forgo discussion of these steps because light sources and viewports are discussed in Chapters 6 and 9 respectively.

THE TARGETWIN::MOVETARGET() FUNCTION

The **MoveTarget()** callback function updates the animation sequence once per system update. The function looks like this:

```
void TargetWin::MoveTarget(LPDIRECT3DRMFRAME, void* p, D3DVALUE)
{
    LPDIRECT3DRMANIMATION animation=(LPDIRECT3DRMANIMATION)p;
    static D3DVALUE time;
    time+=D3DVALUE(.5);
    animation->SetTime( time );
}
```

First, the function prepares a pointer to the **Direct3DRMAnimation** instance that controls the target's movement. A static counter variable is used to track the current position in the animation sequence. The variable is incremented and then used as an argument to the **Direct3DRMAnimation SetTime()** function.

THE TARGETWIN::ORIENTFRAME() FUNCTION

The **OrientFrame()** callback function is used to modify the missile frames according to the movement of the target. This is accomplished with the **Direct3DRMFrame LookAt()** function. The **LookAt()** function orients one frame to "look at" another. The **OrientFrame()** function is defined this way:

```
void TargetWin::OrientFrame(LPDIRECT3DRMFRAME frame, void* p, D3DVALUE)
{
    LPDIRECT3DRMFRAME targetframe=(LPDIRECT3DRMFRAME)p;
    LPDIRECT3DRMFRAME scene;
    frame->GetScene( &scene );
    frame->LookAt( targetframe, scene, (D3DRMFRAMECONSTRAINT)0 );
}
```

First, a pointer to the target frame is prepared. The pointer is initialized with the user-determined second parameter. Next, the scene's root frame is retrieved. The root frame is required because the **LookAt()** function, like many of the **Direct3DRMFrame** member functions, requires that a reference frame be supplied (actually, you can use zero if you want to use the scene's root frame as a reference frame).

Finally, the **LookAt()** function is called. The first **LookAt()** argument is a pointer to the frame that is to be followed. The second argument is the reference frame. The third argument can be used to indicate that the frame's axes be constrained. We want our missile frames to enjoy full freedom of movement, so we use zero rather than supply any constraint flags.

CONCLUSION

This chapter introduces animation topics that Direct3D supports. The demos use Direct3D's animation support in as simple a way as possible (without being too boring). For real-life applications, however, this may be simplistic. A key-framing sequence, for example, is not usually arrived at by trial and error. More often, an animation tool is used to develop the sequence. The animation data is then exported from the animation tool and used from within an application to create the actual animation sequence. This chapter is not intended as a discussion of how to design an animation sequence. Instead, the discussion concentrates on how to use the Direct3D API to implement an animation sequence once it has been designed.

In Chapter 8, we'll take a closer look at meshes. In particular, we will study sub-mesh animation. That is, rather than animating a mesh's position, we'll be animating a mesh's vertex positions. This technique is useful for a number of applications, including morphing.

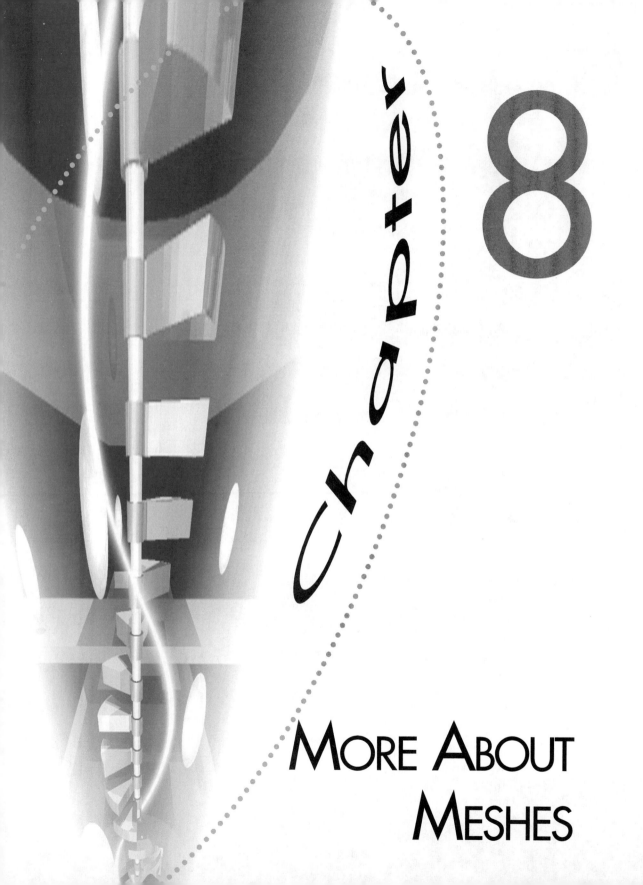

Chapter

8

MORE ABOUT
MESHES

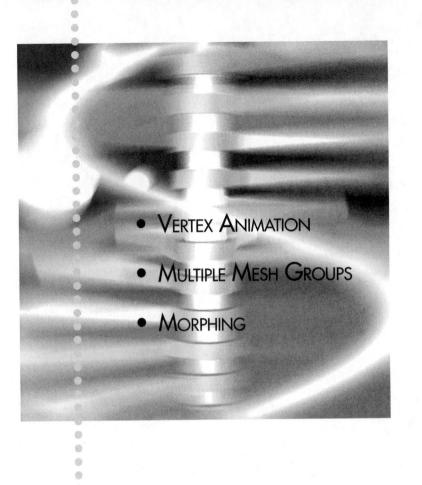

- VERTEX ANIMATION

- MULTIPLE MESH GROUPS

- MORPHING

CHAPTER

8

MORE ABOUT MESHES

At this point, we've talked about animation in considerable detail. We've animated meshes starting with Chapter 4, using rotation attributes. In Chapter 5, we performed texture animation. In Chapter 7, we discussed frame-based animation and key-framing.

All of the animation techniques that we've looked at performed animation either by animating a texture on a mesh, or by moving or rotating the mesh itself. In this chapter, we'll look at sub-mesh, or vertex, animation.

Vertex animation involves manipulating the location of vertices within a mesh to change the shape of the mesh at runtime. This technique has many applications, the most notable of which is morphing.

We'll study these demos in this chapter:

*   Cube

*   Cube2

*   MorphPlay

We'll use the Cube demo to introduce vertex animation. The Cube2 demo illustrates how to create and maintain multiple groups of faces within the same mesh. Finally, we'll study morphing with the MorphPlay demo.

VERTEX ANIMATION

Vertex animation is the animation of one or more vertices within a single mesh, and is relatively simple to implement. The challenging part is not the moving of vertices, but deciding where and when to move the vertices.

Vertex animation can be performed by both the **Direct3DRMMeshBuilder** and **Direct3DRMMesh** interfaces. Because of the extra performance and memory overhead associated with the **Direct3DRMMeshBuilder** interface, however, we will be using the **Direct3DRMMesh** interface exclusively.

THE CUBE DEMO

The Cube demo uses vertex animation to stretch and skew a cube. The demo is intended to be simple rather than impressive, so only two of the cube's vertices are animated. The Cube demo appears in Figure 8.1.

In addition to the vertex animation, a random rotation vector is used to spin the cube. This goes a long way to disguise the simplicity of the vertex

Figure 8.1
The Cube demo.

animation. The Cube demo also supports the typical Render menu that allows the rendering method of the mesh to be changed at runtime.

The Cube demo demonstrates the following techniques:

- Constructing a mesh from scratch (the mesh is not loaded from disk, but assembled at program startup)

- Using the **Direct3DRMMesh** to perform vertex animation

- Changing the mesh's rendering method with menu commands

THE CUBEWIN CLASS

The Cube demo provides its functionality in the **CubeWin** class:

```
class CubeWin : public RMWin
{
public:
    CubeWin();
    BOOL CreateScene();
protected:
    //{{AFX_MSG(CubeWin)
    afx_msg void OnRenderWireframe();
    afx_msg void OnRenderFlat();
    afx_msg void OnRenderGouraud();
    afx_msg void OnUpdateRenderWireframe(CCmdUI* pCmdUI);
    afx_msg void OnUpdateRenderFlat(CCmdUI* pCmdUI);
    afx_msg void OnUpdateRenderGouraud(CCmdUI* pCmdUI);
    //}}AFX_MSG
    DECLARE_MESSAGE_MAP()
private:
    static void UpdateCube(LPDIRECT3DRMFRAME, void*, D3DVALUE);
private:
    LPDIRECT3DRMMESH mesh;
    D3DRMGROUPINDEX group;
};
```

The class declares two public functions: a constructor and the **CreateScene()** function. The constructor is used to initialize the class's data members. The **CreateScene()** function constructs the demo's scene. We'll look at **CreateScene()** soon.

Six protected member functions are declared. They provide Render menu functionality.

One callback function is declared: **UpdateCube**(). We'll use this callback to perform the actual vertex animation.

Finally, two data members are declared. The first is a pointer to the **Direct3DRMMesh** interface and will be initialized to point to the demo's single mesh. The second is a mesh group identifier. We'll use this data member to manipulate the cube mesh once it has been created.

THE CUBEWIN::CREATESCENE() FUNCTION

The Cube demo's scene is constructed by the **CreateScene**() function. The function appears in Listing 8.1.

Listing 8.1 The CubeWin::CreateScene() function.

```
BOOL CubeWin::CreateScene()
{
    // ------- MESH --------
    d3drm->CreateMesh( &mesh );
    mesh->AddGroup( 24, 6, 4, vertorder, &group );
    mesh->SetVertices( group, 0, 24, vertexlist );
    mesh->Translate( D3DVALUE(-0.5), D3DVALUE(-0.5), D3DVALUE(-0.5) );
    mesh->Scale( D3DVALUE(12), D3DVALUE(12), D3DVALUE(12) );

    //-------- TEXTURE ------
    HRSRC texture_id = FindResource( NULL,
            MAKEINTRESOURCE(IDR_WIN95TEXTURE), "TEXTURE" );
    LPDIRECT3DRMTEXTURE texture;
    d3drm->LoadTextureFromResource( texture_id, &texture );
    mesh->SetGroupTexture( group, texture );
    mesh->SetGroupMapping( group, D3DRMMAP_PERSPCORRECT );
    texture->Release();
    texture=0;

    //------- FRAME --------
    LPDIRECT3DRMFRAME frame;
    d3drm->CreateFrame( scene, &frame );
    frame->AddVisual( mesh );
    frame->SetRotation( scene,
            D3DVALUE(0), D3DVALUE(1), D3DVALUE(0),
            D3DVALUE(.04) );

    static CallbackData cbdata;
    cbdata.mesh=mesh;
    cbdata.group=group;
    frame->AddMoveCallback( UpdateCube, &cbdata );
```

```
frame->Release();
frame=0;

// --------- LIGHTS --------
LPDIRECT3DRMLIGHT dlight;
d3drm->CreateLightRGB(D3DRMLIGHT_DIRECTIONAL,
        D3DVALUE(1.00), D3DVALUE(1.00), D3DVALUE(1.00),
        &dlight );

LPDIRECT3DRMLIGHT alight;
d3drm->CreateLightRGB(D3DRMLIGHT_AMBIENT,
        D3DVALUE(0.50), D3DVALUE(0.50), D3DVALUE(0.50),
        &alight );

LPDIRECT3DRMFRAME lightframe;
d3drm->CreateFrame( scene, &lightframe );
lightframe->SetOrientation( scene,
        D3DVALUE(0), D3DVALUE(-1), D3DVALUE(1),
        D3DVALUE(0), D3DVALUE(1), D3DVALUE(0) );

lightframe->AddLight( dlight );
lightframe->AddLight( alight );

dlight->Release();
dlight=0;
alight->Release();
alight=0;
lightframe->Release();
lightframe=0;

//------ CAMERA----------
d3drm->CreateFrame( scene, &camera );
camera->SetPosition( scene,
        D3DVALUE(0), D3DVALUE(0), D3DVALUE(-50) );
d3drm->CreateViewport( device, camera, 0, 0,
        device->GetWidth(), device->GetHeight(),
        &viewport );

return TRUE;
}
```

The **CreateScene()** function performs five steps:

1. Creates the cube mesh

2. Creates and applies a texture to the mesh

3. Creates a frame for the mesh and installs a callback function

4. Creates two light sources

5. Creates a viewport

The first step uses the **Direct3DRMMesh** interface to create the cube mesh. Let's take a closer look:

```
d3drm->CreateMesh( &mesh );
mesh->AddGroup( 24, 6, 4, vertorder, &group );
mesh->SetVertices( group, 0, 24, vertexlist );
mesh->Translate( D3DVALUE(-0.5), D3DVALUE(-0.5), D3DVALUE(-0.5) );
mesh->Scale( D3DVALUE(12), D3DVALUE(12), D3DVALUE(12) );
```

First, the **Direct3DRM Createmesh()** function is used to initialize the **mesh** pointer. Notice that in previous demos that used the **Direct3DRMMesh** interface, the mesh was created with the **Direct3DRMMeshBuilder CreateMesh()** function and not **Direct3DRM CreateMesh()**. Creating a mesh with a meshbuilder is easy because the **Direct3DRMMeshBuilder Load()** function can be used in advance to load a mesh from a file. Because we are using the **Direct3DRM CreateMesh()** function, we have created an empty mesh.

Next, the **Direct3DRMMesh AddGroup()** function is used to initialize the mesh. This step creates a mesh group. A mesh group is a set of faces within a mesh that can be manipulated as a single entity. The first **AddGroup()** argument is the number of vertices in the group. Our cube has 24 vertices because it contains 6 faces, each defined with 4 vertices. The second **AddGroup()** argument is the number of faces in the group, and the third argument is the number of vertices used to represent each face. The fourth **AddGroup()** argument is an array of vertex indices. The **vertorder** array used as the fourth argument is defined like this:

```
unsigned vertorder[] = { 0,1,2,3,4,5,6,7,8,9,10,11,
        12,13,14,15,16,17,18,19,20,21,22,23 };
```

This array establishes the order of the vertices. The indices shown represent the simplest possible order because the order is sequential. When constructing meshes from scratch, like we are doing, there would be little advantage in using non-sequential vertex ordering. Mesh data exported from 3D modelers such as 3D Studio, however, is not likely to use sequential vertex ordering.

The fifth and final **AddGroup()** argument is a pointer to the **group** data member. The **AddGroup()** function initializes the group data member with an identifier that can be used to identify the new mesh group in subsequent function calls. Meshes that contain only one group (such as the one we are creating) use zero as the group identifier.

The **AddGroup()** function adds faces to a mesh and establishes vertex ordering, but the faces all have default values. All of the vertices in a new group have position and normal values of zero, and the new faces have a default color of white and no assigned texture. In order to assign initial vertex settings, we will use the **SetVertices()** function:

```
mesh->SetVertices( group, 0, 24, vertexlist );
```

The **SetVertices()** function is used to assign the position, normal, and texture coordinates of one or more vertices within a mesh group. The first **SetVertices()** argument specifies the mesh group to be modified. We are using **group** data member that was initialized by the **AddGroup()** function. The second argument is the index of the vertex where the changes are to begin (the index of the first vertex to be modified). The third argument is the number of vertices that are to be modified. We are going to assign all 24 vertices in the mesh group, so the values 0 and 24 are used. The fourth argument is an array of **D3DRMVERTEX** structures that contain the new vertex properties.

Before we look at the **vertexlist** array (used as the fourth **SetVertices()** argument), we should talk about the **D3DRMVERTEX** structure. Direct3D defines the structure like this:

```
typedef struct _D3DRMVERTEX
{
    D3DVECTOR position;
    D3DVECTOR normal;
    D3DVALUE  tu, tv;
    D3DCOLOR  color;
} D3DRMVERTEX;
```

The **position** vector is used to describe the vertex's position. The **normal** vector indicates a normal vector for the vertex. The **tu** and **tv** fields indicate texture coordinates. If a texture is applied to the mesh, the two fields indicate what portion of the texture is to be applied at the vertex. Finally, the color field indicates the vertex's color.

The cube demo must supply an array of **D3DRMVERTEX** structures in order to define the cube mesh. We'll use a macro to simplify the array initialization. The macro looks like this:

```
#define VERTEX(px,py,pz,nx,ny,nz,tu,tv)  \
    { { D3DVALUE(px),D3DVALUE(py),D3DVALUE(pz) }, \
      { D3DVALUE(nx),D3DVALUE(ny),D3DVALUE(nz), }, \
      D3DVALUE(tu),D3DVALUE(tv),D3DCOLOR(0) }
```

The macro takes eight arguments and produces a single **D3DRMVERTEX** entry. The main advantage to using a macro in this way is that it saves us the trouble of casting each **D3DRMVERTEX** field with the **D3DVALUE** type specifier. The **vertexlist** array is the array of vertices that the Cube demo uses to initialize its mesh:

```
static D3DRMVERTEX vertexlist[]=
{
    // left face
    VERTEX( 0,0,0, -1,0,0,  0,1 ), // vertex 0
    VERTEX( 0,0,1, -1,0,0,  0,0 ),
    VERTEX( 0,1,1, -1,0,0,  1,0 ),
    VERTEX( 0,1,0, -1,0,0,  1,1 ),
    // right face
    VERTEX( 1,0,0,  1,0,0,  0,0 ),
    VERTEX( 1,1,0,  1,0,0,  1,0 ),
    VERTEX( 1,1,1,  1,0,0,  1,1 ), // vertex 6
    VERTEX( 1,0,1,  1,0,0,  0,1 ),
    // front face
    VERTEX( 0,0,0,  0,0,-1, 0,0 ), // vertex 8
    VERTEX( 0,1,0,  0,0,-1, 1,0 ),
    VERTEX( 1,1,0,  0,0,-1, 1,1 ),
    VERTEX( 1,0,0,  0,0,-1, 0,1 ),
    // back face
    VERTEX( 0,0,1,  0,0,1,  0,1 ),
    VERTEX( 1,0,1,  0,0,1,  0,0 ),
    VERTEX( 1,1,1,  0,0,1,  1,0 ), // vertex 14
    VERTEX( 0,1,1,  0,0,1,  1,1 ),
```

```
    // top face
    VERTEX( 0,1,0,  0,1,0,  0,0 ),
    VERTEX( 0,1,1,  0,1,0,  1,0 ),
    VERTEX( 1,1,1,  0,1,0,  1,1 ), // vertex 18
    VERTEX( 1,1,0,  0,1,0,  0,1 ),
    // bottom face
    VERTEX( 0,0,0,  0,-1,0, 0,0 ), // vertex 20
    VERTEX( 1,0,0,  0,-1,0, 1,0 ),
    VERTEX( 1,0,1,  0,-1,0, 1,1 ),
    VERTEX( 0,0,1,  0,-1,0, 0,1 ),
};
```

The listing defines six groups of four vertices. Each group of four vertices defines a different face of the cube. The first three arguments used with each vertex define the vertex's position. The second three arguments indicate a normal for the vertex. Notice that the normals are identical for each vertex within the same face. This provides a sharp contrast between connecting faces. The final two arguments are texture coordinates.

Notice that comments appear to the right of six of the vertices. These comments indicate which vertices will be animated.

Returning to the mesh creation code (Step 1) in the **CreateScene()** function, the last two function calls look like this:

```
mesh->Translate( D3DVALUE(-0.5), D3DVALUE(-0.5), D3DVALUE(-0.5) );
mesh->Scale( D3DVALUE(12), D3DVALUE(12), D3DVALUE(12) );
```

The **Translate()** function is used to adjust the mesh's axis. The cube was created with one of its corners located at <0, 0, 0>. We use the **Translate()** function to center the cube on its local axis. The **Scale()** function is used to scale the cube to 12 times its original size. Notice that the order of these two function calls is important. If we performed the scale operation before the translation, the cube would hardly be centered on its local axis.

The second step performed by the **CreateScene()** function is the creation and application of a texture to the new mesh:

```
HRSRC texture_id = FindResource( NULL,
        MAKEINTRESOURCE(IDR_WIN95TEXTURE), "TEXTURE" );
LPDIRECT3DRMTEXTURE texture;
d3drm->LoadTextureFromResource( texture_id, &texture );
```

```
mesh->SetGroupTexture( group, texture );
mesh->SetGroupMapping( group, D3DRMMAP_PERSPCORRECT );
texture->Release();
texture-0;
```

The texture is loaded from the program's resources with the **Direct3DRM LoadTextureFromResource()** function. The **Direct3DRMMesh SetGroupTexture()** function is then used to associate the texture with the mesh. Perspective correction is enabled with the **Direct3DRMMesh SetGroupMapping()** function. Notice that both of these functions expect a mesh group identifier as the first argument.

Step 3 creates a frame for the mesh:

```
LPDIRECT3DRMFRAME frame;
d3drm->CreateFrame( scene, &frame );
frame->AddVisual( mesh );
frame->SetRotation( scene,
        D3DVALUE(0), D3DVALUE(1), D3DVALUE(0),
        D3DVALUE(.04) );

static CallbackData cbdata;
cbdata.mesh=mesh;
cbdata.group=group;
frame->AddMoveCallback( UpdateCube, &cbdata );
frame->Release();
frame=0;
```

The frame is created as a child of the **scene** frame using the **Direct3DRM CreateFrame()** function. The demo's mesh is attached to the new frame with the **Direct3DRMFrame AddVisual()** function. A rotation attribute is assigned to the new frame with the **SetRotation()** function. This rotation attribute is arbitrary because the demo's callback function will periodically assign a new rotation attribute for the mesh frame.

Next, a **static CallbackData** structure is declared. This structure is used by the Cube demo to pass pertinent data items to the callback function. It is declared **static** because the structure will be used long after the **CreateScene()** function returns and its local variables go out of scope.

A pointer to the mesh and the mesh group identifier are stored in the structure. The callback function (**UpdateCube()**) is then installed using the **Direct3DRMFrame AddMoveCallback()** function. A pointer to the **CallbackData** structure is used as the second **AddMoveCallback()** argument.

Steps 4 and 5 of the **CreateScene()** function create the lights and a viewport for the demo. We'll skip discussion of these steps because these topics are covered in other chapters and have little to do with vertex animation.

THE CUBEWIN::UPDATECUBE() FUNCTION

The **UpdateCube()** function is a callback function that performs the vertex animation for the Cube demo. The **UpdateCube()** function is defined like this:

```
void CubeWin::UpdateCube(LPDIRECT3DRMFRAME frame, void* p, D3DVALUE)
{
    CallbackData* data=(CallbackData*)p;
    static const D3DVALUE lim=D3DVALUE(5);
    static D3DVALUE control;
    static D3DVALUE inc=D3DVALUE(.25);
    static D3DRMVERTEX vert[24];

    data->mesh->GetVertices( data->group, 0, 24, vert );

    vert[0].position.x+=inc;
    vert[0].position.y+=inc;
    vert[0].position.z+=inc;
    vert[6].position.x+=inc;
    vert[6].position.y+=inc;
    vert[6].position.z+=inc;
    vert[8].position.x+=inc;
    vert[8].position.y+=inc;
    vert[8].position.z+=inc;
    vert[14].position.x+=inc;
    vert[14].position.y+=inc;
    vert[14].position.z+=inc;
    vert[18].position.x+=inc;
    vert[18].position.y+=inc;
    vert[18].position.z+=inc;
    vert[20].position.x+=inc;
    vert[20].position.y+=inc;
    vert[20].position.z+=inc;

    data->mesh->SetVertices( data->group, 0, 24, vert );
```

```
    control+=inc;
    if (control>lim || control<-lim)
        inc=-inc;

    static UINT delay;
    if (++delay<20)
        return;
    delay=0;

    LPDIRECT3DRMFRAME scene;
    frame->GetScene( &scene );

    D3DVECTOR spinvect;
    D3DRMVectorRandom( &spinvect );
    D3DVALUE spin=D3DDivide( rand()%50+1, 400 );
    frame->SetRotation( scene,
            spinvect.x, spinvect.y, spinvect.z,
            spin );
}
```

The function first prepares a pointer to the **CallbackData** structure:

```
CallbackData* data=(CallbackData*)p;
```

The **p** parameter is a pointer to the static **cbdata** structure that is declared by the **CreateScene()** function. The **p** pointer, however, is a pointer to **void,** so we are declaring a local pointer. We'll use the local **data** pointer to access the callback data later in the function.

Next, four static variables are declared:

```
static const D3DVALUE lim=D3DVALUE(5);
static D3DVALUE control;
static D3DVALUE inc=D3DVALUE(.25);
static D3DRMVERTEX vert[24];
```

The **lim** variable is a constant we'll use to limit the distance that the vertices will travel. The **control** variable is used to determine the current location of the animated vertices. The **inc** variable is used to increment the control variable. Finally, the **vert** variable is an array of **D3DRMVERTEX** structures. We'll use the **vert** array to retrieve, manipulate, and assign vertex data.

Next, the **Direct3DRMMesh GetVertices()** function is used to retrieve the current vertex settings:

```
data->mesh->GetVertices( data->group, 0, 24, vert );
```

The argument list for the **GetVertices()** function is identical to the **SetVertices()** function. Notice that both the pointer to the mesh and the mesh group identifier are retrieved via the data pointer. The **GetVertices()** function fills the **vert** array with the mesh's current vertex settings.

The newly retrieved vertex positions can now be updated:

```
vert[0].position.x+=inc;
vert[0].position.y+=inc;
vert[0].position.z+=inc;
vert[6].position.x+=inc;
vert[6].position.y+=inc;
vert[6].position.z+=inc;
vert[8].position.x+=inc;
vert[8].position.y+=inc;
vert[8].position.z+=inc;
vert[14].position.x+=inc;
vert[14].position.y+=inc;
vert[14].position.z+=inc;
vert[18].position.x+=inc;
vert[18].position.y+=inc;
vert[18].position.z+=inc;
vert[20].position.x+=inc;
vert[20].position.y+=inc;
vert[20].position.z+=inc;
```

The **inc** variable is used to increment specific vertex positions. The order that the vertices are updated is irrelevant because the changes don't take place until the **SetVertices()** function is called:

```
data->mesh->SetVertices( data->group, 0, 24, vert );
```

The **SetVertices()** function updates the mesh given the modified vertex data.

Next, the **control** variable is updated:

```
control+=inc;
if (control>lim || control<-lim)
    inc=-inc;
```

This code uses the **lim** variable to change the sign of the **inc** variable when the **control** value reaches its limit.

The remainder of the **UpdateCube()** function is dedicated to periodically changing the frame's rotation attribute:

```
static UINT delay;
if (++delay<20)
    return;
delay=0;

LPDIRECT3DRMFRAME scene;
frame->GetScene( &scene );

D3DVECTOR spinvect;
D3DRMVectorRandom( &spinvect );
D3DVALUE spin=D3DDivide( rand()%50+1, 400 );
frame->SetRotation( scene,
        spinvect.x, spinvect.y, spinvect.z,
        spin );
```

Every 20 system updates, this code calculates a new rotation vector and speed. The new values are installed with the **Direct3DRMFrame SetRotation()** function.

THE CUBEWIN RENDER FUNCTIONS

The remaining **CubeWin** functions provide the demo's Render menu support. These functions appear like this:

```
void CubeWin::OnRenderWireframe()
{
    if (mesh)
        mesh->SetGroupQuality( group, D3DRMRENDER_WIREFRAME );
}

void CubeWin::OnRenderFlat()
{
    if (mesh)
        mesh->SetGroupQuality( group, D3DRMRENDER_FLAT );
}

void CubeWin::OnRenderGouraud()
{
```

```
    if (mesh)
        mesh->SetGroupQuality( group, D3DRMRENDER_GOURAUD );
}

void CubeWin::OnUpdateRenderWireframe(CCmdUI* pCmdUI)
{
    if (mesh)
    {
        D3DRMRENDERQUALITY meshquality = mesh->GetGroupQuality( group );
        pCmdUI->SetCheck( meshquality==D3DRMRENDER_WIREFRAME );
    }
}

void CubeWin::OnUpdateRenderFlat(CCmdUI* pCmdUI)
{
    if (mesh)
    {
        D3DRMRENDERQUALITY meshquality = mesh->GetGroupQuality( group );
        pCmdUI->SetCheck( meshquality==D3DRMRENDER_FLAT );
    }
}

void CubeWin::OnUpdateRenderGouraud(CCmdUI* pCmdUI)
{
    if (mesh)
    {
        D3DRMRENDERQUALITY meshquality = mesh->GetGroupQuality( group );
        pCmdUI->SetCheck( meshquality==D3DRMRENDER_GOURAUD );
    }
}
```

Notice that the mesh group identifier **group** is used to set and retrieve the mesh's rendering settings.

You may also notice that when you use the demo's Render menu, there is little or no difference between the flat and Gouraud settings. Typically, Gouraud rendering softens edges and corners. With the Cube demo, however, the edges of the mesh stay distinct in Gouraud mode. This is because the normals that we used to create the mesh are not calculated in the same way that the **Direct3DRMMeshBuilder** interface would have calculated the normals had it been used. The normals we use in the Cube demo are perpendicular to the face that the vertex is part of. Had the **Direct3DRMMeshBuilder GenerateNormals()** function been used, the normals would have been calculated based on all of the faces surrounding a vertex.

MULTIPLE MESH GROUPS

In the Cube demo, we create a mesh that has one group. All six of the cube's faces are part of the group and are modified as a single entity.

Meshes support multiple groups. Each group must be added to the mesh with the **Direct3DRMMesh AddGroup()** function. The group can later be queried and modified using a group identifier that the **AddGroup()** function assigns. Using multiple groups in a mesh allows different colors, textures, and materials to be used simultaneously by a single mesh.

THE CUBE2 DEMO

The Cube2 demo has its name for two reasons. First, the demo is a direct adaptation from the Cube demo. Second, the Cube2 demo represents its cube using two mesh groups.

The mesh in the Cube2 demo is animated in the same way as the cube in the Cube demo, but the color of the second group (three of the cube's faces) is animated. The Cube2 demo appears in Figure 8.2.

Figure 8.2
The Cube2 demo.

The Cube2 demo demonstrates the following techniques:

- Constructing a mesh from scratch using multiple mesh groups

- Using the **Direct3DRMMesh** to perform vertex and color animation

- Changing each of the two mesh groups' rendering methods with menu commands

We'll talk about each of these techniques as we walk through the Cube2 code.

THE CUBE2WIN CLASS

The Cube2 demo provides its functionality with the **Cube2Win** class:

```
class Cube2Win : public RMWin
{
public:
    Cube2Win();
    BOOL CreateScene();
protected:
    //{{AFX_MSG(Cube2Win)
    afx_msg void OnRenderGroup1Flat();
    afx_msg void OnRenderGroup1Wireframe();
    afx_msg void OnRenderGroup1Gouraud();
    afx_msg void OnRenderGroup2Wireframe();
    afx_msg void OnRenderGroup2Flat();
    afx_msg void OnRenderGroup2Gouraud();
    afx_msg void OnUpdateRenderGroup1Wireframe(CCmdUI* pCmdUI);
    afx_msg void OnUpdateRenderGroup1Flat(CCmdUI* pCmdUI);
    afx_msg void OnUpdateRenderGroup1Gouraud(CCmdUI* pCmdUI);
    afx_msg void OnUpdateRenderGroup2Wireframe(CCmdUI* pCmdUI);
    afx_msg void OnUpdateRenderGroup2Flat(CCmdUI* pCmdUI);
    afx_msg void OnUpdateRenderGroup2Gouraud(CCmdUI* pCmdUI);
    //}}AFX_MSG
    DECLARE_MESSAGE_MAP()
private:
    static void UpdateCube(LPDIRECT3DRMFRAME, void*, D3DVALUE);
    static void UpdateColors(LPDIRECT3DRMFRAME, void*, D3DVALUE);
private:
    LPDIRECT3DRMMESH mesh;
    D3DRMGROUPINDEX group1, group2;
};
```

Two public member functions are declared: a constructor and **CreateScene()**. The constructor initializes the class's data members. The **CreateScene()** function creates the demo's mesh, light sources, and viewport.

THE CUBE2WIN::CREATESCENE() FUNCTION

The Cube2 demo **CreateScene()** function appears in Listing 8.2.

Listing 8.2 The Cube2Win::CreateScene() function.

```
BOOL Cube2Win::CreateScene()
{
    //---------- MESH --------
    d3drm->CreateMesh( &mesh );

    mesh->AddGroup( 12, 3, 4, vertorder, &group1 );
    mesh->AddGroup( 12, 3, 4, vertorder, &group2 );

    mesh->SetVertices( group1, 0, 12, vertexlist );
    mesh->SetVertices( group2, 0, 12, vertexlist+12 );

    mesh->Translate( D3DVALUE(-0.5), D3DVALUE(-0.5), D3DVALUE(-0.5) );
    mesh->Scale( D3DVALUE(15), D3DVALUE(15), D3DVALUE(15) );

    //--------- TEXTURE ----------
    HRSRC texture_id = FindResource( NULL,
            MAKEINTRESOURCE(IDR_WIN95TEXTURE), "TEXTURE" );
    LPDIRECT3DRMTEXTURE texture;
    d3drm->LoadTextureFromResource( texture_id, &texture );
    mesh->SetGroupTexture( group1, texture );
    mesh->SetGroupMapping( group1, D3DRMMAP_PERSPCORRECT );
    mesh->SetGroupTexture( group2, texture );
    mesh->SetGroupMapping( group2, D3DRMMAP_PERSPCORRECT );
    texture->Release();
    texture=0;

    //---------- FRAME ----------
    LPDIRECT3DRMFRAME meshframe;
    d3drm->CreateFrame( scene, &meshframe );
    meshframe->AddVisual( mesh );
    meshframe->SetRotation( scene,
            D3DVALUE(0), D3DVALUE(1), D3DVALUE(0),
            D3DVALUE(-.05) );

    static CallbackData cbdata;
    cbdata.mesh=mesh;
    cbdata.group1=group1;
    cbdata.group2=group2;
    meshframe->AddMoveCallback( UpdateCube, &cbdata );
    meshframe->AddMoveCallback( UpdateColors, &cbdata );
    meshframe->Release();
    meshframe=0;
```

```
// --------LIGHTS--------
LPDIRECT3DRMLIGHT dlight, alight;
d3drm->CreateLightRGB(D3DRMLIGHT_DIRECTIONAL,
        D3DVALUE(1.00), D3DVALUE(1.00), D3DVALUE(1.00),
        &dlight );
d3drm->CreateLightRGB(D3DRMLIGHT_AMBIENT,
        D3DVALUE(0.50), D3DVALUE(0.50), D3DVALUE(0.50),
        &alight );

LPDIRECT3DRMFRAME lightframe;
d3drm->CreateFrame( scene, &lightframe );
lightframe->SetOrientation( scene,
        D3DVALUE(0), D3DVALUE(-1), D3DVALUE(5),
        D3DVALUE(0), D3DVALUE(1), D3DVALUE(0) );
lightframe->AddLight( dlight );
lightframe->AddLight( alight );
dlight->Release();
dlight=0;
alight->Release();
alight=0;
lightframe->Release();
lightframe=0;

//------ CAMERA----------
d3drm->CreateFrame( scene, &camera );
camera->SetPosition( scene,
        D3DVALUE(0), D3DVALUE(0), D3DVALUE(-50));
d3drm->CreateViewport( device, camera, 0, 0,
        device->GetWidth(), device->GetHeight(),
        &viewport );

return TRUE;
}
```

The **CreateScene()** function performs five steps:

1. Creates a mesh using the **Direct3DRMMesh** interface. The mesh is composed of two different groups.

2. Creates a texture for the mesh.

3. Creates a frame for mesh placement and installs update callbacks.

4. Creates two light sources.

5. Creates a viewport.

The first step is the creation of a mesh:

```
d3drm->CreateMesh( &mesh );

mesh->AddGroup( 12, 3, 4, vertorder, &group1 );
mesh->AddGroup( 12, 3, 4, vertorder, &group2 );

mesh->SetVertices( group1, 0, 12, vertexlist );
mesh->SetVertices( group2, 0, 12, vertexlist+12 );

mesh->Translate( D3DVALUE(-0.5), D3DVALUE(-0.5), D3DVALUE(-0.5) );
mesh->Scale( D3DVALUE(15), D3DVALUE(15), D3DVALUE(15) );
```

First, the **mesh** pointer is initialized with the **Direct3DRM CreateMesh()** function. Two groups are then added to the empty mesh. Each group is created with the **AddGroup()** function. Each group has 12 vertices: 3 faces made up of 4 vertices apiece. The **vertorder** array is used as the third **AddGroup()** argument. In the Cube demo, the **vertorder** array contained 24 entries; in the Cube2 demo, the array contains 12 entries:

```
unsigned vertorder[] = { 0,1,2,3,4,5,6,7,8,9,10,11 };
```

The final **AddGroup()** argument is an address to a mesh group identifier. **AddGroup()** assigns a unique value for each mesh group.

Next, the **SetVertices()** function is used to assign values to the vertices in each group. The first **SetVertices()** argument is the identifier for the group. The second argument is the index of the vertex where the changes are to be made. The third argument is the number of vertices that will be assigned. The fourth and final argument is an array of **D3DRMVERTEX** structures. Notice that we are using a single array of vertex structures to initialize two mesh groups. An offset is used in the second **SetVertices()** function, causing the second half of the array to be used for the second mesh group.

Next, the **Direct3DRMMesh Translate()** and **Scale()** functions are called. Unlike the **AddGroup()** and **SetVertices()** functions, the **Translate()** and **Scale()** functions modify all of the groups in a mesh. These function calls are identical to those in the Cube demo.

In Step 2, a texture is created and applied to both meshes:

```
HRSRC texture_id = FindResource( NULL,
        MAKEINTRESOURCE(IDR_WIN95TEXTURE), "TEXTURE" );
LPDIRECT3DRMTEXTURE texture;
d3drm->LoadTextureFromResource( texture_id, &texture );
mesh->SetGroupTexture( group1, texture );
mesh->SetGroupMapping( group1, D3DRMMAP_PERSPCORRECT );
mesh->SetGroupTexture( group2, texture );
mesh->SetGroupMapping( group2, D3DRMMAP_PERSPCORRECT );
texture->Release();
texture=0;
```

Step 3 is the creation of a frame for the mesh and the installation of two callback functions:

```
LPDIRECT3DRMFRAME meshframe;
d3drm->CreateFrame( scene, &meshframe );
meshframe->AddVisual( mesh );
meshframe->SetRotation( scene,
        D3DVALUE(0), D3DVALUE(1), D3DVALUE(0),
        D3DVALUE(-.05) );

static CallbackData cbdata;
cbdata.mesh=mesh;
cbdata.group1=group1;
cbdata.group2=group2;
meshframe->AddMoveCallback( UpdateCube, &cbdata );
meshframe->AddMoveCallback( UpdateColors, &cbdata );
meshframe->Release();
meshframe=0;
```

The frame is created with the **Direct3DRM CreateFrame()** function and used to place the mesh. The frame is then given a rotation attribute.

Next, a static instance of the **CallbackData** structure is initialized. The structure has been modified to include mesh identifiers for both of the demo's mesh groups.

The **Direct3DRMFrame AddMoveCallback()** function is used to install two callback functions: **UpdateCube()** and **UpdateColors()**. Each callback function will be supplied with the pointer to the callback data structure whenever

it is invoked. The **UpdateCube()** function will perform vertex animation
for both mesh groups. The **UpdateColors()** function will perform color
animation for the second mesh group.

Steps 4 and 5 create two light sources and a viewport. We'll omit discussion
of these steps in this chapter.

THE CUBE2WIN::UPDATECUBE() FUNCTION

The **UpdateCube()** function serves two purposes. It performs vertex animation, and it periodically changes the mesh's rotational attributes:

```
void Cube2Win::UpdateCube(LPDIRECT3DRMFRAME frame,
                                      void* p, D3DVALUE)
{
    CallbackData* data=(CallbackData*)p;
    static const D3DVALUE lim=D3DVALUE(5);
    static D3DVALUE control;
    static D3DVALUE inc=D3DVALUE(.25);
    static D3DRMVERTEX vert[12];

    data->mesh->GetVertices( data->group1, 0, 12, vert );
    vert[0].position.x+=inc;
    vert[0].position.y+=inc;
    vert[0].position.z+=inc;
    vert[6].position.x+=inc;
    vert[6].position.y+=inc;
    vert[6].position.z+=inc;
    vert[8].position.x+=inc;
    vert[8].position.y+=inc;
    vert[8].position.z+=inc;
    data->mesh->SetVertices( data->group1, 0, 12, vert );

    data->mesh->GetVertices( data->group2, 0, 12, vert );
    vert[2].position.x+=inc;
    vert[2].position.y+=inc;
    vert[2].position.z+=inc;
    vert[6].position.x+=inc;
    vert[6].position.y+=inc;
    vert[6].position.z+=inc;
    vert[8].position.x+=inc;
    vert[8].position.y+=inc;
    vert[8].position.z+=inc;
    data->mesh->SetVertices( data->group2, 0, 12, vert );
```

```
        control+=inc;
        if (control>lim || control<-lim)
            inc=-inc;

        static UINT delay;
        if (++delay<20)
            return;
        delay=0;

        LPDIRECT3DRMFRAME scene;
        frame->GetScene( &scene );

        D3DVECTOR spinvect;
        D3DRMVectorRandom( &spinvect );
        D3DVALUE spin=D3DDivide( rand()%50+1, 400 );
        frame->SetRotation( scene,
                spinvect.x, spinvect.y, spinvect.z,
                spin );
}
```

The **UpdateCube()** function uses static variables to update the mesh's vertex locations:

```
static const D3DVALUE lim=D3DVALUE(5);
static D3DVALUE control;
static D3DVALUE inc=D3DVALUE(.25);
static D3DRMVERTEX vert[12];
```

The **lim, control,** and **inc** variables are used to control the vertex animation. The **vert** array is used as temporary storage for each mesh group's vertex data. Notice that the array has 12 entries; in the Cube demo, the **vert** array had 24.

Each of the two mesh groups contains vertices that are animated, so the **GetVertices()** and **SetVertices()** functions are used to adjust each mesh group's settings:

```
data->mesh->GetVertices( data->group1, 0, 12, vert );
vert[0].position.x+=inc;
vert[0].position.y+=inc;
vert[0].position.z+=inc;
vert[6].position.x+=inc;
vert[6].position.y+=inc;
vert[6].position.z+=inc;
```

```
vert[8].position.x+=inc;
vert[8].position.y+=inc;
vert[8].position.z+=inc;
data->mesh->SetVertices( data->group1, 0, 12, vert );

data->mesh->GetVertices( data->group2, 0, 12, vert );
vert[2].position.x+=inc;
vert[2].position.y+=inc;
vert[2].position.z+=inc;
vert[6].position.x+=inc;
vert[6].position.y+=inc;
vert[6].position.z+=inc;
vert[8].position.x+=inc;
vert[8].position.y+=inc;
vert[8].position.z+=inc;
data->mesh->SetVertices( data->group2, 0, 12, vert );
```

The **vert** array is used to store the vertex data for both of the mesh groups. The remainder of the **UpdateCube()** function is the same as the Cube demo's **UpdateCube()** function.

THE CUBE2WIN::UPDATECOLORS() FUNCTION

The **UpdateColors()** function performs color animation for the second mesh group. The function looks like this:

```
void Cube2Win::UpdateColors(LPDIRECT3DRMFRAME, void* p, D3DVALUE)
{
    CallbackData* data=(CallbackData*)p;
    static D3DVALUE clr=D3DVALUE(.5);
    static D3DVALUE inc=D3DVALUE(.2);
    clr+=inc;
    if (clr<D3DVALUE(.3) || clr>D3DVALUE(1))
    {
        inc=-inc;
        clr+=inc;
    }
    data->mesh->SetGroupColorRGB( data->group2,
            clr, D3DVALUE(0), D3DVALUE(0) );
}
```

The **clr** variable is used to calculate and store the mesh group's current color. Once the **clr** value has been determined, it is installed with the

Direct3DRMMesh SetGroupColorRGB() function. Only the red portion of the mesh group's color is animated. The green and blue portions are always zero.

THE CUBE2WIN RENDER FUNCTIONS

The Cube2 demo uses a slight variation on the typical Render menu because each mesh group has its own render settings. The Render menu, therefore, contains two submenus—one for each mesh group. This menu structure appears in Figure 8.3.

Twelve functions are required to implement the Cube2 demo's Render menu, but the functions differ from each other only slightly. An example of a function that is invoked when a menu entry is selected looks like this:

```
void Cube2Win::OnRenderGroup1Wireframe()
{
    if (mesh)
        mesh->SetGroupQuality( group1, D3DRMRENDER_WIREFRAME );
}
```

This function responds to the Render|Group1|Wireframe menu entry and uses the **Direct3DRMMesh SetGroupQuality**() function to assign the **wireframe** rendering method. Notice that the **group1** group identifier is used as the first **SetGroupQuality**() argument.

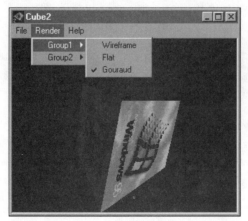

Figure 8.3
The Cube2 Render menu.

An example of a function that is called to activate menu check marks looks like this:

```
void Cube2Win::OnUpdateRenderGroup1Flat(CCmdUI* pCmdUI)
{
    if (mesh)
    {
        D3DRMRENDERQUALITY meshquality = mesh->GetGroupQuality( group1 );
        pCmdUI->SetCheck( meshquality==D3DRMRENDER_FLAT );
    }
}
```

This is the function that determines if the first mesh group's rendering setting is flat.

MORPHING

The term morphing has come to be associated with TV ads and movie effects where one shape "morphs" into another shape. Usually, the starting and destination shapes are quite different. In this section, we discuss morphing on a more general level.

For our purposes, we aren't too concerned with how different the two morph shapes are, just that it is possible to morph one into the other (and vice versa). In order for two shapes (meshes) to be morphable, they must contain the same number of vertices. Meeting this criteria does not guarantee that the resulting morph sequence will look good. Matching vertex counts just means that a morph sequence will be possible.

Practically speaking, the vertex count is only half the story. The faces in the two meshes should be arranged similarly. In fact, most morphable meshes are variations on the same mesh.

A mesh that is part of a set of morphable meshes is called a morph target. The design and creation of morph targets, however, is not the focus of this discussion. Here, we will concentrate on how to perform morphing given two or more compatible morph targets.

Technically, morphing involves calculating vertex positions for a mesh based on three criteria:

- The position of the vertices in the starting morph target.

- The position of the vertices in the destination morph target.

- A value indicating the stage in between the two morph targets that should be represented.

Let's say, for example, that the starting morph mesh is a bird, the destination morph mesh is an airplane, and the "betweening" value ranges from 1 to 100. If we use a value of 1, then the resulting mesh is a bird. If we use a value of 100, the resulting mesh is a plane. If, however, we use a value of 50, then the result will be a shape that is halfway between a bird and a plane. As the value approaches 1, the mesh looks more like a bird. As the value approaches 100, the mesh looks more like a plane.

Morph targets do not have to be entirely different shapes. Visually compelling morph sequences can involve shapes that bend, twist, curl, taper, or stretch.

Also, there is no reason that the number of morph targets has to be limited to two. Any number of morph targets can be used. For example, a bird can be morphed into a ball and then into a plane by adding a spherical morph target between the bird and the plane. As long as a set of morph targets has the same number of vertices, a morph sequence can be created.

THE MORPHPLAY DEMO

The MorphPlay demo is a generic morph sequence player. The demo allows morph files (.MRF) to be loaded and played. The CD-ROM that comes with this book contains MRF files in the **meshes** directory.

The MRF files are X files that meet the following criteria:

- The file contains at least two meshes.

- The meshes in the file all have the same vertex count.

- The meshes are named with single, lowercase letters, starting with the letter *a*.

The MRF file extension is optional. MorphPlay will load files with either X or MRF file extensions. When a file is loaded, the meshes in the file are used as morph targets. The file can include up to 26 morph targets—one for each letter of the alphabet. The morph targets are used in alphabetical order.

The demo provides a Morph menu, which offers three selections: Forward, Reverse, and Both. Forward means the that the morph mesh assumes the shape of the first mesh (mesh a) and then morphs to the second mesh (mesh b). The morphing continues until the morph mesh has conformed to the shape of the last mesh in the file. The sequence then begins over with the first mesh. Playing a morph sequence in reverse causes the morph target sequence to reverse. The default setting, Both, plays the morph sequence forward and backward continuously.

The speed of the morph sequence can be adjusted using the demo's Speed menu. The demos includes five morph speed settings. Slow speeds are accomplished by incrementing the morph time slowly. This results in very smooth motion.

The morph mesh can be rotated and spun using the mouse. Holding the left mouse–button down and moving the mouse will allow you to view the morph sequence from any angle.

The MorphPlay demo appears in Figure 8.4.

The MorphPlay demo demonstrates the following techniques:

- Creating morph sequences using one or more meshes as morph targets

- Using the **Direct3DRMAnimation** interface to perform vertex animation

- Using the window title bar to display program information

- Using MFC's **CFileDialog** class

CLASS DESIGN

Unlike most of the demos on the CD-ROM, the MorphPlay demo functionality is divided between two classes. General morphing functionality is provided by the **MorphWin** class, while the demo specific functionality is provided by the **MorphPlayWin** class. The demo's class hierarchy is shown in Figure 8.5.

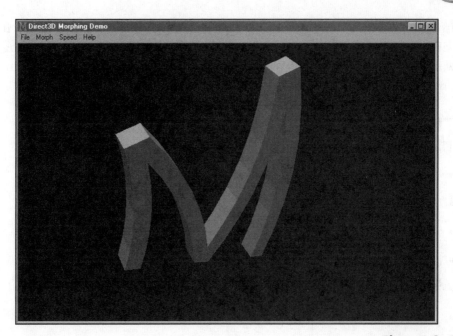

Figure 8.4
The MorphPlay demo.

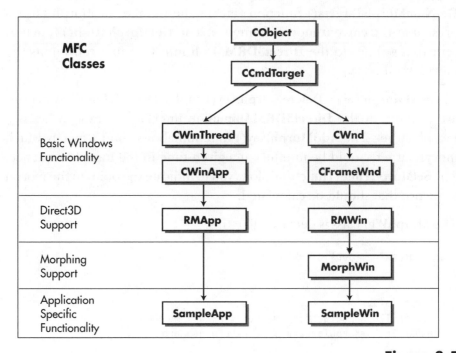

Figure 8.5
The MorphPlay class hierarchy.

Isolating the morphing functionality in the **MorphWin** class means that it will be easy for you to write your own morphing applications. Deriving window classes from **MorphWin** (instead of **RMWin**) means that your window class inherits morphing capability.

THE MORPHWIN CLASS

The **MorphWin** class provides its functionality with these functions:

- LoadMorphSequence()

- GetNumMorphTargets()

- GetMorphMesh()

- AddMorphKey()

- DeleteMorphKey()

- SetMorphTime()

The **LoadMorphSequence()** takes the name of an MRF or X file and attempts to construct a morph sequence based on the file contents. The **GetNumMorphTargets()** function returns the number of morph targets present in the current morph sequence. The **GetMorphMesh()** function returns a pointer to the **Direct3DRMMesh** interface that represents the morph mesh.

The **AddMorphKey()**, **DeleteMorphKey()**, and **SetMorphTime()** functions are inspired by the **Direct3DRMAnimation** interface. A morph key is a morph target. The **AddMorphKey()** function allows you to specify which morph target should be in effect at a given time in the morph sequence. The **SetMorphTime()** function allows you to indicate the point in the morph sequence that should be calculated.

The **MorphWin** class is declared like this:

```
class MorphWin : public RMWin
{
public:
    MorphWin();
    LPDIRECT3DRMMESH GetMorphMesh() { return morphmesh; }
    DWORD GetNumMorphTargets()  { return nummorphtargets; }
```

```
    BOOL LoadMorphSequence( const CString& filename );
    BOOL AddMorphKey( DWORD target, D3DVALUE time );
    BOOL DeleteMorphKey( D3DVALUE time );
    BOOL SetMorphTime( D3DVALUE time );
private:
    BOOL LoadMeshes( const CString& filename );
    BOOL CreateAnimations();
    BOOL PrepareMorphVertices();
    BOOL ReleaseAnimations(int count);
protected:
    //{{AFX_MSG(MorphWin)
    afx_msg void OnDestroy();
    //}}AFX_MSG
    DECLARE_MESSAGE_MAP()
private:
    LPDIRECT3DRMMESH morphmesh;
    D3DRMVERTEX* morphmeshdata[MAXMORPHTARGETS];
    D3DRMVERTEX* morphvertex;
    DWORD nummorphvertices;
    DWORD nummorphtargets;
    LPDIRECT3DRMANIMATION* posanimation;
    LPDIRECT3DRMFRAME* posframe;
    LPDIRECT3DRMANIMATION* normanimation;
    LPDIRECT3DRMFRAME* normframe;
    BOOL morphing;
};
```

The six functions that we have discussed, along with the class constructor, are declared **public.** Four private helper functions are also declared. The class declares the **OnDestroy()** message handler function to perform cleanup tasks.

The **morphmeshdata** array will be used to store the vertex data for each morph target in a morph sequence. The **morphvertex** array is used to store the vertex data for the mesh that will be used to perform the actual morphing.

The **nummorphvertices** data member will be used to store the number of vertices in the morph targets. We don't have to store a separate vertex count for each morph target because it is required that all morph targets have the same vertex count. The **nummorphtargets** is used to store the number of targets in the morph sequence.

The **posanimation** and **posframe** arrays are used to calculate new vertex positions. The **posanimation** array is an array of pointers to the **Direct3DRMAnimation** interface. Vertex positions are determined by generating an animation sequence for each vertex in the morph mesh.

The **posframe** array is an array of frames that serve as dummy frames. The frames are used solely to retrieve animation data from the **Direct3DRM-Animation** objects.

The **normanimation** and **normframe** arrays are used to calculate normals for each vertex. This is necessary for correct lighting during the sequence. The vertex normals are morphed along with the vertex positions using the same technique.

Finally, the boolean **morphing** data member is used to indicate if a morph sequence has been loaded.

THE MORPHWIN::LOADMORPHSEQUENCE() FUNCTION

The **LoadMorphSequence()** function takes the name of a file as an argument. The function attempts to construct a morph sequence given the contents of the file:

```
BOOL MorphWin::LoadMorphSequence( const CString& filename )
{
    CString windowtext;
    GetWindowText( windowtext );

    CString txt="Loading: " + filename;
    SetWindowText( txt );

    BOOL ret=FALSE;
    if (LoadMeshes( filename ))
        if (CreateAnimations())
            ret=PrepareMorphVertices();

    SetWindowText( windowtext );

    return ret;
}
```

First, the function retrieves the text that is currently displayed in the window's title bar. The window title text is retrieved with the MFC **GetWindowText()** function and stored in the **windowtext** object. The text is then replaced with a string that indicates the name of the file to be loaded. The **SetWindowText()** function is used to display the string. Notice that before the **LoadMorphSequence()** function returns, the **SetWindowText()** function is used again—this time to restore the title bar's original text.

Next, the **LoadMorphSequence()** function makes three function calls, each dependent on the last. The **LoadMeshes()** function is used to extract the meshes from the file. The **CreateAnimation()** function is used to prepare an animation sequence for each vertex. The **PrepareMorphVertices()** function is used to initialize the array of vertices that will be used to store the calculated vertex data. If any of these functions fail, the **LoadMorphSequence()** function returns **FALSE**.

THE MORPHWIN::LOADMESHES() FUNCTION

The **LoadMeshes()** function is responsible for loading meshes from the supplied file. In addition to making sure that each mesh has the same vertex count, the **LoadMeshes()** function must extract and store vertex data. It is for this reason that the function is rather long (and ugly). The **LoadMeshes()** function appears as Listing 8.3.

Listing 8.3   The MorphWin::LoadMeshes() function.

```
BOOL MorphWin::LoadMeshes( const CString& filename )
{
    for (DWORD i=0;i<nummorphtargets;i++)
        delete [] morphmeshdata[i];
    nummorphtargets=0;

    if (morphmesh)
    {
        morphmesh->Release();
        morphmesh=0;
    }

    BOOL load_ok=TRUE;
    for (i=0;i<MAXMORPHTARGETS && load_ok;i++)
    {
        CString msg;
```

```
HRESULT r;
LPDIRECT3DRMMESHBUILDER builder;
d3drm->CreateMeshBuilder( &builder );

r=builder->Load( (void*)(LPCTSTR)filename,
        (void*)morphmeshname[i],
        D3DRMLOAD_FROMFILE | D3DRMLOAD_BYNAME, NULL, NULL );
load_ok=r==D3DRM_OK;
if (r==D3DRMERR_FILENOTFOUND)
{
    TRACE("file not found\n");
    CString msg=filename + ": file not found";
    AfxMessageBox( msg );
    morphing=FALSE;
}
if (!load_ok)
    goto nomoremeshes;

D3DVALUE scale;
if (i==0)
    scale=ScaleMesh( builder, D3DVALUE(25) );
else
    builder->Scale( scale, scale, scale );

builder->SetQuality( D3DRMRENDER_FLAT );

LPDIRECT3DRMMESH mesh;
builder->CreateMesh( &mesh );

unsigned vcount, fcount;
DWORD ds;
mesh->GetGroup( 0, &vcount, &fcount, 0, &ds, 0);

if (i==0)
    nummorphvertices=vcount;
else if(vcount!=nummorphvertices && load_ok)
{
    TRACE("invalid vertex count\n");
    AfxMessageBox("Invalid vertex count");
    morphing=FALSE;
    return FALSE;
}

morphmeshdata[i]=new D3DRMVERTEX[nummorphvertices];
```

```
r=mesh->GetVertices( 0, 0, nummorphvertices, morphmeshdata[i] );
if (r!=D3DRM_OK)
    TRACE("mesh->GetVertices() failed\n");

msg.Format("Mesh %d - %d vertices, %d faces",
        i+1, vcount, fcount );
SetWindowText( msg );

if (i==0)
    morphmesh=mesh;
else
{
    mesh->Release();
    mesh=0;
}

nomoremeshes:

builder->Release();
builder=0;

}
nummorphtargets=i-1;
morphing=TRUE;

return TRUE;
}
```

This function is called whenever a new morph sequence is loaded, so morph sequences may already be loaded when **LoadMeshes()** is called. The first thing that the function does is release any previously allocated resources.

The function uses a loop to attempt the loading of 26 targets. The loop stops if a given mesh is not found or if meshes with different vertex counts are discovered. When a mesh is loaded, its vertex data is extracted with the **Direct3DRMMesh GetVertices()** function. After each mesh is loaded, a new message is displayed on the window title bar. The **nummorphvertices** and **nummorphtargets** data members are both initialized by the **LoadMeshes()** function.

THE MORPHWIN::CREATEANIMATIONS() FUNCTION

The **CreateAnimations()** function is called only if the **LoadMeshes()** function is successful. **CreateAnimations()** is responsible for the initialization of the **Direct3DRMAnimation** objects that will perform the morphing calculation for both vertex locations and vertex normals. The function looks like this:

```
BOOL MorphWin::CreateAnimations()
{
    static int vertexcount;
    ReleaseAnimations( vertexcount );
    vertexcount=nummorphvertices;

    posanimation=new LPDIRECT3DRMANIMATION[nummorphvertices];
    posframe=new LPDIRECT3DRMFRAME[nummorphvertices];

    normanimation=new LPDIRECT3DRMANIMATION[nummorphvertices];
    normframe=new LPDIRECT3DRMFRAME[nummorphvertices];

    for (DWORD vert=0; vert<nummorphvertices; vert++)
    {
        d3drm->CreateAnimation( &posanimation[vert] );
        posanimation[vert]->SetOptions( D3DRMANIMATION_LINEARPOSITION |
                D3DRMANIMATION_POSITION );
        d3drm->CreateFrame( scene, &posframe[vert] );
        posanimation[vert]->SetFrame( posframe[vert] );

        d3drm->CreateAnimation( &normanimation[vert] );
        normanimation[vert]->SetOptions( D3DRMANIMATION_LINEARPOSITION |
                D3DRMANIMATION_POSITION );
        d3drm->CreateFrame( scene, &normframe[vert] );
        normanimation[vert]->SetFrame( normframe[vert] );
    }

    return TRUE;
}
```

The function first releases any previously created resources with the **ReleaseAnimations()** function. The number of vertices is stored in the static **vertexcount** variable for future calls to the **ReleaseAnimations()** function.

Next, the **posanimation**, **posframe**, **normanimation**, and **normframe** arrays are initialized. A loop is used to create two instances of the **Direct3DRMAnimation** object for each vertex. The animation objects in the **posanimation** array will be used to calculate vertex positions, and the animation objects in the **normanimation** array will be used to calculate vertex normals.

THE MORPHWIN::PREPAREMORPHVERTICES() FUNCTION

The **PrepareMorphVertices()** function allocates an array that will be used to store calculated vertex data:

```
BOOL MorphWin::PrepareMorphVertices()
{
    if (morphvertex)
    {
        delete [] morphvertex;
        morphvertex=0;
    }

    morphvertex=new D3DRMVERTEX[nummorphvertices];

    return TRUE;
}
```

As with the previous two functions, if existing resources are detected, they are released before any new resources are allocated.

THE MORPHWIN::GETNUMMORPHTARGETS() FUNCTION

The **GetNumMorphTargets()** function is declared in the **MorphWin** class definition:

```
DWORD GetNumMorphTargets()  { return nummorphtargets; }
```

The function simply returns the value stored in the **nummorphtargets** data member.

THE MORPHWIN::ADDMORPHKEY() FUNCTION

The **AddMorphKey()** function associates a morph target with a specific time within the animation. The function expects a target index and a time index as arguments.

```
BOOL MorphWin::AddMorphKey( DWORD target, D3DVALUE time )
{
    if (target<0 || target>nummorphtargets)
        return FALSE;

    for (DWORD i=0;i<nummorphvertices;i++)
    {
        D3DVECTOR& pos=morphmeshdata[target][i].position;
        posanimation[i]->AddPositionKey( time,
                pos.x, pos.y, pos.z );

        D3DVECTOR& norm=morphmeshdata[target][i].normal;
        normanimation[i]->AddPositionKey( time,
                norm.x, norm.y, norm.z );
    }
    return TRUE;
}
```

First, the morph target index is checked for validity. If the index is not valid, the function returns **FALSE**. Otherwise, the supplied morph target index is used to add position keys into the position and normal animation objects for each vertex. The keys are added with the **Direct3DRMAnimation AddPositionKey()** function. Notice that the **time** parameter is used as the first argument to **AddPositionKey()**.

THE MORPHWIN::SETMORPHTIME() FUNCTION

The **SetMorphTime()** function is responsible for generating and installing the vertex positions and normals. The function looks like this:

```
BOOL MorphWin::SetMorphTime( D3DVALUE time )
{
    for (DWORD v=0; v<nummorphvertices; v++)
    {
        posanimation[v]->SetTime( time );
```

```
        D3DVECTOR pos;
        posframe[v]->GetPosition( scene, &pos );
        morphvertex[v].position=pos;

        normanimation[v]->SetTime( time );
        D3DVECTOR norm;
        normframe[v]->GetPosition( scene, &norm );
        morphvertex[v].normal=norm;
    }
    morphmesh->SetVertices( 0, 0, nummorphvertices, morphvertex );

    return TRUE;
}
```

A loop is used to iterate once for each vertex. The **Direct3DRMAnimation SetTime()** function is used to update the animation sequence for both the vertex position and the vertex normal. The frame attached to each animation object is then used to assign the **morphvertex** array entries.

Once a new location and normal has been generated for each vertex, the new data is assigned with the **Direct3DRMMesh SetVertices()** function.

THE MORPHWIN::GETMORPHMESH() FUNCTION

The **GetMorphMesh()** function simply returns a pointer to the mesh that is being used to represent the morph sequence. The function is defined inline like this:

```
LPDIRECT3DRMMESH GetMorphMesh() { return morphmesh; }
```

This function allows classes derived from **MorphWin** to display and manipulate the mesh. You'll see how this is done next.

THE MORPHPLAYWIN CLASS

The **MorphPlayWin** class builds on the **MorphWin** class to create a complete application. The class is defined this way:

```
class MorphPlayWin : public MorphWin
{
public:
    MorphPlayWin();
    BOOL CreateScene();
```

```
protected:
    //{{AFX_MSG(MorphPlayWin)
    afx_msg void OnFileOpen();
    afx_msg void OnMorphForward();
    afx_msg void OnMorphReverse();
    afx_msg void OnMorphBoth();
    afx_msg void OnUpdateMorphForward(CCmdUI* pCmdUI);
    afx_msg void OnUpdateMorphReverse(CCmdUI* pCmdUI);
    afx_msg void OnUpdateMorphBoth(CCmdUI* pCmdUI);
    afx_msg void OnSpeedExtrafast();
    afx_msg void OnSpeedFast();
    afx_msg void OnSpeedMedium();
    afx_msg void OnSpeedSlow();
    afx_msg void OnSpeedExtraslow();
    afx_msg void OnUpdateSpeedExtrafast(CCmdUI* pCmdUI);
    afx_msg void OnUpdateSpeedFast(CCmdUI* pCmdUI);
    afx_msg void OnUpdateSpeedMedium(CCmdUI* pCmdUI);
    afx_msg void OnUpdateSpeedSlow(CCmdUI* pCmdUI);
    afx_msg void OnUpdateSpeedExtraslow(CCmdUI* pCmdUI);
    afx_msg void OnLButtonDown(UINT nFlags, CPoint point);
    afx_msg void OnLButtonUp(UINT nFlags, CPoint point);
    //}}AFX_MSG
    DECLARE_MESSAGE_MAP()
private:
    BOOL InitMorphSequence( const CString& );
    static void UpdateMorph(LPDIRECT3DRMFRAME frame, void*, D3DVALUE);
    static void UpdateDrag(LPDIRECT3DRMFRAME frame, void*, D3DVALUE);
    void OnIdle(LONG);
private:
    LPDIRECT3DRMFRAME frame;
    LPDIRECT3DRMMESH mesh;
    int morphspeed;
    D3DVALUE morphtimeinc;
    D3DVALUE maxmorphtime;
    static D3DVALUE morphtime;

    static BOOL drag;
    static BOOL end_drag;
    static int last_x, last_y;
};
```

Two public member functions are declared: a constructor and the
CreateScene() function. The constructor initializes the class's data members. The **CreateScene()** function initializes the demo's light sources
and viewport.

The class provides an **OnFileOpen()** function to react to File|Open menu commands. The function uses the MFC **CFileDialog** class to present a file selection dialog.

Three menu command handler functions provide support for the demo's Morph menu: **OnMorphForward()**, **OnMorphReverse()**, and **OnMorph-Both()**. Five menu command handler functions provide Speed menu functionality: **OnSpeedExtrafast()**, **OnSpeedFast()**, **OnSpeedMedium()**, **OnSpeedSlow()**, and **OnSpeedExtraslow()**. Each of these functions has a complimentary **OnUpdate()** function. The **OnLButtonDown()** and **OnLButtonUp()** functions will be used to initiate and terminate mouse drag operations (for mesh rotation).

Next, the **InitMorphSequence()** function is declared. We'll use this function to load new morph sequences. The **UpdateMorph()** callback function is used to control the speed and direction of the morph sequence. The **UpdateDrag()** callback function is used to implement mouse drag operations where the mesh is rotated according to mouse movement. The **OnIdle()** function is used to stabilize the mesh rotation during drag operations.

Next, the class's data members are declared. The **frame** and **mesh** data members are pointers to the morph mesh frame and the morph mesh, respectively. The **morphspeed**, **morphtimeinc**, **maxmorphtime**, and **morphtime** data members are used to control the morph sequence. The **drag**, **end_drag**, **last_x**, and **last_y** data members are used to rotate the mesh frame during drag operations.

THE MORPHPLAYWIN::CREATESCENE() FUNCTION

The **MorphPlayWin::CreateScene()** function looks like this:

```
BOOL MorphPlayWin::CreateScene()
{
    // --------DIRECTIONAL LIGHT--------
    LPDIRECT3DRMLIGHT dlight;
    d3rm->CreateLightRGB( D3DRMLIGHT_DIRECTIONAL,
            D3DVALUE(1.00), D3DVALUE(1.00), D3DVALUE(1.00),
            &dlight);
```

```
LPDIRECT3DRMLIGHT alight;
d3drm->CreateLightRGB( D3DRMLIGHT_AMBIENT,
        D3DVALUE(0.40), D3DVALUE(0.40), D3DVALUE(0.40),
        &alight);

LPDIRECT3DRMFRAME lightframe;
d3drm->CreateFrame( scene, &lightframe );
lightframe->AddLight( dlight );
lightframe->AddLight( alight );
lightframe->SetOrientation( scene,
        D3DVALUE(0), D3DVALUE(-1), D3DVALUE(1),
        D3DVALUE(0), D3DVALUE(1), D3DVALUE(0));
alight->Release();
alight=0;
dlight->Release();
dlight=0;
lightframe->Release();
lightframe=0;

//------ CAMERA----------
d3drm->CreateFrame( scene, &camera );
camera->SetPosition( scene, D3DVALUE(0), D3DVALUE(0), D3DVALUE(-50));
d3drm->CreateViewport( device, camera, 0, 0,
        device->GetWidth(), device->GetHeight(),
        &viewport);

return TRUE;
}
```

Unlike most of the other **CreateScene()** functions that we've looked at in
this book, the **MorphPlayWin** version performs just two steps. The first
step is creating two light sources. The second step is creating a viewport.

Because we haven't added any visual objects to the scene, the demo dis-
plays an empty window when it is first executed. The File|Open menu com-
mand must be used to load a morph sequence.

THE MORPHPLAYWIN::ONFILEOPEN() FUNCTION

Selecting the File|Open menu entry causes MFC to invoke the
OnFileOpen() function. The function looks like this:

```
void MorphPlayWin::OnFileOpen()
{
    static char BASED_CODE filter[] =
            "Morph Files (*.mrf)|*.mrf|X Files (*.x)|*.x||";
    CFileDialog opendialog( TRUE, 0, 0, OFN_FILEMUSTEXIST,
            filter, this );
    if ( opendialog.DoModal() == IDOK )
    {
        CString filename = opendialog.GetPathName();
        CWaitCursor cur;
        InitMorphSequence( filename );
    }
}
```

The function uses the MFC **CFileDialog** class to present a file selection dialog that lists only MRF and X files. If the user selects or enters a file name, the **InitMorphSequence()** function is called with the file name as an argument.

THE MORPHPLAYWIN::INITMORPHSEQUENCE() FUNCTION

The **InitMorphSequence()** function uses member functions inherited from the **MorphWin** class to initiate a new morph sequence:

```
BOOL MorphPlayWin::InitMorphSequence( const CString& filename )
{
    if (frame)
        frame->DeleteVisual( mesh );
    else
    {
        d3drm->CreateFrame( scene, &frame );
        frame->AddMoveCallback( UpdateDrag, NULL );
        frame->AddMoveCallback( UpdateMorph, this );
    }

    if (LoadMorphSequence( filename )==FALSE)
        return FALSE;

    DWORD targets=GetNumMorphTargets();
    for (DWORD i=0;i<targets;i++)
        AddMorphKey( i, D3DVALUE(i) );
    maxmorphtime=D3DVALUE(targets-1);
    morphtime=D3DVALUE(0.0);
```

```
mesh=GetMorphMesh();
mesh->SetGroupColorRGB( 0,
        D3DVALUE(.67), D3DVALUE(.82), D3DVALUE(.94) );
frame->AddVisual( mesh );

return TRUE;
}
```

The function first checks the **frame** data member. If the **frame** pointer is not initialized, the function creates a new frame and installs two callback functions: **UpdateDrag()** and **UpdateMorph()**. If the **frame** pointer was initialized by a previous call, the current mesh is removed from the scene with the **Direct3DRMFrame DeleteVisual()** function.

Next, the **LoadMorphSequence()** function is called. If the **LoadMorph-Sequence()** function fails (returns **FALSE**), the **InitMorphSequence** function returns immediately.

Next, a loop is used to install a morph key for each morph target. Also, the **maxmorphtime** and **morphtime** data members are initialized.

Finally, a pointer to the newly created morph mesh is retrieved with the **MorphWin::GetMorphMesh()** function. The color of the mesh is modified, and the mesh is added to the scene.

THE MORPHPLAYWIN::UPDATEMORPH() FUNCTION

The morph sequence is controlled by the **UpdateMorph()** callback function:

```
void MorphPlayWin::UpdateMorph(LPDIRECT3DRMFRAME, void* ptr, D3DVALUE)
{
    MorphPlayWin* win=(MorphPlayWin*)ptr;
    const D3DVALUE maxtime=win->maxmorphtime;
    const int morphspeed=win->morphspeed;
    const D3DVALUE morphtimeinc=win->morphtimeinc;

    if (morphspeed==MORPH_FORWARD)
    {
        morphtime+=morphtimeinc;
        if (morphtime>maxtime)
            morphtime=D3DVALUE(0);
    }
```

```
    else if (morphspeed==MORPH_REVERSE)
    {
        morphtime-=morphtimeinc;
        if (morphtime<D3DVALUE(0))
            morphtime=maxtime;
    }
    else if (morphspeed==MORPH_BOTH)
    {
        static BOOL forward=TRUE;
        if (forward)
            morphtime+=morphtimeinc;
        else
            morphtime-=morphtimeinc;
        if (morphtime<D3DVALUE(0) || morphtime>maxtime)
            forward=1-forward;
    }

    win->SetMorphTime( morphtime );
}
```

A time is calculated for the morph sequence based on the **morphspeed** data member. If the **morphspeed** member is set to **MORPH_FORWARD**, the morph sequence time is incremented until it reaches the maximum time index. The value is then reset to zero. The morph time index is stored with the **morphtime** data member.

If the **morphspeed** data member is set to **MORPH_REVERSE**, the time value is calculated by subtracting values from the **morphtime** data member. The **MORPH_BOTH** constant causes the sequence to be played first forward, then in reverse.

Once the **morphtime** data member has been assigned, the **MorphWin:: SetMorphTime()** function is called. This call calculates the vertex data and updates the morph mesh.

THE MORPHPLAYWIN MOUSE FUNCTIONS

The MorphPlay demo uses four functions to implement mesh rotation: **OnLButtonDown()**, **OnLButtonUp()**, **UpdateDrag()**, and **OnIdle()**. Let's look at the **OnLButtonDown()** function first:

```
void MorphPlayWin::OnLButtonDown(UINT nFlags, CPoint point)
{
    if (!drag)
```

```
    {
        drag=TRUE;
        last_x = GetMouseX();
        last_y = GetMouseY();
        ShowCursor( FALSE );
        SetCapture();
    }
    MorphWin::OnLButtonDown(nFlags, point);
}
```

The function starts a new drag sequence if one is not already in progress. The **drag** data member is used to indicate the current drag status. If a new sequence is initiated, the current mouse position is stored, the mouse cursor is hidden, and the mouse capture mode is started with the MFC **SetCapture()** function. **SetCapture()** causes all mouse-related messages to be sent to the program's window class, regardless of where on the screen the mouse is moved.

The **OnLButtonUp()** function looks like this:

```
void MorphPlayWin::OnLButtonUp(UINT nFlags, CPoint point)
{
    if (drag)
    {
        end_drag=TRUE;
        ReleaseCapture();
        ShowCursor( TRUE );
    }
    MorphWin::OnLButtonUp(nFlags, point);
}
```

The **OnLButtonUp()** function determines if a drag operation is in effect. If so, the **end_drag** data member is set to signal that the drag operation is to be terminated. Also, the mouse capture mode is terminated with the **ReleaseCapture()** function, and the mouse cursor is displayed.

The **UpdateDrag()** callback function is responsible for rotating the morph mesh during a drag operation. The code looks like this:

```
void MorphPlayWin::UpdateDrag(LPDIRECT3DRMFRAME frame, void*, D3DVALUE)
{
    if (drag)
    {
```

```
            double delta_x, delta_y;
            int x=GetMouseX();
            int y=GetMouseY();
            delta_x = x - last_x;
            delta_y = y - last_y;
            last_x = x;
            last_y = y;

            double delta_r = sqrt(delta_x * delta_x + delta_y * delta_y);
            double radius = 50;
            double denom;

            denom = sqrt(radius * radius + delta_r * delta_r);

            if (!(delta_r == 0 || denom == 0))
                frame->SetRotation( 0,
                    D3DDivide(D3DVAL((float)-delta_y), D3DVAL((float)delta_r)),
                    D3DDivide(D3DVAL((float)-delta_x), D3DVAL((float)delta_r)),
                    D3DVAL(0.0),
                    D3DDivide(D3DVAL((float)delta_r), D3DVAL((float)denom)));
        }

    if (end_drag)
    {
        drag=FALSE;
        end_drag=FALSE;
    }
}
```

The **UpdateDrag()** function converts the two dimensional mouse movement data (stored in the **x**, **y**, **last_x**, and **last_y** variables) to calculate a rotational vector for the mesh. The new rotation attribute is assigned with the **Direct3DRMFrame SetRotation()** function.

Finally, the **OnIdle()** function is used to prevent excessive mesh movement during drag operations:

```
void MorphPlayWin::OnIdle(LONG)
{
    if (drag && frame)
        frame->SetRotation( 0,
                D3DVAL(0.0), D3DVAL(1.0), D3DVAL(0.0), D3DVAL(0.0) );
}
```

CONCLUSION

It would probably be derelict of me to close this chapter without saying any more about how to create morph targets of your own. So, without getting into the details, here are a few suggestions:

- The easiest way to create compatible mesh targets is to create multiple instances of a single mesh and modify each instance. This is typically true regardless of what modeller you are using.

- The meshes in the scene do not have to be linked in a hierarchy. Naming them with single lowercase letters starting with 'a' will suffice.

- It is sometimes useful to use the "ignore frame transformation" options when converting 3DS files to X files using the DirectX CONV3DS utility.

Well, that's it for meshes. We've taken a long look at vertex animation and used it in three demos. In Chapter 9, we'll study viewports in—possibly painful—detail.

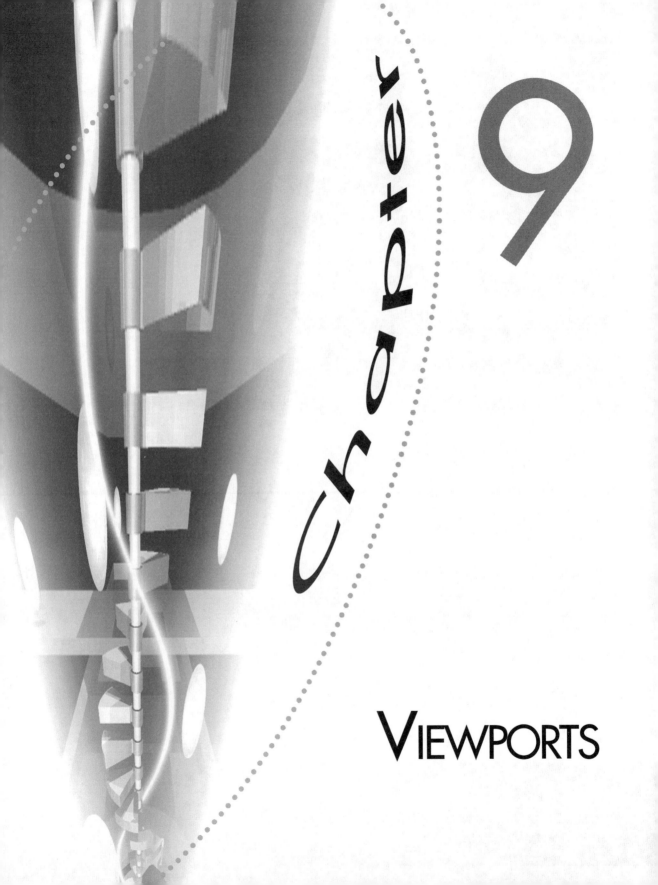

Chapter

9

VIEWPORTS

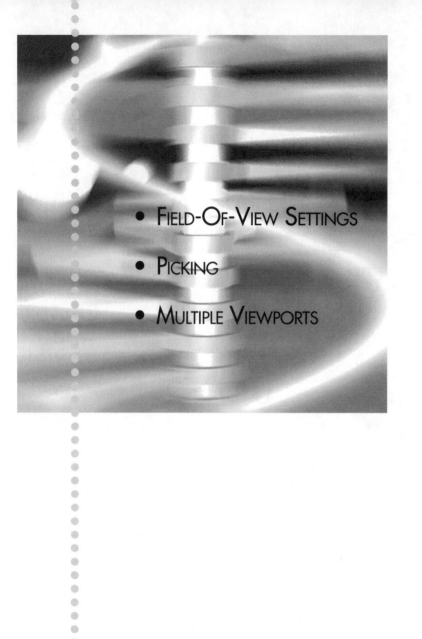

- Field-Of-View Settings

- Picking

- Multiple Viewports

VIEWPORTS

Most of the demos on the CD-ROM require that a viewport be created, so you are already familiar with viewports. In this chapter, we'll take a closer look, demonstrating viewport features and techniques using the following demos:

- Zoom
- MeshPick
- FacePick
- MultiView

For review, a viewport is the component through which Direct3D scenes are viewed. Viewports are the cameras that we use to see our 3D creations. In order to use a viewport, it must be given a location and orientation. This requirement is met when a viewport is attached to a frame. The frame's location and orientation determine the portion of the scene that is displayed.

FIELD-OF-VIEW

In the demos that we looked at in previous chapters, we didn't specify a field-of-view, or camera angle. This means that we were using the default field-of-view setting of 0.5.

A viewport's field-of-view can be changed with the **Direct3DRMViewport SetField()** function. Small values reduce the viewport's field-of-view and have a telephoto effect. Large values widen the viewport's field-of-view, causing a wide-angle effect.

THE ZOOM DEMO

In photography, a lens that has an adjustable field-of-view is called a zoom lens. Zoom lenses allow you to "zoom in" on distant objects and "zoom out" to accommodate more scenery.

The Zoom demo uses the **SetField()** function to adjust the viewport's field-of-view. The demo places a mesh at the origin and zooms in on the mesh from a stationary position. The Zoom demo appears in Figure 9.1 (but it is very unlikely that you will be able to see any changes in field-of-view by looking at the figure).

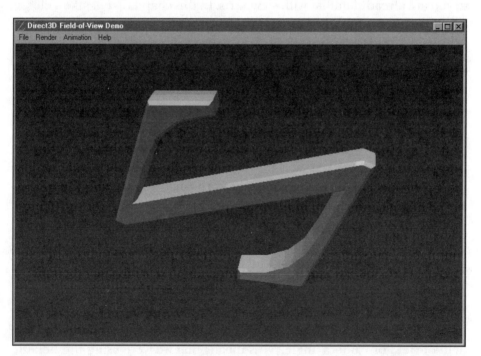

Figure 9.1
The Zoom demo.

If you run the Zoom demo, it appears that the mesh is moving. Although the mesh is rotating, its position is stationary. The illusion is caused by the fact that the viewport field-of-view is being changed.

The Zoom demo supports the typical Render menu that allows the rendering method of the mesh to be changed at runtime. Also, an Animation menu is supported. The Animation menu allows you to change the style of the animation (linear versus spline).

The Zoom demo demonstrates the following techniques:

- Using the **Direct3DRMViewport SetField()** function

- Using the **Direct3DRMAnimation** to perform general purpose (non-frame) animation.

- Changing a mesh's rendering method at runtime

- Using the **Direct3DRMMaterial** interface to alter a mesh's appearance

THE ZOOMWIN CLASS

The Zoom demo provides its functionality in the **ZoomWin** class:

```
class ZoomWin : public RMWin
{
public:
    ZoomWin();
    BOOL CreateScene();
protected:
    //{{AFX_MSG(ZoomWin)
    afx_msg void OnRenderWireframe();
    afx_msg void OnRenderFlat();
    afx_msg void OnRenderGouraud();
    afx_msg void OnUpdateRenderFlat(CCmdUI* pCmdUI);
    afx_msg void OnUpdateRenderGouraud(CCmdUI* pCmdUI);
    afx_msg void OnUpdateRenderWireframe(CCmdUI* pCmdUI);
    afx_msg void OnAnimationLinear();
    afx_msg void OnAnimationSpline();
    afx_msg void OnUpdateAnimationLinear(CCmdUI* pCmdUI);
    afx_msg void OnUpdateAnimationSpline(CCmdUI* pCmdUI);
    //}}AFX_MSG
    DECLARE_MESSAGE_MAP()
private:
    static void AdjustField(LPDIRECT3DRMFRAME frame, void*, D3DVALUE);
```

```
private:
    LPDIRECT3DRMMESHBUILDER meshbuilder;
    static LPDIRECT3DRMFRAME zoomframe;
    static LPDIRECT3DRMANIMATION animation;
};
```

The class declares two public functions: a constructor and the **CreateScene()** function. The constructor is used to initialize the class's non-static data members. (The static data members are initialized to zero automatically, so constructor initialization is not necessary.) Only one non-static data member is present, so the code looks like this:

```
ZoomWin::ZoomWin()
{
    meshbuilder=0;
}
```

The **CreateScene()** function constructs the demo's scene. We'll look at **CreateScene()** soon.

Ten protected member functions are declared. The first six are the message handling functions that provide Render menu functionality. The remaining four implement the demo's Animation menu. We'll look at the Animation menu functions later. The Render menu functions are the same functions that appear in almost all of the demos.

One callback function is declared: **AdjustField()**. We'll use this callback to change the viewport's field-of-view during the program's execution.

Finally, three private data members are declared:

```
LPDIRECT3DRMMESHBUILDER meshbuilder;
static LPDIRECT3DRMFRAME zoomframe;
static LPDIRECT3DRMANIMATION animation;
```

The **meshbuilder** pointer is used to access the demo's mesh. It is used by the **CreateScene()** function and by the six Render menu command-handling functions. The **zoomframe** data member is a pointer to a dummy frame, and the **animation** data member is a pointer to the **Direct3DRMAnimation** interface. We'll use the animation interface and the dummy frame to "animate" the viewport's field-of-view. You'll see how this works when we look at the **AdjustField()** function.

THE ZOOMWIN::CREATESCENE() FUNCTION

The Zoom demo's scene is constructed by the **CreateScene()** function. The function appears in Listing 9.1.

Listing 9.1   The ZoomWin::CreateScene() function.

```
BOOL ZoomWin::CreateScene()
{
    // ------- MESH --------
    D3DRMLOADRESOURCE resinfo;
    resinfo.hModule=NULL;
    resinfo.lpName=MAKEINTRESOURCE( IDR_Z_MESH );
    resinfo.lpType="MESH";
    d3drm->CreateMeshBuilder( &meshbuilder );
    meshbuilder->Load( &resinfo, NULL, D3DRMLOAD_FROMRESOURCE,
            NULL, NULL );
    meshbuilder->SetColorRGB(D3DVALUE(.67),
            D3DVALUE(.82), D3DVALUE(.94) );
    ScaleMesh( meshbuilder, D3DVALUE(25) );

    // ------- MATERIAL ----------
    LPDIRECT3DRMMATERIAL material;
    d3drm->CreateMaterial( D3DVALUE(10), &material );
    meshbuilder->SetMaterial( material );
    material->Release();
    material=0;

    // ------ MESH FRAME ------
    LPDIRECT3DRMFRAME meshframe;
    d3drm->CreateFrame( scene, &meshframe );
    meshframe->SetRotation( scene,
            D3DVALUE(1), D3DVALUE(.4), D3DVALUE(0),
            D3DVALUE(.1) );
    meshframe->AddVisual( meshbuilder );
    meshframe->Release();
    meshframe=0;

    // ------- ANIMATION --------
    d3drm->CreateAnimation( &animation );
    animation->SetOptions(  D3DRMANIMATION_SPLINEPOSITION |
            D3DRMANIMATION_CLOSED |
            D3DRMANIMATION_POSITION );
    animation->AddPositionKey( D3DVALUE(0),
            D3DVALUE(.4), D3DVALUE(0), D3DVALUE(0) );
```

```
animation->AddPositionKey( D3DVALUE(24),
        D3DVALUE(5), D3DVALUE(0), D3DVALUE(0) );
animation->AddPositionKey( D3DVALUE(49),
        D3DVALUE(1), D3DVALUE(0), D3DVALUE(0) );
animation->AddPositionKey( D3DVALUE(74),
        D3DVALUE(5), D3DVALUE(0), D3DVALUE(0) );
animation->AddPositionKey( D3DVALUE(99),
        D3DVALUE(.4), D3DVALUE(0), D3DVALUE(0) );

d3drm->CreateFrame( scene, &zoomframe );
animation->SetFrame( zoomframe );

// --------- LIGHT --------
LPDIRECT3DRMLIGHT dlight;
d3drm->CreateLightRGB( D3DRMLIGHT_DIRECTIONAL,
        D3DVALUE(1.00), D3DVALUE(1.00), D3DVALUE(1.00),
        &dlight );

LPDIRECT3DRMLIGHT alight;
d3drm->CreateLightRGB( D3DRMLIGHT_AMBIENT,
        D3DVALUE(.40), D3DVALUE(.40), D3DVALUE(.40),
        &alight );

LPDIRECT3DRMFRAME lightframe;
d3drm->CreateFrame( scene, &lightframe );
lightframe->SetOrientation( scene,
        D3DVALUE(0), D3DVALUE(-1), D3DVALUE(1),
        D3DVALUE(0), D3DVALUE(1), D3DVALUE(0) );

lightframe->AddLight( dlight );
lightframe->AddLight( alight );

dlight->Release();
dlight=0;
alight->Release();
alight=0;
lightframe->Release();
lightframe=0;

//------ CAMERA----------
d3drm->CreateFrame( scene, &camera );
camera->SetPosition( scene,
        D3DVALUE(0), D3DVALUE(0), D3DVALUE(-50) );
d3drm->CreateViewport( device, camera, 0, 0,
        device->GetWidth(), device->GetHeight(),
        &viewport );
```

```
    camera->AddMoveCallback( AdjustField, NULL );
    return TRUE;
}
```

The **CreateScene()** function performs six steps:

1. Creates and loads a mesh

2. Creates and applies a material to the mesh

3. Creates a frame for the mesh

4. Constructs an animation sequence that will be used to control the viewport's field-of-view

5. Creates two light sources

6. Creates a viewport and installs a callback function

The first step uses the **Direct3DRMMeshBuilder** interface to load a mesh from a file. Let's take a closer look:

```
D3DRMLOADRESOURCE resinfo;
resinfo.hModule=NULL;
resinfo.lpName=MAKEINTRESOURCE( IDR_Z_MESH );
resinfo.lpType="MESH";
meshbuilder->Load( &resinfo, NULL, D3DRMLOAD_FROMRESOURCE, NULL, NULL );
meshbuilder->SetColorRGB(D3DVALUE(.67), D3DVALUE(.82), D3DVALUE(.94) );
ScaleMesh( meshbuilder, D3DVALUE(25) );
```

A **D3DRMLOADRESOURCE** is used to identify the resource entry that contains the mesh. The **meshbuilder** data member is initialized with the **Direct3DRM CreateMeshBuilder()** function. The **Load()** function is then used to load the mesh. The color of the mesh is assigned with the **SetColorRGB()** function. Finally, the mesh is scaled to 25 units with the **ScaleMesh()** function.

Next, a material is applied to the mesh:

```
LPDIRECT3DRMMATERIAL material;
d3drm->CreateMaterial( D3DVALUE(10), &material );
meshbuilder->SetMaterial( material );
material->Release();
material=0;
```

Materials allow us to fine-tune the mesh's appearance by changing the behavior and color of specular highlights. In this case, we are using a material to give the mesh a shiny appearance.

Testing material settings

Xpose is an elaborate object viewer that was created using the techniques in this book. Both it and the code to create it are on the book's CD-ROM. The fastest way to learn about material settings and how they affect a mesh's appearance is to use Xpose to experiment. The Xpose Material Settings dialog allows you to change material settings and see the results immediately.

The **Direct3DRM CreateMaterial()** function is used to create the material. The new material is applied to the mesh with the **Direct3DRMMeshBuilder SetMaterial()** member function. The local **material** pointer is then released.

Step 3 is the creation of a frame for the mesh:

```
LPDIRECT3DRMFRAME meshframe;
d3drm->CreateFrame( scene, &meshframe );
meshframe->SetRotation( scene,
        D3DVALUE(1), D3DVALUE(.4), D3DVALUE(0),
        D3DVALUE(.1) );
meshframe->AddVisual( meshbuilder );
meshframe->Release();
meshframe=0;
```

The frame is created with the **Direct3DRM CreateFrame()** function. The new frame is given a rotation attribute with the **SetRotation()** function. This rotation attribute is the only animation that is applied to the mesh frame. The frame will stay at the origin (by default) throughout the demo's execution. The **meshframe** pointer is released after the meshbuilder has been attached to the new frame with the **AddVisual()** function.

Next, an animation sequence is constructed that we will use to control the viewport's field-of-view. The code looks as follows:

```
d3drm->CreateAnimation( &animation );
animation->SetOptions(  D3DRMANIMATION_SPLINEPOSITION |
        D3DRMANIMATION_CLOSED |
        D3DRMANIMATION_POSITION );
animation->AddPositionKey( D3DVALUE(0),
        D3DVALUE(.4), D3DVALUE(0), D3DVALUE(0) );
animation->AddPositionKey( D3DVALUE(24),
        D3DVALUE(5), D3DVALUE(0), D3DVALUE(0) );
animation->AddPositionKey( D3DVALUE(49),
        D3DVALUE(1), D3DVALUE(0), D3DVALUE(0) );
animation->AddPositionKey( D3DVALUE(74),
        D3DVALUE(5), D3DVALUE(0), D3DVALUE(0) );
animation->AddPositionKey( D3DVALUE(99),
        D3DVALUE(.4), D3DVALUE(0), D3DVALUE(0) );

d3drm->CreateFrame( scene, &zoomframe );
animation->SetFrame( zoomframe );
```

First, the animation is created with the **Direct3DRM CreateAnimation()** function. The **Direct3DRMAnimation SetOptions()** function is then used to specify the characteristics of the animation. We are using the **D3DRMANIMATION_SPLINEPOSITION** constant to indicate that we want a spline-based animation (as opposed to linear). This setting can be modified from the Zoom demo's Animation menu. The **D3DRMANIMATION_CLOSED** constant is used to indicate that the animation sequence should repeat itself. This lets us use a continually increasing value to execute the animation sequence repeatedly. The **D3DRMANIMATION_POSITION** constant is used to indicate that we are interested in the animation's positional output (we are not using the **D3DRMANIMATION_SCALEANDROTATION** constant because, as you will see, we are not using the animation's scaling or rotational output).

Next, five position keys are added to the animation with the **AddPositionKey()** function. The first **AddPositionKey()** argument is the key value, which indicates where in the animation the given key is to take effect. The remaining three arguments indicate the position of the new key. Notice that the keys that we are installing vary only on the X axis. This is arbitrary. We could have used the Y or Z axis because we are creating a linear, or one-dimensional, animation sequence. We will be using only the X axis portion of the animation sequence.

Next, a frame called **zoomframe** is created. The new frame is attached to the animation sequence with the **Direct3DRMAnimation SetFrame()** function.

The **zoomframe** frame is a dummy frame, but not in the same sense as the dummy frames that we used in the Firefly (Chapter 6) or Decal (Chapter 5) demos. This dummy frame will not be used as a parent for other frames. The frame will be animated by the animation sequence that we just created, and its position will be used to assign field-of-view settings to the viewport. Notice that the X axis values in the animation sequence range from 0.4 to 5.0. These values will not be treated as positions. Instead, they will be used as field-of-view settings and used as arguments to the **Direct3DRMViewport SetField()** function.

Returning to the six steps performed by the **CreateScene()** function, the fifth step is the creation of two light sources. We'll forgo discussing this step. Light sources are the subject of Chapter 6.

The sixth, and final, step is the creation of a viewport:

```
d3drm->CreateFrame( scene, &camera );
camera->SetPosition( scene,
        D3DVALUE(0), D3DVALUE(0), D3DVALUE(-50) );
d3drm->CreateViewport( device, camera, 0, 0,
        device->GetWidth(), device->GetHeight(),
        &viewport );
camera->AddMoveCallback( AdjustField, NULL );
return TRUE;
```

First, the **camera** pointer is initialized and positioned. The frame is then used as an argument to the **Direct3DRM CreateViewport()** function. The last thing that the **CreateScene()** function does is install the **AdjustField()** callback function with the **AddMoveCallback()** function. We use the **camera** frame to install the callback, but any frame in the scene would suffice.

THE ZOOMWIN::ADJUSTFIELD() FUNCTION

The **AdjustField()** function is the callback function that controls the viewport's field-of-view. The function looks like this:

```
void ZoomWin::AdjustField(LPDIRECT3DRMFRAME, void*, D3DVALUE)
{
```

```
    static D3DVALUE time;
    time+=D3DVALUE(.5);
    animation->SetTime( time );

    D3DVECTOR pos;
    zoomframe->GetPosition( 0, &pos );

    viewport->SetField( pos.x );
}
```

The function uses a static variable (**time**) to control the animation sequence. The **time** variable is incremented each time that the **AdjustField()** function is invoked. Once the **time** variable has been incremented, the new time is installed into the animation with the **Direct3DRMAnimation SetTime()** function.

Next, the position of the animated frame (**zoomframe**) is retrieved. Recall that the **zoomframe** frame's position is controlled by the animation. When we set the new animation time with the **SetTime()** function, the **zoomframe** was repositioned according to the animation sequence. The frame's new position is retrieved with the **GetPosition()** function.

Finally, the X axis position of the frame is used as a new field-of-view setting for the viewport. The new setting is installed with the **Direct3DRMViewport SetField()** function. Recall that **viewport** is a static **RMWin** class data member. This is why we have access to it from within a callback function.

THE ZOOMWIN ANIMATION FUNCTIONS

The Zoom demo allows you to change animation sequence settings (linear versus spline) from the Animation menu. This is done by setting different options using the **Direct3DRMAnimation SetOptions()** function. The two functions that respond to Animation menu entries appear like this:

```
void ZoomWin::OnAnimationLinear()
{
    animation->SetOptions( D3DRMANIMATION_LINEARPOSITION |
            D3DRMANIMATION_CLOSED |
            D3DRMANIMATION_POSITION );
}

void ZoomWin::OnAnimationSpline()
{
```

```
animation->SetOptions( D3DRMANIMATION_SPLINEPOSITION |
        D3DRMANIMATION_CLOSED |
        D3DRMANIMATION_POSITION );
}
```

The Animation menu functionality is made complete with the addition of check marks that appear on the menu to the left of the currently active animation mode. The two functions that determine if the check marks are to be displayed appear here:

```
void ZoomWin::OnUpdateAnimationLinear(CCmdUI* pCmdUI)
{
    D3DRMANIMATIONOPTIONS options = animation->GetOptions();
    pCmdUI->SetCheck( options & D3DRMANIMATION_LINEARPOSITION );
}

void ZoomWin::OnUpdateAnimationSpline(CCmdUI* pCmdUI)
{
    D3DRMANIMATIONOPTIONS options = animation->GetOptions();
    pCmdUI->SetCheck( options & D3DRMANIMATION_SPLINEPOSITION );
}
```

The functions use the **Direct3DRMAnimation GetOptions()** function to retrieve the active animation settings. The **SetCheck()** function is used to activate the check marks if the setting of interest is detected.

PICKING

Direct3D viewports provide support for picking. Picking is the selecting of an object through the selection of a location on the viewport. Typically, the mouse is used to select a location within the viewport. The viewport uses the location of the mouse to determine which object, if any, was "picked." Picking is useful for applications that require precise and intuitive object selection.

Picking brings a performance hit. Picking requires that Direct3D sorts though its internal structures and buffering data. This search is nontrivial. In fact, there is often a visible delay in animation when a picking operation is executed.

On the other hand, picking is accurate to the pixel. Direct3D can determine exactly which object was selected based on the mouse's location. If the object is visible, then the object can be selected with a pick operation.

THE MESHPICK DEMO

The MeshPick demo displays nine spherical meshes and allows you to use the mouse to pick and drag any of the meshes. The meshes can be placed very near to each other, allowing you to test the accuracy of the picking mechanism. The MeshPick demo appears in Figure 9.2.

The MeshPick demo demonstrates the following techniques:

• Using the **Direct3DRMViewport Pick()** function

• Using mouse input to manipulate visual objects

We'll talk about each of these techniques as we walk through the MeshPick code.

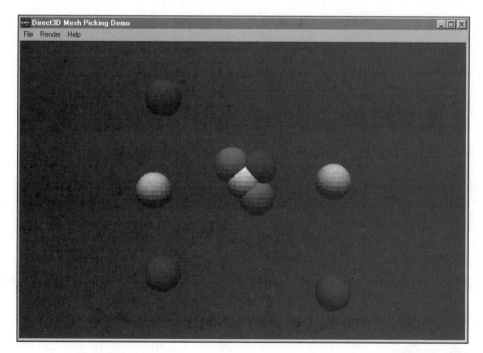

Figure 9.2
The MeshPick demo.

THE MESHPICKWIN CLASS

The MeshPick demo provides its functionality with the **MeshPickWin** class:

```
class MeshPickWin : public RMWin
{
public:
    MeshPickWin();
    BOOL CreateScene();
protected:
    //{{AFX_MSG(MeshPickWin)
    afx_msg void OnLButtonDown(UINT nFlags, CPoint point);
    afx_msg void OnLButtonUp(UINT nFlags, CPoint point);
    //}}AFX_MSG
    DECLARE_MESSAGE_MAP()
private:
    static void UpdateDrag(LPDIRECT3DRMFRAME frame, void*, D3DVALUE);
    BOOL PickMesh( const CPoint& point );
private:
    static DragData drag;
};
```

The class declares two public member functions: a constructor and the **CreateScene()** function. The constructor initializes the class's single data member, and the **CreateScene()** function constructs the demo's scene.

Two protected message handling functions are declared, **OnLButtonDown()** and **OnLButtonUp()**. MFC calls these functions to notify the application of changes in the left mouse button's status. We'll use the **OnLButtonDown()** function to perform the picking procedure and initiate a drag mode that allows the picked object to be moved with the mouse. The **OnLButtonUp()** function is used to terminate the drag mode.

There are two private member functions: **UpdateDrag()** and **PickMesh()**. **UpdateDrag()** is a callback function that will be used to poll the current state of the application. If the application is in a drag mode, the **UpdateDrag()** function will adjust the location of the currently "picked" mesh based on the position of the mouse. The **PickMesh()** function is used to perform the actual picking operation.

The class's only data member is a structure of type **DragData**. The structure is defined like this:

```
struct DragData
{
    LPDIRECT3DRMFRAME frame;
    POINT mousedown;
    D3DVALUE origx,origy;
};
```

The structure contains data that is pertinent during a drag operation. The structure's **frame** data member will point to the frame that is attached to the mesh that is being dragged. The **mousedown** field is used to store the mouse location where the drag operation was initiated. The **origx** and **origy** data members are used to store the location of the frame when the drag operation started.

THE MESHPICKWIN::CREATESCENE() FUNCTION

The MeshPick demo **CreateScene()** function appears in Listing 9.2.

Listing 9.2 The MeshPickWin::CreateScene() function.

```
BOOL MeshPickWin::CreateScene()
{
    // ------- MESH BUILDER --------
    D3DRMLOADRESOURCE resinfo;
    resinfo.hModule=NULL;
    resinfo.lpName=MAKEINTRESOURCE( IDR_SPHEREMESH );
    resinfo.lpType="MESH";
    LPDIRECT3DRMMESHBUILDER meshbuilder;
    d3drm->CreateMeshBuilder( &meshbuilder );
    meshbuilder->Load( &resinfo, NULL, D3DRMLOAD_FROMRESOURCE,
            NULL, NULL );
    meshbuilder->SetQuality( D3DRMRENDER_FLAT );

    //------ NINE MESHES ----------
    for (int x=0;x<3;x++)
    {
        for (int y=0;y<3;y++)
        {
            LPDIRECT3DRMMESH mesh;
            meshbuilder->CreateMesh( &mesh );
            mesh->SetGroupColorRGB( 0,
                    D3DVALUE(x%2), D3DVALUE(y%2), D3DVALUE(1) );

            LPDIRECT3DRMFRAME meshframe;
            d3drm->CreateFrame( scene, &meshframe );
```

```
        meshframe->AddVisual( mesh );
        int xoffset=(rand()%3)-1;
        int yoffset=(rand()%3)-1;
        meshframe->SetPosition( scene,
                D3DVALUE((x-1)*10+xoffset),
                D3DVALUE((y-1)*10+yoffset),
                D3DVALUE(0) );
        meshframe->SetRotation( scene,
                D3DVALUE(0), D3DVALUE(1), D3DVALUE(0),
                D3DVALUE(.1) );

        meshframe->Release();
        meshframe=0;
        mesh->Release();
        mesh=0;
    }
}

meshbuilder->Release();
meshbuilder=0;

//------- CALLBACK --------
scene->AddMoveCallback( UpdateDrag, NULL );

// --------DIRECTIONAL LIGHT--------
LPDIRECT3DRMLIGHT dlight;
d3drm->CreateLightRGB( D3DRMLIGHT_DIRECTIONAL,
        D3DVALUE(1.00), D3DVALUE(1.00), D3DVALUE(1.00),
        &dlight );

LPDIRECT3DRMFRAME dlightframe;
d3drm->CreateFrame( scene, &dlightframe );
dlightframe->AddLight( dlight );
dlightframe->SetOrientation( scene,
        D3DVALUE(0), D3DVALUE(-1), D3DVALUE(1),
        D3DVALUE(0), D3DVALUE(1), D3DVALUE(0) );

dlight->Release();
dlight=0;
dlightframe->Release();
dlightframe=0;

//------ CAMERA----------
d3drm->CreateFrame( scene, &camera );
camera->SetPosition( scene,
        D3DVALUE(0), D3DVALUE(0), D3DVALUE(-50) );
```

```
d3drm->CreateViewport( device, camera, 0, 0,
        device->GetWidth(), device->GetHeight(),
        &viewport );

return TRUE;
}
```

The **CreateScene**() function performs five steps:

1. Uses the **Direct3DRMMeshBuilder** interface to load a spherical mesh

2. Creates nine meshes, each with a frame

3. Installs the **UpdateDrag**() callback function

4. Creates a light source

5. Creates a viewport

The first step is the creation of a meshbuilder:

```
D3DRMLOADRESOURCE resinfo;
resinfo.hModule=NULL
resinfo.lpName=MAKEINTRESOURCE( IDR_SPHEREMESH );
resinfo.lpType="MESH";
LPDIRECT3DRMMESHBUILDER meshbuilder;
d3drm->CreateMeshBuilder( &meshbuilder );
meshbuilder->Load( &resinfo, NULL, D3DRMLOAD_FROMRESOURCE,NULL, NULL );
meshbuilder->SetQuality( D3DRMRENDER_FLAT );
```

The mesh is loaded from the demo's resources with the **Direct3DRMMesh-Builder Load**() function. The **SetQuality**() function is used to demote the **meshbuilder**'s default Gouraud rendering quality setting to flat.

In Step 2, a loop is used to create nine meshes. The previously initialized **meshbuilder** is used:

```
for (int x=0;x<3;x++)
{
    for (int y=0;y<3;y++)
    {
        LPDIRECT3DRMMESH mesh;
        meshbuilder->CreateMesh( &mesh );
        mesh->SetGroupColorRGB( 0,
                D3DVALUE(x%2), D3DVALUE(y%2), D3DVALUE(1) );
```

```
LPDIRECT3DRMFRAME meshframe;
d3drm->CreateFrame( scene, &meshframe );
meshframe->AddVisual( mesh );
int xoffset=(rand()%3)-1;
int yoffset=(rand()%3)-1;
meshframe->SetPosition( scene,
        D3DVALUE((x-1)*10+xoffset),
        D3DVALUE((y-1)*10+yoffset),
        D3DVALUE(0) );
meshframe->SetRotation( scene,
        D3DVALUE(0), D3DVALUE(1), D3DVALUE(0),
        D3DVALUE(.1) );

meshframe->Release();
meshframe=0;
mesh->Release();
mesh=0;
    }
}

meshbuilder->Release();
meshbuilder=0;
```

The nine meshes are created with a nested loop. The body of the inner loop uses the **Direct3DRMMeshBuilder CreateMesh()** function to create a mesh. The mesh's color is assigned depending on the loop's current iteration. Next, a frame is created and attached to the mesh with the **AddVisual()** function. The frame's location is dependent on the loop's current iteration but is altered with random values (this is done to suggest to the user that the meshes can be moved). Each frame is given a rotation attribute before the **meshframe** and **mesh** pointers are released.

Next, a callback function is installed:

```
scene->AddMoveCallback( UpdateDrag, NULL );
```

The callback function is installed using the **scene** frame (the root frame). This is arbitrary; any frame in the scene will do.

Step 4 is the creation of a light source:

```
LPDIRECT3DRMLIGHT dlight;
d3drm->CreateLightRGB( D3DRMLIGHT_DIRECTIONAL,
        D3DVALUE(1.00), D3DVALUE(1.00), D3DVALUE(1.00),
        &dlight );
```

```
LPDIRECT3DRMFRAME dlightframe;
d3drm->CreateFrame( scene, &dlightframe );
dlightframe->AddLight( dlight );
dlightframe->SetOrientation( scene,
        D3DVALUE(0), D3DVALUE(-1), D3DVALUE(1),
        D3DVALUE(0), D3DVALUE(1), D3DVALUE(0) );

dlight->Release();
dlight=0;
dlightframe->Release();
dlightframe=0;
```

This code creates a directional light and positions it facing between the positive Z and negative Y axes. The light is attached to the frame using the **Direct3DRMFrame AddLight()** function.

Finally, a viewport is created:

```
d3drm->CreateFrame( scene, &camera );
camera->SetPosition( scene,
        D3DVALUE(0), D3DVALUE(0), D3DVALUE(-50) );
d3drm->CreateViewport( device, camera, 0, 0,
        device->GetWidth(), device->GetHeight(),
        &viewport );
```

The **camera** frame pointer is initialized with the **Direct3DRM CreateFrame()** function and positioned with the **Direct3DRMFrame SetPosition()** function. The **viewport** pointer is initialized with the **Direct3DRM CreateViewport()** function.

THE MESHPICKWIN MOUSE FUNCTIONS

The MeshPick demo uses two message handling member functions to react to changes of the mouse button state. The **OnLButtonDown()** function is invoked by MFC whenever the user presses the left mouse button. The function looks like this:

```
void MeshPickWin::OnLButtonDown(UINT nFlags, CPoint point)
{
    if (PickMesh( point ))
    {
        ShowCursor( FALSE );
        SetCapture();
```

```
    }
    RMWin::OnLButtonDown( nFlags, point );
}
```

MFC passes two arguments to the **OnLButtonDown()** function. The first is a set of flags that indicates the status of certain keys (CRTL, SHIFT, etc.) at the time of the mouse click. The second parameter, **point**, indicates the location of the mouse when the button was pressed. The **OnLButtonDown()** function uses the **point** parameter as an argument to the **PickMesh()** function. **PickMesh()** determines whether an object is present at the specified location, and, if so, initiates a drag sequence. If such a sequence is initiated, **PickMesh()** returns **TRUE**, and the **ShowCursor()** function is used to hide the mouse cursor (the cursor is hidden during the drag operation). Also, the **SetCapture()** function is used to notify Windows that we expect to receive all mouse-related messages, even if the mouse is moved outside of our window. Finally, the base class version of **OnLButtonDown()** is called.

The **OnLButtonUp()** function is called whenever the left mouse button is released. The function looks like this:

```
void MeshPickWin::OnLButtonUp(UINT nFlags, CPoint point)
{
    if (drag.frame)
    {
        drag.frame=0;
        ShowCursor( TRUE );
        ReleaseCapture();
    }
    RMWin::OnLButtonUp( nFlags, point );
}
```

The function checks the value of the **drag.frame** data member. This member is used to indicate (1) whether a drag sequence is currently in effect, and (2) what frame is being dragged. The **drag.frame** data member is initialized by the **PickMesh()** function if an object is detected at the given mouse position.

If the **drag.frame** data member is not equal to zero, a drag sequence is currently in effect and must now be terminated (because the mouse button was released). The data member is assigned to zero, the mouse cursor is displayed, and the mouse capture is released.

THE MESHPICKWIN::PICKMESH() FUNCTION

As we saw in the **OnLButtonDown()** function, the **PickMesh()** function is used to check if an object has been selected:

```
BOOL MeshPickWin::PickMesh( const CPoint& point )
{
    HRESULT r;
    LPDIRECT3DRMPICKEDARRAY pickarray;

    viewport->Pick( point.x, point.y, &pickarray );

    BOOL ret=FALSE;
    DWORD numpicks=pickarray->GetSize();
    if (numpicks>0)
    {
        LPDIRECT3DRMVISUAL visual;
        LPDIRECT3DRMFRAMEARRAY framearray;
        D3DRMPICKDESC pickdesc;

        r=pickarray->GetPick( 0, &visual, &framearray, &pickdesc );
        if (r==D3DRM_OK)
        {
            framearray->GetElement( framearray->GetSize()-1,
                    &drag.frame );
            D3DVECTOR pos;
            drag.frame->GetPosition( 0, &pos );
            drag.origx=pos.x;
            drag.origy=pos.y;
            drag.mousedown.x=point.x;
            drag.mousedown.y=point.y;
            visual->Release();
            framearray->Release();
            ret=TRUE;
        }
    }
    pickarray->Release();
    return ret;
}
```

The first step that the **MeshPick()** function performs is calling the **Direct3DRMViewport Pick()** function. The **Pick()** function takes three arguments. The first two arguments indicate the location within the viewport that is to be checked. The third argument is a pointer to the

Direct3DRMPickedArray interface. This pointer is initialized with an array of objects that appear at the given viewport location (even if the objects are completely hidden by other objects).

The **Direct3DRMPickedArray** interface supports two member functions: **GetSize()** and **GetPick()**. The **GetSize()** member returns the number of elements in the array. The **GetPick()** function retrieves a pointer to the visual object that was picked and a pointer to an array from **Direct3DRMFrame** pointers.

The array of frames retrieved by the **GetPick()** function is a list of all of the selected object's frames, starting with the root frame. The last frame in the array is the frame to which the object is attached. We retrieve this array and use the **GetElement()** function to retrieve a pointer to the last frame in the array.

Once it has been determined that a new drag operation is to be initiated, the members of the **DragData** structure are assigned. The **drag.frame** member is used to store a pointer to the frame that is to be moved by the drag operation. The frame's position and the mouse click coordinate are also stored. This data will be required later when we are calculating new positions for the frame based on mouse movement.

Once the drag structure has been prepared, the pointers to the various interfaces are released. The **MeshPick()** function returns **TRUE** if an object has been picked.

THE MESHPICKWIN::UPDATEDRAG() FUNCTION

The **UpdateDrag()** function is a callback function that is installed by the **CreateScene()** function. We'll use it to poll the status of the application and to relocate meshes when a drag operation is underway.

```
void MeshPickWin::UpdateDrag(LPDIRECT3DRMFRAME frame, void*, D3DVALUE)
{
    if (drag.frame)
    {
        int x=GetMouseX();
        int y=GetMouseY();
```

```
        D3DVALUE newx=
                -D3DVALUE(drag.mousedown.x-x)*D3DVALUE(.07)+drag.origx;
        D3DVALUE newy=
                D3DVALUE(drag.mousedown.y-y)*D3DVALUE(.07)+drag.origy;
        drag.frame->SetPosition( 0, newx, newy, D3DVALUE(0) );
    }
}
```

The **UpdateDrag()** function checks the **drag.frame** member function to determine if a frame (and the object that is attached to the frame) is being dragged. If so, the **GetMouseX()** and **GetMouseY()** functions are used to retrieve the current mouse position (the **GetMouseX()** and **GetMouseY()** functions are inherited from the **RMWin** class).

A new location for the frame is calculated based on the current location of the mouse, the location of the mouse when the drag sequence started, and the frame's original location. The frame is repositioned with the **Direct3DRMFrame SetPosition()** function.

PICKING FACES

Now we know how to use viewports to pick meshes. What if, however, we wanted to pick individual faces in a mesh? No problem. In fact, the code looks very similar to the code for picking meshes.

THE FACEPICK DEMO

The FacePick demo displays a mesh and allows you to pick individual faces within the mesh. Selected faces change to a color that you can specify from the Colors menu. The mesh can be rotated by selecting any portion of the viewport not occupied by the mesh and moving the mouse. This allows you to reposition the mesh, giving you the ability to change the color of any face in the mesh. Also, the demo's File menu allows you to load and save meshes. The FacePick demo appears as Figure 9.3.

The FacePick demo demonstrates the following techniques:

- Using the **Direct3DRMViewport Pick()** function for face-picking operations

- Using mouse input to manipulate visual objects

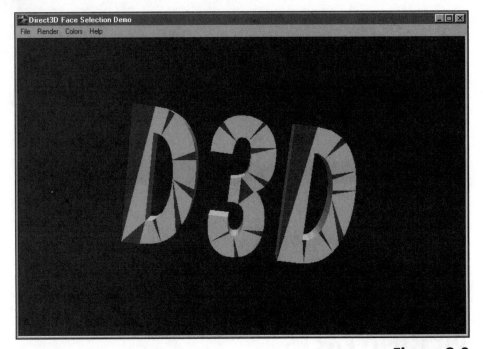

Figure 9.3
The FacePick demo.

- Loading and saving mesh files

- Using MFC's **CFileDialog** class

- Using MFC's **CColorDialog** class

THE FACEPICKWIN CLASS

The **FacePickWin** class provides the FacePick demo's functionality:

```
class FacePickWin : public RMWin
{
public:
    FacePickWin();
    BOOL CreateScene();
protected:
    //{{AFX_MSG(FacePickWin)
    afx_msg void OnRenderWireframe();
    afx_msg void OnRenderGouraud();
    afx_msg void OnRenderFlat();
```

```
        afx_msg void OnUpdateRenderWireframe(CCmdUI* pCmdUI);
        afx_msg void OnUpdateRenderFlat(CCmdUI* pCmdUI);
        afx_msg void OnUpdateRenderGouraud(CCmdUI* pCmdUI);
        afx_msg void OnLButtonDown(UINT nFlags, CPoint point);
        afx_msg void OnLButtonUp(UINT nFlags, CPoint point);
        afx_msg void OnColorsFace();
        afx_msg void OnColorsMesh();
        afx_msg void OnFileOpen();
        afx_msg void OnFileSave();
        //}}AFX_MSG
        DECLARE_MESSAGE_MAP()
private:
        static void UpdateDrag(LPDIRECT3DRMFRAME, void*, D3DVALUE);
        int PickFace(const CPoint& point);
        void OnIdle(long);
private:
        LPDIRECT3DRMMESHBUILDER meshbuilder;
        LPDIRECT3DRMFRAME meshframe;
        D3DCOLOR pickcolor;
        D3DVALUE meshscale;
        static BOOL drag;
        static BOOL end_drag;
        static int last_x, last_y;
};
```

The class declares two public member functions: a constructor and the **CreateScene()** function. The constructor is used to initialize the class's non-static data members. The **CreateScene()** function constructs the demo's initial scene.

Twelve protected member functions are declared. The first six are the Render menu message handlers that are present in most of the demos. The **OnLButtonDown()** and **OnLButtonUp()** functions are used to react to changes in the mouse button's status.

The **OnColorsFace()** and **OnColorsMesh()** functions implement the Colors menu functionality. Both functions display color selection dialogs using MFC's **CColorDialog**.

The **OnFileOpen()** and **OnFileSave()** both use MFC's **CFileDialog** to allow the user to select or enter file names.

Three private member functions are declared: **UpdateDrag()**, **PickFace()**, and **OnIdle()**. The **UpdateDrag()** function is a callback function that is used to regularly update the mesh's position. The **PickFace()** function is similar to the **PickMesh()** function that we used in the PickMesh demo. **PickFace()** is responsible for the demos' picking operations.

THE FACEPICKWIN::CREATESCENE() FUNCTION

The FacePick demo scene is constructed with the **FacePickWin::CreateScene()** function, as shown in Listing 9.3.

Listing 9.3 The FacePickWin::CreateScene() function.

```
BOOL FacePickWin::CreateScene()
{
    // ------- MESH --------
    D3DRMLOADRESOURCE resinfo;
    resinfo.hModule=NULL;
    resinfo.lpName=MAKEINTRESOURCE( IDR_D3DMESH );
    resinfo.lpType="MESH";
    d3drm->CreateMeshBuilder( &meshbuilder );
    meshbuilder->Load( &resinfo, NULL, D3DRMLOAD_FROMRESOURCE,
            NULL, NULL );
    meshbuilder->SetQuality( D3DRMRENDER_FLAT );
    ScaleMesh( meshbuilder, D3DVALUE(25) );

    //------- FRAME ------
    d3drm->CreateFrame( scene, &meshframe );
    meshframe->SetRotation( scene,
            D3DVALUE(1), D3DVALUE(0), D3DVALUE(0),
            D3DVALUE(.05) );
    meshframe->AddVisual( meshbuilder );
    meshframe->AddMoveCallback( UpdateDrag, NULL );

    // --------- LIGHTS --------
    LPDIRECT3DRMLIGHT dlight;
    d3drm->CreateLightRGB( D3DRMLIGHT_DIRECTIONAL,
            D3DVALUE(1.00), D3DVALUE(1.00), D3DVALUE(1.00),
            &dlight );

    LPDIRECT3DRMLIGHT alight;
    d3drm->CreateLightRGB( D3DRMLIGHT_AMBIENT,
            D3DVALUE(0.40), D3DVALUE(0.40), D3DVALUE(0.40),
            &alight );

    LPDIRECT3DRMFRAME lightframe;
    d3drm->CreateFrame( scene, &lightframe );
```

```
lightframe->AddLight( dlight );
lightframe->AddLight( alight );
lightframe->SetOrientation( scene,
        D3DVALUE(0), D3DVALUE(-1), D3DVALUE(1),
        D3DVALUE(0), D3DVALUE(1), D3DVALUE(0) );

dlight->Release();
dlight=0;
alight->Release();
alight=0;
lightframe->Release();
lightframe=0;

//------ CAMERA----------
d3drm->CreateFrame( scene, &camera );
camera->SetPosition( scene,
        D3DVALUE(0), D3DVALUE(0), D3DVALUE(-50) );
d3drm->CreateViewport( device, camera, 0, 0,
        device->GetWidth(), device->GetHeight(),
        &viewport );

return TRUE;
}
```

The **CreateScene()** function performs four steps:

1. Creates a mesh

2. Creates a frame for the mesh

3. Creates two light sources

4. Creates a viewport

The code for the first step looks like this:

```
D3DRMLOADRESOURCE resinfo;
resinfo.hModule=NULL;
resinfo.lpName=MAKEINTRESOURCE( IDR_D3DMESH );
resinfo.lpType="MESH";
d3drm->CreateMeshBuilder( &meshbuilder );
meshbuilder->Load( &resinfo, NULL, D3DRMLOAD_FROMRESOURCE,
        NULL, NULL );
meshbuilder->SetQuality( D3DRMRENDER_FLAT );
ScaleMesh( meshbuilder, D3DVALUE(25) );
```

A default mesh is stored in the demo's resources and identified by the **IDR_D3DMESH** constant. Although the **CreateScene()** function loads this internal mesh automatically, this mesh can be replaced using the File|Open menu selection. Notice that the **SetQuality()** function is used to change the mesh's rendering method to flat. The flat rendering method is used because individual faces are more distinct with the flat method than with other rendering methods.

Step 2 is the creation of a frame for the mesh:

```
d3drm->CreateFrame( scene, &meshframe );
meshframe->SetRotation( scene,
        D3DVALUE(1), D3DVALUE(0), D3DVALUE(0),
        D3DVALUE(.05) );
meshframe->AddVisual( meshbuilder );
meshframe->AddMoveCallback( UpdateDrag, NULL );
```

The **meshframe** pointer is a **FacePickWin** data member, so it is not declared within the **CreateScene()** function. The pointer is initialized with the **Direct3DRM CreateFrame()** function. The frame is given a rotation attribute with the **SetRotation()** function, but this is only an initial setting. The rotation attribute can be changed at any time by rotating the mesh with the mouse (you'll see how this is done when we look at the **UpdateDrag()** function). After the **SetRotation()** function is called, the previously constructed mesh is attached to the new frame with the **AddVisual()** function. Lastly, the **UpdateDrag()** callback function is installed with the **AddMoveCallback()** function.

Next, two light sources are created:

```
LPDIRECT3DRMLIGHT dlight;
d3drm->CreateLightRGB( D3DRMLIGHT_DIRECTIONAL,
        D3DVALUE(1.00), D3DVALUE(1.00), D3DVALUE(1.00),
        &dlight );

LPDIRECT3DRMLIGHT alight;
d3drm->CreateLightRGB( D3DRMLIGHT_AMBIENT,
        D3DVALUE(0.40), D3DVALUE(0.40), D3DVALUE(0.40),
        &alight );

LPDIRECT3DRMFRAME lightframe;
d3drm->CreateFrame( scene, &lightframe );
```

```
lightframe->AddLight( dlight );
lightframe->AddLight( alight );
lightframe->SetOrientation( scene,
        D3DVALUE(0), D3DVALUE(-1), D3DVALUE(1),
        D3DVALUE(0), D3DVALUE(1), D3DVALUE(0) );
```

A directional and an ambient light are created using the **Direct3DRM CreateLightRGB()** function. The ambient light will emit a gray light because of the reduced RGB values used in its creation. A frame is created, and the light sources are attached with the **AddLight()** function. Finally, the **SetOrientation()** function is used to orient the directional light. The frame's orientation will have no effect on the ambient light source.

The fourth and final step is the creation of a viewport:

```
d3drm->CreateFrame( scene, &camera );
camera->SetPosition( scene,
        D3DVALUE(0), D3DVALUE(0), D3DVALUE(-50) );
d3drm->CreateViewport( device, camera, 0, 0,
        device->GetWidth(), device->GetHeight(),
        &viewport );
```

The **camera** pointer is initialized with the **Direct3DRM CreateFrame()** function and positioned with the **SetPosition()** function. The frame is then used as an argument to the **Direct3DRM CreateViewport()** function.

THE FACEPICKWIN MOUSE FUNCTIONS

The FacePick demo relies heavily on the mouse. The mouse is used not only to pick faces, but also to rotate and position the mesh. The **FacePickWin** class uses the **OnLButtonDown()** and **OnLButtonUp()** functions to track the status of the left mouse button. The **OnLButtonDown()** function looks like this:

```
void FacePickWin::OnLButtonDown(UINT nFlags, CPoint point)
{
    int faceindex=PickFace( point );
    if (faceindex!=-1)
    {
        LPDIRECT3DRMFACEARRAY facearray;
        meshbuilder->GetFaces( &facearray );

        LPDIRECT3DRMFACE face;
        facearray->GetElement( faceindex, &face );
        face->SetColor( pickcolor );
```

```
        face->Release();
        facearray->Release();
    }
    else if (!drag)
    {
        drag=TRUE;
        last_x = GetMouseX();
        last_y = GetMouseY();
        SetCapture();
        ShowCursor( FALSE );
    }
    RMWin::OnLButtonDown( nFlags, point );
}
```

The first thing that the **OnLButtonDown()** function does is call the **PickFace()** function. **PickFace()** handles the actual picking operation. **PickFace()** is very similar to the **PickMesh()** function in the MeshPick demo except that **PickFace()** returns the index of a selected face (or -1, if no face was selected).

If a face is selected, the face index is used to color the face. First, the **Direct3DRMMeshBuilder GetFaces()** function is used to retrieve an array of faces. The index of the selected face is used to retrieve a pointer to the face that was selected. The **Direct3DRMFace SetColor()** function is used to change the face's color.

If no face is selected, a drag sequence is initiated. In the MeshPick demo, drag operations were used to move the selected mesh. In the FacePick demo, a drag operation is used to rotate the mesh. Here, when a drag sequence is started, the current mouse position is stored with the **last_x** and **last_y** data members, and the **SetCapture()** and **ShowCursor()** functions are called.

Now, let's look at the **OnLButtonUp()** function:

```
void FacePickWin::OnLButtonUp(UINT nFlags, CPoint point)
{
    if (drag)
    {
        end_drag=TRUE;
        ReleaseCapture();
        ShowCursor( TRUE );
```

```
    }
    RMWin::OnLButtonUp( nFlags, point );
}
```

Intuitively, you would expect the **OnLButtonUp()** function to terminate a drag operation (if one is in effect). Unfortunately, this would prevent one of FacePick's features. The FacePick demo allows the user to spin the displayed mesh. The mesh can be rotated during the drag operation, but it can also be set into motion by flicking the mouse and releasing the button at the same time. This feature wouldn't be possible if we terminated the drag operation here because the code needs a chance to install the latest rotation attribute. The rotation attribute code appears in the **UpdateDrag()** callback function. Rather than duplicate the code, we will use a flag that signals that the drag operation is to terminate. In the meantime, we'll restore the mouse cursor and mouse capture state, as these settings do not affect the rotation attribute code.

THE FACEPICKWIN::PICKFACE() FUNCTION

The **PickFace()** function uses the **Direct3DRMViewport Pick()** function to perform the actual picking operation. If an object is returned as a result of the picking operation, its face index is returned. The **PickFace()** function looks like this:

```
int FacePickWin::PickFace( const CPoint& point )
{
    HRESULT r;
    LPDIRECT3DRMPICKEDARRAY pickarray;

    viewport->Pick( point.x, point.y, &pickarray );

    int faceindex=-1;
    DWORD numpicks=pickarray->GetSize();
    if (numpicks>0)
    {
        LPDIRECT3DRMVISUAL visual;
        LPDIRECT3DRMFRAMEARRAY framearray;
        D3DRMPICKDESC pickdesc;

        r=pickarray->GetPick( 0, &visual, &framearray, &pickdesc );
        if (r==D3DRM_OK)
        {
```

```
            faceindex=pickdesc.ulFaceIdx;
            visual->Release();
            framearray->Release();
        }
    }
    pickarray->Release();
    return faceindex;
}
```

First, the **Direct3DRMViewport Pick()** function is called. The function takes the mouse cursor location as the first two arguments. The third argument is the address of a pointer to the **Direct3DRMPickedArray** interface.

Next, the **GetSize()** function is used to determine if any objects were picked. If the array is empty, the **pickarray** pointer is released, and the function returns -1. If there are items in the array, the first is extracted with the **GetPick()** function. We only need the first item because the array is sorted by Z order, and we are only interesting in the object closest to the viewer.

The **GetPick()** function initializes two pointers and a structure. The first pointer points to the visual object that was picked. In our case, the **visual** pointer will point to the mesh that was created in the **CreateScene()** function (because the mesh is the scene's only visual object). We are not, however, interested in a pointer to the visual object. We would be if the scene contained multiple meshes (as with the MeshPick demo). The second pointer that **GetPick()** initializes is a pointer to an array of frames. We aren't interested in this data either, for the same reasons that we aren't interested in the pointer to the visual object.

The data that we need is the index of the face that was picked. The **GetPick()** function stores this value in the **ulFaceIdx** field of the **D3DRMPICKDESC** structure. The **PickFace()** function stores and returns this value after releasing its local pointers, thereby completing its task.

Incidentally, the **D3DRMPICKDESC** structure contains two other fields that might be of use:

- **lGroupIdx**: Indicates the face's group index. The **Direct3DRMMesh** interface supports multiple groups of faces. The group index identifies the group to which the selected face belongs.

- **vPosition**: The orientation of the face. This vector indicates the facing direction of the selected face.

THE FACEPICKWIN::UPDATEDRAG() FUNCTION

The **UpdateDrag()** function is a callback that is installed by the **CreateScene()** function. **UpdateDrag()** is responsible for calculating new rotation attributes for the mesh during drag operations. The function looks like this:

```
void FacePickWin::UpdateDrag(LPDIRECT3DRMFRAME frame, void*, D3DVALUE)
{
    if (drag)
    {
        double delta_x = GetMouseX() - last_x;
        double delta_y = GetMouseY() - last_y;
        last_x = GetMouseX();
        last_y = GetMouseY();
        double delta_r = sqrt( delta_x * delta_x + delta_y * delta_y );
        double radius = 50;
        double denom = sqrt( radius * radius + delta_r * delta_r );

        if (!(delta_r == 0 || denom == 0))
            frame->SetRotation( 0,
                    D3DDivide( -delta_y, delta_r ),
                    D3DDivide( -delta_x, delta_r ),
                    D3DVALUE(0.0),
                    D3DDivide( delta_r, denom) );
    }

    if (end_drag)
    {
        drag=FALSE;
        end_drag=FALSE;
    }
}
```

The function uses the current mouse position and the position of the mouse when the drag sequence was initiated to calculate a rotation vector and a rotation speed. In essence, the two-dimensional mouse movement data is converted into a vector, while the difference between the old and new mouse positions is used to calculate a rotation speed. These values are installed using the **Direct3DRMFrame SetRotation()** function.

Notice that each time the **UpdateDrag()** function is called, it checks the **end_drag** flag. This is the flag that is set by the **OnLButtonUp()** function to indicate that the drag operation should be terminated. If the **end_drag** flag is set, the drag operation is terminated.

THE FACEPICKWIN COLOR FUNCTIONS

The FacePick demo supports two color selection dialogs. These dialogs are managed by the **OnColorsFace()** and **OnColorsMesh()** functions. The **OnColorsFace()** function is responsible for allowing the user to select a color that will be applied to any faces selected with the mouse. The **OnColorsMesh()** function allows the user to select a color to be applied to the entire mesh. Both functions use MFC's **CColorDialog** class. The **OnColorsFace()** function looks like this:

```
void FacePickWin::OnColorsFace()
{
    CColorDialog dialog( 0, CC_RGBINIT );
    dialog.m_cc.rgbResult = D3DCOLOR_2_COLORREF( pickcolor );
    if (dialog.DoModal()==IDOK)
    {
        COLORREF clr = dialog.GetColor();
        pickcolor = COLORREF_2_D3DCOLOR( clr );
    }
}
```

The **CColorDialog** allows us to specify a color that will be selected when the dialog appears. This allows us to display the dialog with the current face color selected (actually, this only works if the color you specify is one of the dialog's displayed colors).

The **CC_RGBINIT** constant is used as an argument to the constructor's dialog to indicate that we will specify a default color. The default color is assigned to the **m_cc.rgbResult** data member. The **pickcolor** variable is a **MeshPickWin** data member that indicates the current face color. The **pickcolor** data member is of type **D3DCOLOR**, and the dialog expects colors to be expressed as **COLORREF**, so a conversion function is required to make the assignment valid. The **RMWin** class provides the **D3DCOLOR_2_COLORREF()** and **COLORREF_2_D3DCOLOR()** for this purpose. (See Chapter 4.)

We use the **DoModal()** member function for modal dialog operation. If the user dismisses the dialog in any way other than pressing OK, the function returns without performing further action. If the **IDOK** constant is returned, the new color is assigned to the **pickcolor** data member.

The **OnColorsMesh()** function is similar:

```
void FacePickWin::OnColorsMesh()
{
    CColorDialog dialog;
    if (dialog.DoModal()==IDOK)
    {
        COLORREF clr = dialog.GetColor();
        D3DCOLOR meshcolor = COLORREF_2_D3DCOLOR( clr );
        meshbuilder->SetColor( meshcolor );
    }
}
```

Unlike the **OnColorsFace()** function, the **OnColorsMesh()** function does not specify a default color for the dialog. If the user pressed the OK button, the new color is extracted from the dialog class with the **GetColor()** function. The resulting **COLORREF** is converted with the **COLORREF_2_ D3D-COLOR()** function and installed with the **Direct3DRMMeshBuilder Setcolor()** function.

THE FACEPICKWIN FILE FUNCTIONS

The FacePick demo allows meshes to be loaded and saved from the File menu. The **FacePickWin** class provides the **OnFileOpen()** and **OnFileSave()** functions for this purpose. The **OnFileOpen()** function looks like this:

```
void FacePickWin::OnFileOpen()
{
    static char BASED_CODE filter[] =
            "X Files (*.x)|*.x|All Files (*.*)|*.*||";
    CFileDialog opendialog( TRUE, 0, 0, OFN_FILEMUSTEXIST,
            filter, this );
    if (opendialog.DoModal()==IDOK)
    {
        CWaitCursor cur;
        CString filename = opendialog.GetPathName();

        LPDIRECT3DRMMESHBUILDER builder;
        d3drm->CreateMeshBuilder( &builder );
        HRESULT r=builder->Load( (void*)(LPCTSTR)filename,
                NULL, D3DRMLOAD_FROMFILE, NULL, NULL );
```

```
    if (r!=D3DRM_OK)
    {
        CString msg;
        msg.Format( "Failed to load file\n'%s'", filename );
        AfxMessageBox( msg );
        return;
    }

    meshframe->DeleteVisual( meshbuilder );
    meshbuilder->Release();
    meshbuilder=builder;
    meshframe->AddVisual( meshbuilder );
    meshscale=ScaleMesh( meshbuilder, D3DVALUE(25) );
}
}
```

The function uses MFC's **CFileDialog** class. Notice that the **filter** string is used as an argument to the class's constructor. The string informs the dialog of the types of files that will be loaded.

The **DoModal()** function is used to execute the dialog. If the **IDOK** constant is returned, the filename is extracted from the dialog class with the **GetPathName()** function. Notice that the file's existence is not verified. This is because we used the **OFN_FILEMUSTEXIST** constant to construct the dialog object. The constant indicates to the dialog class that file names entered manually should be checked for existence. This dialog will not allow the user to specify a file that doesn't exist (this is no guarantee that the file will be valid, only that it exists).

Next, the function attempts to load the new mesh. If the attempt fails, a message box is displayed, and the function returns. This failure is fairly graceful because the scene's existing mesh will still be displayed.

If the new mesh is loaded successfully, the existing mesh is removed from the scene with the **Direct3DRMFrame DeleteVisual()** function, and the existing **meshbuilder** is released. The new **meshbuilder** is then added to the scene with the **AddVisual()** function.

The last step is a call to the **ScaleMesh()** function. We've seen this function used in the other demos, but this is a little different. Recall that **ScaleMesh()** scales meshes to a desired size. In this case, we are scaling any mesh we load to 25 units. This worked fine in the other demos, and it works here, but if the scaled mesh is saved back to disk, its size will have changed. This requires that we return the mesh to its original size before saving it. The **ScaleMesh()** function returns a value that indicates the scale factor that was used to scale the mesh. Storing this value allows us to restore the mesh to its original size. We'll see how this is done because we are going to talk about the **OnFileSave()** function next.

The **OnFileSave()** function is defined this way:

```
void FacePickWin::OnFileSave()
{
    static char BASED_CODE filter[] = "X Files (*.x)|*.x||";
    CFileDialog opendialog( FALSE, ".x", "",
            OFN_HIDEREADONLY | OFN_OVERWRITEPROMPT, filter );
    if ( opendialog.DoModal() == IDOK )
    {
        CWaitCursor cur;
        CString filename = opendialog.GetPathName();
        D3DVALUE restorescale=D3DVALUE(1)/meshscale;
        meshbuilder->Scale( restorescale, restorescale, restorescale );
        meshbuilder->Save( filename,
                D3DRMXOF_BINARY, D3DRMXOFSAVE_ALL );
        meshbuilder->Scale( meshscale, meshscale, meshscale );
    }
}
```

The **OnFileSave()** function also uses the **CFileDialog** class, but uses different constants with the dialog class constructor. The **OFN_HIDEREADONLY** constant indicates that the "Open as Read Only" check box should not be displayed. The **OFN_OVERWRITEPROMPT** constant causes the dialog to require a confirmation when overwriting existing files.

The **DoModal()** function is used to execute the dialog. If the **IDOK** constant is returned, the current mesh is saved. The **CWaitCursor** class is used to display the hourglass mouse cursor during the save operation. The name of the file that is to be created or overwritten is retrieved with the **GetPathName()** function. Next, the mesh is returned to its original size. The **restorescale** value is calculated so that it negates the scale operation that the mesh underwent when it was loaded. The **Direct3DRMMeshBuilder Scale()** function is used to scale the mesh according to the **restorescale** value. The mesh is saved using the **Save()** member function. Then, the mesh is returned to its previous size. Skipping this last step might cause the displayed mesh to become huge or microscopic following a save operation.

USING MULTIPLE VIEWPORTS

All of the demos that we've looked at in this book have used a single viewport to view a scene. This works fine for most applications, but multiple viewports can be used to view a single scene from multiple vantage points.

THE MULTIVIEW DEMO

The MultiView demo displays a single rotating mesh, but three viewports are used to view the mesh. The demo provides menus that allow you to configure and disable each viewport. The demo also allows external meshes to be loaded. The MultiView demo appears in Figure 9.4.

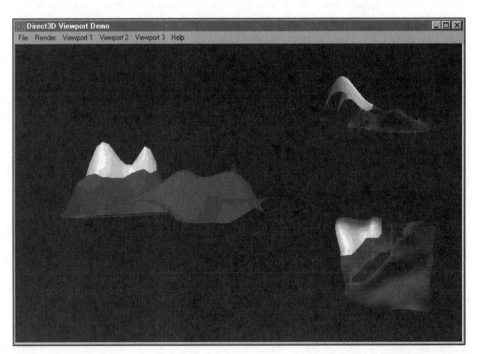

Figure 9.4
The MultiView demo.

The MultiView demo demonstrates the following techniques:

- Using multiple viewports in a single application

- Using menu options to configure a viewport's position

- Using MFC's **CFileDialog** class to implement File|Open functionality

THE MULTIVIEW CODE

The MultiView demo is written differently than the other demos on the CD-ROM. All of the demos use **RMWin** as a base class for an application specific class. Most of the demos use identical versions of **RMWin**, but the MultiView demo uses a modified version.

The version of the **RMWin** class that is used by the MultiView demo contains support for three viewports. This requires that many of the **RMWin** member functions be modified. Our discussion of the MultiView code will, therefore, involve both the **RMWin** class and the **MultiViewWin** class.

THE MULTIVIEWWIN CLASS

Some (but not all) of the MultiView demo's functionality is provided by the **MultiViewWin** class:

```
class MultiViewWin : public RMWin
{
public:
    MultiViewWin();
    BOOL CreateScene();
protected:
    //{{AFX_MSG(MultiViewWin)
    afx_msg void OnRenderWireframe();
    afx_msg void OnRenderFlat();
    afx_msg void OnRenderGouraud();
    afx_msg void OnUpdateRenderFlat(CCmdUI* pCmdUI);
    afx_msg void OnUpdateRenderGouraud(CCmdUI* pCmdUI);
    afx_msg void OnUpdateRenderWireframe(CCmdUI* pCmdUI);
    afx_msg void OnFileOpen();
    //}}AFX_MSG
    DECLARE_MESSAGE_MAP()
private:
    LPDIRECT3DRMMESHBUILDER meshbuilder;
    LPDIRECT3DRMFRAME meshframe;
};
```

The class declares two public member functions: a constructor and the **CreateScene()** function. The constructor initializes the class's two data members. The **CreateScene()** function constructs the demo's scene but differs from the other demos on the CD-ROM because it does not create any viewports. We'll look at **CreateScene()** soon.

Seven protected member functions are declared. Six are the Render menu message handlers that appear in many of the demos. The seventh is a message handler for the File|Open menu selection. We'll use this function to display a file dialog and load selected meshes from disk.

The two data members are pointers that will be used to access the demo's single mesh and the frame to which it is attached.

THE MULTIVIEWWIN::CREATESCENE() FUNCTION

The MultiView demo's scene is constructed by the **CreateScene()** function as shown in Listing 9.4.

Listing 9.4   The MultiViewWin::CreateScene() function.

```
BOOL MultiViewWin::CreateScene()
{
    // ------- MESH --------
    D3DRMLOADRESOURCE resinfo;
    resinfo.hModule=NULL;
    resinfo.lpName=MAKEINTRESOURCE( IDR_MESH );
    resinfo.lpType="MESH";
    d3drm->CreateMeshBuilder( &meshbuilder );
    meshbuilder->Load( &resinfo, NULL, D3DRMLOAD_FROMRESOURCE,
            NULL, NULL );
    ScaleMesh( meshbuilder, D3DVALUE(30) );

    //------- MESH FRAME ------
    d3drm->CreateFrame( scene, &meshframe );
    meshframe->SetRotation( scene,
            D3DVALUE(0), D3DVALUE(1), D3DVALUE(0),
            D3DVALUE(.1) );
    meshframe->AddVisual( meshbuilder );
    meshframe->Release();

    // --------- LIGHT --------
    LPDIRECT3DRMLIGHT dlight;
```

```
d3drm->CreateLightRGB( D3DRMLIGHT_DIRECTIONAL,
        D3DVALUE(1.00), D3DVALUE(1.00), D3DVALUE(1.00),
        &dlight );
LPDIRECT3DRMLIGHT alight;
d3drm->CreateLightRGB( D3DRMLIGHT_AMBIENT,
        D3DVALUE(0.40), D3DVALUE(0.40), D3DVALUE(0.40),
        &alight );

LPDIRECT3DRMFRAME lightframe;
d3drm->CreateFrame( scene, &lightframe );
lightframe->SetOrientation( scene,
        D3DVALUE(0), D3DVALUE(-1), D3DVALUE(1),
        D3DVALUE(0), D3DVALUE(1), D3DVALUE(0) );

lightframe->AddLight( dlight );
lightframe->AddLight( alight );

dlight->Release();
dlight=0;
alight->Release();
alight=0;
lightframe->Release();
lightframe=0;

return TRUE;
}
```

The **CreateScene()** function performs these three steps:

1. Creates a mesh

2. Creates a frame for the mesh

3. Creates and places two light sources

Notice that no viewport is created. As you'll see, we've moved all of the viewport-related code to the **RMWin** class. The **CreateScene()** function prepares a scene, but doesn't specify how the scene is to be viewed.

The first step is the creation of a mesh. The **Direct3DRMMeshBuilder** interface is used to load a mesh from the demo's resources. The **ScaleMesh()** function is used to resize the mesh if necessary.

The next step is the creation of a frame for the mesh. The frame is given a rotation attribute with the **SetRotation()** function and attached to the previously created mesh with the **AddVisual()** function.

Finally, two light sources are created and added to a frame of their own.

THE MODIFIED RMWIN CLASS

The version of the **RMWin** class that is employed by the MultiView demo is
defined as shown in Listing 9.5.

Listing 9.5 The RMWin class definition.

```
class RMWin : public CFrameWnd
{
public:
    RMWin();
    RMWin(int w,int h);
    BOOL Create(const CString& sTitle,int icon,int menu);
    void SetColorModel( D3DCOLORMODEL cm )  { colormodel=cm; }
    inline COLORREF D3DCOLOR_2_COLORREF(D3DCOLOR d3dclr);
    inline D3DCOLOR COLORREF_2_D3DCOLOR(COLORREF cref);
    void Render();
protected:
    static int GetMouseX()     { return mousex; }
    static int GetMouseY()     { return mousey; }
    void ScaleMesh( LPDIRECT3DRMMESHBUILDER, D3DVALUE );
protected:
    //{{AFX_MSG(RMWin)
    afx_msg int OnCreate(LPCREATESTRUCT lpCreateStruct);
    afx_msg void OnDestroy();
    afx_msg void OnActivate(UINT state, CWnd* other, BOOL minimize);
    afx_msg void OnPaint();
    afx_msg void OnSize(UINT type, int cx, int cy);
    afx_msg void OnMouseMove(UINT state, CPoint point);
    afx_msg BOOL OnEraseBkgnd(CDC* pDC);
    afx_msg void OnViewport1Disabled();
    afx_msg void OnViewport1Front();
    afx_msg void OnViewport1Left();
    afx_msg void OnViewport1Right();
    afx_msg void OnViewport1Top();
    afx_msg void OnViewport2Disabled();
    afx_msg void OnViewport2Front();
    afx_msg void OnViewport2Left();
    afx_msg void OnViewport2Right();
    afx_msg void OnViewport2Top();
    afx_msg void OnViewport3Disabled();
    afx_msg void OnViewport3Front();
    afx_msg void OnViewport3Left();
    afx_msg void OnViewport3Right();
    afx_msg void OnViewport3Top();
    afx_msg void OnUpdateViewport1Disabled(CCmdUI* pCmdUI);
```

```
    afx_msg void OnUpdateViewport1Front(CCmdUI* pCmdUI);
    afx_msg void OnUpdateViewport1Left(CCmdUI* pCmdUI);
    afx_msg void OnUpdateViewport1Right(CCmdUI* pCmdUI);
    afx_msg void OnUpdateViewport1Top(CCmdUI* pCmdUI);
    afx_msg void OnUpdateViewport2Disabled(CCmdUI* pCmdUI);
    afx_msg void OnUpdateViewport2Front(CCmdUI* pCmdUI);
    afx_msg void OnUpdateViewport2Left(CCmdUI* pCmdUI);
    afx_msg void OnUpdateViewport2Right(CCmdUI* pCmdUI);
    afx_msg void OnUpdateViewport2Top(CCmdUI* pCmdUI);
    afx_msg void OnUpdateViewport3Disabled(CCmdUI* pCmdUI);
    afx_msg void OnUpdateViewport3Front(CCmdUI* pCmdUI);
    afx_msg void OnUpdateViewport3Left(CCmdUI* pCmdUI);
    afx_msg void OnUpdateViewport3Right(CCmdUI* pCmdUI);
    afx_msg void OnUpdateViewport3Top(CCmdUI* pCmdUI);
    //}}AFX_MSG
    DECLARE_MESSAGE_MAP()
private:
    void Initvars();
    virtual BOOL CreateScene() = 0;
    BOOL CreateDevice();
    GUID* GetGUID();
    void ConfigViewport(LPDIRECT3DRMFRAME camera, int view);
    void CreateViewports();
protected:
    static LPDIRECT3DRM d3drm;
    LPDIRECT3DRMFRAME scene;
    LPDIRECT3DRMDEVICE device;
    D3DCOLORMODEL colormodel;
private:
    LPDIRECT3DRMFRAME camera1, camera2, camera3;
    LPDIRECT3DRMVIEWPORT viewport1, viewport2, viewport3;
    int view1setting, view2setting, view3setting;
    CRect winrect;
    LPDIRECTDRAWCLIPPER clipper;
    static int mousex;
    static int mousey;
    static UINT mousestate;
    friend class RMApp;
};
```

Obviously, this is a complex class, and we won't be discussing all of the member functions in this section. We'll concentrate on the portions of the class that are different from the original **RMWin** class. See Chapter 4 for a complete discussion of the **RMWin** class.

Three data members have been added: **camera1**, **camera2**, and **camera3**. These are **Direct3DRMFrame** pointers that will be used to create and move the demo's three viewports. The fact that these data members are declared as **private** tells us that classes derived from **RMWin** will not be expected to manipulate these pointers. This task is left solely to the **RMWin** class.

The **viewport1**, **viewport2**, and **viewport3** data members will be used to access the demo's three viewports. These data members are also private, so we can expect the **RMWin** member functions to initialize them.

Three more data members have been added: **view1setting**, **view2setting**, and **view3setting**. These values will be used to indicate how each viewport is to be placed. These data members are used in conjunction with the following constants (defined in resource.h):

- VIEWPORT_DISABLED
- VIEWPORT_FRONT
- VIEWPORT_LEFT
- VIEWPORT_RIGHT
- VIEWPORT_TOP

Two private member functions have been added: **ConfigViewport()** and **CreateViewports()**. The **ConfigViewport()** function is used to assign specific orientations for a viewport, given its current configuration. The **CreateViewports()** function is used to initialize the three viewports.

The reminder of added member functions are menu message handlers that were added to the class with ClassWizard. As you'll see, these functions are used to change the viewport's positions and orientations.

THE RMWIN::CREATEDEVICE() FUNCTION

Additional data members and functions aren't the only way that the **RMWin** class has changed. One of the functions that has changed is the **CreateDevice()** function. The **CreateDevice()** function is responsible for the creation of several key elements to Direct3D programs. The version of **CreateDevice()** used by the MultiView demo appears as Listing 9.6.

Listing 9.6   The RMWin::CreateDevice() function.

```
BOOL RMWin::CreateDevice()
{
    HRESULT r;

    r = DirectDrawCreateClipper( 0, &clipper, NULL );
    if (r!=D3DRM_OK)
    {
        AfxMessageBox( "DirectDrawCreateClipper() failed" );
        return FALSE;
    }

    r = clipper->SetHWnd( NULL, m_hWnd );
    if (r!=DD_OK)
    {
        AfxMessageBox( "clipper->SetHWnd() failed" );
        return FALSE;
    }

    RECT rect;
    ::GetClientRect( m_hWnd, &rect );

    r = d3drm->CreateDeviceFromClipper( clipper, GetGUID(),
            rect.right, rect.bottom,
            &device );
    if (r!=D3DRM_OK)
    {
        AfxMessageBox( "CreateDeviceFromClipper() failed" );
        return FALSE;
    }

    device->SetQuality( D3DRMRENDER_GOURAUD );

    HDC hdc = ::GetDC( m_hWnd );
    int bpp = ::GetDeviceCaps( hdc, BITSPIXEL );
    ::ReleaseDC( m_hWnd, hdc );

    switch ( bpp )
    {
    case 1:
        device->SetShades( 4 );
        d3drm->SetDefaultTextureShades( 4 );
        device->SetDither( TRUE );
        break;
```

```
case 8:
    // ...
    break;
case 16:
    device->SetShades( 32 );
    d3drm->SetDefaultTextureColors( 64 );
    d3drm->SetDefaultTextureShades( 32 );
    device->SetDither( FALSE );
    break;
case 24:
case 32:
    device->SetShades( 256 );
    d3drm->SetDefaultTextureColors( 64 );
    d3drm->SetDefaultTextureShades( 256 );
    device->SetDither( FALSE );
    break;
}

d3drm->CreateFrame( NULL, &scene );

if (CreateScene()==FALSE)
{
    AfxMessageBox( "CreateScene() failed" );
    return FALSE;
}

d3drm->CreateFrame( scene, &camera1 );
ConfigViewport( camera1, view1setting );

d3drm->CreateFrame( scene, &camera2 );
ConfigViewport( camera2, view2setting );

d3drm->CreateFrame( scene, &camera3 );
ConfigViewport( camera3, view3setting );

CreateViewports();

return TRUE;
}
```

Rather than discuss the entire function here, we'll concentrate on the modifications. The portion of the function that is of interest to us is the last portion, following the initialization of the **scene** frame pointer:

```
if (CreateScene()==FALSE)
{
    AfxMessageBox( "CreateScene() failed" );
    return FALSE;
}

d3drm->CreateFrame( scene, &camera1 );
ConfigViewport( camera1, view1setting );

d3drm->CreateFrame( scene, &camera2 );
ConfigViewport( camera2, view2setting );

d3drm->CreateFrame( scene, &camera3 );
ConfigViewport( camera3, view3setting );

CreateViewports();
```

This portion of code first calls the **CreateScene()** function. If the **CreateScene()** function returns **FALSE**, a message box is displayed, and the **CreateDevice()** function returns **FALSE** as well.

If the **CreateScene()** function is successful, the **CreateDevice()** function initializes three frames: **camera1**, **camera2**, and **camera3**. These frames will be used to create and position the demo's three viewports. After each frame is created, it is passed to the **ConfigViewport()** function along with the integer that stores the viewport's configuration. The **ConfigViewport()** function positions the frames differently, depending on the value that is used as the second argument. The values shown are initialized like this:

```
view1setting=VIEWPORT_FRONT;
view2setting=VIEWPORT_LEFT;
view3setting=VIEWPORT_TOP;
```

The values indicate that the first viewport will provide a front view of the scene. The second viewport will view the scene from the left, and the third viewport will provide a top-down view.

After the three **camera** frames are initialized, and **ConfigViewport()** is called for each one, the actual viewport creation is performed by the **CreateViewports()** function.

THE RMWIN::CONFIGVIEWPORT() FUNCTION

The **ConfigViewport()** function takes two arguments: a pointer to a **Direct3DRMFrame** interface and an integer value that indicates the frame's desired positioning. The function looks like this:

```
void RMWin::ConfigViewport(LPDIRECT3DRMFRAME camera, int view)
{
    if (view==VIEWPORT_FRONT)
    {
        camera->SetPosition( scene,
                D3DVALUE(0), D3DVALUE(0), D3DVALUE(-50) );
        camera->SetOrientation( scene,
                D3DVALUE(0), D3DVALUE(0), D3DVALUE(1),
                D3DVALUE(0), D3DVALUE(1), D3DVALUE(0) );
    }
    else if (view==VIEWPORT_LEFT)
    {
        camera->SetPosition( scene,
                D3DVALUE(-50), D3DVALUE(0), D3DVALUE(0) );
        camera->SetOrientation( scene,
                D3DVALUE(1), D3DVALUE(0), D3DVALUE(0),
                D3DVALUE(0), D3DVALUE(1), D3DVALUE(0) );
    }
    else if (view==VIEWPORT_RIGHT)
    {
        camera->SetPosition( scene,
                D3DVALUE(50), D3DVALUE(0), D3DVALUE(0) );
        camera->SetOrientation( scene,
                D3DVALUE(-1), D3DVALUE(0), D3DVALUE(0),
                D3DVALUE(0), D3DVALUE(1), D3DVALUE(0) );
    }
    else if (view==VIEWPORT_TOP)
    {
        camera->SetPosition( scene,
                D3DVALUE(0), D3DVALUE(50), D3DVALUE(0) );
        camera->SetOrientation( scene,
                D3DVALUE(0), D3DVALUE(-1), D3DVALUE(0),
                D3DVALUE(0), D3DVALUE(0), D3DVALUE(1) );
    }
}
```

The function uses the **SetPosition()** and **SetOrientation()** functions to place the frame. The position and orientation depend on the **view** parameter.

The **ConfigViewport**() function is used both in the **CreateDevice**() function (as we have seen) and in the Viewport menu message handling functions (as you will see).

THE RMWIN::CREATEVIEWPORTS() FUNCTION

The **CreateViewports**() function creates the demo's three viewports:

```
void RMWin::CreateViewports()
{
    int newwidth = device->GetWidth();
    int newheight = device->GetHeight();
    int onethird=newwidth/3;
    int halfheight=newheight/2;
    d3drm->CreateViewport( device, camera1,
            0, 0,
            onethird*2, newheight,
            &viewport1 );
    d3drm->CreateViewport( device, camera2,
            onethird*2, 0,
            onethird, halfheight,
            &viewport2 );
    d3drm->CreateViewport( device, camera3,
            onethird*2, halfheight,
            onethird, halfheight,
            &viewport3 );
}
```

The function divides the space available on the device into three parts. The first viewport occupies the first two thirds of the device space, and the last two viewports share the remaining third. The viewports are each created with the **Direct3DRM CreateViewport**() function.

THE RMWIN::RENDER() FUNCTION

We've discussed the code that creates and configures the demo's scene and internal components. Now, we need to address what happens after initialization.

An important issue is updating the scene and rendered output during the program's execution. In the other demos, this task is performed by the **RMApp::OnIdle**() function. The **OnIdle**() function for the regular demos look like this:

```
BOOL RMApp::OnIdle(LONG count)
{
    ASSERT( RMWin::d3drm );
    ASSERT( rmwin );
    rmwin->OnIdle( count );
    RMWin::d3drm->Tick( D3DVALUE(1) );
    return TRUE;
}
```

The **Direct3DRM Tick()** function is used to update the program's data
and produce a new image based on the changes. This method works fine
when you have only one viewport, but for our purposes, we need more
control. The MultiView demo uses this version of **RMApp::OnIdle()**:

```
BOOL RMApp::OnIdle(LONG lCount)
{
    ASSERT( rmwin );
    rmwin->Render();
    return TRUE;
}
```

This version passes the responsibility of updating the program to the
RMWin::Render() function, which looks like this:

```
void RMWin::Render()
{
    scene->Move( D3DVALUE(1.0) );
    if (view1setting!=VIEWPORT_DISABLED)
    {
        viewport1->Clear();
        viewport1->Render( scene );
    }
    if (view2setting!=VIEWPORT_DISABLED)
    {
        viewport2->Clear();
        viewport2->Render( scene );
    }
    if (view3setting!=VIEWPORT_DISABLED)
    {
        viewport3->Clear();
        viewport3->Render( scene );
    }
    device->Update();
}
```

Recall that the **Direct3DRM Tick()** function handles both updating the program's data and producing new visual output. Because we aren't using the **Tick()** function, we have to handle this task ourselves.

First, the **Direct3DRMFrame Move()** function is used to update the program's data. This function applies motion attributes and invokes callback functions for a frame hierarchy. We are using the scene's root frame (**scene**), so this function call ensures that the entire scene is updated.

Next, we must produce new visual output. This is done with the **Direct3-DRMViewport Clear()** and **Render()** functions. Unless the viewport is disabled, the **Clear()** function is used to reset the viewport, and the **Render()** function is used to produce new output.

Although new visual output is produced with the **Direct3DRMViewport Render()** function, it is not visible yet. The **Direct3DRMDevice Update()** function is used to perform the actual display of the rendered output.

THE RMWIN::ONSIZE() FUNCTION

The **OnSize()** function is called whenever the window is resized. This is important because Direct3D devices cannot be resized. This means that the **OnSize()** function must destroy and rebuild the device whenever the window is resized. Since viewports are attached to devices, the viewports must also be destroyed and rebuilt. The **OnSize()** function for the MultiView demo looks like this:

```
void RMWin::OnSize(UINT type, int cx, int cy)
{
    CFrameWnd::OnSize( type, cx, cy );

    if (!device)
        return;

    int newwidth = cx;
    int newheight = cy;

    if (newwidth && newheight)
    {
        int old_dither = device->GetDither();
        D3DRMRENDERQUALITY old_quality = device->GetQuality();
        int old_shades = device->GetShades();
```

```
        viewport1->Release();
        viewport2->Release();
        viewport3->Release();
        device->Release();
        d3drm->CreateDeviceFromClipper( clipper, GetGUID(),
                newwidth, newheight, &device );

        device->SetDither( old_dither );
        device->SetQuality( old_quality );
        device->SetShades( old_shades );

        CreateViewports();
    }
}
```

The function first stores the current device settings. These settings are used to configure the new device once it has been created. The **Direct3DRMDevice GetDither**(), **GetQuality**(), and **GetShades**() functions are used to retrieve the device settings.

Next, all three viewports and the device are released. A new device is then created using the **Direct3DRM CreateDeviceFromClipper**() function. The new device is configured with the previously saved settings.

Notice that it isn't necessary to destroy and create the three camera frames. The **CreateViewports**() function (the last function call in the **OnSize**() function) will use the existing camera frames to createand position the new viewports.

THE RMWIN VIEWPORT FUNCTIONS

The MultiView demo provides menu options that allow each viewport to be configured. One menu is provided for each of the three viewports. We'll discuss the message-handling functions for the first viewport here. The code for the remaining two viewports is virtually identical to these functions.

```
void RMWin::OnViewport1Disabled()
{
    view1setting=VIEWPORT_DISABLED;
    viewport1->Clear();
}

void RMWin::OnViewport1Front()
```

```
{
    view1setting=VIEWPORT_FRONT;
    ConfigViewport( camera1, view1setting );
}

void RMWin::OnViewport1Left()
{
    view1setting=VIEWPORT_LEFT;
    ConfigViewport( camera1, view1setting );
}

void RMWin::OnViewport1Right()
{
    view1setting=VIEWPORT_RIGHT;
    ConfigViewport( camera1, view1setting );
}

void RMWin::OnViewport1Top()
{
    view1setting=VIEWPORT_TOP;
    ConfigViewport( camera1, view1setting );
}
```

Each of the functions assigns a different value to the **view1setting** data member. The **OnViewportDisabled()** function uses the **Direct3DRMViewport Clear()** function to reset the viewport. The remaining functions use the **ConfigViewport()** function to configure the viewport according to the new setting.

CONCLUSION

It is entirely possible the applications you are going to write with Direct3D will use viewports solely for viewing scenes. If, however, you need to implement viewport operations such as zooming or picking, this chapter will give you a strong start.

In the next chapter, we'll talk about using DirectDraw and Direct3D together, to create applications that push Windows out of the way and take over the whole screen.

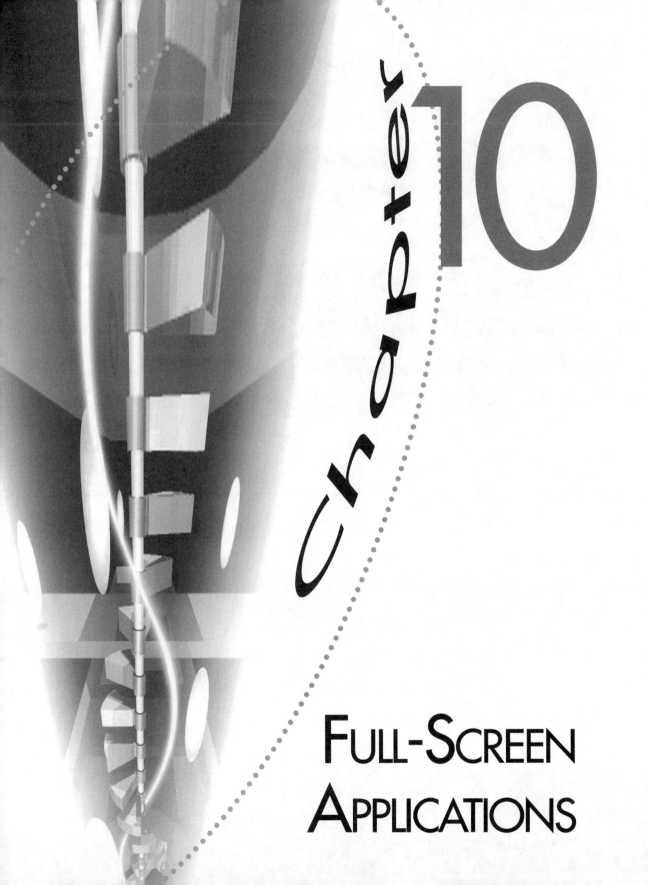

Chapter 10

FULL-SCREEN
APPLICATIONS

- DirectDraw

- Upgrading The RMWin Class

- The FullScreen Demo

CHAPTER
10

FULL-SCREEN APPLICATIONS

The demos that we've looked at so far have all been windowed applications. They appear in and among windows on the Windows desktop, and can be overlapped, minimized, and maximized. Because windowed applications must integrate themselves into the desktop, they are forced to use the current Windows display mode. In this chapter, we'll look at full-screen applications.

A full-screen application is a program that ignores the Windows desktop and all of the desktop's rules. Full-screen applications take full control of the video card and can use whatever display modes the video card supports.

Internally, windowed and full-screen applications are quite different. Full-screen applications are generally more complicated than their windowed counterparts. There are a number of practical differences, as well.

Probably the biggest difference is that with full-screen applications, we must perform our own screen updates and palette handling. With the windowed variety of Direct3D programs, we don't have to worry about these tasks. The good news is that only 8-bit modes require palettes (16-, 24-, and 32-bit display modes do not).

Another difference is that Windows doesn't "understand" full-screen applications. Normal Windows screen updates are performed by the Windows Graphics Device Interface (GDI). The GDI doesn't have any knowledge of full-screen applications; it assumes that it is in control at all times. This is a problem because if the GDI displays a menu or window in full-screen mode, it does so without regard for the current display mode and palette. Some full-screen applications use the GDI to display menus despite its lack of support for full-screen operation, but it is usually best not to use the GDI while in full-screen mode. The GDI can be made to behave (remain inactive) by placing a TOPMOST-style menuless window over the whole screen.

Our discussion will start with brief, focused coverage of DirectDraw. From there, we will modify the **RMWin** class to support full-screen operation. We will then use the new version of the **RMWin** class to create the FullScreen demo.

DIRECTDRAW

DirectDraw is a generic video card control API that allows you to detect and exploit any two-dimensional features that a video card supports. DirectDraw also includes software emulation capabilities that are used to compensate for lacking video card features.

The following discussion of DirectDraw is by no means complete, but it needn't be. We will discuss only the DirectDraw functionality that we will need in our full-screen applications.

THE DIRECTDRAW INTERFACE

DirectDraw, like Direct3D, provides the bulk of its functionality through a master interface. For Retained-Mode Direct3D, the master interface is the **Direct3DRM** interface. For DirectDraw, the master interface is the **DirectDraw** interface.

The **DirectDraw** interface is created with the **DirectDrawCreate()** function, like this:

```
LPDIRECTDRAW ddraw;
DirectDrawCreate( 0, &ddraw, 0 );
```

COOPERATIVE LEVELS

DirectDraw's control of the video card can be adjusted with the **SetCooperativeLevel()** function. The cooperative level indicates to what extent DirectDraw will cooperate with other applications. For our purposes, we will use the **SetCooperativeLevel**() function to obtain exclusive, full-screen control.

DISPLAY MODES

The **DirectDraw** interface allows us to detect and activate display modes. Display modes are detected using the **EnumDisplayModes**() function. Detected display modes can be activated with the **SetDisplayMode**() function. The **RestoreDisplayMode**() function can be used to return the video card to the display mode that was active before our application was launched. Later, when we write the FullScreen demo, we'll use these functions to write a demo that allows any detected display mode to be activated.

PAGE FLIPPING

One important DirectDraw feature is page flipping. Page flipping is an animation technique where images are prepared in an off-screen buffer and then displayed on the screen. This method is useful for two reasons. First, the preparation of the image in a hidden buffer allows for flicker-free animation because each screen image is fully assembled before it becomes visible. The second advantage is speed. Page flipping is performed by video hardware, so the screen update is virtually instantaneous.

Page flipping requires two buffers: a primary buffer and a back buffer. The primary buffer contains the data that is currently visible on the screen. The back buffer contains image data that can be moved to the primary buffer with a single operation. Later, we'll create both a primary buffer and a back buffer. We'll copy 3D and 2D images to the back buffer, and then perform page flipping to make the new images visible.

SURFACES

In DirectDraw, a surface is a portion of memory designed to store image data. The memory that a surface uses can exist either on the video card or in system memory. Only surfaces that reside in video card memory, however, can be displayed on the screen.

Surfaces are represented by the **DirectDrawSurface** interface, and can be created with the **DirectDraw CreateSurface**() function. The **CreateSurface**()

function takes arguments that specify the type, size, and capabilities of the surface to be created.

There are three basic types of surface: flipping surfaces, off-screen surfaces, and Z-buffers. Flipping surfaces are used to perform page flipping. The primary and back buffers in our code will be represented by flipping surfaces. Off-screen surfaces are used to store and manipulate image data, such as backgrounds and sprites. We'll talk about Z-buffers next.

Z-BUFFERING

One of the luxuries of using Direct3D in a windowed environment is the automatic creation of Z-buffers. With full-screen applications, we must create Z-buffers explicitly.

Z-buffers are DirectDraw surfaces that have Z-buffering capabilities. Like regular surfaces, Z-buffers are created with the **DirectDraw CreateSurface()** function. Once a Z-buffer has been created and installed, Direct3D makes use of the Z-buffer without further intervention.

PALETTES

Eight-bit display modes require palettes. With windowed applications, Direct3D creates and installs a palette automatically. With full-screen applications, we must supply the palette.

 Palettes in captivity
The easiest way to produce a palette for your application is to create a windowed version of the application and use a capture program (such as Paint Shop Pro) to capture the window contents. The resulting file will contain the colors that are necessary to display a full-screen version. You'll learn how to extract palettes from BMP files in this chapter.

Palettes are represented with the **DirectDrawPalette** interface and created with the **DirectDraw CreatePalette()** function.

MODIFYING THE RMWIN CLASS

In Chapter 4, we discussed the strategy behind the class design that was used to write the demos in this book. Our strategy was to create two MFC-derived classes that provide Direct3D support. We named these classes **RMWin** and **RMApp.** Each demo supplies two more classes, one derived from **RMWin** and the other derived from **RMApp.** These application-specific classes augment and modify the functionality of the base classes. Figure 10.1 displays the class inheritance tree with respect to this division of labor.

In moving to full-screen applications, we want to keep the architecture shown in the figure. This way, any new features that we add to the **RMWin** and **RMApp** classes will automatically be inherited by derived classes. This will make it much easier to use the added features in subsequent applications.

Because full-screen applications are so different internally from windowed applications, the Direct3D classes (**RMWin** in particular) must be heavily modified.

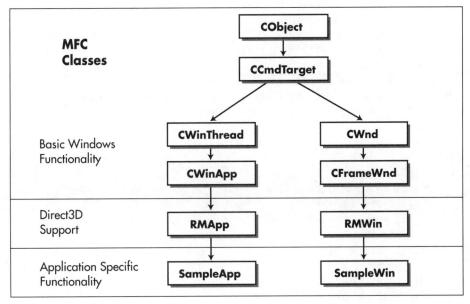

Figure 10.1
The class hierarchy used in this book.

THE RMWIN CLASS

The extent of the modifications becomes clear if you compare the **RMWin** class definition in Chapter 4 to the full-screen version in this chapter. The full-screen **RMWin** class definition appears in Listing 10.1.

Listing 10.1   The RMWin class.

```
class RMWin : public CFrameWnd
{
public:
    RMWin();
    RMWin( int w, int h );
    BOOL Create( const CString& sTitle, int icon, int menu);
    void SetColorModel( D3DCOLORMODEL cm )  { colormodel=cm; }
    virtual void Render() = 0;
protected:
    int GetNumDisplayModes()  { return totaldisplaymodes; }
    BOOL ActivateDisplayMode( int index );
    int GetCurDisplayMode()  { return curdisplaymode; }
    BOOL GetDisplayModeDims( int index, DWORD& w, DWORD& h, DWORD& d );
    BOOL GetCurDisplayModeDims( DWORD& w, DWORD& h, DWORD& d );
    static void CheckResult( HRESULT );
    static void CheckDirectDrawResult( HRESULT );
    virtual void OnIdle(LONG)  { }
    static int GetMouseX()     { return mousex; }
    static int GetMouseY()     { return mousey; }
    D3DVALUE ScaleMesh( LPDIRECT3DRMMESHBUILDER, D3DVALUE );
    void UsePalette( CString filename ) { palettefile=filename; }
    LPDIRECTDRAWSURFACE CreateSurface( DWORD w, DWORD h );
    BOOL ClearSurface(LPDIRECTDRAWSURFACE surf, DWORD clr);
    void SaveSurface( LPDIRECTDRAWSURFACE surf, int number );
protected:
    //{{AFX_MSG(RMWin)
    afx_msg int OnCreate( LPCREATESTRUCT lpCreateStruct );
    afx_msg void OnDestroy();
    afx_msg void OnMouseMove( UINT state, CPoint point );
    //}}AFX_MSG
    DECLARE_MESSAGE_MAP()
private:
    BOOL InitMainSurfaces();
    BOOL InitDisplayMode();
    BOOL ActivateDisplayMode(DWORD,DWORD,DWORD);
    void Initvars();
    virtual BOOL CreateScene() = 0;
    BOOL CreateDevice();
    GUID* GetGUID();
```

```
    BOOL InstallPalette();
    static HRESULT WINAPI DisplayModeAvailable(LPDDSURFACEDESC, LPVOID);
    static int CompareModes( const void *arg1, const void *arg2 );
protected:
    LPDIRECTDRAW ddraw;
    LPDIRECTDRAWSURFACE primsurf;
    LPDIRECTDRAWSURFACE backsurf;
    LPDIRECTDRAWSURFACE zbufsurf;
    LPDIRECTDRAWPALETTE palette;
    static LPDIRECT3DRM d3drm;
    static LPDIRECT3DRMFRAME scene;
    static LPDIRECT3DRMFRAME camera;
    static LPDIRECT3DRMDEVICE device;
    static LPDIRECT3DRMVIEWPORT viewport;
private:
    static DWORD modewidth, modeheight, modedepth;
    D3DCOLORMODEL colormodel;
    CRect winrect;
    LPDIRECTDRAWCLIPPER clipper;
    static int mousex;
    static int mousey;
    static UINT mousestate;
    static int totaldisplaymodes;
    static videomode displaymode[MAXDISPLAYMODES];
    static int curdisplaymode;
    CString palettefile;
};
```

Let's look first at how this class definition differs from the windowed version of the **RMWin** class. We can do this by looking at functions that were present in the windowed version but are not present here. After that, we'll look at functions that have been added to support the full-screen capability.

REMOVING OBSOLETE FUNCTIONS

The first difference is that the following four member functions that appeared in the windowed version do not appear here because they aren't necessary for full-screen operation:

- OnActivate()

- OnPaint()

- OnSize()

- OnEraseBkgnd()

These four functions serve as message handlers in the windowed demos. The **OnActivate**() function is called by MFC when an application gets or loses focus. We used the **OnActivate**() function to notify Direct3D of the **WM_ACTIVATE** message using the **Direct3DRMWinDevice HandleActivate**() function. With full-screen applications, this notification isn't necessary.

The same is true with the **OnPaint**() function. In the windowed demos, we used the **OnPaint**() function to call the **Direct3DRMWinDevice HandlePaint**() function. This allowed Direct3D to perform screen updates. Because we will be handling our own screen updates, the **OnPaint**() function isn't required.

Although the **OnActivate**() and **OnPaint**() functions have been removed, the **WM_ACTIVATE** and **WM_PAINT** messages that they handle are still passed to our application. This is not true of the **WM_SIZE** message. The reason that the **OnSize**() function has been removed is because our application cannot be resized. It is a full-screen application and provides no means for resizing.

Finally, the **OnEraseBkgnd**() function has been removed because its purpose was to erase the window background. Although our application does create a window, it isn't necessary to erase its contents. The window is present primarily to quiet the Windows GDI.

ADDING DISPLAY MODE SUPPORT

The full-screen version of **RMWin** provides several functions that facilitate display mode detection and switching. These functions are:

- GetNumDisplayModes()

- ActivateDisplayMode()

- GetCurDisplayMode()

- GetDisplayModeDims()

- GetCurDisplayModeDims()

Internally, the **RMWin** class assembles a list of supported display modes. The number of entries in the list can be determined with the **GetNumDisplayModes**() function. Specific display modes can be activated with the **ActivateDisplayMode()** function. The **GetCurDisplayMode()** function returns the currently active display mode. The **GetDisplayModeDims()** and **GetCurDisplayModeDims()** functions return the dimensions (width, height, and depth) of the display modes.

SURFACE SUPPORT FUNCTIONS

The **RMWin** class creates and manages the DirectDraw surfaces that are necessary for Direct3D full-screen operations. It is, as you will see later in this chapter, sometimes useful to create and display extra surfaces. Two surface-related functions have been added to the **RMWin** class: **CreateSurface()** and **ClearSurface()**. The **CreateSurface()** function creates a new surface given the surface's dimensions. The **ClearSurface()** function clears the contents of an existing surface.

PALETTE SUPPORT

Full-screen applications running in 8-bit modes require that a palette be constructed and attached to each surface. Palettes can be supplied to the **RMWin** class in the form of a BMP file. The **UsePalette()** function is provided for this purpose.

Internally, the **RMWin** class uses the **InstallPalette()** function to extract the palette data from the BMP file and create a DirectDraw palette. The new palette is then attached to the surfaces.

THE ONCREATE() FUNCTION

The **OnCreate()** function is called by MFC to allow window initialization. In the windowed version of **RMWin,** we used **OnCreate()** only to initialize the **Direct3DRM** interface. In the full-screen version, the **OnCreate()** function initializes Direct3D, DirectDraw, the DirectDraw surfaces, and the Direct3D device. The function also constructs any application-specific elements. The **OnCreate()** function is shown in Listing 10.2.

Listing 10.2   The OnCreate() function.

```
int RMWin::OnCreate(LPCREATESTRUCT)
{
    ShowCursor( FALSE );
    Direct3DRMCreate( &d3drm );
```

```
    DirectDrawCreate( 0, &ddraw, 0 );
    ddraw->SetCooperativeLevel( GetSafeHwnd(),
              DDSCL_EXCLUSIVE | DDSCL_FULLSCREEN | DDSCL_ALLOWMODEX );
    InitDisplayMode();
    InitMainSurfaces();
    InstallPalette();
    CreateDevice();
    d3drm->CreateFrame( 0, &scene );
    CreateScene();
    return 0;
}
```

First, the Win32 **ShowCursor()** function is used to hide the mouse cursor. The mouse can be used in full-screen mode, but not as reliably as in windowed mode. Some display modes (Mode X display modes in particular) garble the mouse cursor.

Next, the **Direct3DRMCreate()** function is used to initialize Direct3D, and the **DirectDrawCreate()** function is used to initialize DirectDraw. Once DirectDraw has been initialized, the **SetCooperativeLevel()** function is used to specify that we will be running in full-screen, exclusive mode. The **DDSCL_ALLOWMODEX** constant is included to allow use of any supported Mode X display modes.

Next, the **InitDisplayMode()** function is called. This function creates a list of supported display modes and selects an initial mode.

The **InitMainSurfaces()** function creates the primary and back surfaces along with the Z-buffer. These three surfaces (the Z-buffer is a special type of surface) always have the same width and height. These dimensions are determined by the current display mode, so it is important that the intended display mode be active when these surfaces are created.

The **InstallPalette()** function is then used to create and attach a palette to the primary and back surfaces. The **InstallPalette()** function extracts a palette from a BMP file. The name of the BMP file must first be supplied with the **UsePalette()** function.

Next, the **CreateDevice()** function is called to create and configure the Direct3D device.

Finally, a root frame is created (using the **scene** pointer), and **CreateScene()**
is called. You'll recognize the **CreateScene()** function as the focus of our
studies in previous chapters.

THE INITDISPLAYMODE() FUNCTION

The **InitDisplayMode()** function uses DirectDraw to determine which display modes are supported by the installed video card. This data is used to
create a list of display modes. The list is then used to determine an initial
display mode. The **InitDisplayMode()** function appears in Listing 10.3.

Listing 10.3   The InitDisplayMode() function.

```
BOOL RMWin::InitDisplayMode()
{
    curdisplaymode=0;

    CDC* dc=GetDC();
    DWORD curdisplaydepth=dc->GetDeviceCaps( BITSPIXEL );
    dc->DeleteDC;

    ddraw->EnumDisplayModes( 0, 0, 0, DisplayModeAvailable );
    qsort( displaymode, totaldisplaymodes, sizeof(videomode),
            CompareModes );

    for ( int i=0; i<totaldisplaymodes; i++ )
    {
        DWORD w, h, d;
        GetDisplayModeDims( i, w, h, d );
        if (w==640 && h==480 && d==curdisplaydepth)
            curdisplaymode=i;
    }

    GetDisplayModeDims( curdisplaymode,
            modewidth, modeheight, modedepth );
    ddraw->SetDisplayMode( modewidth, modeheight, modedepth );
    return totaldisplaymodes!=0;
}
```

First, the function determines the current Windows display mode depth.
This is retrieved with the **GetDeviceCaps()** function. The **BITSPIXEL** constant is used to indicate that we are interested in the display mode's bits

per pixel. The resulting value is stored in the **curdisplaydepth** variable. This value is used later in the function to select an initial display mode.

Next, the **DirectDraw EnumDisplayModes()** function is called. The last **EnumDisplayModes()** argument is a callback function that DirectDraw will invoke each time a supported display mode is detected. The **InitDisplayMode()** function uses the following callback function to react to detected display modes:

```
HRESULT WINAPI RMWin::DisplayModeAvailable(LPDDSURFACEDESC desc, LPVOID)
{
    int& count=totaldisplaymodes;
    if (count==MAXDISPLAYMODES)
        return DDENUMRET_CANCEL;

    displaymode[count].width=desc->dwWidth;
    displaymode[count].height=desc->dwHeight;
    displaymode[count].depth=desc->ddpfPixelFormat.dwRGBBitCount;

    count++;
    return DDENUMRET_OK;
}
```

The **DisplayModeAvailable()** callback function receives a pointer to a **DDSURFACEDESC** structure. This structure describes the detected mode. The callback function uses the structure to initialize elements of the **displaymode** array. After the element has been initialized, the **totaldisplaymodes** variable is incremented (via the **count** alias). Finally, the **DDENUMRET_OK** constant is returned, indicating that DirectDraw should continue searching for supported display modes. Using **DDRNUMRET_CANCEL** as a return value causes DirectDraw to discontinue display mode enumeration.

Returning to the **InitDisplayMode()** function, after all available display modes have been detected, the **Win32 qsort()** function is used to sort the array of display modes. The function call looks like this:

```
qsort( displaymode, totaldisplaymodes, sizeof( videomode ), CompareModes );
```

The **displaymode** array, the total number of display modes, the size of each **displaymode** element, and a comparison function are all passed to the **qsort()** function. The comparison function (**CompareModes()**) is a callback function invoked by **qsort()** to determine correct order. The **CompareModes()** function appears as shown in Listing 10.4.

Listing 10.4 The CompareModes() function.

```
int RMWin::CompareModes( const void *arg1, const void *arg2 )
{
    videomode* mode1=(videomode*)arg1;
    videomode* mode2=(videomode*)arg2;

    DWORD volume1=mode1->width*mode1->height;
    DWORD volume2=mode2->width*mode2->height;

    if (volume1<volume2)
        return -1;
    else if (volume1>volume2)
        return 1;

    if (mode1->depth<mode2->depth)
        return -1;
    else if (mode1->depth>mode2->depth)
        return 1;

    return 0;
}
```

The **CompareModes()** function uses the display mode's dimensions to compare the two modes passed as parameters. This allows the **displaymode** array to be sorted according to display mode dimension.

Next, an initial display mode is selected from the **displaymode** array:

```
for ( int i=0; i<totaldisplaymodes; i++ )
{
    DWORD w, h, d;
    GetDisplayModeDims( i, w, h, d );
    if (w==640 && h==480 && d==curdisplaydepth)
        curdisplaymode=i;
}
```

A 640×480 display mode is sought (640×480 being a display mode that virtually every video card supports). The current Windows display depth is used for the initial bit depth.

Once a display mode has been selected, its dimensions are retrieved and used to change the current display mode:

```
GetDisplayModeDims( curdisplaymode,
        modewidth, modeheight, modedepth );
ddraw->SetDisplayMode( modewidth, modeheight, modedepth );
```

The **GetDisplayModeDims()** function retrieves the dimensions for the display mode indicated by the first argument. The **modewidth**, **modeheight**, and **modedepth** variables are **RMWin** data members used to store the dimensions of the current video mode. Once the dimensions are retrieved, they are used as arguments to the **DirectDraw SetDisplayMode()** function. This function call performs the actual display mode activation and completes the task of the **InitDisplayMode()** function.

THE INITMAINSURFACES() FUNCTION

Now, let's look at the **InitMainSurfaces()** function. For review, the **InitMainSurfaces()** function is called by the **OnCreate()** function after **InitDisplayMode()** is called. The **InitMainSurfaces()** function creates the primary and back surfaces along with a Z-buffer surface, as shown in Listing 10.5.

Listing 10.5   The InitMainSurfaces() function.

```
BOOL RMWin::InitMainSurfaces()
{
    if (primsurf)
    {
        primsurf->Release();
        primsurf=0;
    }
    if (zbufsurf)
    {
        zbufsurf->Release();
        zbufsurf=0;
    }

    DDSURFACEDESC desc;
    desc.dwSize = sizeof( desc );
    desc.dwFlags = DDSD_BACKBUFFERCOUNT | DDSD_CAPS;
    desc.dwBackBufferCount = 1;
```

```
desc.ddsCaps.dwCaps = DDSCAPS_PRIMARYSURFACE |
        DDSCAPS_3DDEVICE |
        DDSCAPS_FLIP |
        DDSCAPS_COMPLEX;
ddraw->CreateSurface( &desc, &primsurf, 0 );

DDSCAPS ddscaps;
ddscaps.dwCaps = DDSCAPS_BACKBUFFER;
primsurf->GetAttachedSurface( &ddscaps, &backsurf );

memset( &desc, 0, sizeof(desc) );
desc.dwSize = sizeof(DDSURFACEDESC);
desc.dwFlags =
        DDSD_WIDTH | DDSD_HEIGHT |
        DDSD_CAPS | DDSD_ZBUFFERBITDEPTH;
desc.dwWidth = modewidth;
desc.dwHeight = modeheight;
desc.dwZBufferBitDepth = 16 ;
desc.ddsCaps.dwCaps= DDSCAPS_ZBUFFER | DDSCAPS_SYSTEMMEMORY;
ddraw->CreateSurface( &desc, &zbufsurf, 0 );
backsurf->AddAttachedSurface( zbufsurf );

return TRUE;
}
```

First the **InitMainSurfaces()** function releases any existing primary surface and Z-buffer:

```
if (primsurf)
{
    primsurf->Release();
    primsurf=0;
}
if (zbufsurf)
{
    zbufsurf->Release();
    zbufsurf=0;
}
```

The **OnCreate()** function (which calls the **InitMainSurfaces()** function) is called only once—when the program's window is created—so no primary surface or Z-buffer will be present. The **InitMainSurfaces()** function is, however, used by other functions to change the initial display mode. Existing primary surfaces and Z-buffers will be released before new ones are created. It is not necessary to release the back surface because it gets released along with the primary surface.

Next, the primary surface is created:

```
DDSURFACEDESC desc;
desc.dwSize = sizeof( desc );
desc.dwFlags = DDSD_BACKBUFFERCOUNT | DDSD_CAPS;
desc.dwBackBufferCount = 1;
desc.ddsCaps.dwCaps = DDSCAPS_PRIMARYSURFACE |
        DDSCAPS_3DDEVICE |
        DDSCAPS_FLIP |
        DDSCAPS_COMPLEX;
ddraw->CreateSurface( &desc, &primsurf, 0 );
```

The surface we are interested in creating must be described with a **DDSURFACEDESC** structure. The structure's **dwSize** field must contain the size of the structure. The **dwFlags** field is used to store flags that indicate which structure fields we will be initializing. In this case, we will be using the **dwBackBufferCount** and **ddsCaps** fields, so the **DDSD_BACK-BUFFERCOUNT** and **DDSD_CAPS** flags are used.

The surface capability flags (**DDSCAPS_PRIMARYSURFACE, DDSCAPS_ FLIP,** and **DDSCAPS_COMPLEX**) indicate that we are creating a primary surface that is capable of page flipping. The **DDSCAPS_3DDEVICE** flag indicates to DirectDraw that we will be using the new surface to create a Direct3D device.

The **DirectDraw CreateSurface()** function performs the actual surface creation. The **DDSURFACEDESC** structure that we prepared is used as the first argument. The address of a pointer to the **DirectDrawSurface** interface is used as the second argument. The pointer (**primsurf**) is an **RMWin** data member that we will use later to perform page flipping.

Notice that the **DDSURFACEDESC dwBackBufferCount** field is assigned to one. This means that we have already informed DirectDraw that the primary surface has one back buffer. In fact, DirectDraw created the back buffer along with the primary surface. All we have to do now is retrieve a pointer to the back buffer:

```
DDSCAPS ddscaps;
ddscaps.dwCaps = DDSCAPS_BACKBUFFER;
primsurf->GetAttachedSurface( &ddscaps, &backsurf );
```

Later, we'll use the **backsurf** pointer to store visual output before it is moved, or flipped, to the primary surface.

Next, we create a Z-buffer and attach it to the **backsurf** surface:

```
memset( &desc, 0, sizeof(desc) );
desc.dwSize   = sizeof(DDSURFACEDESC);
desc.dwFlags =
        DDSD_WIDTH | DDSD_HEIGHT |
        DDSD_CAPS | DDSD_ZBUFFERBITDEPTH;
desc.dwWidth  = modewidth;
desc.dwHeight = modeheight;
desc.dwZBufferBitDepth = 16 ;
desc.ddsCaps.dwCaps = DDSCAPS_ZBUFFER | DDSCAPS_SYSTEMMEMORY;
ddraw->CreateSurface( &desc, &zbufsurf, 0 );
backsurf->AddAttachedSurface( zbufsurf );
```

We need to describe the Z-buffer surface with an instance of the **DDSURFACEDESC** structure. Rather than declare another copy, we can use the **desc** instance that was used to create the primary surface. We reset the structure with a call to the **memset()** function, assigning zero to all of the structure's fields. The **dwSize** and **dwFlags** fields are then assigned.

The flags assigned to the **dwFlags** field indicate that we will be supplying the surface's width, height, capabilities, and depth of the desired Z-buffer. The appropriate fields are then assigned. The Z-buffer's dimensions must be equal to the dimensions of the primary and back buffers. Because the size of the primary and back buffers is always equal to the current display mode dimensions, we can use **modewidth** and **modeheight** to assign the **dwWidth** and **dwHeight** fields.

We specify a 16-bit Z-buffer by assigning the **dwZBufferBitDepth** field. The depth of the Z-buffer determines the accuracy of the hidden surface removal code. An 8-bit Z-buffer would provide only 256 different Z, or distance values, and that is too conservative. A 16-bit Z-buffer offers 65,536 different values, so it will work for general purpose Z-buffering. Complex scenes may require 24- or 32-bit Z-buffers.

The **DDSCAPS_SYSTEMMEMORY** constant is used to indicate that the Z-buffer memory should be allocated from system memory rather than from video card memory. With 3D graphics, video card memory is scarce (especially with 2 megabyte video cards). Storing the Z-buffer in system memory leaves more space in video card memory for visual surfaces such as sprites and backgrounds. Storing visual data in video card memory is preferable because accelerated video cards usually copy video memory faster than system memory.

The last step is to create the Z-buffer surface and attach it to the **backsurf** surface:

```
ddraw->CreateSurface( &desc, &zbufsurf, 0 );
backsurf->AddAttachedSurface( zbufsurf );
```

Once the Z-buffer surface is attached, Direct3D makes use of it automatically. No further Z-buffer manipulation is required.

THE PALETTE FUNCTIONS

The **RMWin** class provides two member functions that facilitate the use of palettes. The **UsePalette()** function is a protected function that instructs **RMWin** to use the palette stored in a BMP file. The **UsePalette()** function is declared in the **RMWin** class definition:

```
void UsePalette( CString filename ) { palettefile=filename; }
```

The function simply stores the supplied file name. The file is used by the **RMWin** class when a palette must be created.

You may recall that the **OnCreate()** function calls the private function **InstallPalette()**. The **InstallPalette()** function uses the file name supplied by the **UsePalette()** function to extract and install a palette based on the contents of the BMP file. **InstallPalette()** is shown in Listing 10.6.

Listing 10.6   The InstallPalette() function.

```
BOOL RMWin::InstallPalette()
{
    BITMAPFILEHEADER bmpfilehdr;
    BITMAPINFOHEADER bmpinfohdr;
    RGBQUAD quad[256];
    PALETTEENTRY pe[256];
    int ncolors;

    if (palettefile.GetLength()<=0)
        return FALSE;
```

```
if (modedepth!=8)
    return FALSE;

if (palette)
{
    palette->Release();
    palette=0;
}

ifstream bmp( palettefile, ios::binary | ios::nocreate );

bmp.read( (char*)&bmpfilehdr, sizeof(bmpfilehdr) );
bmp.read( (char*)&bmpinfohdr, sizeof(bmpinfohdr) );

char* ptr=(char*)&bmpfilehdr.bfType;
if (*ptr!='B' || *++ptr!='M')
{
    TRACE("invalid bitmap\n");
    return FALSE;
}

if (bmpinfohdr.biBitCount!=8)
{
    TRACE("not 8 bit file!\n");
    return FALSE;
}

if (bmpinfohdr.biClrUsed==0)
    ncolors=256;
else
    ncolors=bmpinfohdr.biClrUsed;

bmp.read( (char*)quad, sizeof(RGBQUAD)*ncolors );

for( int i=0; i<ncolors; i++)
{
    pe[i].peRed   = quad[i].rgbRed;
    pe[i].peGreen = quad[i].rgbGreen;
    pe[i].peBlue  = quad[i].rgbBlue;
    pe[i].peFlags = D3DPAL_READONLY;
}

HRESULT r=ddraw->CreatePalette( DDPCAPS_8BIT, pe, &palette, 0 );
if (r!=DD_OK)
{
    TRACE("failed to load palette data from file\n");
```

```
        return FALSE;
    }

    primsurf->SetPalette( palette );
    backsurf->SetPalette( palette );

    return TRUE;
}
```

Before we discuss the **InstallPalette()** function, it should be mentioned that only the palette portion of the BMP file is extracted. The image data in the file is ignored.

The **InstallPalette()** function first declares several data instances:

```
BITMAPFILEHEADER bmpfilehdr;
BITMAPINFOHEADER bmpinfohdr;
RGBQUAD quad[256];
PALETTEENTRY pe[256];
```

The **BITMAPFILEHEADER** structure appears at the beginning of every BMP file. We'll use the structure to load file-specific data from the BMP file. In particular, the **BITMAPFILEHEADER** structure contains signature data that identifies BMP files. The **BITMAPFILEHEADER** structure is defined like this:

```
typedef struct tagBITMAPFILEHEADER {
        WORD      bfType;
        DWORD     bfSize;
        WORD      bfReserved1;
        WORD      bfReserved2;
        DWORD     bfOffBits;
} BITMAPFILEHEADER;
```

The **bfType** field contains the characters "BM" in a valid BMP file. If this signature is incorrect, we will know that the file that we are loading is not valid.

The **BITMAPINFOHEADER** structure appears immediately after the **BITMAPFILEHEADER** structure in a BMP file. We'll use this structure to load image-specific data from the file. The **BITMAPINFOHEADER** structure is defined as follows:

```
typedef struct tagBITMAPINFOHEADER {
    DWORD    biSize;
    LONG     biWidth;
    LONG     biHeight;
    WORD     biPlanes;
    WORD     biBitCount
    DWORD    biCompression;
    DWORD    biSizeImage;
    LONG     biXPelsPerMeter;
    LONG     biYPelsPerMeter;
    DWORD    biClrUsed;
    DWORD    biClrImportant;
} BITMAPINFOHEADER;
```

The **biWidth** and **biHeight** fields contain the image dimensions. The **biBitCount** field indicates the image's bit depth. The **biBitCount** field is used to ensure that we are loading an 8-bit file.

An array of **RGBQUAD** structures is declared because BMP files store palette data as **RGBQUAD** entries. The array is declared with 256 entries because that is the maximum number of color entries that will be stored in the file.

Next, an array of **PALETTEENTRY** structures is declared. We'll use this array to create the DirectDraw palette. The **RGBQUAD** and **PALETTEENTRY** structures are similar. The definitions look like this:

```
typedef struct tagRGBQUAD {
    BYTE    rgbBlue;
    BYTE    rgbGreen;
    BYTE    rgbRed;
    BYTE    rgbReserved;
} RGBQUAD;

typedef struct tagPALETTEENTRY {
    BYTE    peRed;
    BYTE    peGreen;
    BYTE    peBlue;
    BYTE    peFlags;
} PALETTEENTRY;
```

The biggest difference is the order in which the red, green, and blue color elements appear. We'll use a loop to copy the contents of the **RGBQUAD** array to the **PALETTEENTRY** array.

The **InstallPalette()** first function checks the **palettefile** string:

```
if (palettefile.GetLength()<=0)
    return FALSE;
```

Recall that the **palettefile** string is assigned by the **UsePalette()** function. If classes derived from **RMWin** do not use **UsePalette()** to announce the name of a BMP file, no palette is created and the **InstallPalette()** function returns **FALSE**. This isn't as bad as it sounds, because only 8-bit modes require a palette. Applications that use only 16-, 24-, and 32-bit modes will execute properly without using the **UsePalette()** function.

Next, the current display mode depth is checked:

```
if (modedepth!=8)
    return FALSE;
```

Palettes aren't necessary for display mode depths other than eight, so the **InstallPalette()** function returns if the current display mode depth is not eight.

The **InstallPalette()** function then releases any existing palette:

```
if (palette)
{
    palette->Release();
    palette=0;
}
```

The BMP file is then opened, and the file and image data structures are loaded:

```
ifstream bmp( palettefile, ios::binary | ios::nocreate );

bmp.read( (char*)&bmpfilehdr, sizeof(bmpfilehdr) );
bmp.read( (char*)&bmpinfohdr, sizeof(bmpinfohdr) );
```

The freshly loaded data is used to check the BMP file's signature and the file's bit depth:

```
char* ptr=(char*)&bmpfilehdr.bfType;
if (*ptr!='B' || *++ptr!='M')
{
```

```
        TRACE("invalid bitmap\n");
        return FALSE;
}

if (bmpinfohdr.biBitCount!=8)
{
        TRACE("not 8 bit file!\n");
        return FALSE;
}
```

If the "BM" signature is not present, then the file is either corrupted or not a BMP file at all. In that case, a diagnostic message is displayed and the function returns **FALSE**.

Files that have bit depths less than eight will do us little good. Four-bit files, for instance, use only 16 colors, which would be a waste in a 256-color mode. Files with bit depths of 16 or more don't have palettes at all. If the file's bit depth is not equal to eight, the function returns.

Next, the number of colors in the palette is calculated:

```
if (bmpinfohdr.biClrUsed==0)
    ncolors=256;
else
    ncolors=bmpinfohdr.biClrUsed;
```

It is not uncommon for the **biClrUsed** field to be zero, indicating that the file contains the maximum number of colors for the given bit depth. We assign our local **ncolors** integer to 256 if the **biClrUsed** field is zero. Otherwise, the **biClrUsed** field is used to assign the **ncolors** integer.

The next step that the **InstallPalette()** function performs is loading the palette from disk and initializing the array of **PALETTEENTRY** structures:

```
bmp.read( (char*)quad, sizeof(RGBQUAD)*ncolors );
for( int i=0; i<ncolors; i++)
{
    pe[i].peRed    = quad[i].rgbRed;
    pe[i].peGreen  = quad[i].rgbGreen;
    pe[i].peBlue   = quad[i].rgbBlue;
    pe[i].peFlags  = D3DPAL_READONLY;
}
```

The **quad** array is used to load the palette. A loop then copies values from the **quad** array to the **pe** array. The **D3DPAL_READONLY** constant is used to indicate that the colors in the array should not be modified.

Now, we can create the DirectDraw palette:

```
HRESULT r=ddraw->CreatePalette( DDPCAPS_8BIT, pe, &palette, 0 );
if (r!=DD_OK)
{
    TRACE("failed to load palette data from file\n");
    return FALSE;
}
```

The palette is created with the **DirectDraw CreatePalette()** function. The **DDPCAPS_8BIT** constant indicates to DirectDraw that the palette data we are supplying is 8-bit data. The **pe** array is supplied as the second argument. The third **CreatePalette()** argument is the address of a pointer to the new palette.

Finally, the new palette is attached to the primary and back surfaces:

```
primsurf->SetPalette( palette );
backsurf->SetPalette( palette );
```

This step completes the task of the **InstallPalette()** function. The BMP file is closed automatically when the function returns because the **ifstream** object used to open the file will go out of scope.

THE CREATEDEVICE() FUNCTION

The **CreateDevice()** function is called by the **OnCreate()** function. Its task is to create the Direct3D device:

```
BOOL RMWin::CreateDevice()
{
    d3drm->CreateDeviceFromSurface( 0, ddraw, backsurf, &device );
    device->SetQuality( D3DRMRENDER_GOURAUD );

    return TRUE;
}
```

The **CreateDeviceFromSurface()** function is used to create the device. The function takes four arguments. The first is a GUID (Globally Unique

Identifier) that identifies the device. Using zero causes Direct3D to choose a device automatically. You'll need to use a specific GUID only if you want to override Direct3D's default selection. The **GetGUID()** function can be used to retrieve specific GUIDs. See Chapter 4 for a discussion of the **GetGUID()** function.

The second **CreateDeviceFromSurface()** argument is a pointer to the **DirectDraw** interface. The third argument is the surface that is to be used in creating the device. We are using the **backsurf** surface that we created with the **InitMainSurfaces()** function. This means that Direct3D will use the **backsurf** surface as a rendering target.

The final **CreateDeviceFromSurface()** argument is the address of the **device** pointer. After the device is created, the **Direct3DRMDevice SetQuality()** function is used to set the device's rendering quality to Gouraud (flat rendering quality is used by default).

THE ACTIVATEDISPLAYMODE() FUNCTION

The **RMWin** class provides two versions of the **ActivateDisplayMode()** function. One is declared **protected** and is used by derived classes to signal **RMWin** to activate specific display modes. The second version is declared **private** and is used by the **protected** version to perform the actual display mode activation. The **protected** version of the **ActivateDisplayMode()** function looks like this:

```
BOOL RMWin::ActivateDisplayMode( int index )
{
    DWORD w=displaymode[index].width;
    DWORD h=displaymode[index].height;
    DWORD d=displaymode[index].depth;

    curdisplaymode=index;
    return ActivateDisplayMode( w, h, d );
}
```

The **ActivateDisplayMode()** function takes a single integer as an argument. The integer is an index into the list of supported display modes that was created by the **InitDisplayMode()** function.

ActivateDisplayMode() uses the **index** integer to retrieve the display mode dimensions for the given entry in the **displaymode** array. The **private** **curdisplaymode** data member is updated, and the **private** version of **Activate-**

DisplayMode() is called. The **private** version of **ActivateDisplayMode()** is defined as shown in Listing 10.7.

Listing 10.7   The private version of ActivateDisplayMode().

```
BOOL RMWin::ActivateDisplayMode(DWORD w,DWORD h,DWORD d)
{
    if (modewidth==w && modeheight==h && modedepth==d)
        return TRUE;

    modewidth=w;
    modeheight=h;
    modedepth=d;

    if (scene)
    {
        scene->Release();
        scene=0;
    }
    if (device)
    {
        device->Release();
        device=0;
    }
    if (primsurf)
    {
        primsurf->Release();
        primsurf=0;
    }
    if (zbufsurf)
    {
        zbufsurf->Release();
        zbufsurf=0;
    }

    ddraw->SetDisplayMode( modewidth, modeheight, modedepth );

    InitMainSurfaces();

    InstallPalette();

    CreateDevice();

    d3drm->CreateFrame( 0, &scene );
    CreateScene();

    return TRUE;
}
```

This version is more complicated than the previous version because it is responsible for destroying and rebuilding the internal application constructs.

First, a check is made to see if the requested mode is not already in effect. If the requested display mode is no different from the current display mode, the function returns. If a new display mode is being requested, the **modewidth**, **modeheight**, and **modedepth** data members are updated.

Next, the existing root frame, Direct3D device, primary surface, and Z-buffer are released. The back buffer is released along with the primary surface, so it should not be released explicitly.

Then, the **DirectDraw SetDisplayMode()** function is used to activate the new display mode. The **modewidth**, **modeheight**, and **modedepth** data members are used as arguments.

The next five function calls are identical to the portion of the **OnCreate()** function following the call to **InitDisplayMode()**:

```
InitMainSurfaces();

InstallPalette();

CreateDevice();

d3drm->CreateFrame( 0, &scene );
CreateScene();
```

In the case of **OnCreate()**, the five calls initialize the application following the activation of the initial display mode. In this case, the calls reconfigure the application following a change in display mode.

THE GETNUMDISPLAYMODES() FUNCTION

The **GetNumDisplayModes()** is a **protected** function that returns the number of display modes detected by the **InitDisplayMode()** function. The function is declared and defined in the **RMWin** class definition:

```
int GetNumDisplayModes()  { return totaldisplaymodes; }
```

THE GETCURDISPLAYMODE() FUNCTION

The **GetCurDisplayMode**() returns the index of the currently activated mode:

```
int GetCurDisplayMode()   { return curdisplaymode; }
```

As with the **GetNumDisplayModes**() function, the simplicity of the **GetCurDisplayMode**() function makes it a good candidate for in-class (**inline**) declaration.

THE GETDISPLAYMODEDIMS() FUNCTION

The **GetDisplayModeDims**() function returns the dimensions of a specific display mode:

```
BOOL RMWin::GetDisplayModeDims( int index, DWORD& w, DWORD& h, DWORD& d )
{
    if (index<0 || index>=totaldisplaymodes)
        return FALSE;

    w=displaymode[index].width;
    h=displaymode[index].height;
    d=displaymode[index].depth;

    return TRUE;
}
```

The first **GetDisplayModeDims**() parameter is the index of the display mode in question. The index is used to retrieve the display mode's dimensions from the **displaymode** array.

Later in this chapter, we'll use this function to retrieve the dimensions of each supported display mode. The dimensions will be used to construct a menu of display modes.

THE GETCURDISPLAYMODEDIMS() FUNCTION

The **GetCurDisplayModeDims**() function is defined as follows:

```
BOOL RMWin::GetCurDisplayModeDims( DWORD& w, DWORD& h, DWORD& d )
{
    if (curdisplaymode<0 || curdisplaymode>=totaldisplaymodes)
        return FALSE;
```

```
    w=displaymode[curdisplaymode].width;
    h=displaymode[curdisplaymode].height;
    d=displaymode[curdisplaymode].depth;

    return TRUE;
}
```

The function is almost identical to **GetDisplayModeDims()** except that this function retrieves the dimensions of the current display mode and not an arbitrary mode. This is a convenience function. The same data can be retrieved by using the **GetDisplayModeDims()** function in conjunction with the **GetCurDisplayMode()** function.

THE CREATESURFACE() FUNCTION

Speaking of convenience functions, the **CreateSurface()** function is also a convenience function. The **CreateSurface()** function constructs an off-screen DirectDraw surface given the surface's desired width and height. The function looks like this:

```
LPDIRECTDRAWSURFACE RMWin::CreateSurface( DWORD w, DWORD h )
{
    DDSURFACEDESC desc;
    memset( &desc, 0, sizeof(desc) );
    desc.dwSize = sizeof(desc);
    desc.dwFlags = DDSD_WIDTH | DDSD_HEIGHT | DDSD_CAPS;
    desc.dwWidth = w;
    desc.dwHeight = h;
    desc.ddsCaps.dwCaps = DDSCAPS_OFFSCREENPLAIN;

    LPDIRECTDRAWSURFACE surf;
    HRESULT r=ddraw->CreateSurface( &desc, &surf, 0 );
    if (r!=DD_OK)
        return 0;

    return surf;
}
```

A local **DDSURFACEDESC** structure is used to describe an off-screen surface with dimensions equal to those provided as parameters. The **DirectDraw CreateSurface()** function is used to create the surface. If the **CreateSurface()** function succeeds, a pointer to the new surface is returned.

The **CreateSurface()** function is designed to be used by classes derived from the **RMWin** class, but is not used by **RMWin** itself. We'll use this function in the FullScreen demo.

THE CLEARSURFACE() FUNCTION

Like the **CreateSurface()** function, the **ClearSurface()** function is provided in order to make classes derived from **RMWin** easier to write. The **ClearSurface()** function assigns a specified value to each element in a surface. The function is defined like this:

```
BOOL RMWin::ClearSurface(LPDIRECTDRAWSURFACE surf, DWORD clr)
{
    DDBLTFX bltfx;
    memset( &bltfx, 0, sizeof(bltfx) );
    bltfx.dwSize = sizeof(bltfx);
    bltfx.dwFillColor = clr;
    surf->Blt( 0, 0, 0, DDBLT_COLORFILL | DDBLT_WAIT, &bltfx );
    return TRUE;
}
```

The function takes two arguments: a pointer to the surface to be cleared and the value to be used to clear the surface.

The **DirectDrawSurface Blt()** function is used to erase the contents of the surface. Typically, the **Blt()** function is used to copy surfaces or portions of surfaces to other surfaces. However, the **Blt()** function can perform special operations such as mirroring, rotating, and Z-buffer operations. In this case, we are using the **DDBLTFX** structure and the **DDBLT_COLORFILL** constant to indicate to the **Blt()** function that we want a color fill operation to be applied to the given surface.

THE RENDER() FUNCTION

The **Render()** function is the last (and the simplest) **RMWin** function that we'll study. The **Render()** function is declared, but not defined:

```
virtual void Render() = 0;
```

Render is a *pure virtual* function. This means that **Render()** must be overridden by classes derived from **RMWin.** Our reasons for declaring the **Render()**

function this way is to ensure that classes derived from **RMWin** handle the application's screen updates. Among other things, the **Render()** function should perform page flipping.

THE FULLSCREEN DEMO

For the remainder of this chapter, we will be studying the FullScreen demo. The FullScreen demo is a full-screen Direct3D application. The FullScreen demo uses the full-screen version of the **RMWin** class to allow display-mode switching and page flipping. The demo appears in Figure 10.2.

The FullScreen demo animates the familiar swirl mesh across the screen using the **Direct3DRMAnimation** interface. Of more interest, however, is the fact that the demo displays all of the detected display modes and allows each to be activated. The arrow keys can be used to select any of the display modes, and the ENTER key activates the selected mode.

When you run the FullScreen demo, any display modes that your video card supports will appear. The display modes shown in Figure 10.2 are display modes detected on an ATI Mach 64 video card.

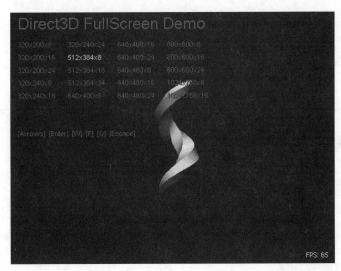

Figure 10.2
The FullScreen Demo.

Monitor—your limitations
Both your monitor and your video card must support a display mode if the display mode is to work properly. The FullScreen demo displays display modes supported by your video card. The modes may or may not be supported by your monitor. If you select a mode and your screen turns blank for longer than 10 seconds, you can press ESCAPE to exit the demo and return to the Windows desktop.

The demo also displays the program's current display speed, or frames-per-second (FPS).

The FullScreen demo demonstrates the following techniques:

- Creating full-screen Direct3D applications

- Page flipping

- Integrating 2D surfaces into 3D scenes

- Using Win32 functions to draw text on DirectDraw surfaces

- Calculating a program's frames-per-second (FPS)

- Alternatives to traditional Windows menus

THE FULLSCREENWIN CLASS

The FullScreen demo provides its functionality with the **FullScreenWin** class. The **FullScreenWin** class uses **RMWin** as a base class, as shown in Listing 10.8.

Listing 10.8 The FullScreenWin class.

```
class FullScreenWin : public RMWin
{
public:
    FullScreenWin();
protected:
    //{{AFX_MSG(FullScreenWin)
    afx_msg void OnKeyDown(UINT nChar, UINT nRepCnt, UINT nFlags);
    //}}AFX_MSG
    DECLARE_MESSAGE_MAP()
```

```
private:
    void OnRenderWireframe();
    void OnRenderFlat();
    void OnRenderGouraud();

    BOOL CreateScene();
    void Render();
    static void UpdateAnimation(LPDIRECT3DRMFRAME, void*, D3DVALUE);

    BOOL CreateMenuSurface();
    BOOL UpdateMenuSurface();

    BOOL CreateFPSSurface();
    BOOL UpdateFPSSurface();
private:
    LPDIRECT3DRMMESHBUILDER meshbuilder;
    static LPDIRECT3DRMANIMATION animation;

    HFONT smallfont, largefont;

    LPDIRECTDRAWSURFACE menusurf;
    RECT menurect;
    int selectmode;

    LPDIRECTDRAWSURFACE fpssurf;
    RECT fpsrect;
    BOOL displayfps;
};
```

The class's only public member function is a constructor. The constructor is responsible for initializing the class's non-static data members.

One message handler is declared: **OnKeyDown**(). MFC calls this function whenever a key is pressed. We'll use this function to implement the demo's menu functionality.

Notice that the usual Render menu functions aren't present in the MFC **afx_msg** section. Instead, they appear as regular member functions, as the first three **private** functions. This is because we aren't using a traditional Windows menu. We will have to invoke these functions manually instead of relying on MFC to call them.

The **CreateScene**() function is declared next. As with the demos in previous chapters, the **CreateScene**() function is responsible for constructing the application's visual constructs.

Next, the **Render()** function is declared. Remember that the **RMWin** version of **Render()** is declared as a pure virtual function. This requires us to provide a version in the **FullScreenWin** class. We'll use this function to render and display the visual output that the demo produces.

A **static** callback function called **UpdateAnimation()** is declared. This function will be used to update the demo's animation sequence.

The next four functions that the **FullScreenWin** class declares deserve some extra discussion:

```
BOOL CreateMenuSurface();
BOOL UpdateMenuSurface();

BOOL CreateFPSSurface();
BOOL UpdateFPSSurface();
```

When you run the FullScreen demo, a list of available display modes appears in the top-left corner, and, after a second or two, the demo's frames-per-second (FPS) appears in the lower-right corner.

Each of these displays is accomplished with a surface, and both surfaces are created and maintained by the **FullScreenWin** class. The **CreateMenuSurface()** and **UpdateMenuSurface()** functions create and maintain the list (or menu) of display modes. The **CreateFPSSurface()** and **UpdateFPSSurface()** functions create and maintain the FPS readout.

The remainder of the class definition declares data members. Pointers to the **Direct3DRMMeshBuilder** and **Direct3DRMAnimation** interfaces are declared. Next, two **HFONT** instances are declared. The **HFONT** type is a handle to a Windows font. We'll use these handles to draw the text that appears in the display mode menu and FPS readout.

Data members that are specifically used to implement the display mode menu are declared next:

```
LPDIRECTDRAWSURFACE menusurf;
RECT menurect;
int selectmode;
```

The **menusurf** pointer will be used to manipulate the surface that implements the display mode menu. The **menurect** structure is used to store the menu surface's dimensions. The **selectmode** integer will be used to track the currently selected display mode. This should not be confused with the currently active display mode. Entries in the display mode menu can be highlighted with the arrow keys. The selected display mode does not, however, get activated until you press ENTER.

Data members specific to the FPS readout appear like this:

```
LPDIRECTDRAWSURFACE fpssurf;
RECT fpsrect;
BOOL displayfps;
```

The **fpssurf** pointer will be used to display and update the FPS display surface. The **fpsrect** structure is used to store the dimensions of the **fpssurf** surface. The **displayfps** boolean is used to delay the display of the FPS readout each time the display mode is changed. This is done because initial FPS calculations are typically erratic. Once the speed of the demo has stabilized, the FPS readout is displayed.

THE FULLSCREENWIN() FUNCTION

The FullScreenWin constructor is shown in Listing 10.9.

Listing 10.9   The FullScreenWin() function.

```
FullScreenWin::FullScreenWin()
{
    meshbuilder = 0;
    animation   = 0;
    menusurf    = 0;
    fpssurf     = 0;
    selectmode  = -1;
    displayfps  = FALSE;

    UsePalette( "palette.bmp" );

    largefont = CreateFont( 28, 0, 0, 0,
        FW_NORMAL, FALSE, FALSE, FALSE,
        ANSI_CHARSET,
        OUT_DEFAULT_PRECIS,
        CLIP_DEFAULT_PRECIS,
        DEFAULT_QUALITY,
        VARIABLE_PITCH,
        "Arial" );
```

```
smallfont = CreateFont( 14, 0, 0, 0,
    FW_NORMAL, FALSE, FALSE, FALSE,
    ANSI_CHARSET,
    OUT_DEFAULT_PRECIS,
    CLIP_DEFAULT_PRECIS,
    DEFAULT_QUALITY,
    VARIABLE_PITCH,
    "Arial" );
}
```

First, the class's data members are initialized. Next, the **UsePalette()** function is used to provide the name of a BMP file that contains a palette to be used with 8-bit display modes.

The two font handles, **largefont** and **smallfont**, are initialized with the Win32 **CreateFont()** function. The only difference between the two fonts is the size. The larger font will be used for the demo's title banner (on the upper portion of the display mode menu). The small font will be used for both the display mode entries and the FPS readout.

THE CREATESCENE() FUNCTION

The **CreateScene()** function is shown in Listing 10.10.

Listing 10.10   The CreateScene() function.

```
BOOL FullScreenWin::CreateScene()
{
    //-------- MENU AND FPS SURFACES --------
    selectmode=GetCurDisplayMode();

    CreateMenuSurface();
    UpdateMenuSurface();

    CreateFPSSurface();

    // ------- MESH --------
    D3DRMLOADRESOURCE resinfo;
    resinfo.hModule=0;
    resinfo.lpName=MAKEINTRESOURCE( IDR_SWIRLMESH );
    resinfo.lpType="MESH";
    d3drm->CreateMeshBuilder( &meshbuilder );
    meshbuilder->Load( &resinfo, 0, D3DRMLOAD_FROMRESOURCE, 0, 0 );
    ScaleMesh( meshbuilder, D3DVALUE(15) );
```

```
//------- MESH FRAME --------
LPDIRECT3DRMFRAME meshframe;
d3drm->CreateFrame( scene, &meshframe );
meshframe->AddVisual( meshbuilder );
meshframe->SetRotation( scene,
        D3DVALUE(0), D3DVALUE(1), D3DVALUE(0),
        D3DVALUE(.1) );
meshframe->AddMoveCallback( UpdateAnimation, 0 );

//-------- ANIMATION --------
d3drm->CreateAnimation( &animation );

for (int i=0; i<11; i++)
{
    D3DRMQUATERNION    quat;
    D3DRMQuaternionFromRotation( &quat, &vect[i], rot[i] );
    animation->AddRotateKey( D3DVALUE(i), &quat );
    animation->AddPositionKey( D3DVALUE(i),
            trans[i].x, trans[i].y, trans[i].z );
}

animation->SetOptions( D3DRMANIMATION_SPLINEPOSITION |
        D3DRMANIMATION_CLOSED |
        D3DRMANIMATION_POSITION |
        D3DRMANIMATION_SCALEANDROTATION );
animation->SetFrame( meshframe );

meshframe->Release();
meshframe=0;

// --------DIRECTIONAL LIGHT--------
LPDIRECT3DRMFRAME dlightframe;
LPDIRECT3DRMLIGHT dlight;

d3drm->CreateLightRGB(D3DRMLIGHT_DIRECTIONAL,
        D3DVALUE(1.00), D3DVALUE(1.00), D3DVALUE(1.00),
        &dlight );

d3drm->CreateFrame( scene, &dlightframe );
dlightframe->SetOrientation( scene,
        D3DVALUE(0), D3DVALUE(-1), D3DVALUE(1),
        D3DVALUE(0), D3DVALUE(1), D3DVALUE(0) );
dlightframe->AddLight( dlight );

dlightframe->Release();
dlightframe=0;
```

```
    dlight->Release();
    dlight=0;

    //------ CAMERA----------
    d3drm->CreateFrame( scene, &camera );
    camera->SetPosition( scene,
            D3DVALUE(0), D3DVALUE(0), D3DVALUE(-50) );
    d3drm->CreateViewport( device, camera, 0, 0,
            device->GetWidth(), device->GetHeight(),
            &viewport );

    return TRUE;
}
```

The **CreateScene()** function performs six steps:

1. Initializes the display menu and FPS readout surfaces

2. Creates and loads a mesh

3. Creates a frame for the mesh

4. Creates and configures an animation sequence using the **Direct3DRMAnimation** interface

5. Creates a light source

6. Creates a viewport

We'll forgo a discussion of steps 2 through 6. These steps have been covered by previous chapters. Step 1, however, is of interest because this is where the display mode menu and FPS read-out surfaces are initialized. The surfaces are initialized with these function calls:

```
selectmode=GetCurDisplayMode();
CreateMenuSurface();
UpdateMenuSurface();

CreateFPSSurface();
```

The **GetCurDisplayMode()** function is used to initialize the **selectmode** integer. This is done so the display mode menu can highlight the current display mode. The **CreateMenuSurface()** function creates the surface that will be used to display the display mode menu. The **UpdateMenuSurface()**

function creates the menu surface contents. The **CreateFPSSurface()** function creates the FPS readout surface, but no FPS values are calculated because no frames have been displayed at this point in the demo's execution.

THE CREATEMENUSURFACE() FUNCTION

The **CreateMenuSurface()** function appears like this:

```
BOOL FullScreenWin::CreateMenuSurface()
{
    menusurf=CreateSurface( menuwidth, menuheight );

    menurect.left=0;
    menurect.top=0;
    menurect.right=menuwidth;
    menurect.bottom=menuheight;

    DDCOLORKEY ddck;
    ddck.dwColorSpaceLowValue = 0;
    ddck.dwColorSpaceHighValue = 0;
    menusurf->SetColorKey( DDCKEY_SRCBLT, &ddck );

    return TRUE;
}
```

First, the **RMWin::CreateSurface()** function is used to create the surface. The **menuwidth** and **menuheight** constants are used as arguments. The **CreateSurface()** function returns a pointer to the new surface.

The **menurect** structure is initialized. The rectangle doesn't contain the surface's location, only its dimensions.

Next, a color key is assigned to the surface. Color keys indicate which pixel value or values should be treated as transparent. In this case, we are specifying that display menu surface pixels that have the value zero should be transparent. If you watch the FullScreen demo in action, you can see that except for the text the menu surface is transparent. This is because all of the surface's pixels are assigned to zero before the text is drawn.

While we are on the subject of surface contents, it should be pointed out that the surface we just created has random contents. The surface creation claims memory to represent the surface, but does not initialize the memory itself.

THE UPDATEMENUSURFACE() FUNCTION

The role of the **UpdateMenuSurface()** function is to initialize the contents of the display mode menu surface, as shown in Listing 10.11.

Listing 10.11 The UpdateMenuSurface() function.

```
BOOL FullScreenWin::UpdateMenuSurface()
{
    char buf[80];
    int len;
    RECT rect;

    ClearSurface( menusurf, 0 );

    HDC hdc;
    menusurf->GetDC( &hdc );
    SelectObject( hdc, largefont );
    SetBkMode( hdc, TRANSPARENT );

    SetTextColor( hdc, textshadow );
    ExtTextOut( hdc, 1, 1, 0, 0, headertext, strlen(headertext), 0 );
    SetTextColor( hdc, textcolor );
    ExtTextOut( hdc, 0, 0, 0, 0, headertext, strlen(headertext), 0 );

    SelectObject( hdc, smallfont );

    int nmodes=GetNumDisplayModes();
    if (nmodes>maxmodes)
        nmodes=maxmodes;

    int rows=nmodes/menucols;
    if (nmodes%menucols)
        rows++;

    for (int i=0; i<nmodes; i++)
    {
        rect.left=(i/rows)*colwidth;
        rect.top=(i%rows)*rowheight+reservedspace;
        rect.right=rect.left+colwidth;
        rect.bottom=rect.top+rowheight;

        DWORD w,h,d;
        GetDisplayModeDims( i, w, h, d );

        len=sprintf( buf, "%dx%dx%d", w, h, d );
```

```
        SetTextColor( hdc, textshadow );
        ExtTextOut( hdc, rect.left+1, rect.top+1, 0, &rect, buf,
                len, 0 );

        if (i==selectmode)
            SetTextColor( hdc, highlightcolor );
        else
            SetTextColor( hdc, textcolor );
        ExtTextOut( hdc, rect.left, rect.top, 0, &rect, buf, len, 0 );
    }

    rect.left=0;
    rect.right=319;
    rect.top=179;
    rect.bottom=199;

    len=sprintf( buf, "[Arrows] [Enter] [W] [F] [G] [Escape]" );
    SetTextColor( hdc, textshadow );
    ExtTextOut( hdc, 1, 180, 0, &rect, buf, len, 0 );
    SetTextColor( hdc, textcolor );
    ExtTextOut( hdc, 0, 179, 0, &rect, buf, len, 0 );

    menusurf->ReleaseDC( hdc );

    return TRUE;
}
```

The first step that the **UpdateMenuSurface()** function takes is clearing the entire surface to zero. This is done with the **RMWin::ClearSurface()** function. Zero is passed as the second argument to **ClearSurface()**, indicating the desired pixel value. Because a color key of zero was specified for this surface, the entire surface is now transparent.

Next, the **DirectDrawSurface GetDC()** function is used to retrieve a Windows device context for the surface. The resulting HDC (Handle for a Device Context) allows us to use Windows device context functions. In our case, we are going to use the device context handle to draw text on the surface.

The bulk of the **UpdateMenuSurface()** function is dedicated to drawing text on the **menusurf** surface. First, the Win32 **ExtTextOut()** function is used to display a banner for the demo. Then, a string for each detected video mode is created and drawn. Finally, a list of keys that the demo responds to is displayed at the bottom of the surface.

Notice that all of the text is displayed twice, each time using a different color and a slightly different location. This creates a subtle text shadow effect.

Before the **UpdateMenuSurface()** function returns, the **DirectDrawSurface ReleaseDC()** function is called. This is very important because Windows itself is shut down between **GetDC()** and **ReleaseDC()** function calls. Forgetting to release the device context handle for a DirectDraw surface results in an impressive crash (believe me—I know!).

THE CREATEFPSSURFACE() FUNCTION

The **CreateFPSSurface()** function approaches surface creation a little differently than the **CreateMenuSurface()** function. The **CreateFPSSurface()** function first determines the size of the surface and then creates the surface, as shown in Listing 10.12. The surface size depends on the size of the text that is to be displayed:

Listing 10.12   The CreateFPSSurface() function.

```
BOOL FullScreenWin::CreateFPSSurface()
{
    static const char dummystr[]="FPS: 0000";

    HDC hdc = ::GetDC( 0 );
    SelectObject( hdc, smallfont );
    SIZE size;
    GetTextExtentPoint( hdc, dummystr, strlen(dummystr), &size );
    ::ReleaseDC( 0, hdc );

    fpsrect.left=0;
    fpsrect.top=0;
    fpsrect.right=size.cx;
    fpsrect.bottom=size.cy;

    fpssurf=CreateSurface( size.cx, size.cy );

    DDCOLORKEY  ddck;
    ddck.dwColorSpaceLowValue=0;
    ddck.dwColorSpaceHighValue=0;
    fpssurf->SetColorKey( DDCKEY_SRCBLT, &ddck );

    return TRUE;
}
```

A dummy string is used to determine the text size. The string is initialized with a worst-case scenario. That is, the dummy string contains more characters than the actual string will have to display. Therefore, the size of the text will be sufficient for any frame rate (up to 9,999 frames per second).

A temporary device context is created for the text size calculation. The smaller of the demos two fonts is selected, and the **GetTextExtentPoint()** function is used to retrieve the text size in pixels. The text size is then used to initialize the **fpsrect** structure and to create the **fpssurf** surface.

Finally, a color key is assigned to the surface. As with the display mode menu surface, pixels with values of zero are transparent.

THE UPDATEFPSSURFACE() FUNCTION

The **UpdateFPSSurface()** function is called for each screen update, as shown in Listing 10.13.

Listing 10.13   The UpdateFPSSurface() function.

```
BOOL FullScreenWin::UpdateFPSSurface()
{
    static const long interval=100;
    static long framecount;
    framecount++;

    if (framecount==interval)
    {
        static DWORD timenow;
        static DWORD timethen;
        timethen=timenow;
        timenow=timeGetTime();

        double seconds=double(timenow-timethen)/(double)1000;
        int fps=(int)((double)framecount/seconds);

        static char buf[10];
        int len=sprintf( buf, "FPS: %d", fps);

        HDC hdc;
        fpssurf->GetDC( &hdc );
        SelectObject( hdc, smallfont );
        SetTextColor( hdc, RGB(255,255,255) );
        SetBkColor( hdc, RGB(0,0,0) );
```

```
        SetBkMode( hdc, OPAQUE );
        ExtTextOut(hdc, 0, 0, ETO_OPAQUE, &fpsrect, buf, len, 0 );
        fpssurf->ReleaseDC( hdc );

        displayfps=TRUE;
        framecount=0;
    }

    return TRUE;
}
```

This function uses a **static** counter variable (**framecount**) to count the number of screen updates, or frames. When the frame count reaches 100 (an arbitrary delay), the FPS for the last 100 frames is calculated and displayed.

The high-performance Win32 multimedia **timeGetTime()** function is used to determine the amount of time that has elapsed since the previous FPS calculation. A string containing the calculated FPS is created and used to draw text on the **fpssurf** surface. Once the surface has been updated, the **framecount** variable is reset to zero.

THE RENDER() FUNCTION

Now, it's time to look at how the visual output from our demo is created and displayed. The **Render()** function is called by the **RMApp::OnIdle()** function, and is responsible for updating the back buffer surface and performing a page flip. The **Render()** function is shown in Listing 10.14.

Listing 10.14 The Render() function.

```
void FullScreenWin::Render()
{
    if ( primsurf->IsLost() == DDERR_SURFACELOST )
    {
        TRACE("Restoring primsurf...\n");
        primsurf->Restore();
    }

    if ( menusurf->IsLost() == DDERR_SURFACELOST )
    {
        TRACE("Restoring menusurf...\n");
        menusurf->Restore();
        UpdateMenuSurface();
    }
```

```
if ( fpssurf->IsLost() == DDERR_SURFACELOST )
{
    TRACE("Restoring fpssurf...\n");
    fpssurf->Restore();
}

DDBLTFX bltfx;
memset( &bltfx, 0, sizeof(bltfx) );
bltfx.dwSize = sizeof(bltfx);
bltfx.dwFillColor = 0;
backsurf->Blt( 0, 0, 0, DDBLT_COLORFILL | DDBLT_WAIT, &bltfx );

scene->Move(D3DVALUE(1.0));
viewport->Clear();
viewport->Render( scene );
device->Update();

UpdateFPSSurface();
if (displayfps)
{
    DWORD w, h, d;
    GetCurDisplayModeDims( w, h, d );
    backsurf->BltFast( w-fpsrect.right,
            h-fpsrect.bottom, fpssurf, &fpsrect,
            DDBLTFAST_SRCCOLORKEY | DDBLTFAST_WAIT );
}

backsurf->BltFast( 0, 0, menusurf, &menurect,
        DDBLTFAST_SRCCOLORKEY | DDBLTFAST_WAIT );

primsurf->Flip( 0, DDFLIP_WAIT );
}
```

The first portion of the function is dedicated to the loss of surfaces. Surface loss occurs when the memory used by a surface is required by Windows for another purpose. Only the surface memory is lost, not the surface itself. Surface loss typically occurs when the ALT+TAB sequence is used to switch to another program.

The **DirectDrawSurface IsLost()** function returns **TRUE** if the surface memory has been lost. Recovering the surface memory is fairly simple. The **DirectDrawSurface Restore()** function must be called. This reclaims the surface memory, but it does not restore the contents of the memory. Notice how the display mode menu surface is restored:

```
if ( menusurf->IsLost() == DDERR_SURFACELOST )
{
    TRACE("Restoring menusurf...\n");
    menusurf->Restore();
    UpdateMenuSurface();
}
```

If surface loss has occurred, the **Restore()** function is called. This recovers the surface memory, but a call to the **UpdateMenuSurface()** function is necessary to restore the surface's contents.

Next, the contents of the **backsurf** surface are erased:

```
DDBLTFX bltfx;
memset( &bltfx, 0, sizeof(bltfx) );
bltfx.dwSize = sizeof(bltfx);
bltfx.dwFillColor = 0;
backsurf->Blt( 0, 0, 0, DDBLT_COLORFILL | DDBLT_WAIT, &bltfx );
```

Similar code is used in the **RMWin::ClearSurface()** function. The **Blt()** function is used to perform a color fill. The fill color is zero, but no color key has been assigned to this surface so the surface pixels are all set to zero.

Now, the Direct3D portion of the scene can be drawn:

```
scene->Move(D3DVALUE(1.0));
viewport->Clear();
viewport->Render( scene );
device->Update();
```

The **Direct3DRMFrame Move()** function updates the frame hierarchy's internal values and executes any frame movement callbacks used by the hierarchy. The **Direct3DRMViewport** function calls (**Clear()** and **Render()**) clear the viewport contents (this has no effect on our surface) and calculate the new visual output. The **Direct3DRMDevice Update()** function copies the calculated output to the **backsurf** surface. This may not seem intuitive because the **backsurf** surface does not appear in the code snippet. But remember that the **backsurf** surface was used to create the Direct3D device. This association causes the **Update()** function to render output directly to the **backsurf** surface.

The FPS surface is now displayed over, or on top of, the Direct3D output:

```
UpdateFPSSurface();
if (displayfps)
{
    DWORD w, h, d;
    GetCurDisplayModeDims( w, h, d );
    backsurf->BltFast( w-fpsrect.right,
            h-fpsrect.bottom, fpssurf, &fpsrect,
            DDBLTFAST_SRCCOLORKEY | DDBLTFAST_WAIT );
}
```

The **UpdateFPSSurface()** is invoked to update the **fpssurf** surface. Then, if the **displayfps** boolean is set to **TRUE**, the contents of the surface are copied to the **backsurf** surface via the **BltFast()** function (the **BltFast()** function is an optimized version of the **Blt()** function).

The **fpssurf** surface is to appear in the lower-right corner of the screen, so the display mode dimensions are used in calculating the surface's destination on the back surface.

The display mode menu surface is then copied to the **backsurf** surface:

```
backsurf->BltFast( 0, 0, menusurf, &menurect,
        DDBLTFAST_SRCCOLORKEY | DDBLTFAST_WAIT );
```

This code is simple because the display mode menu surface is always visible and appears in the upper-left corner of the screen.

Finally, the contents of the **backsurf** surface are moved to the primary surface with a page flip operation:

```
primsurf->Flip( 0, DDFLIP_WAIT );
```

It is this function call that makes the contents of the **backsurf** surface visible.

THE KEYDOWN() FUNCTION

We need to talk about one more function before we can fully understand the FullScreen demo. The **KeyDown()** function is the message handler that gets called whenever a key is pressed. Listing 10.15 displays the **KeyDown()** function.

Listing 10.15   The KeyDown() function.

```
void FullScreenWin::OnKeyDown(UINT nChar, UINT nRepCnt, UINT nFlags)
{
    static int screencapture;
    int newindex;
    int nmodes=GetNumDisplayModes();
    if (nmodes>maxmodes)
        nmodes=maxmodes;

    int rows=nmodes/menucols;
    if (nmodes%menucols)
        rows++;

    switch (nChar)
    {
    case VK_ESCAPE:
        PostMessage( WM_CLOSE );
        break;
    case VK_UP:
        newindex=selectmode-1;
        if (newindex>=0)
        {
            selectmode=newindex;
            UpdateMenuSurface();
        }
        break;
    case VK_DOWN:
        newindex=selectmode+1;
        if (newindex<nmodes)
        {
            selectmode=newindex;
            UpdateMenuSurface();
        }
        break;
    case VK_LEFT:
        newindex=selectmode-rows;
        if (newindex>=0)
        {
            selectmode=newindex;
            UpdateMenuSurface();
        }
        break;
    case VK_RIGHT:
```

```
            newindex=selectmode+rows;
            if (newindex<nmodes)
            {
                selectmode=newindex;
                UpdateMenuSurface();
            }
            break;
        case VK_RETURN:
            if (menusurf)
            {
                menusurf->Release();
                menusurf=0;
            }
            if (fpssurf)
            {
                fpssurf->Release();
                fpssurf=0;
            }
            ActivateDisplayMode( selectmode );
            displayfps=FALSE;
            CreateMenuSurface();
            UpdateMenuSurface();
            CreateFPSSurface();
            break;
        case 'W':
            OnRenderWireframe();
            break;
        case 'F':
            OnRenderFlat();
            break;
        case 'G':
            OnRenderGouraud();
            break;
    }

    RMWin::OnKeyDown( nChar, nRepCnt, nFlags );
}
```

In essence, the **KeyDown()** function uses the arrow keys to highlight new
display modes on the display mode menu. The ENTER key is used to activate selected display modes. The "W," "F," and "G" keys are used to change
the rendering quality of the demo's only mesh (wireframe, flat, and
Gouraud). The ESCAPE key is used to terminate the demo.

CONCLUSION

Well, that's it—this is the last chapter in this book. I hope you learned what you wanted to know and maybe a little bit more. Good luck!

WORKING WITH THE DEMO PROGRAMS

Programming books are interesting because they vary so much. Most include a disk or CD-ROM. Some, especially those that include a CD-ROM, include various shareware, freeware, and trial versions of semi-related products. These extras are fine, but ultimately it is the code that makes a disk valuable. After all, shareware and freeware software is almost always available elsewhere.

The quality of the code that comes with books also varies. Some books include code that doesn't even compile. Others provide code that compiles but doesn't run. Other books provide high-quality professional code that serves as a valuable resource for many readers.

The CD-ROM that comes with this book has virtually no shareware and freeware software. That, quite frankly, is because I didn't have time. The vast majority of my time was spent on the book's demos. I reasoned that you'd rather have demos than shareware, so that is how I spent my time. I'll leave surfing the Internet in search of more tools to you.

THE CD-ROM CONTENTS

The contents of the CD-ROM can be divided into three categories:

- Source code for the book's demos
- Data files for meshes and textures
- Extra software

The CD-ROM includes full source code for the 22 demo programs, Xpose the mesh viewer, and the Direct3D AppWizard. Source code is also included for all of the meshes and textures that are used in the demos. The meshes are included in both X and 3DS form. Finally, two utilities are included: Texture Magic and 3DS2POV.

INSTALLATION

The CD-ROM is autoplay enabled, meaning that an installation program is executed automatically when the disk is inserted into your CD-ROM drive. The installation program, with your permission, performs these steps:

- Copies the source code and executables for the book's demos to your hard drive (to a drive and directory of your choice)

- Adds a folder to your Windows Start menu to allow the demos to be executed easily

- Installs the Direct3D AppWizard (if Visual C++ is installed)

- Associates X files with Xpose so that clicking on an X file runs Xpose automatically

The installation program also allows you to run the demos directly from the CD-ROM.

DIRECTORY STRUCTURE

The CD-ROM directory structure is shown in Figure A.1.

All of the book's source code is stored in the SRC directory. The demo executable files are stored in the BIN directory. The contents of these two directories are what is installed on your hard drive by the CD-ROM installation program.

The 3ds directory contains the 3D Studio files that were used to create the meshes for the demos. These files aren't required to use the book's source code, but might be handy if you use 3D Studio or if you use utilities that read the 3DS file format.

The meshes directory contains X and MRF files. X files can contain meshes, animations, frame hierarchies, and entire scenes. Most of the meshes in

Figure A.1
The CD-ROM directory structure.

the meshes directory, however, merely contain meshes. MRF files are X files that contain meshes that make up a morph sequence. Chapter 8 discusses MRF files and how you can make your own. The textures directory contains BMP and PPM files that can be used as textures.

The files in the meshes and textures directories are not used by the demos, so it isn't necessary for these directories to be installed on your hard drive. Each demo provides its own copy of the meshes and textures that it requires.

The EXTRAS directory contains two software utilities: Texture Magic and 3DS2POV. We'll talk about these utilities later in this appendix.

THE DEMO CODE

The demo source code is located in the src directory. Each demo's source code is stored in a separate src sub-directory. These sub-directories appear in Figure A.2.

Each directory contains a number of files, each of which is necessary for the successful compilation of the demo. These files are discussed next.

CPP AND H FILES

CPP and H files contain the C++ source code that is used in this book.

Figure A.2
The contents of the src directory.

MDP FILES

MDP files are known as project, or workspace, files. They contain all of the information that is required to compile the demo. These workspace files are created and modified by Visual C++. Loading these files with Visual C++ is the fastest and easiest way to compile, test, and modify an application.

MAK

MAK files are makefiles that can be used to compile the demos. These files are created automatically by Visual C++ and are usually ignored. They can be invaluable, however, if for some reason an MDP file is not available. MAK files allow projects to be compiled with either the command-line compiler (cl), or with Visual C++. MAK files can be used to create MDP files. Use the File|Open Workspace menu, and load the MAK file with the file dialog.

CLW

Visual C++'s ClassWizard tool stores its data in CLW files. Normally, Visual C++ uses these files without your knowledge. There are situations, however, when CLW files become corrupt and cannot be read by Visual C++. If this happens, close the workspace, delete the CLW file, and re-open the workspace. Then invoke the ClassWizard tool. You will be presented with a dialog that allows you to specify the source code files that should be used to create new ClassWizard data.

RC FILES

RC files are used by Visual C++ to store information specific to the application's resources (menus, icons, bitmaps, meshes, etc.). Visual C++ modifies these files automatically when resources are modified via the Visual C++ interface. Resources can be moved and copied between workspaces by opening multiple RC files, and then cutting and pasting resources between the two files.

X, BMP, AND PPM FILES

In the case of the demos on the CD-ROM, X, BMP, and PPM files contain Direct3D specific resources that are compiled into the resulting EXE file, and accessed during program operation. The meshes and textures that a demo uses can be changed by replacing these files with new versions and re-compiling the demo.

MODIFYING THE DEMOS

Each demo sub-directory contains all of the necessary files for compilation of the demo. This means that the demos are completely independent from each other. Any combination of demos can be moved or copied, and they will continue to compile.

Chapter 4 explains that almost all of the demos use the same versions of the **RMWin** and **RMApp** C++ classes. This is true, but each demo uses its own copy. In fact, 21 of the 23 demos use identical copies of the RMWin.cpp, RMWin.h, RMApp.cpp, and RMApp.h files. The exceptions are the FullScreen and MultiView demos.

EXTRA STUFF

While I was working on this book, I found these two tools to be very useful. I hope you get as much use out of them as I did.

TEXTURE MAGIC

Surfing the Internet, as it has come to be known, is generally overrated. There are times, however, when it pays off. This is true with Texture Magic. Texture Magic is a texture-creation tool that I found online and with which I have been very impressed. Texture Magic was written by Scott Pultz. Scott has created a Web page for Texture Magic at www.eskimo.com/~scott/povtext.html. You'll need to have a copy of the POV-ray ray-tracer to use Texture Magic. POV-ray is available on CompuServe (GO POVRAY), or at ftp.povray.org.

Texture Magic is cleverly written because, although its specialty is creating textures, it can be used as a front end to POV-ray. It allows both texture settings and POV-ray source code to be modified from within a comfortable and well organized interface. Texture Magic appears in Figure A.3.

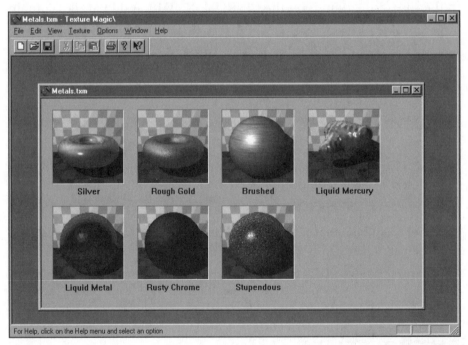

Figure A.3
Texture Magic.

3DS2POV

The 3DS2POV utility converts 3DS scenes to POV-ray scenes. The utility is short a few features, but provides an easy way to use modellers to design POV-ray scenes. The utility is usually best used to create a first draft of the scene. The resulting POV-ray source code can then be modified. 3DS2POV was written by Steve Anger and Jeff Bowermaster.

A WORD ABOUT VISUAL C++ 4.2

Before finishing this book, I uploaded the Direct3D AppWizard to several CompuServe forums. I got positive feedback, but some Visual C++ 4.2 users were unable to compile the projects that the AppWizard created.

The problem turned out to be that DirectX 1 is part of Visual C++ 4.2. The compiler was locating the DirectX 1 version of ddraw.h. DirectX 1 didn't include Direct3D, so naturally the compilation failed.

The best solution to this problem is to go to the Tools|Options, and select the Directories tab. The dialog allows you to move the directory where DirectX is located above the standard directory entries. This causes the compiler to locate the correct version of ddraw.h.

INDEX

D

M